Gertrude Stein and the Making of an American Celebrity

Studies in Major Literary Authors
WILLIAM E. CAIN, *General Editor*

"Unnoticed in the Casual Light of Day"
Philip Larkin and the Plain Style
Tijana Stojković

Queer Times
Christopher Isherwood's Modernity
Jamie M. Carr

Edith Wharton's "Evolutionary Conception"
Darwinian Allegory in Her Major Novels
Paul J. Ohler

The End of Learning
Milton and Education
Thomas Festa

Reading and Mapping Hardy's Roads
Scott Rode

Creating Yoknapatawpha
Readers and Writers in Faulkner's Fiction
Owen Robinson

No Place for Home
Spatial Constraint and Character Flight in the Novels of Cormac McCarthy
Jay Ellis

The Machine that Sings
Modernism, Hart Crane, and the Culture of the Body
Gordon A. Tapper

Influential Ghosts
A Study of Auden's Sources
Rachel Wetzsteon

D.H. Lawrence's Border Crossing
Colonialism in His Travel Writings and "Leadership" Novels
Eunyoung Oh

Dorothy Wordsworth's Ecology
Kenneth R. Cervelli

Sports, Narrative, and Nation in the Fiction of F. Scott Fitzgerald
Jarom Lyle McDonald

Shelley's Intellectual System and its Epicurean Background
Michael A. Vicario

Modernist Aesthetics and Consumer Culture in the Writings of Oscar Wilde
Paul L. Fortunato

Milton's Uncertain Eden
Understanding Place in *Paradise Lost*
Andrew Mattison

Henry Miller and Religion
Thomas Nesbit

The Magic Lantern
Representation of the Double in Dickens
Maria Cristina Paganoni

The Environmental Unconscious in the Fiction of Don DeLillo
Elise A. Martucci

James Merrill
Knowing Innocence
Reena Sastri

Yeats and Theosophy
Ken Monteith

Pynchon and the Political
Samuel Thomas

Paul Auster's Postmodernity
Brendan Martin

Editing Emily Dickinson
The Production of an Author
Lena Christensen

Cormac McCarthy and the Myth of American Exceptionalism
John Cant

Our Scene is London
Ben Jonson's City and the Space of the Author
James D. Mardock

Poetic Language and Political Engagement in the Poetry of Keats
Jack Siler

Politics and Aesthetics in *The Diary of Virginia Woolf*
Joanne Campbell Tidwell

Homosexuality in the Life and Work of Joseph Conrad
Love Between the Lines
Richard J. Ruppel

Shakespeare in the Victorian Periodicals
Kathryn Prince

Shakespeare and the Economic Imperative
"What's aught but as 'tis valued?"
Peter F. Grav

Wallace Stevens and the Realities of Poetic Language
Stefan Holander

Milton and the Spiritual Reader
Reading and Religion in Seventeenth-Century England
David Ainsworth

Everybody's America
Thomas Pynchon, Race, and the Cultures of Postmodernism
David Witzling

Dickens, Journalism, and Nationhood
Mapping the World in *Household Words*
Sabine Clemm

Narrative Conventions and Race in the Novels of Toni Morrison
Jennifer Lee Jordan Heinert

Philip K. Dick
Canonical Writer of the Digital Age
Lejla Kucukalic

The Historical Imagination of G.K. Chesterton
Locality, Patriotism, and Nationalism
Joseph R. McCleary

The Politics of Humiliation in the Novels of J.M. Coetzee
Hania A.M. Nashef

Gertrude Stein and the Making of an American Celebrity
Karen Leick

Gertrude Stein and the Making of an American Celebrity

Karen Leick

Taylor & Francis Group

LONDON AND NEW YORK

First published 2009 by Routledge
2 Park Square, Milton Park, Abingdon, Oxon OX14 4RN
52 Vanderbilt Avenue, New York, NY 10017

First published in paperback 2012

Routledge is an imprint of the Taylor & Francis Group, an informa business

© 2009 Taylor & Francis

All rights reserved. No part of this book may be reprinted or reproduced or utilised in any form or by any electronic, mechanical, or other means, now known or hereafter invented, including photocopying and recording, or in any information storage or retrieval system, without permission in writing from the publishers.

Trademark Notice: Product or corporate names may be trademarks or registered trademarks, and are used only for identification and explanation without intent to infringe.

Library of Congress Cataloging-in-Publication Data
Leick, Karen.
  Gertrude Stein and the making of an American celebrity / by Karen Leick.
    p. cm. — (Studies in major literary authors)
  Includes bibliographical references and index.
  1. Stein, Gertrude, 1874–1946—Criticism and interpretation. 2. Women and literature—United States—History—20th century. I. Title.
  PS3537.T323Z696 2009
  818'.5209—dc22
                                                        2009000764

Typeset in Sabon by IBT Global.

ISBN 13: 978-0-415-65497-5 (pbk)
ISBN 13: 978-0-415-99472-9 (hbk)

for Scott

Contents

List of Figures   xi
Acknowledgments   xiii

1   Introduction   1

2   The 1910s: Experimental Art and the American Public   24

3   The 1920s: Modernism and the Mainstream Press   67

4   The 1930s: Bestselling Modernism   131

     Conclusion: Stein and Hollywood   191

Notes   199
Selected Bibliography   227
Index   235

Figures

1	*Life* cartoon.	70
2	Djuna Barnes caricature, *Herald Tribune*.	84
3	*Atlantic* advertisement (December 1933): "A Notable List of Outstanding Biography."	139
4	*Publishers' Weekly* advertisement.	145
5	Bergdorf Goodman advertisement.	175

Acknowledgments

This project grew out of a dissertation that focused on the popular American reception of Gertrude Stein, Ezra Pound, and T. S. Eliot. I am exceptionally grateful to Christine Froula for directing that dissertation, asking the right questions throughout the process, and in every way helping me to improve my skills as a writer and thinker. Many people read chapters and drafts of the book as it progressed. I would like to thank Len Diepeveen for carefully reading entire book and making smart suggestions and observations. Debra Moddelmog, Brian McHale, and Jessica Prinz all read parts of the manuscript at different stages and helped me to sharpen the project in various ways. I also enjoyed many conversations about modernism at Steve Kern's house, with Jesse Matz, Brian McHale, Jim Phelan, Sebastian Knowles, Murray Beja, Ellen Jones, Jessica Prinz, Paul Reitter, Bill Palmer, Martin Hipsky, and Kate Elkins. The many lively discussions we had were intellectually stimulating every time, and helped me rethink many parts of the book. I am also thankful for the discussions about modernism, celebrity and personality that I've shared with Celia Marshik, whose friendship and support has meant much to me for many years.

I received a Coca-Cola Critical Difference for Women Faculty Grant for Research on Women, Gender, and Gender Equity from The Ohio State University in 2005 that generously funded trips to the Beinecke Rare Book and Manuscript Library at Yale University and at the Addison M. Metcalf Collection of Gertrude Steiniana at Claremont College. I would like to thank everyone at the Beinecke Rare Book and Manuscript Library who helped with my many requests. Special thanks goes to Patricia Willis, who offered cheerful advice and encouragement when I needed it most. I appreciated the courtesy of Judy Harvey Sahak at Claremont College, who helped me to be very comfortable there. The librarians at The Ohio State University at Lima also were indispensable throughout the writing of this book. Lori Schleeter made countless interlibrary loan requests for me without complaint, and was always there to answer my questions.

I am grateful to the Estate of Gertrude Stein, and its Literary Executor, Mr. Stanford Gann, Jr. of Levin & Gann, P. A., for permission to quote from the works of Gertrude Stein. Random House kindly granted permission to quote from *The Autobiography of Alice B. Toklas*, *Lectures in America*, and *Everybody's Autobiography*, and to use two advertisements for *The Autobiography of Alice B. Toklas* that appeared in 1933. Parts of chapters one and two were published in *PMLA* 123.1 (January 2008) and are reprinted by permission of the Modern Language Association of America.

Thanks most of all is due to my family. My husband, Scott, has been consistently supportive of this project and my academic career. His generous and easy-going attitude has made our life in rural Ohio a pleasurable experience. My children, Henry and Paige, were both born during the years I wrote and revised this book, and they have made this time infinitely joyful and special in ways I can hardly begin to articulate. Thank you for sleeping through the night, greeting me with such smiles every day, and for making my life into a new, happy thing.

1 Introduction

Gertrude Stein was an American icon in the 1930s. As John Malcolm Brinnin observes, "her eminence on the American scene was for a time shared only by gangsters, baseball players and movie stars."[1] In fact, the vast majority of studies about Gertrude Stein begin by announcing that she is primarily notable as a personality, celebrity or icon and seldom has been, at least until the last several decades, taken seriously as a writer. Frequently described by epithets such as "widely ridiculed and seldom enjoyed" and "most publicized but least-read writer" of the twentieth century, Stein's reception has been considered somewhat mysterious, particularly because scholars assume that it differs considerably from other modernist writers such as James Joyce, T. S. Eliot, and Virginia Woolf, who successfully achieved canonical status in their own lifetimes but apparently avoided success with popular audiences.[2]

After attending college at Harvard Annex from 1893–97, failing to graduate from Johns Hopkins medical school in 1901, and moving to Paris with her brother, Leo, in 1903, Gertrude Stein did not return to her native United States until 1934. Her celebrated lecture tour strategically capitalized on the great interest in Stein's work and personality that had gradually developed in the 1910s and 1920s, culminating in the huge sales of her bestselling *Autobiography of Alice B. Toklas* (1933) and the enormous publicity that surrounded her opera, *Four Saints and Three Acts* (1934). There was a press conference with reporters from all the major New York papers upon Stein's arrival from Paris on 24 October 1934; her name was illuminated in Times Square; people asked her for autographs everywhere she went; she gave a radio interview over New York's WJZ and was filmed for a Pathé newsreel; Stein and Toklas were entertained at the White House by Eleanor Roosevelt. These visible and well-known evidences of Stein's celebrity in the 1930s are often discussed as remarkable events, since most critics erroneously believe that Stein was unknown in mainstream America until the publication of the *Autobiography*. In fact, the public had been hearing about this enigmatic writer—and possible hoaxtress—for two decades. Although none of the books Stein published in the 1910s and 1920s sold well in the United States, columnists and book reviewers were attentive to modernism and discussed whatever obscure and difficult work they could find. Stein's work, like that of other modernist writers, was published in a variety of magazines and anthologies that were regularly discussed and quoted by columnists all over the country.

In this era before television began to monopolize the leisure time of Americans, people closely followed news about books and writers. The public spotlight could shine on an author for many reasons. A writer could quickly become a household name if, for example, his or her book became a bestseller or a book club selection, was investigated for obscenity, was made into a film, or was so unusual that the famous columnists or radio commentators of the day took notice. The assumption that, unlike Stein, Joyce and Woolf did not achieve this recognition is mistaken. Like Stein, Joyce was catapulted into the American public eye in the 1930s, in his case as a result of the sensational obscenity trial that surrounded *Ulysses* in 1933; as Catherine Turner notes, "all the major literary newspaper inserts and magazines, including the *New York Times*, the New York *Herald Tribune*, and the *Saturday Review of Literature*, reviewed [*Ulysses*] on their front covers" when it was finally released in January 1934.[3] Joyce, like Stein, was already a familiar name to Americans who had read discussions, parodies and quotations from his work in mainstream newspapers and periodicals throughout the 1920s, even if his writing initially appeared in obscure little magazines. Woolf too had been the subject of numerous discussions about modern literature by American reviewers and columnists, and she also became a bestseller in the 1930s. *Flush* was serialized in the *Atlantic* monthly in the some of the same issues of the magazine that Stein's *Autobiography of Alice B. Toklas* appeared in 1933 and was Book-of-the-Month Club selection in October, while Stein's *Autobiography* was a selection of the Literary Guild, the Book-of-the-Month Club's largest competitor, in September. That James Joyce, Virginia Woolf, and Gertrude Stein all produced bestsellers in the United States in a six month period (1933–34) is evidence of the remarkable mainstreaming of modernism. As 1922 is considered a seminal year for modernism with the publication of T. S. Eliot's *The Waste Land*, Joyce's *Ulysses*, and Woolf's *Jacob's Room*, 1933–34 can be recognized as the moment that modernist writers became truly popular. As *Vanity Fair* observed in 1934:

> There may have been a few far-seeing souls who were prepared for the lifting of the governmental ban on *Ulysses*, and the consequent huge sale of the master-work; but we doubt if any one—even Miss Stein herself—ever envisaged a time when a Stein book would, month after month, grace the best seller lists, and a Stein opera run four solid weeks at a Broadway theatre, to re-open three weeks later at *popular demand*. But this is 1934, and the twin miracles have happened.[4]

As miraculous as this popular recognition might seem, in fact this enthusiastic response to the first widely available works by Stein and Joyce might have been anticipated. Their names were so familiar to readers that parodies in the *Saturday Evening Post*, the *New Yorker*, or daily newspapers in the 1920s guaranteed easy laughs; serious debates about the value of their writing also frequently appeared in the mainstream press. Book columnists and reviewers, such important middle-men in the making of modernist culture, were overwhelmed with literary news about modernism to disseminate to readers in the 1920s and 1930s; they were bombarded with advertisements and press releases from publishers, numerous literary magazines published in the period, book club selections, and discussions by their peers in newspapers, periodicals and on the radio. Indeed, the diverse and pervasive media that analyzed, reproduced or otherwise advertised modern literature in the 1910s, 1920s and 1930s brought about not only a mainstream public knowledge of Gertrude Stein and her work, but modernism generally.

Some recent studies look at celebrity writers in the twentieth-century. Loren Glass's *Authors Inc.: Literary Celebrity in the Modern United States*, considers how "celebrity troubled many American authors' sense of their relation to their texts and audiences" (including Stein) and Aaron Jaffe's *Modernism and the Culture of Celebrity* analyzes the reactions of Ezra Pound, Wyndham Lewis, T. S. Eliot, and James Joyce to modern celebrity culture.[5] Other critics, including Kirk Curnutt, Susan M. Schultz, and Bryce Conrad discuss Stein's quest for an audience and the effects of her eventual popularity on her work and philosophy.[6] Although these scholars have described the effect of celebrity on some modernist writers, none have looked closely at the market conditions in America that facilitated this success and brought about a remarkable mainstream interest in new literary developments in the modernist period. Glass is certainly correct that Stein "entered into an already-established authorial star system in which the marketable 'personalities' of authors were frequently as important as the quality of their literary production."[7] Indeed, as Theodore Greene has observed, literary figures received considerable attention by periodicals at the turn of the century.[8] However, important changes in the literary marketplace in the 1920s enabled the effective dissemination of the experimental work of high modernism to mainstream America.

This study focuses on America's response to Gertrude Stein, not Gertrude Stein's response to America. Undoubtedly, Stein was attentive to popular culture and did not live in an elite, highbrow subculture in Paris, untouched by mainstream books and conversation, although the mistaken idea that modernists like Stein intentionally isolated themselves from the mainstream continues to be repeated by critics. John Xiros Cooper, for example, has recently argued that "From the soirées at the Stein salon, number 32 rue Fleurus in Paris, or the gatherings of Bloomsbury at number 50 Gordon Square in London, or the 'Ezra-versity' in Rapallo, Italy, the modernist avant-garde not only told itself the story of its own difference and superiority, but enacted it as well in the making of private communities."[9] Similarly, Barbara Will argues in her study of Stein that:

Perhaps most importantly, the notion of "genius" for high modernism served as a key term in articulating an oppositional stance toward one of the major developments of social and economic modernization from the mid-nineteenth century on: the emergence of an enormous, literature mass that seemed to threaten the very conditions of possibility of modern art.[10]

In fact, Stein read detective novels for pleasure and was fascinated by Hollywood, advertising, and other popular discourses when she was in the United States for her lecture tour. "She reads anything and everything," Alice points out in *The Autobiography of Alice B. Toklas*.[11] As Sara Blair has argued, Stein's salon was democratic, rather than elitist: "Its distinctive social life allowed participants of many stripes—GI Joes and regular Joes, tourists and art students and ticket-of-leave-men, collectors of art and of experience and other refugees from Protestant rigidity."[12] Alice observes that Stein "always says that she is very grateful not to have been born of an intellectual family, she has a horror of what she calls intellectual people." Instead, "she was democratic, one person was a good as another."[13] Stein explained to a reporter in 1935: "I like ordinary people who don't bore me. Highbrows do, you know, always do."[14]

Until the last decade, modernist literature has been treated by scholars as an elite literature that was only understandable by literary specialists in the university, but new methodologies have begun to challenge the idea that there was a distinct separation between high-brow and mainstream American readers. Recent studies of middle-brow readers and books have expanded the range of texts that scholars study the in modernist period, and explorations of the material conditions (such as the role of publishers or advertising) that facilitated the development of modernism have also brought about a rethinking of what "modernism" means. Fredric Jameson and Andreas Huyssen have been particularly influential in suggesting that modernists negatively constructed mass culture as the distinct, defining other of modernism.[15] Following this lead, analyses of modernism's relation to the popular by Jennifer Wicke, David Chinitz, Michael Coyle and others have examined the ways popular culture has informed the content of certain modernist texts.[16] As Maria DiBattista observes, many modernists "regarded low cultural phenomena and entertainments unique to their times—the popular press, cinema, music hall, and the 'art' of advertising—as an inalienable part of modern life, hence unavoidable subject matter whose forms as well as content might be assimilated or reworked, playfully imitated or seriously criticized, in their own art."[17] These studies tend to focus on the attitudes of modernist artists toward mainstream culture by looking at references in their writing to popular culture. Although critics do not consistently agree on precisely what differences between mass, popular, or high culture are, each privileges an elite perspective, positing a binary division between popular and high culture. By examining not the ways that Stein portrayed the popular in her work, but the ways the popular portrayed her, this study shows that that there was an intimate relationship between literary modernism and mainstream culture and that modernist writers and texts were much more well-known than has been previously acknowledged.

I am rethinking Fredric Jameson's description in of a "postmodern view of the 'great modernist creators,'" which, he argues,

> ought not to argue away the social and historical specificity of those now doubtful "centered subjects," but rather provide new ways of understanding their conditions of possibility. A beginning is made on that process by grasping the once-famous names no longer as characters larger than life or great souls of one kind or another, but rather—non- and anti-anthropomorphically—as careers, that is to say as objective situations in which an ambitious young artist around the turn of the century could see the objective possibility of turning himself into the "greatest painter" (or poet or novelist or composer) "of the age."[18]

Jameson anticipates the recent trend in socio-historical criticism that focuses on the material conditions that facilitated the development of modernism. These critics ask questions such as: what strategic moves within the marketplace did writers make? How did certain publishing practices enable or hinder the popularity or success of particular writers? When Stein's career is considered with these questions in mind, her celebrity status becomes less surprising. She did not, as some scholars have suggested, become an overnight success with *The Autobiography of Alice B. Toklas*. Debates about Stein's writing had been appearing regularly since the 1910s. Because the mainstream press habitually discussed cultural events and developments connected to Stein, such as the 1913 Armory Show or the shocking new free verse appearing in *Poetry* magazine and elsewhere in the 1910s, her name was often in the public eye. In the 1920s, the mainstream interest in experimental work, whether it appeared in little magazines, anthologies, or was published by obscure presses, continued to keep Stein's name before the public. Surely there would have been little interest in an autobiography by unknown eccentric writer; instead, Stein's accessible memoir seemed to explain the fascinating twenty-year long riddle of Stein's poetry and prose.

American modernism had a public cultural meaning that has been left out of many discussions, although modernist artists and literary trends were certainly considered "news" by periodicals and newspapers throughout the country; mainstream debates about modernism were familiar to all kinds of American readers. The importance of middlebrow book reviewers in the 1910s-1950s has been described in books including Joan Shelley Rubin's *The Making of Middlebrow Culture* and Janice Radway's *A Feeling for Books*.[19] Both, however, mistakenly suggest that the mainstream press was not attentive to modernism. Having stated that the *New York*

Herald Tribune's *Books* section tended to "bury reviews of works by major experimental poets" and did not review modernist works "on page one," Rubin is forced to describe Louis Bromfield's front page story in the *Books* section about *The Autobiography of Alice B. Toklas* as exceptional.[20] She does not mention Katherine Anne Porter's 1927 cover story about the *Making of Americans,* the 1939 front page review of Stein's children's book, *The World is Round,* or Janet Flanner's review of *Paris France* that appeared on page one of *Books* in 1940.[21] It may be true that modernist works rarely appeared on the cover of the *Herald Tribune*'s influential *Books* supplement, but Rubin's focus on this one weekly book section, rather than considering the many other supplements and book pages that appeared nationwide, results in a distorted picture. She fails to recognize the enormous attention that modernist writers received by other newspapers and periodicals across the country. In fact, before the *Herald* and the *Tribune* merged, a caricature of Gertrude Stein by Djuna Barnes appeared on the cover of the *New York Tribune*'s Sunday book section, "Book News and Reviews," on November 2, 1923, after her *Geography and Plays* had been extensively discussed in mainstream newspapers and periodicals.

Because Janice Radway confines her study to the Book-of-the-Month Club rather than looking at the other many clubs of the period, she also suggests that middle-brow readers did not have an interest in experimental modernist works. She neglects to mention that Virginia Woolf's *Flush* was one of the "dual" selections of the Book-of-the-Month Club in October 1933, or that Stein's *Autobiography of Alice B. Toklas* was the September 1933 selection of the Literary Guild.[22] In fact, writers like James Joyce and Virginia Woolf were frequently mentioned by popular columnists and were very well-known public figures, even celebrities, in the 1920s and 1930s. In 1927 the *Saturday Review of Literature,* a mainstream, popular review, chose for its cover story a discussion of the first issue of *transition* magazine, focusing on the contributions by Stein and Joyce. "Many take Miss Stein seriously (she is already a cult) and so will we," declared the conservative magazine.[23]

Furthermore, the appearance of Stein and Joyce on the cover of *Time* (11 September 1933; 29 January 1934) confirmed not only the celebrity status of each, but also their mainstream cultural significance. Both cover stories attempt to dispel the possible impression readers might have that each writer is unintelligible, and introduce helpful advice for understanding the work of each. Edmund Wilson is the critical expert cited in Gertrude Stein's cover story, while Stuart Gilbert's analysis dominates Joyce's. But *Time*'s writers need not have read *Ulysses* or Gilbert's accessible book to research the article. Random House's enormous two-page advertisement for *Ulysses,* "How to Enjoy James Joyce's Great Novel, *Ulysses,*" quotes Gilbert's analysis and gives a chapter-by-chapter summary of the novel's plot, as does *Time.*[24] Woolf, too, was celebrated by *Time*; she would grace its cover in 1937.[25]

Critics who are attentive to Stein's popularity in the 1930s have tended to suggest that her reputation was entirely different from that of other modernist writers, and that her exceptional reception does not shed light on the way Americans generally understood and reacted to modernist literature in this period. In fact, Stein and Joyce were frequently grouped together by columnists and book reviewers in newspapers that appeared all over the United States in the 1920s and 1930s. Newspapermen such as Harry Hansen (whose daily column in the 1920s and 1930s, "The First Reader," syndicated by Scripps Howard, reached millions of readers in such a wide range of cities as Tulsa, Oklahoma; Norfolk, Virginia; Minneapolis, Minnesota; San Francisco, California) took notice of any authors or books that were considered "news." It is clear that the experimental writings of Stein and Joyce were interesting (and amusing) for columnists to discuss, and they quoted from modernist work regularly. Whether Stein published in *transition* (a literary, avant-garde publication), *Vanity Fair* (a chic, mainstream magazine), or the *Saturday Evening Post* (with the largest circulation of any American magazine), columnists mentioned her contributions, at times poking fun at her radical style and at others suggesting that her innovations were so unusual that they were newsworthy. Furthermore, newspapers often detailed the literary contents of magazines in order to aid readers who might be looking for fiction or poetry by a favorite author. The *New York Times Book Review* printed a weekly discussion of "Current Magazines" that reported the contents of both popular and avant-garde periodicals. The contents of the May-June 1924 *transatlantic review* were listed there—which included an installment of Stein's "The Making of Americans"—alongside the contents of the current issues of *Harper's*, *McClure's*, *Red Book*, and *McCall's*.[26] "Current Magazines" also printed entire poems or lengthy quotes from articles and stories appearing in that week's magazines. Not only did newspapers alert readers to Stein's latest publications in little magazines by listing the contents of these publications, journalists also read each other's literary columns and quoted from discussions about the contributions to little magazines, frequently introducing the public to an author's most radical works (such as Joyce's "Work in Progress," the working title for *Finnegans Wake*). This literary conversation was often comic; nevertheless, mainstream readers regularly encountered excerpts from Stein's work in *Broom*, *transition*, and the *Little Review*. In the 1920s, some of Stein's more difficult writing appeared in popular anthologies that were widely reviewed and sold in significant numbers, further contributing to this ongoing national conversation about Stein's unusual work.[27] This literary "imagined community," to use Benedict Anderson's phrase, consisted of a culturally informed public that in the 1920s would understand perfectly any popular reference to Gertrude Stein in the daily paper.[28]

Although some of Stein's earliest work appeared in *Life* magazine and *Vanity Fair*, two mainstream periodicals, and her more obscure work was regularly quoted in newspapers and magazines in the 1910s and 1920s, critics continue to assert that her writing was only familiar to limited audiences until she achieved success with *The Autobiography of Alice B. Toklas*. To support this view, Corrine Blackmur observes:

> Until the *Autobiography* was serialized in the *The Atlantic Monthly* and subsequently published by Harcourt Brace in 1933, Stein's work had appeared only in small magazines such as Stieglitz's *Camera Work* and Van Vechten's *Trend*, alternative houses such as Donald Evans's Claire Marie and Leonard and Virginia Woolf's Hogarth Press, vanity presses such as Grafton, and small firms such as Four Seas Company, Daniel Henry Kahnweiler, Payson and Clarke, and Seizen Press.[29]

Similarly, Lawrence Rainey's recent anthology of modernism claims that "*The Autobiography of Alice B. Toklas*, which became a bestseller, turned Stein into a household name," although the reverse is nearer the truth; it was because Stein was a household name that *The Autobiography of Alice B. Toklas* became a bestseller.[30] Because the myth of Stein's obscurity in the 1920s has been perpetuated for so long, critics who are interested in the celebrity status of Stein tend to focus on her reception in the 1930s and to ignore the first twenty years of her career.

The use of Stein's cryptic phrases for humorous effect in newspaper columns became commonplace early in her career when, in 1914, the witty Don Marquis quoted from *Tender Buttons* so frequently in his daily column "The Sun Dial" in the New York *Evening Sun* that one reader wrote on September 24: "Sir: Won't you please stop printing Miss Stein's ravings? I know it makes great column filler, but please, please have a heart !!!" In addition to literary reviewers like Harry Hansen, Stein was discussed by celebrity columnists including Heywood Broun, Isabel Paterson, and Lewis Gannett. Stein cultivated friendships with some of the most famous, including Alexander Woollcott, whose radio show "The Town Crier" reached millions; he shared Stein's love for poodles and wrote her a touching note on Christmas Day, 1938, when he found out that her dog, Basket, had died.

Numerous influential forces in the publishing world, including Henry Luce, publisher of *Time* magazine, and his wife Clare Boothe Luce, Bennett Cerf of Random House, Fanny Butcher of the *Chicago Tribune*, Kate Buss of the *Boston Herald*, and Louis Bromfield of the *Herald Tribune*'s *Books*, not only praised Stein's work in print but were also personal friends who visited her in France. In the 1920s, writers who had already achieved literary success, including Sherwood Anderson and Carl Van Vechten, further alerted the public to Stein's significance. She was discussed by columnists and reviewers as an important influence on Anderson and Ernest Hemingway, two writers who were widely recognized as masters of the short story in the 1920s. Throughout her career, numerous supporters defended Stein's work against trivial attacks on experimental writing in the mainstream press. This campaign was noticeable to mainstream reviewers: as early as 1923, *Life* magazine observed in its review of *Geography and Plays* that "It would be easy to dispose of Gertrude Stein if it were not for the downrightness of her defenders." These conspicuous endorsements were only possible as a result of the American media's focus on the value of books and art, which effectively created a mainstream audience interested in debates about modernism and modernist literature; this popular, democratic interest in American writers and artists in the 1910s—1930s enabled Stein's success.

Books as News

In 1941, Donald Stauffer observed that "The influence of the book review in the daily paper, the Sunday supplement, or the popular periodical is one of the most striking developments of modern literature. Possibly such book reviewing merits the attention of the expert on public opinion, the sociologist, rather than that of the literary critic."[31] The explosion in the number of book reviews, literary columns, book supplements, and advertising by publishers in the 1920s and 1930s was the direct result of what many in the publishing business described as an excessive number of new titles. As early as 1910, *Publishers' Weekly*, who might have been expected to enthusiastically report an increase in book numbers, complained: "More and more appalling becomes the flood of books."[32]

The production of books showed no sign of slowing in the 1920s, when Wayne Gard observed in his guide for book reviewers: "Today the production of books has reached a magnitude without precedent. . . . Obviously the ordinary reader cannot take time to search among all the books offered by competing publishers and to select those that likely would interest him. For this sorting and selection he must depend on the book reviewer."[33] Consumers seemed to be overwhelmed by the choices available in bookstores, and reviewers were called upon to help highlight the most interesting books of each season. Considered by some to be a public service, others recognized that publishers relied upon reviews to publicize and thus help to move product that otherwise would languish in bookstores. As literary columnist Harry Hansen explained shrewdly in 1930, "The literary racket is the direct result of over-production in books. . . . If books are not to disintegrate into pulp on the shelves something must be done to move them."[34]

One important consequence of this effort among publishers to advertise and sell vast quantities of literature was a greater awareness among mainstream America readers about books and book news. The greater space given to book news in newspapers and periodicals did not just fulfill a need, it generated new interest. Rather than seeing huge numbers of new books as a problem, many saw this fact as an exciting opportunity. Publishers like George Doran, who understood that books were a lucrative business, said in a 1921 interview: "Never in the history of literature in America has there been such an increase in the number of readers or, as this may or may not indicate, so widespread an interest in all kinds of books. . . . We are on the threshold of a new American era of novels, plays and poetry."[35]

That reading for pleasure was considered a democratic pursuit rather than an elitist pastime by mainstream Americans cannot be emphasized enough; reading appealed to individuals from all kinds of cultural backgrounds, since it was both an affordable source of entertainment and a sign of culture and sophistication. Although a distinction between certain popular novels and more significant fiction was acknowledged, books generally promised to improve the mind in an enjoyable way. In 1922, publisher John Farrar expressed his view that there was "a healthful display of a general increase in book interest. There is a definite hunger on the part of women—and the appetite is not exclusively feminine—for some indefinite thing which they perhaps call culture. This hunger they are satisfying by a reaching out for books and book information. . . . From practically every city in the country and from small towns in every state come weekly letters which tell us of local literary activities and of local literary heroes. This movement is not urban, it is nationwide."[36] The fact that readers throughout the country craved news about books facilitated the development of modern American literature; new, radical developments were publicized almost immediately as a result of each columnist's desire to quench his reader's hunger for information—not to mention his own professional need to find interesting material to discuss on a daily basis.

The idea that books were news, and thus a natural subject for newspapers to discuss, was common in the first decades of the twentieth century. Adolph Ochs of the *New York Times* reflected the growing sense in the United States that literature was for everybody, not just the elite, when he said that "books themselves are news and therefore within the province of the newspaper"; the purpose of a book review, according to Ochs, was "to keep readers of the *Times* informed of what was going on in the literary world."[37] An individual did not need to go to college, cultivate high-brow friendships in literary circles, or otherwise go out of the way to learn about current literary trends in this period. One simply needed to subscribe to a newspaper and one or more periodicals, as virtually all Americans did.[38] Florin I. McDonald explains the new trend in book reviewing:

> It was perhaps only natural that the newspaper should take up this function of helping readers to answer this query of 'what to read.' The newspaper appealed to all classes of people. The busy executive, the shop girl, the Fifth Avenue debutante, the street laborer—people in all walks of life are regular subscribers. . . . The average reader could not be expected to know how to select from the thousands of published books the ones he wished to read.[39]

Harry Hansen was well aware of the importance of accessibility, and emphasized that his role as a daily columnist on literary subjects was specific and limited. He explained that "A critic may be anything he wishes, but a reviewer possesses no charter to be anything more than an interpreter and an announcer of books. . . . A reviewer wastes good white space unless he remembers that he must be understood equally well in Central Park West and the wilds of Flatbush, on Halsted Street and Lake Shore Drive. . . .Books as news—that is the slogan which has guided many in that increasing army of reviewers for American newspapers."[40]

Hansen's style of review—full of literary gossip—was what most Americans encountered in their newspapers on a daily basis, and it was this kind of review in conjunction with daily book columns that established Gertrude Stein's reputation in the Untied States. By the early 1920s, the literary world realized that there was such interest in this kind of accessible and informative book review that special newspaper supplements were devised to both accommodate and increase the demand for books by dedicating more space not only to reviews but also to book advertising. Reviews in newspapers were only one part of the cultural conversation about books that raged in the 1920s and 1930s. Discussion of books and authors could be found in periodicals, popular columns whose focus was not necessarily literary, and, by the late twenties, the radio. As Robert Morse Lovett observed in the *New Republic* 1921, "No longer does the literary audience consist of a group of connoisseurs, instructed by criticism to make formal comparisons and praise the best. On the contrary, everybody reads, and supplying reading-matter to an immense and voracious public has become a business like supplying it with clothes and food."[41]

The *New York Times* started the first literary supplement in 1896, but other papers did not follow suit until the 1920s. One of most prestigious was the *New York Herald Tribune*'s *Books*, edited by Stuart Sherman, which appeared in September 1924 after Ogden and Helen Reid, who owned the New York *Tribune*, purchased the *Herald*.[42] Irita Van Doren, literary editor of the *Nation* and Sherman's assistant, succeeded Sherman as editor after his death in 1926.[43] In 1920, the New York Evening *Post* began publishing a review section called the *Literary Review* but the literary editors, including Henry Seidel Canby, William Rose Benét, Amy Loveman, and Christopher Morley, were unhappy at the *Post* and decided to start their own literary magazine, the *Saturday Review of Literature*. The *Saturday Review* first appeared in August of 1924 and became a popular, accessible, and reactionary, source for readers.[44] To compete, the *Times* introduced a larger *Book Review* in the 1920s with higher quality photographic reproductions, creating space for more plentiful and attractive advertisements.[45] Most major newspapers throughout the country had a literary page with book news—with names such as "Books and Authors" or "Book News"— and many employed talented writers who went on to have significant careers as critics, reviewers, and novelists.[46] In the 1920s, early in their careers, Harry Hansen was literary editor of the Chicago *Daily News*, Floyd Dell was literary editor at the *Chicago Evening Post*, and Burton Rascoe was literary editor of the New York *World*. Book pages, periodicals, and Sunday supplements printed regular columns by admired writers, so readers could develop relationships with writers whose tastes they especially respected. Christopher Morley's "The Bowling Green" column for the New York *Evening Post* and the *Saturday Review of Literature*, Isabel Paterson's "Turns With a Bookworm" and Lewis Gannett's "Books and Things" for the *Herald Tribune*'s *Books* were popular, gossipy columns exuding the personality, opinions, and sense of humor of each columnist.

There was soon such a selection of review literature that readers were as overwhelmed by the choice of reviews as they were by the quantities of new books; attempts were made to determine which were considered the most valuable sources. In 1924, *Time* magazine published an article on "The Weekly Reviews" which briefly surveyed the *New York Herald Tribune*'s *Books*, the *Saturday Review of Literature*, and the *Post*'s *Literary Review*. John Farrar explains: "Whether or not these supplements survive, it is interesting and important that the public apparently wants them and wants, too, in large quantities the *Book Review* section of the *New York Times*, which, as a purveyor of book news, has never been excelled and is the most lavishly and, I think, tastefully illustrated of all." He wondered: "What does it mean? That we are reading more books than before and reading them more intelligently?"[47] At least it could be said with certainty that more people were reading *about* books than before. The *New York Times* conducted a survey to find out which reviews book buyers most often read to get advice about their literary purchases and happily discovered that they were, in fact, the country's most popular source of book news. *Publishers' Weekly* reported in 1934 that, after tabulating 3,682 questionnaires that had been inserted in books by fourteen publishers, "67% of the 3,682 replies listed the *Times Book Review*, 37% listed the *Atlantic Monthly*, 33% included *Harper's Magazine*, 31% named *Herald Tribune Books* and 23% mentioned the *Saturday Review of Literature*."[48] In the mid-west, the *Atlantic Monthly* received the highest percentage with 49%, while the *New Times Book Review* received 47%; and in New England and the Mid-Atlantic, the *Herald Tribune*'s *Books* was ranked second, after the *Times*.

In addition to the great attention paid to books by newspapers, new periodicals that were not chiefly literary but that also helped promote the cause of books appeared in this period, such as Condé Nast's chic *Vanity Fair*. Without a doubt, the pages of *Vanity Fair* represented what was cutting edge in the literary and artistic world. In addition to the work of modernists including Stein, T. S. Eliot, Djuna Barnes, and Edna St. Vincent Millay, subscribers of *Vanity Fair* were also introduced to the work of Picasso, Matisse, and Gaugin. And the magazine's staff was always impressive. Three Algonquin Wits, Dorothy Parker, Robert Sherwood and Robert Benchley, were employed by *Vanity Fair* for a time, while others in this circle, including Heywood Broun and Alexander Woollcott, regularly published there. Edmund Wilson, one of the earliest critics to recognize Stein's importance, began his distinguished career at *Vanity Fair* in 1920 and became managing editor in 1922; he was then literary editor of the *New Republic* from 1925 to 1940 and a weekly book reviewer for the *New Yorker* from 1943 to 1948. While *Vanity Fair* never competed with the most popular magazines such as the *Saturday Evening Post*, its circulation hovered around a respectable 90,000 until it merged with *Vogue* in 1936.[49]

Vanity Fair printed Stein's "Have They Attacked Mary. He Giggled" in 1917, several poems in 1919, "A Portrait of Jo Davidson" and "Miss Furr and Miss Skeene" in 1923, and "If I Told Him" in 1924, which the editors observed was "A Complete 'Portrait' of Pablo Picasso, in an Eccentric Modern Manner." In addition to two poems that appeared in *Life* magazine in 1917 and 1919, these were her first publications accessible to a large American audience and were widely discussed by the daily press, inspiring the repetitive "Steinese" used by critics and reviewers who parodied Stein's style throughout her career. Even *Vanity Fair* printed an early parody, "When Helen Furr Got Gay With Harold Moos" in October 1923.

The *New Yorker*, founded in February 1925 by Harold Ross, considered *Vanity Fair* its most serious competition. As I have argued elsewhere, both publications attempted to educate the sophisticated reader about current trends in arts and culture, but neither wished to be considered difficult, academic or inaccessible.[50] Ross's prospectus for the magazine emphasized that the magazine was not an avant-garde publication, but instead should appeal to the educated, urban reader:

> It will not be what is commonly called radical or highbrow. It will be what is commonly called sophisticated, in that it will assume a reasonable degree of enlightenment on the part of its readers. . . . The *New Yorker* will be the magazine which is not edited for the old lady in Dubuque. . . . the *New Yorker* is a magazine avowedly published for a metropolitan audience and thereby will escape an influence which hampers most national publications. It expects a considerable national circulation, but this will come from persons who have a metropolitan interest.[51]

Writers who regularly appeared in little magazines like *The Little Review*, *The Dial*, or *Poetry* were rarely published by the *New Yorker*; modernists including Gertrude Stein and James Joyce were instead noticed in book reviews, parodies and cartoons. Although Stein's rejection notice from Katharine White at the *New Yorker* explained that "she was not allowed to buy anything her boss didn't understand," the numerous references to her in the magazine suggest that Stein's work was familiar to the *New Yorker* readers.[52]

In addition to these newcomers, the well-established *Atlantic Monthly*, where quality literature had been published since its premiere in 1857, was an important influence on modern literature. At the turn of the twentieth century, the *Atlantic* published Henry James, Edith Wharton, and W. E. B. Dubois; and, although the *Atlantic* is not usually associated with radical trends in modernist literature, they printed Ernest Hemingway's short story "Fifty Grand" which *Cosmopolitan* had rejected, saying it was too "hardboiled."[53] After Ellery Sedgwick became editor of the *Atlantic* in August 1909, writers understood that serializing part of a work could immediately turn the book into a financial success. The experience of Mildred Aldrich, a friend of Gertrude Stein, may have inspired her to follow this example. Aldrich's collection of wartime letters that describe her view of the Battle of the Marne from her garden during World War I, *A Hilltop on the Marne* (1915), was serialized in the *Atlantic* before the bestselling book was released; once the book was published, it went into seventeen printings.[54] Stein and Virginia Woolf had similar success with *The Autobiography of Alice B. Toklas* and *Flush*.

Time magazine was an arbiter of taste for a more popular audience in the 1920s. Although the magazine was considered distinctly non-literary by some readers, *Time* took a great interest in authors and placed an astonishing number of writers on its cover from 1920 to 1950. When Henry Luce and Britton Hadden founded *Time* in 1923, it was far from clear to the twenty-four year old Yale graduates that the enterprise they had begun would become the enormous, and to some critics, monstrous, Time Inc. After Hadden's premature death in 1929, Luce went on to introduce *Fortune* (1930), *Life* (1936), and the March of Time newsreels, fundamentally changing the way Americans defined "news." Luce and Hadden initially thought that a weekly news magazine would be popular with the businessmen whom they saw taking public transportation to work, who never had time to finish reading a complete *New York Times* before they arrived at their destination. But once they began to develop the idea of a magazine that condensed the most important information for a well-informed person to know—*De omni re sciblili et quibusdam aliis*—they saw that the magazine could appeal to a much broader audience than just businessmen.[55] Unlike the *New Yorker*, *Time* specifically *was* "for the lady from Dubuque. . . . And for the President of the United States."[56]

According to the magazine's prospectus, *Time* would show that important figures "are something more than stage-figures with a name. It is important to know what they drink. It is important to know to what gods they pray and what kinds of fights they love." Luce and Hadden declared that "the personalities of politics make public affairs live," and the magazine spectacularly followed through with this promise to expose the personal habits of the individuals they discussed, including the writers who were profiled.[57] In addition to Gertrude Stein (1933), the impressive list of authors who appeared on the cover includes: Joseph Conrad (1923), G. B. Shaw (1923), Eugene O'Neill (1924, 1928, 1931, 1946), Amy Lowell (1925), Rudyard Kipling (1926), H. G. Wells (1926), Sinclair Lewis (1927, 1945), Willa Cather (1931), Noel Coward (1933), Upton Sinclair (1934), Thomas Mann (1934), James Joyce (1934, 1939), John Dos Passos (1936), Ernest Hemingway (1937), Virginia Woolf (1937), Carl Sandburg (1939),

William Faulkner (1939), Van Wyck Brooks (1944), Rebecca West (1947), C. S. Lewis (1947), Robert Frost (1950), and T. S. Eliot (1950).

Time alerted readers to modernist experimentation in the very first issue in an article that discussed *Ulysses* and *The Waste Land*, although each was treated with scorn. The article began: "There is a new kind of literature abroad in the land, whose only obvious fault is that no one can understand it." Speculating on the method Joyce used to compose *Ulysses*, *Time* suggested that: "Mr. Joyce had taken some half million assorted worlds—many such as are not ordinarily heard in reputable circles—shaken them up in a colossal hat, laid them end to end." The article also reported that "It is rumored that *The Waste Land* was written as a hoax."[58] *Time* may have missed the significance of these works in 1923, but the magazine showed in later years that it was interested in modern literature, and Joyce and Eliot in particular were treated with great respect in their cover stories. Furthermore, in addition to promoting the careers of writers in *Time*, Hadden and Luce were also active in other literary ventures. When they heard that Henry Seidel Canby was starting the *Saturday Review of Literature*, they offered to share their offices with the new magazine while giving the venture a significant financial boost by buying a large amount of the *Saturday Review*'s stock.[59] In fact, Time Inc. considered starting its own literary magazine in 1945 that would print the work of writers including "W. H. Auden, R. P. Blackmur, T. S. Eliot, Reinhold Niebuhr, George Orwell, and Lionel Trilling." Dwight Macdonald, who spent his career writing protests about the spread of mass culture, was horrified by the idea and wrote a memo to Henry Luce. He complained that "if the new periodical succeeded in acquiring contributions from some of the intellectuals suggested. . . . it would compete with 'little magazines' such as *Partisan Review, Kenyon Review, Sewanee Review* and *Politics*. This invasion of a field hitherto, because of its notoriously unprofitable nature, left to irresponsible intellectuals is part of that present-day tendency toward a merging of commercialized culture and serious (or 'high-brow') culture which I analyzed in 'A Theory of Popular Culture.'"[60]

The venture was abandoned, but the proposal for such a magazine and Macdonald's reaction to it suggest that the distinction between high culture and popular culture was blurred in ways that Macdonald was unwilling to acknowledge. While we might sympathize with Macdonald's fear that such a magazine would put little magazines out of business, it is not clear why it would be undesirable for a larger audience to encounter the "serious" culture that Macdonald reveres. The frequent notices in *Time* of many serious intellectuals suggests that these categories were meaningless, even if readers could only read about (but not actually read the work of) "serious" literature in the Luce publications. Edmund Wilson's complaint that "the attitude of the Luce publications has been infectious though it is mainly negative" similarly suggested that the kind of superficial exposure *Time* offered writers was in itself to blame for the absence of serious, high culture in the United States.[61]

Reviewers and Columnists

Critics frequently argued that the methods by which books were advertised or reviewed was a moral responsibility, because readers could easily be misled by manufactured hype. The importance of reviews for the reading public was enormous, and positive and negative reviews clearly influenced book sales. It was no secret that publishers constantly sent advertising and other promotional devices to reviewers to manipulate their opinions. The suspicion that reviewers were actually printing thinly disguised advertisements for books rather than serious appraisals loomed, although Harry Hansen and other reviewers consistently denied this charge. He explained that the undeniable relationship between publishers and reviewers was necessary, rather than evidence of insidious pressure: "That the reviewer is in closer touch with the publisher than the critic who does not take release dates into account there is no doubt. His work demands it. He must know what the new books are and when they are coming. His newspaper is interested in personalities and wants to know where they can be photographed and interviewed."[62] Although Hansen suggests that reviewers naturally cover authors who are "news," it is not at all clear that literary merit was the most important quality. Without a doubt, a writer whose publishers and agents succeeded in generating interesting tidbits for literary columns, made photographs available, and invented a literary "personality" was given much more attention by the press. Stein, whose writing and personality were so distinctive, was an especially appealing subject for the newspaper columnists.

Even if a review occasionally misrepresented a book's merits by praising it too highly, Hansen did not believe that book sales were skewed. He may be correct that readers were using so many other sources of information, including other reviews and advice from friends or booksellers, that one positive review did not necessarily result in greatly increased sales. "It seems to me that all books invariably get the reviews and the public they deserve. I have read misleading reviews of books, but their sales indicated that the bookseller and the reader did not share the mistaken confidence of the reviewer."[63] Still, the fear that the public could be deceived by reviewers or book clubs persisted. Dorothy Canfield Fisher, bestselling author and one of the Book-of-the-Month Club judges, explained to skeptical consumers in 1944: "There is no such thing as 'putting over' an author on the reading public by any system of reviews, publicity, or distribution plan. In the long run, readers themselves decide the fate of books and authors. All that can be done by praise from book reviewers and such a special system of getting books into the hands of readers as the Book-of-the-Month Club, is to hasten the public recognition of a writer who has something to offer that people want."[64]

Harry Hansen and Dorothy Canfield Fisher both influenced millions, Hansen with his syndicated book column and radio shows, Fisher as a Book-of-the-Month Club judge and bestselling author and essayist. Their names have been neglected by scholars of modernist literature, although Hansen in particular discussed the work of Gertrude Stein and other modernist writers, as well as popular writers: he did not discriminate. Hansen's point of view and background were typical of columnists in the modernist period. Born in Davenport, Iowa in 1884, Hansen attended the University of Chicago and then got a job at the Chicago *Daily News*. While literary editor there he championed the work of the Chicago writers he knew and admired, including Sherwood Anderson, Carl Sandburg, and Ben Hecht.[65] In 1926 he moved to New York as literary editor of the Morning *World*. When the powerful Scripps Howard media corporation purchased the *World* in 1931, his column was syndicated and, for the first time, he reached over a million readers across the nation.[66] Hansen was also known for his weekly book reviews on the radio for NBC from 1931 to 1935. Well-known as a "literary expert" by mainstream readers, he was often asked to sit in on other literary radio shows, contribute to symposia about contemporary literature in magazines or newspapers, and write essays about the state of American letters for periodicals.

Many other newspaper columnists and radio commentators were household names in this period, some with larger than life personalities. Probably the most well known was Alexander Woollcott. Woollcott's "Shouts and Murmurs" column for the *New Yorker* was popular, but his influence on the radio was incredible, both on his first radio show "The Early Bookworm" and then on the program that made him a national celebrity, "The Town Crier," a broadcast during which Woollcott discussed any topic that interested him. Frequently literature interested Mr. Woollcott: in 1934 he was so moved by James Hilton's sentimental *Goodbye, Mr. Chips*, a novella that had appeared in the *Atlantic,* that he convinced Little, Brown to publish it as a book.[67] He then told listeners of his radio show how much he loved the book, and it became an immediate bestseller. *Publishers' Weekly* began to publish notices when Woollcott mentioned a book on the air to alert bookstores to increase their orders; as they observed in 1934, "When Alexander Woollcott recommends a book, the book begins to sell at a breathless speed."[68] His influence was widely acknowledged. Louis Kronenberger complained in a review of an anthology that Woollcott edited in 1935, *The Woollcott Reader*, that "Mr. Woollcott is not only a best-seller in his own right, but with a sentence or two he can make best-sellers of other men. At present he is by far the most influential salesman of books in the United States."[69] Further evidence of Woollcott's great influence comes from Ezra Pound who, like Woollcott, was a graduate of Hamilton College; he wrote Woollcott a letter suggesting that he tell the American people about the "enormous swindle of government" in his efforts in the late 1930s to convince Americans not to trust politicians who seemed likely to lead the country to war. "Why me?" Woollcott wanted to know. Pound explained: "because you are not merely a funny man, but the most influential broadcaster and critic in America."[70] Woollcott's political views could not have been any more different than the Pound's; he was interested in Communism and admired Roosevelt. But when Pound gave his controversial pro-Mussolini broadcasts over Rome Radio starting in 1939, he used Woollcott's famous opening line, changing "This is Woollcott speaking" to "This is Ezra Pound speaking."

Harry Hansen's column was printed on the *World*'s famed op-ed page along with, for a time, Alexander Woollcott, Franklin P. Adams, and Heywood Broun, all well-known celebrity columnists of the 1920s and 1930s.[71] F. P. A.'s "The Conning Tower" and Broun's "It Seems to Me" were not primarily about books, but they did discuss especially newsworthy literary items and cultural developments. These Algonquin Wits developed a personal, funny anecdotal style that gave the reader the impression that he or she was witnessing a witty conversation between urban sophisticates who were aware of all that was relevant in the modern world.

A great influence on a more exclusive audience of educated readers was the iconoclastic H. L. Mencken, who was co-editor of *Smart Set* from 1914 to 1923 and then founded the *American Mercury* in 1924 with George Jean Nathan. *Smart Set*,—"a magazine of cleverness" or "the aristocrat of magazines" as it called itself on its stationary—focused on literature, unlike the *Mercury*, which emphasized political and cultural commentary.[72] Excerpts of *Dubliners* appeared in *Smart Set*, James Joyce's first appearance in America; the magazine also published W. Somerset Maugham, three Eugene O'Neill Plays, and stories by F. Scott Fitzgerald. In addition to these achievements, readers were attracted to Mencken's brash opinions about literature, the arts, and American culture. The irreverent critic coined many expressions, such as the "Bible Belt," and referred to humans as "homo boobiens" and the bourgeoisie as the "booboisie." His impatience with provincialism appealed to young readers particularly, who delighted in his rants about the lack of American taste. Edmund Wilson noted in 1929 that "it may be said that Mencken and [T. S.] Eliot between them rule the students of the Eastern Universities: when the college magazines do not sound like Mencken's *Mercury*, they sound like Eliot's *Criterion*."[73] A sure sign of Mencken's importance, Hemingway's Jake Barnes observes with irritation in *The Sun Also Rises*: "So many young men get their likes and dislikes from Mencken."[74]

Mencken, who lived in Baltimore for his entire life, was not a great admirer of Gertrude Stein, but he did review her work. In 1914, he observed in the *Baltimore Sun* with usual sarcasm: "'Tender Buttons,' by Gertrude Stein, late of Baltimore but now of Paris and the cubist movement, is not a work for boneheads. Its emanations are too delicate to penetrate even the thinnest scum of cranial ivory."[75] He went on to argue in the *Smart Set* in October 1914 that Stein's great achievement was to make English "easier to write and harder to read." Apparently uninterested in promoting Stein's difficult, fashionable work, in 1923 he called *Geography and Plays* "419 pages of drivel."[76]

Don Marquis, another highly paid star columnist who noticed Stein, wrote a satirical column that appeared on the editorial page of the New York *Evening Sun* starting in 1912, "The Sun Dial," which usually included several unrelated observations or commentaries about current events, politics, and the arts. Marquis satirized a certain artificial, high-brow, literary type of young woman by creating a character, Hermione, who commented on cultural developments in his column. "Isn't it *wonderful*! Simply *wonderful*!" she frequently exclaimed; "it" could be free verse, psychoanalysis, Gertrude Stein, or any other "fad" that Marquis wished to lampoon. He also parodied the development of free verse by introducing his most famous commentator in 1916, Archy, a *vers libre* poet who had been reincarnated as a cockroach. Late at night Archy would compose poetry on Mr. Marquis's typewriter by bouncing from key to key, and Marquis would publish his efforts in "The Sun Dial." As Gertrude Stein was well aware, Marquis frequently quoted *Tender Buttons* in his column in 1914 and 1915 for comic effect. Mabel Dodge wrote to her in 1914: "Every little while a Gertrude Stein parody comes out. Stieglitz showed me one the other evening from the Sun which I have ordered & will send you."[77]

These celebrated columnists greatly increased the American public's awareness of literary and cultural developments in this period. Disguising their critical discourse as comedy, Marquis, Mencken, Woollcott, and others made modernist books and authors a relevant topic for the everyday reader. As Henry Canby explains:

> F.P.A. and Don Marquis, the columnists, were making a new type of book familiar to readers who had been content with best-sellers, and with both writers instruction and irony were sweetened by laughter. . . .With no high-brow pretentiousness, they made literature, and art in general, subjects for general conversation. . . . It was in this way, among others, that a new audience was prepared for a new literature. . . . I am not sure whether this widespread interest in a national literature—which has never since abated—was not more important than the books which accompanied it.[78]

In fact, the distinction between high- and low-brow that has been emphasized by recent scholars was not important to most American readers, who saw books as a democratic form of entertainment and enlightenment that were accessible to everyone.

Marketing books and authors to attract these eager readers was a sophisticated business, and by the 1930s publishers used complex strategies to seduce consumers. The success of *The Autobiography of Alice B. Toklas* was certainly encouraged by several publishing strategies. Chapters of the book were serialized in the *Atlantic Monthly* from May—July 1933 before its release and the book was a selection of The Literary Guild for September 1933. The Literary Guild was founded in 1927, a year after the Book-of-the-Month Club and, after World War II, was the largest book club in the United States. In addition, Stein promoted her lecture tour on the radio; William Lundell interviewed her on a coast-to-coast hookup with New York City's WJZ on 11 November 1934, as newspapers all over the country reported in articles and radio schedules for the day. Press releases from Harcourt, Brace in 1933—34 also helped columnists and reviewers to come up with topics related to Stein for daily book columns. During Stein's tour, this publishing house sent out numerous releases, such as one on 1 November 1934 that reported: "Gertrude Stein, visiting her homeland after thirty-one years, is including in her sightseeing the Yale-Dartmouth football game this Saturday afternoon. She and Miss Toklas will accompany Alfred Harcourt and a party to New Haven." This news item was reported nationwide.

Never revealed as a lesbian by the American press in her lifetime, Stein was presented to popular audiences as a wise, witty grandmother during the lecture tour. Her sense of humor was emphasized throughout the tour by columnists, although scholars have neglected this aspect of her public image. Her witty responses to questions after each lecture won audiences over and were reported in detail in the daily newspapers. Bennett Cerf was only one victim of Stein's comedy. When he introduced her on the radio for the 1934 interview with William Lundell, Cerf commented: "I'm very proud to be your publisher, Miss Stein, but as I've always told you, I don't understand very much of what you're saying." Stein remarked cheerfully: "Well, I've always told you, Bennett, you're a very nice boy but you're rather stupid."[79] Radio was one new and essential tool for promoting the work of modern writers, as was film. The Pathé newsreel that featured Stein reading from *Four Saints in Three Acts* was shown in major theaters all over the country, prompting James Thurber's hilarious response to seeing Stein "interpret" several lines from the opera. In his piece for the *New Yorker*, "There's an Owl in my Room," Thurber countered that "Pigeons are definitely not alas."[80]

Stein was so well-known that her image and personality were frequently used in popular culture; it was obvious that any American was expected to know who she was. To note just a few examples: In the 1930s, Gertrude Stein appeared on the cover of a brochure advertising Ford automobiles, Gimbel's window display on Fifth Avenue during Easter 1934, declared: "4 SUITS in 2 ACTS," while an advertisement for Bergdorf Goodman encircled a drawing of a woman wearing a hat with a rose prominently displayed on it: "a rose is a pose is a rose." Stein was mentioned in two popular films in 1935: *Top Hat*, starring Fred Astaire and Ginger Rogers, and *The Man on the Flying Trapeze*, starring W. C. Fields; her name was used in jokes in the 1935 Broadway musical, *Jubilee!*, and in George S. Kaufman's and Moss Hart's play, *The Man Who Came to Dinner* (1939). Cartoons in *Esquire*, the *New Yorker*, and the *Saturday Review of Literature* made reference to her.

Despite these numerous examples of Stein's intimate relationship with popular culture, as early as 1964 Leslie Fiedler lamented "The Death of Avant-Garde Literature," nostalgically writing that Gertrude Stein and James Joyce were part of a legitimate avant-garde in a way that new writers like William S. Burroughs or Allen Ginsburg are not. Fiedler complains about "how quickly their breakthrough to new frontiers of offense has been followed up by imitators and vulgarizers," yet the work of Stein and Joyce was equally imitated, parodied, and recognized by popular audiences in the 1920s. Mistakenly suggesting that Stein and Joyce were unknown to mainstream readers, Fiedler distinguishes them from modernists like Fitzgerald, Faulkner, and Hemingway, who cultivated relationships with popular publications:

> Scott Fitzgerald, we remember, was at home in the *Saturday Evening Post* from the start, and that same magazine opened its arms to Faulkner at the very moment he was completing *Absalom, Absalom!*; while Hemingway, after a brief flirtation with the little magazines and a vicious parody of their modes in *Torrents of Spring*, headed via *Esquire* toward the maximum audience provided by *Life*.[81]

But Stein published in (the early) *Life* magazine in the 1910s; *Vanity Fair* in the 1910s and 1920s; the *Atlantic Monthly* and the *Saturday Evening Post* in the 1930s; *Vogue* and *Collier's* in the 1940s. Her appearance in these periodicals was no accident; as she recalls in *Everybody's Autobiography*, "I had said I always wanted two things to happen to be printed in the Atlantic Monthly and in the Saturday Evening Post."[82]

Since Gertrude Stein's celebrity and popularity in the 1930s are well known, it is surprising that her mainstream reception has not been more carefully considered. Distinctions between high- and low-brow literature are complicated when the response by the popular press to modernist writers is taken into account. As Alyson Tischler observes, the many clippings from newspapers and periodicals that refer to Stein in the Gertrude Stein and Alice B. Toklas Papers at Yale University's Beinecke Rare Book and Manuscript Library "reveal that the producers and consumers of mass culture were ... engaged by modernism."[83] The many other evidences of Stein's commodification and popularization on the American scene that I will discuss do even more damage to any strict definition of modernism as an elite, highbrow literary movement. This study takes issue with Andreas Huyssen's suggestion that "as modernism hides its envy for the broad appeal of mass culture behind a screen of condescension and contempt, mass culture, addled as it is with pangs of guilt, yearns for the dignity of serious culture which forever eludes it." Instead, Stein's example shows that the relationship between mass culture and modernism in America was less antagonistic, more productive and integrated. As

Huyssen explains, "Mass culture has always been the hidden subtext of the modernist project."[84]

Huyssen's description of an intense anxiety among modernist artists about the negative effects of mass culture, however, does not reflect Gertrude Stein's career, nor does Stein's American reception support the idea that mainstream America was forced to highjack certain aspects of modernism to build up its cultural status. Instead, American audiences were much more confident, tolerant, matter-of-fact, and genuinely interested in artistic innovation than Huyssen suggests. Furthermore, the frequent discussions of avant-garde writing in mainstream publications, not to mention the fluid careers of American critics who published in high- middle- and low-brow publications, ensured that no elite readership could legitimately exist in the United States in the 1920s and 1930s. The reviewers and columnists who significantly controlled the fate of certain books and writers were often friends who attended the same literary and cultural functions; there was no social divide between these professional writers, whose work appeared in a variety of publications. Thus in 1934 Harold Ross was invited to a reception for Gertrude Stein by Bennett Cerf of Random House, Stein's new publisher, where he might have expected to see Alexander Woollcott, an old friend who had been a staff writer for *The Stars and Stripes*, the army newspaper Ross edited in Paris during World War I.[85]

Huyssen has recently emphasized the need for a revision of the prevalent idea that there is a clear division between high and low culture, and recommends expanding our methodologies to underscore the intersections between genres. As he points out, "We should raise the issue of medium (oral/aural, written, visual) in all its historical, technical, and theoretical complexity rather than continue to rely on the traditional binary notion of media culture as low and its high literary other in traditional modernist fashion."[86] Examining "media culture," including Stein's radio interviews, appearances on newsreels, and references to her in other popular art forms—and taking these aspects of Stein's American reception seriously—allows critics to reassess the cultural meaning of modernism in America. Moving away from the idea that by the very definition of celebrity, Stein's writing must be inconsequential, an historical approach reveals that the American media created an environment in which the "celebrity writer" could be as "high-brow" as James Joyce or as "low-brow" as Anita Loos, bestselling author of *Gentlemen Prefer Blondes*. It is certainly true, as Daniel Boorstin has observed, that "the celebrity in the distinctive modern sense could not have existed in any earlier age, or in America before the Graphic Revolution," but it does not necessarily follow that Stein should be considered a "pseudo-event" (to use Boorstin's term) and thus an empty, frivolous media construction.[87] The many material reasons for Stein's artistic success in the United States are not insulting to her reputation, nor is her career idiosyncratic when compared with other modernist writers. Her triumph was a natural consequence of this strikingly literary moment in American history. Of course, not all critics were comfortable with Stein's position as both a serious and popular writer. Isaac Rosenfeld observed in a 1952 review of Stein's posthumous *Mrs. Reynolds* that "academic respectability [was being] conferred upon her through the Yale edition of her unpublished works," adding that this new understanding of the popular Stein should really not be a surprise, as the "elite" arts are not sacred: "we have long since grown accustomed to the incorporation of the *avant garde* in the universities, the films and the mass-circulation magazines."[88] In the next decades, critics repressed this dynamic reception of modernist literature, and worked to rewrite the history of modernism as an obscure, high-brow, difficult movement unknown to mainstream Americans.

2 The 1910s
Experimental Art and the American Public

In the 1910s, Gertrude Stein became widely known in America as a *verslibrist* and a writer of cubist prose. Thanks to the lively ongoing national conversation in newspapers and periodicals about books and art, her name was in the news with such frequency that by 1916, mainstream reviewers used Stein's name as the standard for new, radical writing. Other writers who also attempted similarly daring literary experiments were often compared to Stein, creating very early connections between writers that are now easily grouped as "modernist." A 1916 review of Dorothy Richardson in the New York *Evening Globe*, for example, explained that "[Richardson] does not . . . shut herself up in a dark room and put herself in a hypnotic condition like Gertrude Stein and record whatever jumble of words may come to her."[1] Similarly, a review of Ezra Pound's *Gaudier-Brzeska* in the New York *Sun* used Stein as shorthand for incomprehensible, modern writing, a contrast to the more accessible book at hand: "The reader should be duly grateful that it is not written in the new fashioned, obscure, tiresome Gertrude Stein prose." Stein was by no means the only experimental artist discussed by the popular press in this decade, and she greatly benefited from association, sometimes accidental, with other movements or events that caught the attention of reporters and columnists, such as the 1913 Armory Show, the appearance of *Poetry* magazine in 1912, or the championing of Imagism by its most enthusiastic promoter, Amy Lowell. As Stein observed, "the newspapers are always interested"; but they were not interested in her as an isolated phenomenon.[2] Instead, Stein's unusual writing was understood in the context of the much publicized work of Picasso, Matisse, Ezra Pound, Amy Lowell, and others.

Although these reviewers of Pound and Richardson failed to appreciate Stein's radical early work, she did have immediate, serious devotees. Stein's ability to be both respected and chastised by American readers in the 1910s is partly attributable to the stylistic and generic range of writing that she produced and the variety of publications in which her work appeared. From the start of her career, Stein's work could be found in periodicals with wildly divergent readerships, including the extremely popular *Life* magazine and obscure little magazines such as *The Soil* or *Rogue*.

Furthermore, *Three Lives* (1909) and *Tender Buttons* (1914), Stein's first two books, were so distinctive that each might have been written by a different author. The public reaction to each was just as singular. *Three Lives* was immediately recognized by readers and critics as a difficult but successful and moving piece of realism, while *Tender Buttons* was greeted by many reviewers and columnists as an incomprehensible piece of literary futurism or cubism. Although each of Stein's early publications was a radical and innovative linguistic experiment, the press constructed independent contexts for understanding each of her books: *Three Lives* was considered a daring "realistic" novel following an American tradition, while *Tender Buttons* was considered part of the radical European "cubist" movement in art. These opposing views of Stein's artistic value competed throughout her career and contributed to her complex and variable reputation within both mainstream and academic circles.

Three Lives: "a most extraordinary piece of realism"

Three Lives (1909), a collection of three stories, each an intimate portrait of a woman living in Baltimore, was Stein's first book. Although exploring the lives of ordinary, working-class women was unusual, it was not an altogether new idea. Theodore Dreiser's *Sister Carrie* (1900) and Stephen Crane's *Maggie: A Girl of the Streets* (1893) were well-publicized, controversial precursors. Stein's primary innovation in *Three Lives* was stylistic. Flaubert's *Trois Contes*, which describes the life of a servant girl, and Cézanne's portrait of his wife that hung above Stein's desk, were important European influences on Stein's storytelling technique. She explained in 1946:

> Everything I have done has been influenced by Flaubert and Cézanne, and this gave me a new feeling about composition. Up to that time composition had consisted of a central idea, to which everything else was an accompaniment and separate but was not an end in itself, and Cézanne conceived the idea that in composition one thing was as important as another thing. Each part is as important as the whole.[3]

Certainly, *Three Lives* breaks new linguistic ground. As Donald Sutherland observes, "The heroines of *Three Lives*, two German women and a Negress, have no connection whatever with the literary past of the language."[4] The repetitive, simple language that dominates each story seems grounded in immediate experience and avoids narrative digressions or detail that is not directly connected to the action or conversation reported. Emphasizing the present, each narrative primarily reveals what the characters directly think and experience at the expense of past memories, flashbacks, or other narrative devices that often establish a certain context for the motivations or desires of individuals in more traditional writing; each woman's thoughts repetitively dwell on related themes or impressions revealing, as Marianne DeKoven puts it: "the rhythm or pulse of personality."[5] The break with American realism exemplified by writers including Crane and Dreiser is clear, although the first critics of Stein's book understandably saw her writing following in this tradition. Delta Bell points out that, "her narrative . . . is notably bare of specificities such as abound in realist writing" but even the publisher characterized *Three Lives* as "a most extraordinary piece of realism."[6]

Of Stein's writing, *Three Lives* is one of the works students are most likely to read in a college course today, although this collection of three character studies was not the book that made Stein famous. It was, however, especially important for launching her career because several influential writers and critics, including Carl Van Vechten and Edmund Wilson, were impressed by these stories and subsequently championed her work. The attention of Van Vechten, who was such an important promoter of Harlem Renaissance writers, also contributed to the interest among African Americans in Stein's work in the 1920s. Many black writers were impressed by Stein's ability to reproduce what they felt were authentic speech patterns in "Melanctha," a bi-racial woman's story. Richard Wright and Nella Larsen were particular admirers of the book, but were not aware of its existence until the 1920s. As John Malcolm Brinnin observes, when *Three Lives* was first published, it "did little to carry [Stein's] name abroad in the terms she had hoped for, yet its appearance was nevertheless a salutary event in literary history. . . . Gradually it became famous."[7]

Because of the book's unusual repetitive style, it was not easy for Stein to interest publishers in *Three Lives*. Leo Stein's friend Hutchins Hapgood, a writer and critic most known for his sociological studies *The Spirit of the Ghetto* (1902) and *The Spirit of Labor* (1907), was the first friend Gertrude Stein recruited to place *Three Lives*. Hapgood accurately predicted that publishers would hesitate to take a risk with Stein's first book. He first sent it to Pitts Duffield of Duffield & Co., who seemed to recognize the influence of Flaubert, explaining in his rejection letter that "The book is too unconventional, for one thing, and if I may say so, too literary. Where one person would be interested in your application of French methods to American low life, a hundred, ignorant of any sense of literary values, would see only another piece of realism; and realism nowadays doesn't go."[8] Duffield suggested a literary agent, Flora Holly, who was also unsuccessful in finding a publisher. Nor could Stein's friend Mabel Weeks generate interest; after spending a year sending the book to publishers, she asked May Bookstaver Knoblauch for ideas.[9] Finally, Knoblauch found a vanity press willing to publish the book at Stein's expense, the Grafton Press of New York. For $660, Stein arranged to have five hundred bound copies of *Three Lives* printed on 30 July 1909.

Although reviews of *Three Lives* by no means dominated the mainstream press, considering the small press run of the book and the fact that it was published by a vanity press, the reviews are impressive. As Alice observes in *The Autobiography of Alice B. Toklas*, "It is rather astonishing the number of newspapers that noticed this book, printed privately and by a perfectly unknown person."[10] Most newspapers did not begin publishing regular book review supplements until the 1920s, but reviews were still an important aspect of mainstream periodicals and interesting publications could attract notice. The range of papers that did print reviews suggests how interested newspapers were in informing readers about new and innovative literature, even if a book was largely unavailable to the public or seemed unlikely to attract a large audience. Indeed, many of today's readers find *Three Lives* intimidating, but Stein's contemporaries exhibited a remarkable willingness to seriously consider the work's contribution to American literature.

Stein most valued the *Kansas City Star*'s review, "Fiction, But Not Novels," a sincere effort to understand and explain her innovative technique:

> "Three Lives," by Gertrude Stein, is fiction which no one who reads it can ever forget, but a book for a strictly limited audience. . . . In this remarkable book one watches humanity groping in the mists of existence. As character study one can speak of it only in superlatives. . . . the reader never escapes from the atmosphere of those lives, so subtly is the incantation wrought into these seeming simple pages. Here is a literary artist of such originality that it is not easy to conjecture what special influences have gone into the making of her.[11]

This insightful review initiated two themes that recur in mainstream assessments of *Three Lives*: the lifelike, intimate quality of the descriptions of the characters, and the unique, challenging prose. Book reviewers read each other's reviews, and it is easy to see how certain notices echoed the sentiments and language used to describe Stein's unusual book. *Three Lives* began to develop a reputation among reviewers and notices began to multiply. *The Nation* followed the *Kansas City Star*'s lead: "These stories of the Good Anna, Melanctha, and the Gentle Lena have a quite extraordinary vitality conveyed in a most eccentric and difficult form. The half-articulated phrases follow unrelentingly the blind mental and temperamental gropings of three humble souls wittingly or unwittingly at odds with life,"[12] and the New York City *Post* reprinted this review.[13] The Brooklyn *Eagle* agreed that Stein's repetitive style effectively captured each character's state of mind; "very realistic" observed the Cleveland *Plain Dealer*.[14]

The Boston *Evening Globe* headlined its review "Notable Piece of Realism," initiating a string of reviews in Boston and other Massachusetts papers.[15] Phillip Hale called *Three Lives* "an extraordinary book" in the Boston *Morning Herald*, explaining that "With its strange, unconventional English, its haltings, its endless repetitions, it furnishes hard reading, and yet somehow its unfamiliar, almost uncanny, style grips the reader firmly. . . . The book should attract notice, for a volume penetrated with such amazing vitality does not come before one in many a long day. It is worth reading with careful patience. Here is something really new."[16] Stein's innovative use of realism was emphasized by many; a reviewer for the *Boston Transcript* wrote that "the characterization in these short stories is unique; the psychology is interesting because of its quaintness, and the themes touch the lives of some commonplace colored people. Miss Stein lays bare their subjective selves in a strong, realistic way."[17] The Springfield (MA) *Union* repeated Hale's phrase in its headline: "An Extraordinary Book," explaining that:

> Gertrude Stein's "Three Lives" is heralded as "a most extraordinary piece of realism" and that is not an overextravagant claim. . . . The style is peculiar and, if intentional, it is certainly a work of art, as the author has succeeded in reproducing commonplace thought and talks, as in the story of Melanctha, with a verbal realism that is astounding, and at the same time is very fatiguing for the reader.[18]

The Springfield (MA) *Republican* agreed, arguing that "It . . . has a peculiar vividness."[19] Positive reviews also appeared in the Chicago *Record Herald*, Philadelphia *Booknews*, and in a particularly sensitive review, the Philadelphia *American,* which asserted with confidence: "the book stands almost by itself in contemporary literature."[20]

Negative reviews focused on the "sordid" nature of the stories rather than the style, and argued that the everyday existence of these women was not subject matter worthy of art. The New York *Sun* complained that "the realism consists in dwelling persistently on the sordid side of the women's lives and in ascribing to their minds the vacancy and monotony which impress their employers. . . . It is obvious that the same stories could have been made bright and cheerful with equal truth, if the author had preferred to tell about other realities."[21] The Pittsburg *Post* also discussed the "sordid, unpretty existence of a trio of lowly women," predicting that "no vast popularity can be predicted for this work."[22] The Washington D.C. *Herald* offered another classist and racist reading; according to this reviewer, Stein presents "minds of low caliber and meager cultivation, the three lives depicted being those of three servant women, one of whom is a mulatto. . . . If she would attempt the same things with minds of a higher caliber, the result might be more entertaining."[23] More succinctly, the Rochester *Post* carped: "Gertrude Stein's book may be 'realistic,' but it seems to us that the pages devoted to a description of the habits of dogs and of maid-servants are both tedious and distasteful.[24]

Stein heard reports about the reception of *Three Lives* from Etta Cone, a friend who had typed the stories in Paris. Some readers had positive reactions, but Cone confessed that

> most people . . . were distinctly disappointed in their lack of style, their easy dispensation with all rules of rhetoric, and their "dreadful immorality." She had even heard some readers criticize Gertrude for allowing the

little dog in the care of the Good Anna to manifest its "natural desires." They thought she dwelt too much on "unpleasant things."[25]

The prudish snobbery that pervaded these reactions was characteristic of the period; Dreiser and Crane suffered similar criticisms, as did Sherwood Anderson, who became Stein's close friend. Anderson recalls that after *Winseburg, Ohio* was published in 1919, he received hate mail "for the most part from women. What names I was called. They spat upon me, shouted at me, used the most filthy of words."[26] Even T. S. Eliot was the victim of such responses. In a 1920 review of "Preludes," a reviewer explained that "General incomprehensibility and sordidness of detail . . . are Mr. Eliot's distinguishing traits. He is usually intelligible only when he is nasty."[27] Indeed, complaints against "modern" writers frequently focused on content rather than form. One fan of the popular, sentimental writer Dorothy Canfield Fisher wrote to her, "We are so disgusted with the sordid, so-called 'realistic' novels of today which are degrading."[28]

Most reviewers knew nothing about Gertrude Stein's life in Paris and based their reactions entirely on the contents of *Three Lives*. This would be the only moment in Stein's career that her writing was almost exclusively judged on its merits, rather than as an extension of her personality. But there were exceptions; a harbinger of the American reaction to Stein in decades to come, a Baltimore paper headlined a profile of Stein "Eccentric Authoress Once a Student Here." Dispensing with serious consideration of *Three Lives*, this reporter described Stein as a "a woman of strong personality, independence of thought and an utter disdain of conventionalities, and by her brilliant qualities and lovable traits she charms all who come in contact with her." Most surprising is the emphasis on Stein's appearance and, more specifically, her clothing.

> The dictatorial rules of fashion have no terrors for her. For a street costume she wears always a brown corduroy suit, a short coat and a small, inconspicuous hat. . . . According to this independent authoress's belief shoes are an unnecessary adjunct and a hindrance to health; consequently summer or winter, no matter how severe the weather, she walks the streets of Paris in brown sandals regardless of the many impertinent glances that she often is forced to encounter. . . . The corset, that modern invention of the suppression of unruly flesh, is an unknown article in the simple wardrobe of the fearless Miss Stein.

New York City *Press* reprinted this description of Stein's wardrobe, as did the San Francisco *Chronicle*, with the headline "Woman Author, Who Disregards the Fashions."[29] These articles avoid discussion of *Three Lives* and instead suggest that the eccentric taste of Stein, a newly discovered author, is newsworthy in itself. This early example of the mainstream treatment of writers as celebrities whose personal habits might be even more interesting than their books only became more pronounced in the 1920s and 1930s.

Three Lives created enough stir that one bookstore in New York specifically advertised that they carried it: "This much talked of, hated and admired book is on sale for one dollar a copy at the Washington Square Gallery."[30] Although it attracted substantial critical and even some commercial attention, *Three Lives* did not sell. Reviewers had benefited from the 78 copies that had been sent out to friends, writers and reviewers for free; by February 10, only 73 copies actually sold. Perhaps the focus of reviewers on the book's difficulty intimidated some potential readers, and interested readers would not have found the book widely available at bookstores. Still, impressed by the strong book reviews, Stein's editor at Grafton Press wrote to suggest that she contribute funds to advertise the book, admitting with surprise that *Three Lives* "certainly appeals very strongly to a class of readers." Apparently discouraged with the limited sales of the book, Stein did not send the additional money.[31]

The Armory Show and Camera Work: "weird art"

Stein was correct that she did not need to finance an advertising campaign to become well-known in America. By the time her next book, *Tender Buttons,* was published in 1914, she had already gained a certain amount of notoriety, especially in literary circles, although most of this new public had missed the publication of *Three Lives*. Stein's next literary venture was to write brief "portraits" of her friends and acquaintances, usually several pages long, in an original and difficult style baffling to many of her acquaintances. Others, such as Mabel Dodge, found Stein's literary creations brilliant; Dodge began an enthusiastic campaign to distribute and publicize Stein's experimental work.

Dodge, of course, may have been biased since she was the subject of one of Stein's early portraits. In the fall of 1912, Stein and Toklas had visited the Dodge's impressive villa in Florence. Stein composed the portrait late at night, apparently inspired by noises from the other side of her bedroom wall which suggested that Dodge was reluctantly rebuffing the advances of her son's attractive, young tutor. The affluent Dodge, who cultivated friendships with artists and writers throughout her life, decided to have the abstract portrait printed and covered in floral paper. These three hundred copies she gave to her many artistic or literary friends in the United States and abroad. Thus Dodge's enthusiastic and motivated response resulted in more copies being distributed of this work that had been sold of *Three Lives*, and she was thrilled at the response generated by her efforts. She wrote to Stein about the early interest of Carl Van Vechten, who would become one of Stein's most intimate friends and advocates.

> There is an article about you coming out in the N. Y. Times this Sunday & the editor sent a young man around to see me & talk about you as

he (the ed.) had got hold of a copy of yr portrait of me & he said he must get hold of it all first at it was new, etc., etc. . . . I have done myself proud in the way I have distributed those Portraits.[32]

Van Vechten, the "young man," first tried and failed to get his piece printed in the Sunday *New York Times* magazine, where it would have been sure to attract attention. He then contacted the *Bookman*, the *Sunday World*, and the *Evening Globe*, but was unable to find an interested editor. Finally the article was printed in the *New York Times* in February 1913 in a most obscure location: the financial page.

Dodge's enthusiasm began to create some interest in literary and artistic circles at the same moment that Stein's word portraits of Picasso and Matisse were printed in Alfred Stieglitz's *Camera Work,* an innovative journal dedicated to art and photography, another endorsement from an important artistic influence. May Bookstaver Knoblauch brought the manuscripts to "291," Stieglitz's New York art gallery, for him to consider, just as she had placed *Three Lives* at the Grafton Press.[33] A pioneering American photographer and artist, Stieglitz was an old acquaintance of Leo and Gertrude Stein, and had been to see their art collection in Paris. Like the Stein's home, "291" was an important gathering place for modern artists; Marsden Hartley, an artist whose first one-man show was at "291" in 1909, wrote to Stein in 1913: "I have somewhat the same feeling toward the number 27 that I have toward the number 291—They both have a magic of their own."[34] Although he claimed not to understand her writing, Stieglitz agreed to publish the portraits and emphasized the importance of her writing in an editorial statement printed in the issue: "It is precisely because, in the articles by Stein, the Post-Impressionist spirit is found expressing itself in literary form that we lay them before readers of *Camera Work* in a specially prepared and supplemental number," he explained.

Like the portrait of Mabel Dodge, these pieces do not present a recognizable narrative or any kind of usual description, but instead emphasize certain epithets by repetition. Stein presented Picasso as "this one":

> This one was one having always something being coming out of him, something having completely a real meaning. This one was one whom some were following. This one was one who was working. This one was one who was working and he was one needing this thing needing to be working so as to be one having some way of being one having some way of working.

Stein was not the only artist to experiment with abstract portraits in *Camera Work*, although she was the only contributor who used words to create her effects. In the October 1914 issue, Marius de Zayas's nonrepresentational drawings of famous individuals appeared. De Zayas had published traditional caricatures of celebrities for the New York *World* since 1907, but the abstract experiments published in *Camera Work* seemed unrelated to their subjects including Francis Picabia, Alfred Stieglitz and Theodore Roosevelt.[35] These examples of the "post-Impressionist spirit" promoted by Stieglitz demonstrated the modern artist's active role in interpreting—not just representing but re-presenting—the essence of the subject matter depicted.

All of Stein's writing was profoundly affected by modern painting, but reviewers simply did not realize this when they struggled to classify *Three Lives*. Since post-Impressionist painting was virtually unknown in the United States in 1909, it would have been surprising if any American had recognized this influence who had not been to Gertrude and Leo Stein's home in Paris, which housed one of the most important collections of contemporary art in the world. Leo Stein had begun collecting modern art in Paris in 1903, when he purchased his first Cézanne, *The Spring House*. After Gertrude arrived in Paris later that year, she and Leo began to seek out the work of post-Impressionists and showed their appreciation for the most radical artistic developments in the decade when they acquired Matisse's *Woman with the Hat* and Picasso's *Jeune Fille* in 1905. As they developed friendships with both Matisse and Picasso, Picasso painted the famous portrait of Gertrude Stein in late 1905 and early 1906 that now hangs in the Metropolitan Museum of Art. Before Stein developed a reputation as a writer, she and her brother were primarily known for the gatherings of artists, intellectuals, and other interested individuals at their home in Paris, who were eager to see the shocking paintings that covered the walls. These eclectic gatherings before the war accommodated all kinds of people of many nationalities: "Everybody could come in and as at that time these pictures had no value and there was no social privilege attached to knowing any one there, only those came who really were interested."[36]

The American ignorance of experimental art and writing abruptly ended in 1912 and 1913, with the premiere of Harriet Monroe's *Poetry* magazine in 1912 and the opening of the famous Armory Show in 1913, the wildly controversial modern art exhibit in New York that introduced Americans to the work of Picasso, Matisse, Van Gogh, Gaugin, Brancusi, and Kandinsky, not to mention Marcel Duchamp's *Nude Descending a Staircase*, the painting that most scandalized audiences and prompted passionate responses from columnists, cartoonists, and art critics nationwide. Both events received considerable attention in the mainstream press and the experimental writers whose *vers libre* appeared in *Poetry* were soon linked to the European artists whose radical works created such public furor in 1913.

Stein's work was not printed in *Poetry* until 1940, but her "portraits" were immediately connected to the art displayed at the Armory Show, thanks to Mabel Dodge's inspired article about her "Portrait of Mabel Dodge at the Villa Curonia." "Speculations, or Post-Impressionism in Prose" appeared in the March 1913 issue of *Arts and Decoration* and was sold at the Armory Show, an exhibit which, as James Mellow puts it, "was a publicist's dream."[37] Milton Brown estimates that about 87,000 visitors attended the exhibit in New York, a whopping 188,000 in Chicago, and a disappointing 13,000 in Boston, where the show had been reduced from about 1250 to about 300 works.[38] The reaction to the exhibition was mixed; the New York *Sun* called the show "something very like a miracle," the *New York Times* reported that "no one within reach of it can afford to ignore it," and the *Globe* explained that "American art will never be the same again."[39] But there were many jokes as well; J. F. Griswald's well-known caricature of Duchamp's painting, "Seeing New York with a Cubist: The Rude Descending a Staircase (Rush Hour in the Subway)," appeared in the *Evening Sun* in March 1913 and was reprinted nationwide. Dodge's essay—bought, read, or skimmed by the show's many visitors—was the first major publicity that Stein received, and initiated the popular understanding of her work as directly related to European cubist art.

"In a large studio in Paris, hung with paintings by Renoir, Matisse and Picasso, Gertrude Stein is doing with words what Picasso is doing with paint," Dodge explained. She included a quotation from Stein's portrait of herself to illustrate her unconventional approach to literary description:

> It is a gnarled division, that which is not under any obstruction, and the forgotten swelling is certainly attracting. It is attracting the whiter division, it is not sinking to be growing, it is not darkening to be disappearing, it is not aged to be annoying. There cannot be sighing. This is this bliss.

Dodge was not the only contributor to this issue of *Arts and Decoration* who mentioned Stein; Jo Davidson anticipated much of the criticism that was immediately leveled at the portrait of Dodge: "This piece of prose—if prose it is—has a certain fascination. But does it convey any idea whatsoever of Mabel Dodge, to even the most intelligent reader? Indeed, if it were not described as a portrait on the cover, who would suspect what it was all about?" he asked.[40] Davidson does not dismiss Stein or what he calls "the new modernist painters and sculptors" altogether; instead, he judiciously warns readers that "it is as much a mistake to accept a thing without understanding it as to reject it without understanding it."[41] This reassurance anticipates the anxiety that Stein's unorthodox word play elicited, even from unexpected quarters. The young E. E. Cummings, an undergraduate at Harvard, was unconvinced by Stein's portrait. "Her art is the logic of literary sound painting to its extremes. While we must admit it is logic, must we admit that it is art?" he asked in the *Harvard Advocate*.[42]

Although Stein's work was essentially unavailable to the public, Mabel Dodge's article prompted numerous mainstream critics and columnists to comment on the connection between her writing and post-Impressionism during the controversy surrounding the Armory exhibition. These discussions usually reprinted the small quotation from "The Portrait of Mabel Dodge" in the article, parts of Dodge's own commentary, and occasionally Stein's contributions to *Camera Work* were referenced and quoted. Indeed, concern over Stein's abstractions was so great that editorials took notice.

Stein's portrait of Picasso was extensively quoted in the *Chicago Daily Tribune*, "whose proofreader is not expected to recover," the paper joked. Despite this dubious introduction, the reporter goes on to explicate several lines, and not without care: "First, that this person . . . was one, not two or three, as so many of us are in this age of multiple personality. In spite of this deplorable shortage he was a person of considerable acquaintance, but the delicate implication is that he had no friends."[43] The following week, Frank Crane responded to this piece with an editorial in the *Tribune,* quoting from "The Portrait of Mabel Dodge" and then arguing that, by contrast to the painters represented in the Armory Show, writers should have less freedom to experiment:

> We recognize that artists sometimes want to play the earnest lunatic and have their fling at hocus pocus with the public and have just as much right to do this as the scientific fad faker or the real estate agent. But when ladies and gentlemen come along and essay to exploit literature in that same way we gently but firmly decline to sit in. . . . No, Gertrude, this will not do. Paint it, sculp it, play it, if you will, but don't write it. (sic)[44]

Other references to Stein in the *Tribune* could be eccentric, even bizarre. One article presented ridiculous drawings of "futurist" clothing, noting that: "We may expect that the influence of such a gown will be in the direction of Futurism in Literature, and that Mrs. [Edith] Wharton will soon be following in the footsteps of Gertrude Stein, the futurist prose writer, who sits in her studio in Paris wearing a futurist dress and surrounded by paintings of Picasso, Matisse, and Picabia."[45] The quotation from Mabel Dodge's article was then reproduced.

Hutchins Hapgood did his best to counter the skeptical responses to Stein's portrait of Dodge (and Dodge's celebration of it) that began to proliferate in the daily papers. In an article for the New York *Globe* on 21 March 1913, "Democratic Criticism," he confessed:

> I myself do not understand this piece of writing. I am sure that Miss Stein is attempting to express something, but I cannot get it. But I happen to have read earlier things by Miss Stein and to know something about her moral and mental and imaginative equipment, which is unusual and distinguished. This helps me to do what I ought to do anyway—try sympathetically to get her and her material, not from the standpoint of my own habits and prejudices as a thinker and writer, but from hers.[46]

Unwilling to let this generous assessment stand, the editors of the *Globe* decided to enter into the conversation, impatiently denying that any serious effort should be required by readers. The editorial complained that:

> What we are worried about is Mr. Hapgood's feeling that he 'ought to ... try to get her material' from her point of view, or, in other words, that he ought respectfully to like what she writes. We cannot for the life of us see any ought about it. . . . Now, Miss Stein's writing affects us like an attempt to play ball with a trout rod, or to unlock a door with a toy balloon. Of course, this proves that we do not understand her, but why need we try?[47]

This animated conversation in the daily press relied almost exclusively on quotations from Dodge's article, and showed that columnists who had never read a complete piece of Stein's work, or the work of other modernist writers, would not hesitate to discuss or parody this strange writing.

Camera Work did reprint "The Portrait of Mabel Dodge" in the June 1913 issue and finally made the work more widely available to reviewers who had only heard about it through these numerous contributions to newspapers and periodicals, but *Camera Work* was by no means a popular or mainstream publication and its small distribution would have reached very few readers. But the issue at least inspired the conservative *Atlantic Monthly* to print extensive excerpts and a generally supportive article about Stein's work and the exciting potential for experimental writing in September.[48]

Many of Stein's friends wrote her letters informing her of the publicity that her writing (and discussions of it) had generated. Marsden Hartley explained that "you are much talked of—even in Philadelphia you are said to be a creator of style—isn't that interesting—you are a new value in the eyes of many—not in the eyes of some."[49] And in January 1914, Claribel Cone wrote to Stein that she had attended a lecture on Whistler during which the speaker made a reference to Stein's collection of modern art and read from her portraits of both Picasso and Matisse.[50] Stein even began to develop a reputation abroad; she received a letter on 24 January 1914 from Oliver Gogarty, James Joyce's friend and the model for memorable Buck Mulligan:

> I wonder if your good nature would not be overtaxed by my requesting a few copies of "The Portrait of Mabel Dodge at the Villa Curonia"? I want one or two for my friends. I am incompetent to offer an opinion on a form of Art so new as yours. . . . Will you soon come so far away from the centres of culture as to visit Dublin?[51]

Certainly, James Joyce may have been one of the "friends" who received a copy.

Stein's "art so new," like the Armory show, immediately impressed many Americans as a sign of a significant change in arts and letters. Although the controversy surrounding the Armory Show is well known, it is especially significant because it suggests that, just as the mainstream press found eccentric or difficult literature to be of interest to general readers, newspapers and magazines were also attentive to new developments in art. As Steven Conn has persuasively shown, museums were just beginning to be understood as high-brow institutions in the 1910s and 1920s; previously, the American public thought of them as democratic venues in which any citizen might benefit from both educational and entertaining exhibits.[52] As books were for everybody, so was the museum. It wasn't clear to the public how this strange kind of abstract art was useful (although it certainly was amusing), but rather than concluding that the new art was for elite tastes and avoiding the Art Institute, masses of Chicagoans went to the Armory Show to see for themselves what the post-Impressionists might be attempting to convey. Even the *Saturday Evening Post*, America's most popular, mainstream magazine—which boasted a circulation of "More Than 2 Million a Week" on its 1913 covers—offered a critical description of the modern art displayed in the Chicago Armory Show: "it makes no difference whether one of a lady's legs is seven feet long while the other is three, or whether her head looks like a soft-boiled egg that some one has mussed up in an attempt to crack the shell." The editorial, "Making Art Popular," explained that "Bevies of people of both sexes and all ages surged by the canvases, catalogue in hand, laughing fit to kill. . . . To make art galleries more popular, we suggest the posting of signs reading: 'You can laugh here whenever you feel like it.'"[53]

In fact, the Armory Show had a greater influence on mainstream Americans than the sponsors ever imagined. As Walt Kuhn explains: "The Armory Show affected the entire culture of America. Business caught on immediately."[54] Not only were advertisements, fashion, and even home decorating transformed by the introduction of modern art to the United States, but another exhibition of post-Impressionist art was developed by Gimbell's Brothers department store, who clearly hoped to cash in on the stir that the Armory Show had created. The exhibit was shown in Milwaukee, New York, Philadelphia, Cleveland, and Pittsburgh, although William Taylor, Son and Company and Boggs and Buhl's took over the exhibits for the final two cities. During the exhibit, the New York department store Wannamakers displayed "cubist" fashion in their windows. By the 1920s, *Vogue* could show "cubist" designs with the certainty that subscribers would all recognize what this label signified.[55] All of these developments illustrate how widespread and immediate the mainstreaming of modern art was in the United States. As a set-designer for the Armory Show explained: "Within a year we disarmed the revolution by domesticating it."[56] The media's ability to familiarize the public with an innovation like cubism—and the commodification of the movement as a recognizable style—was similarly used to publicize Stein's early writing.

"The New Poetry" and the Popular Press

Although there were some visual parodies of cubist art, and Duchamp in particular, a striking number of amused or skeptical responses in the mainstream press were written in verse. *American Art News* offered $10 to anyone who could solve the mystery of Duchamp's painting. What did it really mean? The winning contribution, "It's Only a Man," explained the riddle:

> You've tried to find her,
> And you've looked in vain
> Up the picture and down again,
> You've tried to fashion her of broken bits,
> And you've worked yourself into seventeen fits;
> The reason you've failed to tell you I can,
> It isn't a lady but only a man.[57]

In fact, many critics of the Armory Show used silly rhymes for comic effect. Maurice L. Ahern's "A Post Impression" appeared in the New York *Sun* on March 8:

> Awful lack of technique
> Awful lot of paint
> Makes a Cubist picture
> Look like what it ain't.

And the *Chicago Tribune*'s "Line-O'-Type or Two" column on the editorial page, which regularly published parodic, teasing verse about current events, printed this gem, directly linking Stein to the Armory Show:

> I called the canvas Cow with cud
> And hung it on the line,
> Altho' to me 'twas vague as mud,
> 'Twas clear to Gertrude Stein.[58]

In fact, an entire book of poetry, *The Cubies' ABC*, was published in response to the Armory Show, and Gertrude Stein was prominently featured:

> **G** is for Gertrude Stein's limpid lucidity
> (Eloquent scribe of the Futurist Soul,)
> Cubies devour each word with avidity:
> "Alone words lake sense!" they affirm with placidity
> But how wise we'll be when we've swallowed the whole."
> — G is for Gertrude Stein's limpidity.

S is for Schamberg's fair dame at her 'phone.
Conversing with G. Stein, the Futurist scribe.
The Cubies, eavesdropping, hear Gertrude bemoan:
'This one feeling many far seeing alone,
The bluer the bliss the redder the bribe!'
— S is for Schamberg's fair dame at her 'phone.[59]

The frequent use of poetry to parody the Armory Show might seem surprising, but verse was the form many editorials and letters to the editor used in this period to respond to current events in magazines and newspapers. In fact, it is astonishing how much poetry appeared on every editorial page in any American newspaper in the 1910s and 1920s on a daily basis. Readers still understood literature of all genres to be accessible, and poetry was no exception.

The popular conception of poetry and its use is especially relevant when we consider the reaction to Monroe's *Poetry* magazine and Stein's next publication, *Tender Buttons*, a book of abstract poetry that failed to reflect any of the conventions mainstream readers associated with verse. Harriet Monroe, who was art critic for the *Chicago Tribune* during the Armory Show, also connects the new art with the new poetry that she would print in *Poetry* magazine beginning in 1912. She recalls that when she wrote about the Armory Show for the *Tribune*, "I was fighting the same battle which was then starting or about to start in *Poetry*—a never ending battle for freedom of the creative spirit in the authentic and individual achievement of beauty through the fit expression of its ideas."[60]

Most Americans had spent considerable time in grammar school memorizing poetry for recitation and would have been accustomed to certain formal conventions. Between World War I and II, students most remembered memorizing or reading for school the classic poems William Wordsworth's "Daffodils" and Rudyard Kipling's "If," poems which exemplify the sentimental limits of mainstream America's poetic sensibility in the 1910s.[61] With such poems near to the hearts of many Americans, new developments in poetry threatening this norm were of great concern to the public. As editorials commented on Stein's writing and the value of modern art during the Amory show controversy, they also discussed new trends in poetry, with special attention paid to Harriet Monroe's *Poetry* magazine and the innovative free verse that was published there.

Monroe solicited poems from contemporary poets for the magazine's first issue by sending out letters which explained that she offered them "a chance to be heard in their own place, without the limitations imposed by the popular magazine. In other words, while the ordinary magazines must minister to a large public little interested in poetry, this magazine will appeal to, and it may be hoped will develop, a public primarily interested in poetry as an art."[62] Monroe's suggestion that the only place for poets to publish was in popular magazines, and that there was a great need for a serious place for poets to publish their work, shows that poetry was not considered high-brow or esoteric; the majority of the American public regularly read conventional poems in the pages of *Life* magazine or the *Saturday Evening Post* and would have understood poetry as a popular genre. Ezra Pound immediately and enthusiastically responded to Monroe's new magazine: "there is no other magazine in America which is not an insult to the serious artist and to the dignity of his art."[63]

Even before the first issue was published, *Poetry* was widely discussed nationwide. As Monroe explains, "many papers from New York to San Francisco diverted the midsummer doldrums with sarcastic comments. Even from the China Press in Shanghai came a would-be encouraging pat: 'Chicago, anxious to overshadow its packing-house reputation by repute as an art center, will hereafter be the home of the subsidized muse.'" When the October 1912 premiere issue did appear, editorials such as "Poetry in Porkopolis" appeared in Philadelphia.[64] Readers of the *Chicago Tribune*'s editorial page learned that: "Lots of inquiries are heard for Harriet Monroe's new magazine, which is called 'Poetry.' We're going to subscribe as soon as we get time, and everybody else ought to."[65]

Once the *Tribune* did receive the magazine, it became a target. The "Imagiste" poetry that Monroe promoted was so controversial that, like the Armory Show, it inspired satires on the editorial pages of many newspapers. Ezra Pound's "Salutation," which first appeared in *Poetry*, was parodied in the *Tribune*'s "Line-O'-Type" column, with an explicit reference to the Armory Show:

> O generation of the thoroughly smug
>   and thoroughly uncomfortable,
> I have seen fishermen picnicking in the sun . . .
> And I am happier than you are,
> And they were happier than I am;
> And the fish swim in the lake
>   and do not even own clothing.
> — Ezra Pound
>
> O degenerates in the art of writing,
>   and fallen ones,
> I have seen Cubist splattering their paints . . .
> You are far worse than they are,
> And they are much worse than nothing;
> And the nude descends the staircase,
>   and does not even own clothing.
> —*Chicago Tribune*[66]

The original poem by Pound was not included; readers were expected to understand the joke without instruction.

Other experimental verse began to appear and attracted the notice of the mainstream press. A 1915 article in the New York tribune about *Others*, an experimental little magazine published in New York, reported that, in order to rebel against traditional verse, these "younger poets have banded together in an uprising the purpose of which is to decry the usage of rhyme and metre." Making a direct comparison between free verse and the cubist art of the Armory Show, this journalist explains that: "The poor, harassed public has scarcely adjusted itself to seeing lines and colors, instead of the old story-pictures, and portraits that actually looked like the sitter, when it is called upon by the young poets to assist at a revolution of all its old ideas about verse."[67] But, although there was some outrage expressed at the "Imagiste" *vers libre* printed by Monroe and *Others*, as early as 1915 *Poetry* ceased to be shocking to some journalists. The New York *Sun*'s editorial, "The Business of Poetry," declared that:

> Three years ago Poetry began. We are not of those who scoff at the bright little Chicago magazine of the 'new' verse. . . . The first rapture of publicity is definitely passed, and Miss Monroe, who is a rather conservatively inclined chaperon of the radical brood, speaks soberly for the cause. Modernism in verse, she seems to say, is only a return to first principles. Metric devices that have been regarded as fundamental are only incidental; derived not elemental. . . . This is not sensational.[68]

The proliferation of free verse continued to inspire jokes and discussions in newspapers and magazines, and some remained unconvinced that this new writing should be taken seriously. As Amy Lowell pointed out: "We hear so much about 'new poetry' today, and see it so injudiciously lauded in publishers' catalogues, and so non-understandingly reviled and jeered at in the daily press, that it is no wonder if most people think it a mere advertising term, with no basis in fact."[69]

Perhaps there was no consensus as to the value of this *vers libre*, but public interest did translate into book sales. Monroe's 1917 anthology, co-edited with Alice Corbin Hendersen, *The New Poetry,* a collection of poems that had had not necessarily appeared in *Poetry* but were, according to Monroe and Henderson, representative of the "new poetry," was "a best seller in the poetry field," challenging the enormous popularity of Edgar Lee Masters' *Spoon River Anthology*.[70] A review appeared on the front page of the *New York Times Book Review* and the volume was discussed in the popular, comic *Life* magazine: "Few 'anthologies' (which for the most part are hobby-horses offered for hire) serve so present a need as does this interesting volume."[71] In July 1917, *Poetry* was celebrated in an editorial in the *New York Tribune,* which called it "best magazine of poetry in the English language": this compliment was quoted in the *Chicago Tribune*.[72]

Of course, all of the work that appeared in *Poetry*—significantly subtitled "a magazine of verse"—was not radical. As Jayne Marek observes, "their editorial agenda differed form the elitist position of some modernist writers; *Poetry* provided a democratic space that encouraged inclusiveness and extensive scope in modernism at a crucial time."[73] Harriet Monroe remembers that "The two most widely quoted poems we ever printed, Helen Hoyt's 'Ellis Park' and Joyce Kilmer's 'Trees,' appeared on consecutive pages during our first year" and "Trees" also appeared in *The New Poetry*.[74] Certainly, these sentimental poems broke no new literary ground and "Trees" was famously ridiculed in Cleanth Brooks and Robert Penn Warren's influential New Critical textbook, *Understanding Poetry*, in 1938. Many of the more popular, conservative poems that Monroe printed appeared in newspapers across the country, since they were not copyrighted.[75] But even if Monroe's magazine printed this conventional verse, she was always most interested in the innovative *vers libre* that most readers associated with *Poetry*. And, as art critic for the *Tribune*, she was able to highlight the radical work of modernists including Stein at unexpected moments. She reproduced a large portrait of Stein in December 1913, accompanied by this commentary:

> Miss Grace Gaselle, who has recently retuned from Paris, has a number of interesting portraits in her studio in the Fine Arts building. Among them is one of Gertrude Stein, the famous American woman who has been the patron and friend of Matisse, Picasso, and other post-impressionists, and whose recent prose sketches have aroused comment as an expression of the same movement of revolt in literature.[76]

Tender Buttons: "the latest Cubist joke"

Considering the fact that the subject of poetry was of great interest to reviewers, editors, and American readers, it is no surprise that Gertrude Stein's unusual book of poetry, *Tender Buttons*, received so much attention in 1914. According to Brinnin, *Tender Buttons* "appalled the world of letters, sent readers into fits of unamused laughter, and finally provoked the most exasperated reaction to greet any book of the twentieth century."[77] While Brinnin is certainly correct that the book did provoke a dramatic reaction across the country, Stein did not seem to mind the book's reception. As Alice reports in *The Autobiography of Alice B. Toklas*:

> [Tender Buttons] was a very charming little book and Gertrude Stein was enormously pleased, and it, as every one knows, had an enormous influence on all young writers and started off columnists in the newspapers of the whole country on their long campaign of ridicule. I must say that when the columnists are really funny, and they quite often are, Gertrude Stein chuckles and reads them aloud to me.[78]

Some critics have argued that it is remarkable that the book was noticed in so many newspapers and magazines throughout the United States, since only 1000 copies were printed, suggesting that it is likely that some reviewers had not even seen the book.[79] Even so, in June of 1914, the *Pittsburgh Dispatch* called Stein "the most talked-about creature in the intellectual world today," a characterization suggested by Stein's publisher and repeated by reviewers in Louisville, KY and elsewhere.[80] As Leonard Diepeveen argues, the publication of *Tender Buttons* was an "event."[81] By December, it had been so frequently discussed that the *Boston Evening Transcript* could mention it with confidence that any reader would understand the reference: "The Syracuse Public Library put Gertrude Stein's 'Tender Buttons' under the heading 'Literature.' Surely, there should be limits to the use of sarcasm, even in library bulletins."[82]

Columnists clearly got news of books from other reviews and, since *Tender Buttons* was quoted so extensively in some publications, many had actually read significant samples of Stein's work. The *Chicago Tribune*, for example, printed a spread of 19 of the poems (or sections) in *Tender Buttons*, including the lengthy "A Piece of Coffee" and "A Plate," with a large picture of Stein sitting at her desk.[83] Extensive excerpts also appeared in the Chicago *Evening Post*, the *Chicago Advance*, the *New York Sun*, the *New York World*, the *Philadelphia Press*, the *Boston Transcript*, the *Baltimore Sun*, the *San Antonio Light*, and the St. Louis *Post Dispatch*.[84] As Alice observes in the *Autobiography*: "They always quote it and what is more, they quote it correctly . . . My sentences do get under their skin, only they do not know that they do, she has often said."[85] Any reviewer who had seen these extensive quotations would have much ammunition for parody or respectful analysis. The *Omaha Herald*, for example, made it clear their knowledge of Stein came from other reviews; they explained that Stein was "described, in a review in the Chicago Tribune to which we are indebted, as a literary Cubist."[86]

Mabel Dodge predicted that Stein's decision to publish with Claire Marie Press would bring about a mistaken public impression of her work, that it was "decadent & Broadwayish & that sort of thing," but Stein did not seem to be concerned about this threat.[87] As James Mellow observes, "[Stein] knew the value of publicity—good and bad."[88] In any case, it is doubtful that a major publisher would have accepted the book. Claire Marie was run by the eccentric poet Donald Evans, who proclaimed in the promotional brochure that accompanied review copies of *Tender Buttons* that he published "New Books for Exotic Tastes":

> CLAIRE MARIE believes that there are in America seven hundred civilized people only.
>
> CLAIRE MARIE publishes books for civilized people only.
>
> CLAIRE MARIE'S aim, it follows from the premises, is not even secondarily commercial.

Despite the frivolous reputation of the obscure Claire Marie Press, the publication of *Tender Buttons* was noticed by the mainstream press even before it was reviewed. In their weekly "News of Books" column, the *New York Times Book Review* (mis)reported that "Claire Marie, the recently established publishing house that pays especial attention to belles letters in artistic dress, announces 'Objects : Food : Rooms,' a cubist volume, by Gertrude Stein."[89]

What does "Tender Buttons" mean? The title of Stein's book has been a subject of debate since it appeared in 1914. The Boston *Evening Transcript* asserted that "'Tender Buttons' means French mushrooms—canned. Why 'tender,' you ask? That is the divine irony of it."[90] Another contemporary review offered ideas for what "tender" might signify, and observed that there were three common definitions of the word: "It is not clear whether the 'tender' of the title means a rowboat, a fuel car attached to a locomotive, or is an expression of human emotions."[91] Of course, the confusion does not end with the book's title. Richard Bridgman suggests that "Because in *Tender Buttons* Gertrude Stein seemed to veer off into meaninglessness, the book has a certain notoriety," but it might be more accurate to say that *Tender Buttons* suggests so many possible interpretations that, as Oscar Cargill observes, "the piece has too much meaning."[92] For the most part, recent criticism of *Tender Buttons* can be divided into two camps: interpretations focusing on the poem as an exploration of language and its possibilities, and those that understand the work as an analysis of gender relations, but first readers did not advance these sophisticated readings.[93] It is certainly true that any reader of *Tender Buttons* must put aside conventional literary expectations, and decide how to mange what, at first glance, appears to be nonsense. How, for example, should a reader approach the section titled "Milk"?: "Climb up in sight climb in the whole utter needles, and a guess a whole guess is hanging. Hanging hanging."

In her description of the composition of *Tender Buttons*, Stein explained that no group of words can be designated accurately as nonsense:

> I took individual words and thought about them until I got their weight and volume complete and put them next to another word, and at this same time I found out very soon that there is no such thing as putting them together without sense. It is impossible. . . . Any human being putting down words had to make sense out of them.[94]

But in order to make "sense," audiences must approach reading in a different way. The many, varied readings of the poem may suggest that a reader's preconceived notions are especially significant when interpreting such an evocative work, but this does not necessarily suggest that such interpretations are invalid. Stein explains, "I was not interested in what people would think when they read this poetry; I was entirely taken up with my problem and if it did not tell my story it would tell some story. They might have another conception which would be their affair."[95]

While many reviews that appeared in 1914 used a mocking, bewildered tone to describe the contents of *Tender Buttons*, some defended Stein's linguistic experiment. Reviewers and columnists were clearly influenced by Claire Marie's description of the book in the brochure which accompanied the review copies:

> Her followers believe she has added a new dimension to literature; scoffers call her writings a mad meaningless jumble of words, and there are some who assert that with her tongue in her cheek she is having a sardonic joke at the expense of those who take who take her seriously. It is idle to attempt to pass judgment at the present moment. Time alone can give the verdict. For us it is merely that she is a real force that must be reckoned with—she cannot be ignored. . . . The effect produced on the first reading is something like terror.

Stein's publisher effectively framed the debate; the New York *Evening Sun*'s editorial note explained that:

> The worst that has been said of [Stein's] latest book Tender Buttons is that it is a farrago of nonsense, a meaningless medley of ill assorted words. . . . The defense offered by her admirers is in fact that she has found an entirely new use for words, arranging them indeed without too nice regard for sense, but with clear and telling emotional intent. To this argument her critics have no answer, except her prose means nothing to them. They are obliged, however to admit that it is at least new.[96]

The *Chicago Tribune* directly quoted the first two sentences of Claire Marie's description, with a few minor changes, as an introduction to a lengthy excerpt from the book.[97] The exposé, which filled an entire newspaper page, inspired such responses from *Tribune* readers that a columnist on the op-ed page finally commented to readers: "A great many flippant contributors have sent in comments on Gertrude Stein's cubist stuff, but we don't think it is nice to poke fun at a person who is afflicted as she is."[98]

There had been such stir over Stein's "Portrait of Mabel Dodge" that many reviewers reminded readers of Stein's relationship to the Armory Show. New York's *Commercial Advertiser* noted that "from Claire Marie . . . comes at last a Gertrude Stein volume . . . in the new Stein manner. The old Stein manner, it appears, was too easy. . . . Some of those who read the famous 'Portrait of Mabel Dodge,' for example, are even said to have recognized Mabel Dodge when they meet her at her 'salon' on lower Fifth avenue."[99] In Minnesota, the St. Paul *Pioneer Press* remembered that "When cubist art was first brought to American attention by the international exhibition in New York a year or more ago, the related work in letters of Gertrude Stein came up also for the amused consideration of the public." This reviewer quoted from *Tender Buttons*, then observed: "Sounds a trifle like nonsense, doesn't it? But you must remember that Gertrude Stein is using words to convey sensations, not ideas."[100] Even more enthusiastic was Robert Emons Rogers of the *Boston Transcript*, who urged readers to take Stein's work seriously.

> If we consider her then as a person who is consciously working out an art form and who knows what she is about, a description of her method of work may be illuminating. . . . [S]he hopes to present impressions by arrangements of sounds of familiar words which suggest an emotion rather than define a fact.[101]

Constructive comment also appeared in the Buffalo *Times*: "Those who are avid for the literature of tomorrow will find great satisfaction in this book. It is one of the most unique books of the twentieth century."[102]

Many compared the book to cubist or "futurist" art, clearly an insult. Before quoting Stein, the St. Joseph (MO) *Press* noted that "'Why are the cubists?' is the question the majority of the public ask. It is hard to believe that they take themselves seriously, but they seem to."[103] Emphasizing how familiar the public already was with "futurist" writing, surely as a result of the incredible attention paid to the Armory Show, the New York *Sun* observed:

> The bits and snatches of 'futurist' literature that have been copied into the newspapers for the delectation of the general public may have teased and tickled some part of the susceptible populace in to a curious yearning for a closer, fuller view of this much heralded literary 'novelty'. It can be had in Gertrude Stein's Tender Buttons.[104]

The *Pittsburgh Dispatch* claimed that "Gertrude Stein is to literature what the Cubists and Futurists are to art, maybe worse than that."[105] The *Boston Herald*'s review—"What?"—explained that "Some critics call this little book 'Cubist composition.' We do not think the Cubists deserve it."[106] The Detroit *Free Press* and the Columbus *Dispatch* printed this dismissal:

> It was to be expected that the Futurists, having ceased to dismay us with their art, and having foisted their primary and violent colors upon us in the other fashions of the moment, would address themselves to literature. Forthwith, Doctor Dippy is outdone. Gertrude Stein has perpetrated the latest Cubist joke.[107]

The St. Joseph Missouri *News*, the Philadelphia *North American*, the Pittsburg *Post*, and *Smart Set* all similarly categorized *Tender Buttons* as "Cubist" or "Futurist."[108] The review in the *Los Angeles Times*, "Futurist Essays," pretended to be above the fray, arguing that "[*Tender Buttons*] lends itself to invective and satire; it is an excellent butt for ridicule, and offers a rare opportunity for all sort of sarcasm and funniness. But we restrain ourselves, having little sympathy with those who mock and tease the foolish."[109]

Other reviewers enjoyed poking fun at Stein's book rather than attempting to contextualize or understand it. Indeed, *Tender Buttons* was a columnist's gift, easily inspiring amused comment. The New York City *Call* suggested that Stein was "what the Germans call 'Wort-salad,' a style particularly cultivated by crazy people. . . . The way to make a world-salad is to sit in a dark room, preferably between the silent and mystic hours of midnight and dawn, and let the moving fingers write whatever comes."[110] The *Detroit News* declared that "After reading excerpts from [*Tender Buttons*] a person feels like going out and pulling the Dime Bank building over onto himself."[111] And George Cram Cook wrote that "A week or so ago a characteristic new work of Gertrude Stein's issued from the press of Claire Marie. It is read, it is read aloud, it is talked about. . . . It can be read either backward or forward, for it produces the same impression either way. Three printers gave up their jobs with the Claire Marie Press rather than go on setting type on it."[112] Many reviewers declared the book unreadable; Charles Ashleigh of the Chicago *Evening Post*, the New York City *Press* and the Louisville *Courier* all admitted defeat, the *Courier* arguing that it was impossible to understand the book. "It is claimed by Gertrude Stein's publishers that there are persons who take her seriously. . . . We do not get it, and we are inclined to believe that those who read scraps with delight and do not get anything make up the entire sum of Miss Stein's admirers."[113] The eminent H. L. Mencken's also suggested that some readers only pretended to have an affection for *Tender Buttons* in order to prove their own sophistication. Lampooning "intellectual" readers, he wrote that:

> As the publishers frankly admit, the emotions aroused by a first reading of Miss Stein are "something like terror," but as one proceeds the beauty of these super-sentences begins to caress the refined mind, and in the end the effect is almost electrical. Not, however, upon the bonehead. The common earthworm will gag at such filaments of fancy. They will demand a special education. They presuppose a Cubist and resilient cerebrum.[114]

By contrast, some reviews sarcastically claimed that the incomprehensible book was actually transparent. The *Pittsburg Sun* joked: "This book is almost stupidly conventional. . . .What schoolboy has not written callow poems about the 'handsome cheese which is stone?' Really, we must have something new—these old things are beginning to pall."[115] And the *Chicago Evening Post* thought that *Tender Buttons* would not appeal to literary sophisticates at all: "One would think that the function of words in human experience was pretty well established by this time. But in these days of anti-intellectualism it is, apparently, dangerous to think, if one wishes to be right."[116] Because *Tender Buttons* dispensed with literary convention so thoroughly, there was no consensus among its first readers as to how it should be classified or who its intended readers were. Some reviewers clearly believed that Stein's experiment was beyond understanding and thus threatened serious literature. Indeed, "Futurist Poetry" seemed so silly that anyone could produce it. The *Chicago Tribune* asked readers to send in their own attempts, and printed samples in August 1914. They challenged readers: "Have you ever tried your hand at futurist poetry? . . . Use a vacuum cleaner on your brain . . . get rid of all your former notions of grammar, spelling, and methods of expressing your thoughts and have a try at this newest type of verse," the newspaper challenged readers.[117]

Sensitive to this mainstream interest in Stein's work, her important advocate, Carl Van Vechten, did his best to promote her work in the 1910s although he was relatively unknown as a writer. As his fame began to grow in the late teens and exploded in the 1920s, his confidence in Stein's writing and his consistent willingness to write about her work in newspapers, magazines, and even to make references to her in his best-selling novels helped to maintain public interest and knowledge of Stein's obscure, and sometimes difficult to obtain, publications. His comments about Stein were repeated in the mainstream press; as early as 1918 Fanny Butcher noted in her "News in Brief of Authors and of Their Books" column that

> Carl Van Vechten, whose "Interpreters and Interpretations" (Knopf) are charming, unrivaled little essays on music and life, the other day made the amusing suggestion that a real experiment in the matter of opera would be a collaboration of Gertrude Stein and Irving Berlin. There's never anything mid-Victorian about Carl's point of view. That's why his volumes are such fun.[118]

Van Vechten was friends with Donald Evans of Claire Marie Press and was responsible for Stein's decision to publish *Tender Buttons* there. In response to the mocking attitude found in so many reviews of the book, he published "How to Read Gertrude Stein" in a small, yet respected literary journal in the United States, *The Trend* in August 1914, a piece that offers little practical advice for the reader. He concedes that "Miss Stein has no explanations to offer regarding her work. I have often questioned her, but I have met with no satisfaction. She asks you to read."[119] Introducing two subjects that would become of extraordinary importance to Stein's critics over the years, Van Vechten describes both her personality and her wardrobe:

> As a personality Gertrude Stein is unique. She is massive in physique, a Rabelaisian woman with a splendid thoughtful face; mind dominating her matter. Her velvet robes, mostly brown, and her carpet slippers associate themselves with her indoor appearance. To go out she belts

herself, adds a walking staff, and a trim unmodish turban. This garb suffices for a shopping tour or a box party at the *Opéra*.[120]

Although *The Trend* was considered an avant-garde publication, it was read by mainstream reviewers and columnists who were looking for subjects to discuss. Van Vechten's article attracted enough notice for the *Boston Evening Transcript* to discuss it and dismiss his rather conventional interpretation of Stein's title, *Tender Buttons*: "The three divisions which comprise the book in a way explain the title. They are 'Food; Objects; Rooms,' all things which fasten our lives together, and whose complications may be said to make them tender."[121] The Chicago *Evening Post* also discussed Van Vechten's commentary: "We have just been reading an article in the October Trend on how to read Gertrude Stein—not that we have any desire to read her." The point of this article is to revel at quotations from *Three Lives* that Van Vechten claims are comprehensible.[122] And Don Marquis also referred to Van Vechten's article in his column for the New York *Evening Sun*. He explains that readers "ask us from time to time, 'Is there a real Gertrude Stein?' There is. We clip the following portrait . . . from an article in The Trend written by Carl Van Vechten." The blurb describing Stein's personality and dress is quoted in full.[123]

Hoaxes

Tender Buttons received so much publicity and, at the same time, was so baffling to many critics that some were convinced that the book was a hoax. Emphasizing how well known Stein had already become, Richard Burton asked his Minneapolis readers:

> Was there ever in the known history of man a time when the faker and poseur had as good a chance as he had today? . . . The case in point is Gertrude Stein, 'cubist' of literature, futurist of words, and self-advertiser of pseudo-intellectual antics. . . . It will not do to say that nobody takes her seriously; newspapers do, or they would not give up so much space to her. [124]

Leveling a similar accusation at Stein, Alfred Kreymborg titled an article: "Gertrude Stein—Hoax and Hoaxtress: A Study of the Woman Whose 'Tender Buttons' Has Furnished New York With a New Kind of Amusement." Not surprisingly, Kreymborg, a poet known for his own experimentation, had more patience with *Tender Buttons* than Mr. Burton. He decided that

> serious or hoaxtress, Gertrude Stein has provided the world with a new kind of entertainment for some time past. Whether you wrinkle your brow and curl your tongue for a long, ponderous defense of her work,

or whether you scowl and shoot your tongue for a venomous attack, or whether you merely lean back in your velvet easy chair and open your mouth for a good roaring laugh, Miss Stein will have benefited you. She has given you a new sensation. And sensations are so rare, particularly in these days of warfare that you don't want to deny yourself the opportunity of one.[125]

According to Sherwood Anderson and others who later became admirers of Stein, *Tender Buttons* was considered both so amusing and so original that it became a sensation in literary circles and reading aloud from it became a kind of party game. Anderson explains:

My brother had been at some sort of a gathering of literary people on the evening before and someone had read aloud from Miss Stein's new book.... After a few lines the reader stopped and was greeted by loud shouts of laughter. It was generally agreed that the author had done a thing we Americans call "putting something across"—the meaning being that she had, by a strange, freakish performance, managed to attract attention to herself, get herself discussed in newspapers, become for a time a figure in our hurried, harried lives.[126]

Similarly, Kay Boyle remembers hearing her mother read aloud from *Tender Buttons* to her father's medical colleagues when she was a child. According to Boyle, her mother believed that the men would be "enthralled," by this taste of high culture, but "one of the doctors laughed so hard over Stein that he became ill and had to be taken upstairs to bed.... I remember the doctor's face as he was led, crippled with laughter, up the stairs."[127]

When it was suggested to Stein that *Tender Buttons* was a hoax, she was defensive. In 1914, a reporter in London who had read some of the American reviews of *Tender Buttons* asked Stein if the book had been a "stunt." She explained that "stunts are not created in this way. They are invariably the product of one mind reacting on the work of another or the caricature of a thing somebody else has created.... A stunt is always founded on something that somebody else has done."[128] Indeed, this comment of Stein's was prophetic. In 1916, after *Tender Buttons* and the Imagists had been thoroughly dissected by the mainstream American press, Arthur Davison Ficke and Witter Bynner spectacularly pulled off a literary hoax that has been largely forgotten, but was news throughout the country when it was revealed in 1918. *Spectra: A Book of Poetic Experiments* (1916), by Anne Knish and Emanuel Morgan, was composed by the drunken Ficke and Bynner in February 1916 in an attempt to spoof the new, and to them ridiculous, *vers libre* printed in *Poetry, Others, The Little Review* and elsewhere. The book was immediately accepted for publication by Mitchell Kennerley, who was then let in on the hoax.[129]

The book included an elaborate, over-written introduction that apparently explained the Spectrist philosophy:

> The theme of a poem is to be regarded as a prism, upon which the colorless white light of infinite existence falls and is broken up into glowing, beautiful, and intelligible hues. . . . Just as the colors of the rainbow recombine into a white light,— just as the reflex of the eye's picture vividly haunts sleep,—just as the ghosts which surround reality are the vital part of that existence,—so may the Spectric vision, if successful, synthesize, prolong, and at the same time multiply the emotional images of the reader.

The poems did not seem to have much relation to this theory. Instead, Bynner and Ficke wrote thinly veiled parodies of the *vers libre* that was in such vogue, often targeting specific poets or poems. Knish's "Opus 200" is no exception:

> If I should enter to his chamber
> And suddenly touch him,
> Would he fade to a thin mist,
> Or glow into a fire-ball,
> Or burst like a punctured light-globe?
> It is impossible that he would merely yawn and rub
> And say—"What is it?"[130]

This particular poem clearly mocks T. S. Eliot's "The Love Song of J. Alfred Prufrock," which first appeared in *Poetry* magazine in June 1915. The next line, of course, should be: "Let us go and make our visit." Probably the most frequent victim, however, was Amy Lowell. In the eyes of the American public, Lowell had become the face of the new and controversial free verse that begin to appear. As Catherine Turner observes:

> Her sponsorship of collections such as *Some Imagist Poets* (1915), her critical works such as *Tendencies in Modern American Poetry* (1917), and her lecture tours alerted consumers to the way literature was changing. . . . T. S. Eliot called her a "demon saleswoman," and, while he surely did not mean it as a compliment, this description captures the power and fervor of Lowell's lectures on "the new style."[131]

Lowell's publicity campaign was successful thanks to the attentive mainstream press, but it was her popular public lectures that attracted the most attention and led to her celebrity status in the 1910s and 1920s. Literary lectures significantly contributed to the popular awareness of literary trends in America in the early twentieth century America, attracting audiences who wished not only to be educated but also entertained by lively personalities. In 1947 Henry Seidel Canby recalled of Lowell: "On the lecture platform, or in her vast home in a park at Brookline, or in her suite at the Hotel Belmont in New York, where she held court for a few weeks each year, she make poetry exciting (as of course it ought to be) and stimulated the adrenal glands of her listeners."[132] Lowell was so famous that on 2 March 1925 she appeared on the cover of *Time* magazine.

Although *Spectra* did elicit many negative reviews, like *Tender Buttons* it was given a tremendous amount of attention and, according to Curtis Mac-Dougal, the widely available book became "as close to being a best seller as poetry ever reaches."[133] The *New York Herald* called *Spectra* a "daughter of Futurist poetry, a granddaughter of *vers libre*, and no relation at all to real poetry" while the St. Louis *Post-Dispatch* observed that: "they have a theory of poetry all their own, but the stuff in the volume does not seem to be poetic."[134] Much to his delight, Bynner was asked to review his own creation for the *New Republic*. His praise of the book was primarily at the expense of the Imagists, who he argued were so concerned with "technique" that they "don't connect" with readers. Bynner argued that the Spectrists have "gone deeper than the attempts of any of the other latter-day schools" because they "show more interesting vigor" and "bring to the 'new poetry' a quality it had rather lacked."[135] He also did not hesitate to discuss *Spectra* poets in lectures, during interviews, and in conversations with friends.

Ficke and Bynner began submitting poems under the names Morgan and Knish to the little magazines, a primary object of their literary joke. Alfred Kreymborg's *Others* printed an entire "Spectric" issue in January 1917 and Spectrist poems appeared in the *Little Review* in July 1917. Apparently Kreymborg, who had called *Tender Buttons* a hoax, did not suspect that Knish and Morgan were imposters.[136] Harriet Monroe accepted some of Emanuel Morgan's poems for *Poetry* magazine, and went so far as to request that he send in a few more poems so "reader would have a chance to get it," but when the hoax was revealed she declined to print them. Monroe admits in passing that: "They had a lot of fun being taken seriously and getting accepted here and there. *Poetry* was almost caught, for an 'Emmanuel Morgan' poem was waiting guiltily for publication when careless gossiping betrayed the hoax."[137]

The hoax was finally revealed in a question and answer session at one of Bynner's lectures in April 1918 in Detroit. "Is it not true, Mr. Bynner, that you are Emanuel Morgan and that Arthur Davison Ficke is Anne Knish?" an audience member asked. Bynner simply answered: "Yes."[138] Newspapers around the country commented on the resolution of the affair. The *New York Times Magazine* printed a lengthy story about the hoax in the *New York Times Magazine* with pictures of Ficke and Bynner and the St. Louis *Post-Dispatch* observed that: "it was a huge joke on the part of the two poets."[139] But some responses were less amused. Jane Heap's editorial in the *Little Review* failed to understand why poems that had been admired were suddenly considered poor. "I confess to a deep ignorance of the nature of the hoax. If a man changes his name and writes better stuff, why does that make the public so ridiculous?" she asked. In fact, many editors argued that the hoax was only successful because Ficke and Bynner had succeeded in producing better poetry than they did under their real names.[140] Without embarrassment, William Carlos Williams confessed that he was "completely taken in by the hoax and ... admired them as a whole quite sincerely."[141]

Despite the fact that the Spectra hoax was well known, another book of poetry appeared under the name Emanuel Morgan, *Pins for Wings*, in 1920. More directly, this collection revealed that the Spectrists were critiquing contemporary poets, including Stein:

GERTRUDE STEIN
Wings rotting
under water

CONRAD AIKEN
phosphorescent
plumbing

H.D.
the Winged Victory
hopping

The target of the hoax becomes even more obvious and the volume can be clearly seen as a critique and parody of free verse. Finally, several "posthumous" poems by Morgan appeared in the 1927 *American Caravan*, an anthology that was a Literary Guild selection and thus was widely distributed. The fictitious biographical note observed that after Anne Knish had recently died of an unknown disease, Morgan committed suicide; the real identity of Morgan was not mentioned but readers were expected to understand the joke, and reviewers did comment on the hoax. The *American Caravan* also included Stein's enigmatic "Mildred's Thoughts," a contribution that received much attention in the mainstream reviews of the book.

This public interest in new poetry—including *Poetry* magazine, Imagism, *Tender Buttons* and the new "Spectrist" poets that Ficke and Bynner invented—shows how eager American readers were to learn about exciting literary developments, and how gullible. In 1918, Randolph Bourne complained in *The Dial* that: "The current popularity of verse, the vogue of the little theaters and the little magazines, reveal a public that is almost pathetically receptive to anything which has the flavor or the pretension of literary art.... Almost anyone can win recognition and admiration."[142] Similarly irritated with what he considered indiscriminate literary tastes, in 1940 Curtis MacDougal observed that Ficke's and Bynner's "Spectra" hoax was "soul satisfying to those who find it impossible to swallow such literary fads of the last half century as Vorticism, Imagism, Gertrude Stein, and e. e. cummings."[143] Traditional writers and critics like Ficke and Bynner thought the free verse poets were both lazy and pretentious, but of course these outraged dismay dissenters only succeeded in contributing to the public's general knowledge of—and interest in—these innovative poets.

Don Marquis and "The Sun Dial"

Stein was aware of the critics in New York and elsewhere who regularly discussed her work. In 1945 she recalled that:

> Carl Van Vechten . . . was a great believer in me from the very beginning. Then there was a group of young people in New York. I do not know what has become of them now. They were all friends of Carl Van Vechten. There was a man called Don Marquis, and he in the guise of making fun was very much interested in my work. Henry McBride said "if you laugh with her you have more fun than laughing at her." Protestingly, he used pieces of my work in his paper.[144]

Henry McBride was a critic for the New York *Sun* who took Stein's work seriously, and did what he could to promote her in his columns.[145] "It was Henry McBride," Alice remembers in *The Autobiography of Alice B. Toklas*, "who used to keep Gertrude Stein's name before the public all those tormented years. Laugh if you like, he used to say to her detractors, but laugh with and not at her, in that way you will enjoy it all much better."[146] He not only printed excerpts of Stein's work in the *Sun*, but he also mentioned her contributions to obscure little magazines like *Rogue*. McBride arranged to have her "M. Vollard et Cézanne" printed in the *Sun* in October 1915, accompanied by his analysis and a letter from Stein explaining her relationship to Vollard, the picture dealer who sold Leo and Gertrude Stein their first Cézannes. As Alice points out: "This was the first fugitive piece of Gertrude Stein's to be so printed and it gave both her and Vollard a great deal of pleasure."[147] McBride had such confidence in the lasting value of Stein's writing that in a discussion of the first issue of *Rogue*, where Stein's "Aux Galeries Lafayette" appeared in March 1915, he wrote that "Rogue was certainly astute from a business point of view in engaging the interest of Miss Stein whose extraordinary and attractive art will tide a magazine, if anything can, over the first few anxious trial numbers."[148]

By contrast to McBride, Don Marquis consistently used Stein's work for comic effect. Marquis was a humorist who wrote poetry, short stories and novels, but became famous for his newspaper column "The Sun Dial" that appeared on the editorial page of the New York *Evening Sun* from 1912–22. From 1922–25, he wrote another column, "The Lantern," for the New York *Tribune*, he regularly contributed to *Collier's* in the 1920s and 1930s, and in the early 1930s Marquis wrote a column for the *Saturday Review of Literature*. According to Lynn Lee, "from 1915–1930, it would have been difficult to find an American humorist who was any better known than Don

Marquis" and this seems to be accurate, although his name has been largely forgotten.[149] Today, Marquis is most known for the characters Archy and Mehitabel, who were first introduced in "The Sun Dial" and then appeared in several books, including *Archy and Mehitabel*, *Archy does his Part*, *Archy's Life of Mehitabel*, and *The Lives and Times of Archy and Mehitabel*. In the 1950s, E. B. White remembered Marquis's influence, and how different the culture of newspapers was in "an era before the newspaper column had degenerated. In 1916 to hold a job on a daily paper, a columnist was expected to be something of a scholar and a poet. . . . Buying a paper then was quietly exciting, in a way that it has ceased to be."[150]

I have found over 50 references to Gertrude Stein in "The Sun Dial" from June 1914 to March 1915. As Alyson Tischler observes, Marquis was an "accidental promoter" of Stein and *Tender Buttons* in particular.[151] His relentless use of Stein in the column familiarized readers across the country with excerpts of *Tender Buttons*. One Rhode Island paper wryly observed that "Many hurried readers without the time for the serious study of profound literature for which they have a normal intellectual bent must be greatly indebted to Don Marquis of the *Evening Sun* for his frequent quotations from the works of Gertrude Stein, that great Futurist litterateur."[152] Marquis was not the only columnist on an op-ed page who mentioned Stein; the "Line-O'-Type or Two" column in the *Chicago Tribune* referenced Stein with some frequency, but with nothing like the regularity of Marquis.[153]

Marquis habitually chose a subject to ridicule for an extended period, and Stein was his choice for 1914 and 15. His use of a "running gag" can be equated to the humor we now associate with late-night talk show hosts, who often choose a current event or celebrity and repeatedly make reference to it for an easy laugh. Marquis invented regular characters who offered commentary on specific cultural developments, such as the drunken Old Soak, whose exploits hilariously exposed the drawbacks of prohibition; Archy, a free verse poet who had been reincarnated as a cockroach; Mehitabel, a cat who had been Cleopatra in a previous life; and Hermione, a young woman who was fascinated by any cultural or literary fad. Hermione's enthusiasm for any new school of thought or philosophy effectively exposed the silliness of these trends. She explained, for example:

> I'm taking up Bergson this week.
>   Next week I'm going to take up Etruscan
> Vases and the Montessori system.
>   Oh, no, I haven't lost my interest in sociology.
>   Only the other night we went down in the auto
> And watched the breadline.[154]

It was no surprise that Hermione discovered Gertrude Stein. She declared:

Don't you think Gertrude Stein is wonderful, just simply *wonderful*? We—our little group of serious thinkers, you know—have been giving an entire week to her, and the more we study her the more esoteric she seems, and the more esoteric the more fascinating.

A great many people, you know, pretend they are understanding her when they really aren't. The way to tell is to give them a test sentence, and then watch them as they say it over and over.
If they're only faking they try to *act* emotions—to put expression on their faces, and look delighted, and all that.
But if they really *get* the message, their faces just simply get wooden, and you can see that while their lips are repeating the words their Souls have Gone on a Journey.[155]

Marquis's favorite way to ridicule Stein was simply to quote from *Tender Buttons*. He would introduce a line or two with: "A great thought from Gertrude Stein" or, on July 8, "Yet another esoteric revelation by Gertrude Stein—this one is entitled 'Salad Dressing and an Artichoke': 'Please pale hot, please cover rose, please acre in the red stranger, please butter all the beefsteak with regular feel faces.'"[156] Then he would go on to another subject in his column. Marquis included these brief tastes of Stein throughout the summer of 1914, occasionally quoting longer sections. On August 28 Marquis wrote that "The following thoughts are from an article entitled 'Food,' by Miss Gertrude Stein, the champion scrambler—brain, egg or word—of Futurist literature, will no doubt be of considerable assistance to those who are mobilizing against the well-known price of food" and then printed the first half of the lengthy "Breakfast" that appears in the FOOD section of *Tender Buttons*.[157] By September, quotes from *Tender Buttons* were prefaced by challenges to the reader such as: "We imagine Miss Stein's critics will find it very difficult to disprove this."[158] Or, in December: "A Christmas thought—well, can you prove that it isn't about Christmas?—by Gertrude Stein."[159]

Marquis regularly printed brief letters from readers about the subjects he addressed in the column and he did not fail to print numerous letters about Stein. Some simply commented on the frequency with which he quoted from her work. One reader complained: "Sir: Please publish Gertrude Stein's volume all at once and get done with it, won't you?"[160] But when he did not print any lines by Stein for a week or more, Marquis received concerned queries from Stein readers: "Sir: A whole week has elapsed since you have given us any Gertrude Stein stuff. What do you mean by cutting off the supply just as I was beginning to understand it?"[161] Or: "Sir: Please give us some more of Gertrude Stein."[162]

Many readers who wrote to Marquis had a sense of humor. One wrote: "Sir: What's this here from Gertrude Stein about tend 'er buttons? Why doesn't she tend 'em herself?"[163] And many submitted queries about Stein, parodies of her work, or examples of writing that they thought was reminiscent of Stein. "Sir, for the love of heaven is there such a person as Gertrude Stein? I should like is there why if so or not if any?" one reader wondered.[164] Another wrote: "Sir: I have just found out why is Gertrude Stein. The answer is aphasia. See Kipling's 'Plain Tales From the Hills,; 'The Conversion of Mc Goggin,'. . ..: 'Perfectly conceivable—dictionary—red oak—amenable—cause—retaining—shuttlecock—alone.'"[165] And one reader sent in a recipe for a new drink, called the "Gertrude Stein": "A light a dark a dash a vermouth an ale bitters a stein in a tub cup stout. Serve in a tub cup scuttle, a spoon a straw with a lampshade. Serve with a button hook. Serve hot, serve cold, a tub cup scuttle a bitters and a straw."[166] Others suggested that Stein's writing was no different than a child's:

> Sir: My 8-year-old niece is a devoted admirer of Miss Gertrude Stein's. . . . After a preliminary course of Miss Stein's, my niece wrote me the following letter:
>
> 'Pig you the papa is you by my you bear the Jack you bear is a cat and the cat is.—Elsiette.' I see in this letter a great and revolutionary meaning. Don't you?[167]

But all parodies were not considered equal. When Marquis parodied Stein on June 4, he was critiqued by a reader, who complained that his attempt "distinctly means something."[168] Marquis rejected one reader's "appreciation" of Gertrude Stein as an unsatisfactory imitation: "C'est Magnifique, mais ce n'est pas la Gertrude."[169]

Stein's name also came up in unexpected ways. During the period in which she was quoted so extensively by Marquis, a debate raged in his column about whether women prefer light or dark beer, prompting many sexist comments from male readers. One argued that "women lean to dark beer. And it is quite reasonable to suppose that they should because dark beer is 'sweet' and light beer is 'dry.'" Another suggested that "Color selection of beer by women hinges not upon the woman but upon her escort."[170] One reader believed that "Women like the foamiest beer, whether light or dark, because the foam is so pretty and lace-like."[171] Finally the debate was concluded by a woman—who wondered if Gertrude Stein should be asked her opinion on the matter: "Sir: I have read with much interest the learned discussion regarding ladies and beer. . . . I suggest that you put the question up to Gertrude Stein—she knows everything, doesn't she?"[172]

Marquis, who published several books of poetry, also enjoyed composing comic poems addressing subjects that he found worthy of ridicule. In the 1910s, his most fervent dislike was for *vers libre*, while in the 1920s his wrath was directed at prohibition. The adventures of both Hermione and Archy were used by Marquis to expose what he considered ridiculous about developments in modern poetry. As E. B. White remembers,

"The days of the Sun Dial were, as one gazes back on them, pleasantly preposterous times and Marquis was made for them, or they for him. *Vers libre* was in vogue, and tons of souped-up prose and other dribble poured from young free-verse artists who were suddenly experiencing a gorgeous release in the disorderly highsounding tangle of nonmetrical lines."[173] Indeed, many serious writers objected to the popularity of free verse. Marxist critic Max Eastman complained about "Lazy Verse" in the *New Republic*, arguing that the arbitrary splitting up of lines is indebted to "the new art of display-advertising" and makes poetry much too easy to write.[174]

Gertrude Stein was only one writer who annoyed Marquis. He grouped her with poets usually associated *Poetry* magazine, Imagism, and free verse, including Amy Lowell and Ezra Pound. And, of course, Don Marquis was just as annoyed by *Spectra*, even before the hoax was revealed. In December 1916 he asked: "Are you hep to the Spectric Group? Have you a little Spectrist in Your Home?"[175] Using traditional, rhyming verse, Marquis printed many critiques of modern poetry, such as this homage to Stein and Pound, "To G.S. and E.P.":

>Ye gods, in all these worlds of thine,
>Where shall the Super-Pote be found
>To wed the Thoughts of Gertrude Stein
>Unto the Tunes of Ezra Pound?
>
>Oh Literchoor! Oh Bunk! Oh Art!
>Oh Cubist Bard! Oh Futurist!
>Have we not rent the Trite apart,
>And slapped the Usual on the wrist?
>
>Oh, much-appealed to Muses Nine!
>Where shall the Super-Fake be found
>To put the Thoughts of Gertrude Stein
>Into the Verse of Ezra Pound?[176]

Amy Lowell was another victim of Marquis's satire:

>"Peppercorns and purple sleet
>Enwrap me round from head to feet,
>Wrap me around and make me thine,"
>Said Amy Lowell to Gertrude Stein.
>
>"Buzz-saws, buzzards, curds and glue
>Show my affinity for you.
>You are my golden sister-soul,"
>Said Gertrude Stein to Amy Lowell.

"Brainstorms, bricks and amber bocks
And little mice that dwell in clocks,
I am your brother, I'll be bound."
Said the gooey frère, the Ezra Pound.

And Hermione barked to them, rapt, elate:
"And aren't they all of them simply great!
Of course, the bourgeois can't understand —
But aren't they wonderful? Aren't they grand?"[177]

Marquis discussed Stein with such frequency that he was shocked if readers admitted that her name was unfamiliar to them. He answered a letter from a "puzzled reader" who inquired "Who is Gertrude Stein?" with a nine-stanza poem, concluding: "But preferring to be honest, to adopt the candid line,/ All we know of Gertrude—really—is that she is Gertrude Stein!"[178]

Rarely did Marquis offer any editorial comment on the excerpts he quoted from Stein, but it would be a mistake to assume that the column deliberately avoided political or ideological content. On September 30, Marquis observed that "Gertrude Stein's own title for the lyric outburst that follows is 'Dinner,' but it sounds to us more like it had something to do with the Ku Klux Klan: 'It was a time when in the acres in late there was a wheel that show a burst of land and needless are niggers and a sample set of old eaten butterflies with spoons.'"[179] He accused her of "militant feminism" in these lines: "Startling a starving husband is not disagreeable. . . . Blind and meek and organized and worried and betrothed and resumed and also asked to a fast and always asked to consider and never startled and not at all bloated, this which is no rarer than frequently is not so astonishing when hair brushing is added."[180]

Marquis expressed his own political views regularly. In January of 1915, he observed that "Congress has saved the country from both Woman Suffrage and Prohibition this winter, and Man and Booze can smile wickedly and knowingly and serenely at each other and rest in peace for a few months more."[181] By no means a politically correct columnist, Marquis not only showed his disdain for women's rights, but also included racist jokes, such as this offensive item: "Williams College has just beaten the Chinese University of Hawaii playing baseball. It is a little hard for a Mongolian to get the right slant on the game."[182] Gertrude Stein was just one of many subjects that Marquis rejected with his trademark conservative and tremendously popular humor. His discussion of *Tender Buttons* were so well known that Edmund Pearson noted in a 1923 guide to book collecting that "'Tender Buttons' [is] an extremely serious book, but its permanent value in literature . . . is that it provoked some of the best of Don Marquis's satire."[183]

Life and Vanity Fair

"The Sun Dial" was not the only comic publication which featured Gertrude Stein. In 1917, *Life* magazine, one of the most popular, mainstream magazines in America, began its own campaign to both parody and, perhaps unintentionally, make the public more aware of her work. The original *Life* was essentially a humor magazine and had very different aims than the post-1936 magazine of photojournalism published by *Time* magazine's Henry Luce. Although *Life* was conservative and routinely printed editorial cartoons and other commentary on current events, the magazine employed the Algonquin Wits Robert Benchley and Dorothy Parker before they moved on to jobs at *Vanity Fair*, the *New Yorker*, and elsewhere. Thus, a certain sarcastic wit was a trademark.

Not surprisingly, Stein's poetry was used for comic effect. In four issues, Kenneth L. Roberts published what he called "Cubist Poems—After Gertrude Stein." F. W. Dupee explains that "There used to be something known to all readers as 'Steinese.' Steinese was the peculiar literary idiom invented by Gertrude Stein around 1910 and made familiar to a large American public by her admirers and nonadmirers alike"; certainly, from 1914 to 1918, Roberts, Marquis, and others were responsible for this development. Even *The Little Review*, an experimental "little magazine," printed a parody in 1914 "with apologies to the author of *Tender Buttons*," and this parody was reprinted by the mainstream press.[184] Each of Roberts's parodic poems was titled after a famous person, suggesting that he may have been influenced by Stein's portraits of Picasso and Matisse, although his style has little in common with Stein's. "Theodore Roosevelt" and other poems were full of onomatopoeia that seemed to refer to nothing in particular:

> There is a something a something and everything a tumultuousness.
> I am I am slam bang slametty bang bang boom!
> Wallop, wallop, wallop!
> Zowie![185]

Usually Roberts incorporated some identifying feature of the subject in the poem; his "Emma Goldman" included the line: "Down with everything!" and "John D. Rockefeller" began: "Money gray, money drab, money halt, money feeble, money oily."[186] Stein found these bad parodies so exasperating that she finally sent *Life* some of her own poetry to print. As Alice reports in *The Autobiography of Alice B. Toklas*:

> Gertrude Stein suddenly one day wrote a letter to Mason who was then editor of Life and said to him that the real Gertrude Stein was as Henry McBride had pointed out funnier in every way than the imitation, not to say much more interesting, and why did they not print the original. To her astonishment she received a very nice letter from Mr. Mason

saying that he would be glad to do so. And they did . . . Mr. Mason had more courage than most.[187]

Stein understood that her people found her work to be funny—and did not mind that Mason was most likely willing to publish her work as comedy. She sent him war poems that were composed during the years she and Alice B. Toklas drove a car for the "American Fund for French Wounded," delivering supplies to hospitals around France. As the New York *Sun* reported to interested readers: "The very latest letter to be received from Paris brings the interesting intelligence that Miss Gertrude Stein, the poetess, has 'joined up.' That is to say, she is going to drive a car for one of the American relief ambulances and one of her women friends 'was to sit on the front seat with her as groom.'"[188]

Stein's "Relief Work in France" was printed in *Life* magazine in December of 1917 with this parenthetical qualification by the editors: "Miss Gertrude Stein sends us this contribution from Paris, and it has been set in the style of type in which Miss Stein's verses usually appear." The first section of the poem reads:

> THE ADVANCE
> IN COMING TO A VILLAGE WE ASK THEM CAN THEY
> COME TO SEE US. WE MEAN NEAR ENOUGH TO TALK;
> AND THEN WE ASK THEM HOW DO WE GO THERE.
> THIS IS NOT FANCIFUL.[189]

She also sent *Life* "A League" which was, according to Stein, "about Wilson."[190] The editors printed this explanation: "Miss Gertrude Stein is one of the pioneers of Free Verse. We gladly publish her poem as a fit accompaniment to President Wilson's elucidation of the League of Nations."[191] The editorial remarks are welcome, since it is unlikely any reader would have guessed the subject otherwise:

> Why don't you visit your brother with a girl he doesn't know?
> And in the midst of emigration we have wishes to bestow.
> We gather that the West is wet and fully ready to flow.
> And we gather that the East is wet and very ready to say so.
> We gather that we wonder, and we gather that it is in respect to all of
> us that we think.
> Let us stray.
> Do you want a baby? A round one or a pink one?

Life framed this poem as political, perhaps in a category we might associate with political cartoons. In 1919, President Wilson had been traveling around the United States, trying to garner support for the League of Nations, and his speeches had been much in the news. But what point does

Stein's poem make? That Wilson's argument is nonsense? It seems that both Stein and Wilson are targets of ridicule here.

Thanks to *Life*, Stein's name was introduced to mainstream subscribers across the country. More sophisticated, urban readers who somehow missed the media frenzy that accompanied the publication of *Tender Buttons* and did not subscribe to *Life* learned about Stein from Condé Nast's *Vanity Fair*. The magazine was designed to focus on "the things people talk about at parties—the arts, sports, humor, and so forth" and printed the work of many important writers and artists, including Stein, T. S. Eliot, E. E. Cummings, Djuna Barnes, Aldous Huxley, Sherwood Anderson, and André Gide. As an advertisement for *Vanity Fair* in *Life* declared:

> *Six Months of Vanity Fair will Enable you to Ignite a Dinner Party at Fifty Yards.* . . . Vanity Fair will act as your passport to popularity. It will teach you how to write vers-libre on your shirt-bosom; how to wear a tiara without hatpins; and how to tell a Newport dowager from a sea-lion. In short, it will keep you in touch with everything stimulating, novel and amusing in the brilliant kaleidoscope of American life.[192]

Like *Century* and *Arts and Decoration*, *Vanity Fair* discussed and published work by modern artists such as Picasso and Matisse, and reached a large audience. Roland Marchand has also shown the extent to which mainstream audiences were familiarized with post-Impressionism from the advertising pages of popular magazines like *Ladies' Home Journal* and the *Saturday Evening Post*.[193] Clearly, as Michael Murphy has argued, "*Vanity Fair*'s clear social function . . . was to keep its mass upper-middle-class readership culturally up-to-date." In fact, Murphy argues that the magazine published modernist writing and art so frequently that "the magazine simply became modernism for many of its readers," but this was a modernism that was intimately connected with what Murphy calls "market savvy."[194]

Apparently convinced of Stein's significance, sophistication and market value, *Vanity Fair* printed "Have They Attacked Mary. He Giggled" in June 1917. The subtitle to the piece was: "An Utterance from the High Priestess of Cubist Literature" and it was prefaced with the following guide, explaining how the urbane person (that is, readers of *Vanity Fair*) should react to it:

> Somehow, it seems as if the surest test for the detection of a modern philistine is the poetic work of Gertrude Stein. The reader who takes a delirious joy in the poem which we publish here, who constantly stops his reading to say "Isn't it great?" "Isn't it wonderful?," etc., is not a philistine. On the contrary, the individual, male or female, who begins foaming at the mouth at Miss Stein's second "page," who shrieks "This is insanity" at the third or fourth, and ends by writing a letter of protest to the Editor of Vanity Fair, IS one. Decidedly this second individual is one. Is one decidedly.[195]

This mocking blurb, either a direct reaction to letters to the editor from "philistines" or a strategy to minimize them, accompanied a piece consisting of 32 short sections, titled "Page I", "Page II", and so on. For example:

> Page XVIII
> It is found out.
> Not by me.
>
> Page XIX
> I told you that you were told.
>
> Page XX
> It is outrageous to mention a hotel.
>
> Page XXI
> Can you please me with kisses.

The following year, *Vanity Fair* printed "The Great American Army," explaining that Stein was "the first and most representative of the so-called cubists in prose."[196] Contradicting Don Marquis's conception of Stein as an aesthete incapable of engaging with the real world, according to Bryce Conrad the poem "blatantly popularized the image of Stein as the ultra-American patriot aiding the cause of liberty in Europe."[197] Not only was her war effort publicized, but Stein's literary influence was emphasized; a longer editorial note accompanied "New Poems by Gertrude Stein" in March 1919:

> One of the genuinely interesting figures among those who have attacked the task of revolutionizing modern verse is that of Gertrude Stein, the American woman, who, operating from Paris as her basis, has stirred the critics and people of taste all over the world to the verge of ecstasy—or insensate fury. . . . Whether or not you like her art form—or lack of it, rather, whether or not you understand the cryptic meaning of her verses, there she is, and there is her influence, and there are her changes, and there will they remain.[198]

After her success with these publications, Stein frequently received word from friends like Mabel Dodge and Carl Van Vechten about her growing notoriety in the United States. Dodge reported in January 1915: "Press clippings about you still come in—it is a habit now to quote you 'as Gertrude Stein would say'—I am keeping them in a book which is yours & which you can have whenever you want it. And you have a school. People are copying you."[199] Van Vechten wrote that "Your name pops up in current journalism with great frequency. You are as famous in America as any historical character—and if you came over I think you might have as great a reception as say Jenny Lind."

With such encouragement, it is not surprising that Stein thought that the *Atlantic Monthly* might be interested in her work. In fact, the *Atlantic* discussed and quoted from Stein's portrait of Mabel Dodge in September 1914, defending her experiments as a rebellion against the "flat prose" dominating not only journalism, but also contemporary fiction. Even if reading Stein made one feel as if "some one has applied an egg-beater to [the] brain," the *Atlantic* argued that Stein was "more sinned against than sinning." Her "rebellion" was to be expected: "this is the sort of thing we are bound to get if the lid is kept down on the stylists much longer."[200] Stein claims in the *Autobiography of Alice B. Toklas* that Midlred Aldrich, whose own autobiography had been serialized in the *Atlantic,* inspired Stein to send her work there. Alice remembers that "Mildred always felt and thought that it would be a blue ribbon if the Atlantic consented, which of course it never did."[201] These lines first appeared in the *Atlantic* in 1933, Stein's debut in the venerable periodical.

In 1919 Stein began a long, and at times hilarious, correspondence with the *Atlantic*'s editor, Ellery Sedgwick, who was convinced that her work would not appeal to his subscribers. In October 1919 he wrote: "Your poems, I am sorry to say, would be a puzzle picture to our readers. All who have not the key must find them baffling, and—alack! that key is known to very, very few."[202] Stein did not give up. She explained:

> I am sorry you have not taken the poems for really you ought to. I may say without exaggeration that my stuff has genuine literary quality, frankly let us say the only important literature that has come out of America since Henry James. . . . [D]uring the war I met many and miscellaneous Americans and I confess I was surprised to find how many knew my work and were interested.[203]

Not at all persuaded by Stein's confidence in a great American interest in her work, in December 1919 Sedgwick replied that "your letter . . . seems to show me that you misjudge our public. Here there is no group of *literati* or *illuminati* or *cognoscenti* or *illustrissimi* of any kind, who could agree upon interpretations of your poetry. More than this, you could not find a handful even of careful readers who would think that it was a serious effort. Pardon me if I say this." But Sedgwick was wrong that Stein thought that her work appealed only to elite readers. "But I don't misjudge your public," she wrote back. "I am not interested in their being literati, etc. My work is legitimate literature and I amuse and interest myself in words as an expression of feeling as Shakespeare or anyone else writing it did. This is entirely in the spirit of all that is first class in American letters whether it's newspapers, Walt Whitman or Henry James, or Poe."[204]

Stein's resistance to hierarchical divisions between high- and low-brow literature in this correspondence is especially striking. She not only compares her work to Shakespeare, but also mentions newspapers and Edgar Allan Poe in the same breath. Since her work had already appeared in both

Life magazine and *Vanity Fair*, she understandably thought that there was a wide range of readers who might enjoy her work. Sedgwick introduces the assumption that many critics still maintain and that always surprised Stein: that her difficult writing could only appeal to the elite audiences who subscribed to the many emerging little magazines in this period. Of course, Stein's work did appear in these literary, experimental publications, especially in the 1920s, but it is a mistake to assume that the little magazines were hostile to mainstream readers or the market, as Mark Morrisson has persuasively shown or, even more important, that mainstream reviewers and readers were hostile to or unaware of these little magazines. Many of these publications deliberately printed a combination of high- and lowbrow art and literature, apparently oblivious to such artificial boundaries.

Robert J. Coady's *The Soil*, for example, which appeared from December 1916 to April 1917 in New York, included illustrations by Picasso and Van Gogh, film stills, pictures of film stars and other entertainers, and photographs of the modern city. Because *The Soil* used so many modern photographs, Michael North has suggested that the journal competed with Stieglitz's *Camera Work*, and it is certainly true that the two publications printed work by many of the same artists.[205] But *The Soil* was much more concerned with presenting an unrestricted vision of modern life. As Juan A. Suárez explains: "Pieces by Wallace Stevens, Maxwell Bodenheim, and Gertrude Stein competed for attention with decidedly lowbrow genres: the Nick Carter serial, 'The Pursuit of the Lucky Clew'; sports chronicles; and articles about magic, billiards, dressmaking, shop window arrangements, or the dime novel as literature."[206]

Stein's "Mrs. Th ---y" appeared in the December 1916 issue of *The Soil*, as did an essay about "Censoring the Motion Picture," an installment of "The Pursuit of the Lucky Clew," and an essay by Charlie Chaplin titled "Making Fun" in which he observed that:

> Making fun is serious business. It calls for deep study, for concentrated observation. It is the business of a funny man to know what makes people laugh and why it makes them laugh. He must be a psychologist before he can become a successful comedian.

Chaplin's serious consideration of the art of comedy exemplifies *The Soil's* belief that all kinds of modern creative expression were equally important in the contemporary world. In this issue, Coady celebrated the success of American art in an editorial that included in a lengthy list of accomplishments (and he did not forget Stein): "Ragtime, Syncopation and the Cake-walk. The Window Dressers. Football. Coney Island, the Shooting Galleries, the Beaches, *The Police Gazette*, Krazy Kat, Nick Carter, Deadwood Dick, Walt Whitman and Poe, William Dean Howells, and Gertrude Stein. The Zoo. Staten Island Warehouses. Parkhurst Church and the Woolworth Building. The Movie Posters. The Jack Pot. Dialect and Slang."[207]

According to Coady, the list encompassed "an expression of life—a complicated life—American life." As Hoffman, Allen and Ulrich point out, "[Coady] was impressed by the native vigor of American activity in many fields; and, like Whitman, he found poetry in all of them."[208]

Each issue of *The Soil* also contained a price list of "Books to be Obtained from 'The Soil'" which included Stein's *Three Lives*, works by Joseph Conrad, Oscar Wilde, Robert Louis Stevenson, Lewis Carroll, and the "Nick Carter Library." Although the readership for *The Soil* would have been primarily writers, artists, or collectors in New York (not unlike the audience for *Camera Work* or *Rogue*, where Stein also appeared in the 1910s), the magazine still managed to create a democratic space for artists. Clearly Stein felt comfortable publishing in this visionary periodical whose editor associated her work with Whitman and Poe (as she did numerous times throughout her career), not to mention Krazy Kat, a favorite cartoon of both Stein and Picasso.[209]

Just as newspapers were attentive to interesting books, no matter how difficult they might be to acquire, they also took note of new little magazines like *The Soil* and *Rogue* even if it was unlikely that readers would subscribe to them. The New York *Herald* emphasized the broad definition of art that *The Soil* promoted, explaining that "Evidently the editors believe there is art in all things. So is everything in it. . . . Gertrude Stein is there, and after reading her you are refreshed by the Book of Job. If Job could stand what he did, certainly moderns can tolerate Gertrude Stein."[210] *Publishers' Weekly* similarly described the magazine's focus: "'Art' to it seems to consist of everything from Cezanne to a photograph of a steam hammer, from Gertrude Stein to a description of a 'wild west' show."[211] By contrast, *Rogue* was described as a less inclusive periodical, with a focus on what we now consider high modernism. As the New York *Globe* and Newark *Evening News* explained: "The *Rogue* aims to offer a field for the very youngest school of literary art, particularly those writers given to the composition of free verse and of impressionistic verse." Stein's "Aux Galeries Lafayette" is unhelpfully described as "a nondescript mystery."[212] Not missing an opportunity to poke fun at Stein, the *Los Angeles Times* noted that *Rogue*'s editor, Allen Norton, "seems inclined to offer enticement to readers who have a penchant for things that are different. However, Gertrude Stein slipped in as one of the contributors and between her and monotonous nonsense there is no difference."[213] None of these brief notices identify Gertrude Stein, suggesting that at this early moment in Stein's career, readers already were expected to be familiar with her writing.

Stein received another publicity boost in 1915 when John Lane published an edition of *Three Lives* in England. Again, the event was widely reported because it was news, not because the average American reader could actually find a copy of the book. *Publishers' Weekly*, the *Boston Times*, the New York *Tribune*, The New York *Globe*, the Pittsburg *Sun* and the Philadelphia *Public Ledger* all mentioned the release of the John Lane edition of *Three Lives*, apparently unaware that the book had been published in the U. S. in 1909. The *Boston Times* observed that "the form of this novel is quite new; the book is an important work of art, a native and genuine expression of the author's temperament, of her way of seeing the world."[214] The Philadelphia *Public Ledger* printed a long quote from Melanctha, then offered this assessment:

> If we try to analyze this from the point of view of 'good English' construction it would seem incomprehensible. But analyze if from the viewpoint of effectiveness, character, picture and feeling, and there can be no doubt of the end accomplished. . . . Let us welcome the new art, if it brings such wealth of simplicity and effectiveness as Miss Stein has shown in these sketches.[215]

While it is impossible to gauge precisely how these generous comments contributed to Stein's American reputation, clearly the many references to her work in the 1910s initiated a public interest in her literary output. Because the mainstream press routinely highlighted remarkable cultural events including the Armory Show, the birth of *Poetry* magazine, the Spectra hoax, or the publication of Stein's *Tender Buttons*, Americans were well aware that contemporary definitions of art and literature were being challenged. Even if the future of this modern art and literature was unknowable, at least a significant number of critics, columnists, and reviewers recognized that these new developments were worth taking seriously. The reception of Stein in the 1910 was certainly mixed as she was not exclusively embraced or ridiculed by a high- or low-brow audience; in fact, at this date no such clearly defined audiences existed.

3 The 1920s
Modernism and the Mainstream Press

Gertrude Stein's network of admirers continued to expand in the 1920s. Stein placed her work in both mainstream and more obscure literary publications and, as was the case in the previous decade, each of her publications was greeted with significant publicity. The widely reviewed *Geography and Plays* (1922) introduced a new audience to Stein's work, and several of the pieces from that collection were reprinted: in *Vanity Fair*, further establishing Stein as an exemplar of literary chic, and in popular anthologies such as *Tom Masson's Annual* (1925), a collection of humor. Even the many works by Stein that appeared in little magazines were often discussed by newspaper columnists, who regularly talked about avant-garde literary trends. As Brinnin observes, "popular reviewers kept her name prominent in the columns of American newspapers, and some even spoke of her with respect instead of quoting her sentences for easy laughs."[1] Stein's reputation did not diminish, as her writing remained frequently in the public eye. References to her in the popular press would have been recognizable to any reader. In 1924, the most popular magazine in America, the *Saturday Evening Post*, published a parody with no editorial explanation, "Investigations and Oil (After Gertrude Stein—With Apologies)":

> Little oil wells bubbling up, sometimes over. Oil is oil and this is this. Politicians many, and a lease, very strangely, very Sinclair. A resignation by the son of an American, like his father, wisely; then revelations, revelations many. A tempest in a teapot rises. Falls. Falls mightily. But you cannot understand unless you understand, and you do not.[2]

Myrtle Conger's parody of Stein, like those by Kenneth L. Roberts in *Life* in 1917, is actually a vehicle to make a political point; the nonsense is not nonsense at all, and turns out to be political commentary. In this case the subject is the Teapot Dome scandal that tarnished the Harding administration, but the parody appears to have been inspired by the apolitical parody that first appeared in the *Little Review*, "Oil and Water." By 1927, when *The American Caravan* (ed. Van Wyck Brooks, Lewis Mumford, Alfred Kreymborg, Paul Rosenfeld) was published and distributed by a popular book club, the Literary Guild, it was assumed that readers were familiar with Stein's style. A reviewer could simply assert that "Mildred's Thoughts," Stein's contribution, "is a typical specimen of Miss Stein's absurd interpretation of fluid consciousness."[3]

After World War I, the quickly growing expatriate community in Paris sought out Gertrude Stein, the most well-known radical, modern American writer. It was no secret that Paris was the gathering place for young American writers. In a lengthy 1922 story in the *New York Times Book Review*, Marjorie Reid describes the influence of Sylvia Beach's famous bookstore, Shakespeare and Company, and details Beach's important role as the publisher of *Ulysses*. "If, as Cicero said, the library is the soul of the house, Shakespeare & Co. may be described as the soul of the American literary circle of Paris," Reid explains.[4] Countering this sincere appreciation of the literary developments taking place in Paris, the popular press frequently showed the less serious side of the American invasion of the city. In a typical article, Merle Schuster informed readers of the *Times* in his "Paris, the Literary Capital of the United States" that in addition to the American writers who have been productive in Paris such as Gertrude Stein, there is "always to be found day or night a group of 'young ineffectuals' at the well-known Café Dome. These are the literateurs who spend their time worrying about when they will start their books. While they worry, of course, the saucers under their liqueurs pile up with amazing speed and the hours flit by on wings."[5] Magazines and newspapers amused readers with numerous jokes about young, lazy, drunken expatriates.

Stein made many connections in the early 1920s with poets, novelists, and critics who facilitated her publishing ventures, wrote about her work, and often became lifelong friends. It became commonplace for Stein's friends to bring interesting people to her salon; in this way she met Sherwood Anderson, a great admirer of *Tender Buttons,* whose 1919 *Winesburg, Ohio* was thought to have initiated a new kind of minimalist short story. Stein was the first American to take out an annual subscription at Shakespeare & Company; Sylvia Beach then introduced her to Anderson in 1921.[6] Later that year, Anderson provided a letter of introduction for Ernest Hemingway, who immediately regarded Stein as a literary mentor, although at twenty-two years old he would have been too young to remember the American fervor generated by the publication of Stein's early work. She either met or established relationships with many other powerful literary arbiters, such as Jane Heap and Margaret Anderson (editors of *The Little Review*), Ezra Pound (foreign editor for *Poetry* magazine and the Parisian literary editor for *The Little Review*), and Robert McAlmon, (editor of the *transatlantic review*). Kate Buss, an American journalist, thought to introduce Stein to the editors of *Broom*, Alfred Kreymborg and Harold Loeb. Jane Heap brought T. S. Eliot to Stein's door, Robert McAlmon arranged a visit with William Carlos Williams, and Hemingway set up a meeting with F. Scott Fitzgerald.

It is certainly true that the majority of Stein's publications in the 1920s were in little magazines including *Broom*, *The Little Review*, the *transatlantic review*, T. S. Eliot's *Criterion*, and *transition* and that these works helped her to gain friendships and recognition among writers and artists. Although the American discussion of little magazines was pervasive in newspaper columns, the readership of each was always modest; according to Alyson Tischler, the *transatlantic review* printed about 5000 copes of each issue (although their subscription list would have been much smaller), while "*Broom*'s circulation was approximately 4000, *Poetry* never had more than 3000 subscribers and the *Little Review* 2000."[7] As for *transition*, "no more than 4000 copies of any issue were ever printed and paid subscription never exceeded 1000."[8] Terry Eagleton notes that the *Criterion*'s "circulation probably never topped eight hundred."[9] But critics have too easily taken at face value James Mellow's suggestion that "Throughout the twenties, Gertrude's literary reputation was based on her contributions to the always-precarious 'little magazines'."[10] In addition to periodicals like *Vanity Fair*, her work also appeared in the most respected literary venues with larger circulations, such as *The Dial*, which had about 18,000 subscribers.[11] Mellow goes on to explain that Stein "published only three books in the decade" (as if that were very few!), although each received extraordinary attention in both the mainstream and literary press.[12] Even when Stein began to self-publish under the imprint The Plain Edition, her books were reviewed. The appearance of any book by Gertrude Stein was news.

Critics presented Stein as a representative writer of experimental literature and in the 1920s her work was compared to James Joyce's more than any other writer. The frequency with which their names were linked, especially in mainstream reports of little magazines like *transition*, suggests that the widespread American interest in Stein's work was not exceptional. As Dougald McMillan observes: "[*transition*] came to stand for all that was new in contemporary writing. . . . Most people never saw a copy but nodded in agreement as book review pages of newspapers pronounced it unintelligible or laughed as *Life* magazine satirized it in a cartoon as the quintessence of expatriate extremism."[13] That a cartoon in *Life* about *transition* magazine would have been comprehensible to its mainstream readers reveals how pervasive discussions about new literary developments were. Modernism was a visible, important force to be reckoned with and reviewers and columnists quoted, discussed, and sometimes ridiculed the writing of Stein and Joyce so that all kinds of readers could decide for themselves if such writing was valuable.

In January 1923 *Life* included a caricature of Stein in a two-page cartoon titled "Life's Birthday Party" that depicted the faces of 112 writers, politicians, and celebrities. In a guide that revealed the identities of each figure, Stein was described as "vers-librist"; also attending the party were the writers Sherwood Anderson, Ben Hecht, Edith Wharton, Eugene O'Neill, and James Branch Cabell in the company of President Warren G. Harding

70   Gertrude Stein and the Making of an American Celebrity

Figure 1   *Life* cartoon (1920s, p. 127).

and his wife, Vice-President Calvin Coolidge, Babe Ruth, Ethel Barrymore, Charlie Chaplin, Irving Berlin, Henry Ford, Don Marquis, Frank Crowninshield, and Condé Nast (figure 1).[14] Always attentive to potential publicity, Stein was so encouraged by this cartoon that she suggested to Edmund Brown of the Four Seas Company, publisher of *Geography and Plays*, that he send a copy of the book to *Life*. In February 1923 she wrote to him: "I would suggest if you have not already done so your sending a copy to 'LIFE' for review. I see that they have placed me among the notabilities in the page cartoon of their anniversary dinner and they might do a review of it."[15] And they did. Stein was not troubled that the subscribers to *Life* were not necessarily literary intellectuals, since she did not regard her work as difficult or obscure. Throughout her career, Stein maintained a democratic vision of a diverse American audience for her writing.

Stein's literary friends also played an important role in emphasizing her status as a significant, or at least remarkable, writer. Certainly, Hemingway, Carl Van Vechten, Edmund Wilson, Sherwood Anderson, Louis Bromfield and other well-known writers and critics so consistently affirmed that Stein was a writer to be taken seriously that it would have been difficult for American readers not to take notice. The "downrightness of her defenders" that *Life* had observed was difficult to ignore; according to Irene and Allen Cleaton, "The baffling thing to Miss Stein's bitterest critics was her capacity for exciting the admiration of America's most worth-while writers, aside from that of the esthetes. Sherwood Anderson, Van Vechten, Fitzgerald and Hemingway came and chatted, listened and went away to broadcast highest praise. 'She may be, just *may* be, the greatest wordslinger of our generation,' offered Anderson."[16]

Carl Van Vechten

Even more than Hemingway, who did not achieve literary celebrity until the release of *The Sun Also Rises* in 1926, Van Vechten was the famous writer in the 1920s whose promotion of Stein was most valuable. Stein did not have a paid agent in the United States, but Van Vechten was so generous and unfailing in his efforts to boost her reputation that none was necessary. Stein recalled in an interview that in her "early period":

> I worked on my own quietly starting to write portraits of everybody who came to the house—Picasso, Matisee, Carl Van Vechten, and others. Van Vechten was then unknown. We have become very good friends since. He, perhaps, did more than any other to keep me before the public, though Sherwood Anderson was so very decent when he was at his height and people were only making fun of me.[17]

Before either writer had become a household name, Stein and Van Vechten were in the habit of mentioning each other in their work, clearly with the idea of faithfully advancing the career of the other. In Van Vechten's 1917 collection of essays, *Interpreters and Interpretations*, he used "rose is a rose is a rose" as the epigraph for "Mary Garden," the first time Stein's famous phrase was ever printed. In 1922 Van Vechten found fame and commercial success with *Peter Whiffle*, a novel that contained several references to Stein. The narrator lists his many activities upon his arrival in Paris, concluding the extensive inventory: "I met the Steins." He explains: "In short, you will observe that I did everything that young Americans do when they go to Paris."[18] No further explanation is given; readers are expected to know that "the Steins" housed an extensive collection of modernist art sought out by enterprising American tourists. Van Vechten also includes a character modeled after Mabel Dodge (Edith Dale) who hosts a literary salon in New York after having moved there from Florence. Dodge's Italian villa and the cultural affairs she had hosted in Italy are described; the composition of "The Portrait of Mabel Dodge" even makes an appearance. Blurring the line between history and fiction, Van Vechten's narrator truthfully observes, "Gertrude Stein commemorated the occasion in a pamphlet, printed and bound in Florentine floral wall-paper, which today fetches a good sum in old bookshops, when it can be found at all."[19] That this novel, which describes the narrator's memories of the failed writer, Peter Whiffle, could become a bestseller, suggests that American readers particularly enjoyed reading about the literary life. This is not to say that the public's interest in Peter Whiffle showed an interest in obscure, high-brow culture; in this decade, readers would understand a tale of a hopeful writer to be concerned with both genius *and* celebrity.

Stein wrote to Van Vechten in June 1922, pleased to find herself mentioned in his novel. She admitted that she was always interested to find out when she read his books: "Am I in it." She explained : "There is one certainly one could never be more pleasantly more faithfully nor more gently in it than when one is put in it by you." Van Vechten also expressed pleasure at Stein's choice to include "One (Van Vechten)" in *Geography and Plays*, published later that year. He wrote: "The book is lovely and thank you. . . . *Me* especially I like, but I had seen that before. How nice, nevertheless, to be in a big book by Gertrude Stein. But I *always* put you in my books. You are in the next one, The Blind Bow-Boy, which comes out next August when I shall send you a copy."[20] Stein's big book did not find the audience that Van Vechten's did. After *Peter Whiffle* was praised in the *Herald Tribune*, the *New York Times*, and *The Nation*, sales increased dramatically; the book went through eight printings in the first year. As Bruce Kellner observes, "In terms of readers, Carl Van Vechten had become a popular success; in terms of critics, he had become a significant artist, all of which was very good news."[21] This was all very good news for Stein as well, as Van Vechten did not forget her.

The Blind Bow-Boy (1923) was also a great success. Before the book was released, the first printing had sold out, and it went through three more printings that year.[22] The decadent, sophisticated, and scandalous young New Yorkers in this novel make clear to which highly publicized cultural developments they do and do not subscribe. One complains: "Everything one called modern a year or two ago is old-fashioned: Freud, Mary Garden, Einstein, Wyndham Lewis, Dada . . . vers libres . . . cubism . . . Ezra Pound, The Little Review, vorticism, Marcel Proust, The Dial . . . Sherwood Anderson."[23] And another character, Campaspe, thinks to herself as she decides what to read: "Works like Ulysses are always out of date. At first too modern, they soon grow old-fashioned."[24] Gertrude Stein is one of the only contemporary writers to escape derision. Campaspe, whose taste we are meant to admire, allows her mind to wander from topic to topic, "she made an attempt to define her impression of Gertrude Stein. She uses words, thought Campaspe, for their detonations and their connotations."[25] Then her thoughts immediately jump to another subject. Readers may not have recognized all of the cultural references in Van Vechten's books, but his popular novels were yet another place a large group of readers were educated about new and sophisticated cultural trends.

As a literary celebrity in New York, Van Vechten found himself the subject of many reports about his social and literary life. When he began spending time in Harlem and promoting the work of African American writers and musicians, the mainstream press took notice. As a regular contributor to *Vanity Fair*, Van Vechten had some influence with the editors and arranged for Langston Hughes's work to appear in September 1925; in March 1926, Van Vechten published an article on Bessie Smith, Clara Smith, and Ethel Waters. *Time* magazine described Van Vechten's new interest in 1925: "Sullen-mouthed, silky-haired Author Van Vechten has been playing with Negroes lately, writing prefaces for their poems, having them around the house, going to Harlem."[26] Other publications offered various racist commentaries: "*Vanity Fair* declared that he was getting a heavy tan . . . Covarrubias caricatured him in blackface, titling the drawing A Prediction; in Andy Razaf's popular song of the day, *Go Harlem*, singers advised, 'Go Inspectin' like Van Vechten!'"[27]

This publicity paved the way for the huge popularity of Van Vechten's controversially titled novel about Harlem, *Nigger Heaven* (1926). Again, Van Vechten was faithful to Stein. At one point in the novel, Mary, a librarian who is interested in modern literature, recalls a lengthy passage from "Melanctha" which is quoted in full:

> [Mary] was reminded of a Negro story called Melanctha, in Gertrude Stein's Three Lives. A white assistant in the library had brought this book to her to read and she had been recommending it ever since, but it seemed that no other copies were available. She recalled now a passage from this story which she had committed to memory. Dr. Campbell was speaking to Melanctha: "It ain't very easy for you to understand what I was meaning. . ."[28]

The quotation goes on for over a page. This extensive sample of Stein's work would have reached an enormous audience. *Nigger Heaven*'s initial publication of 16,000 copies immediately sold out, and the book went through nine printings in four months.[29] Stein wrote to Van Vechten: "I am most awfully pleased that Nigger Heaven is being so successful, it is true that there is nobody whose success gives me as much pleasure as yours does, I don't know why but it does."[30] Perhaps Van Vechten's conspicuous advertisement of her own work contributed to this satisfaction. The following year *Three Lives*, which had been unavailable for many years, was released in a new edition. As the *Chicago Tribune* reported:

> Almost ever since she wrote it, Gertrude Stein's "Three Lives" has been out of print and has been constantly in demand in the Books Wanted advertisements. A new edition has just been brought out. "Three Lives" will be a great surprise to those who know only the Gertrude Stein of the last few years, or even only the Gertrude Stein of "Tender Buttons" and "The Portrait of Mabel Dodge." When she began writing Miss Stein wrote as lucid English as any one.[31]

A delighted Van Vechten wrote to Stein on 28 May 1927:

> And I am so glad that Three Lives is again available for now I can again advise people to read Melanctha. Nella Imes [Larsen], one of the most intelligent people I know (you will see her in Paris next winter) says it is the best Negro story she has ever read (she is a Negro herself). . . . Your home in fact is becoming a mecca—an excuse for travel. Americans now go abroad to meet Gertrude Stein.[32]

Many readers in the African-American community were less enthusiastic about *Nigger Heaven*; W. E. B. Dubois in particular was offended by the book, and the title was distasteful to writers including James Weldon Johnson and Langston Hughes.[33]

Van Vechten's work is decidedly of the 1920s and chronicles the excesses of that decade with ease, but by the time his *Parties* was published in 1930 the public interest in such escapades had waned. His years in the literary spotlight were especially important for Stein, who desperately wished to emulate his ability to produce best-sellers. Corrine Blackmur observes that "the focus on Stein and Van Vechten shifted from the content of their work to the scandalous fascination of their personalities, as both became 'famous for being famous,'" but it was not until the 1930s that Stein found the audience that Van Vechten successfully attracted in the 1920s.[34]

Geography and Plays: "the latest thing in prose style"

Stein's experimental *Geography and Plays* was certainly not a best seller, but it was a sensation. In this case, Kate Buss was the friend who placed Stein's book. She suggested that Stein send the manuscript to her own publisher,

Edmund F. Brown of Boston's Four Seas Company, who agreed to publish the book and was enthusiastic about including an introduction by Sherwood Anderson, with the idea that his status as a more accessible, mainstream writer might bring the book more readers.[35] Four Seas was developing a strong reputation for printing interesting, new poetry by writers including William Carlos Williams, Richard Aldington, and Conrad Aiken; in 1924 they would publish William Faulkner's collection of poetry, *The Marble Faun*.[36] As usual, Stein was required to pay for the expense of publishing the book, but her contract did offer her royalties of 15% and a dollar on each book sold, so theoretically she could make money on the venture.[37] Stein optimistically wrote to Brown: "I have a large selling public" and, knowing the reaction her work elicited from the press, this confidence may not have been as egocentric as it might seem.[38] Although the book was not advertised, its publication was noted in the mainstream press. All of the Four Seas Company's fall publications were listed in the "Books News and Reviews" column in the *New York Times* (October 1922) and *Geography and Plays* appeared in a list of "Latest Books" in May.[39] Brown did not appear to have much confidence that the book would generate many sales but he recognized the import of publishing works by Stein, correctly predicting that *Geography and Plays* would be widely discussed by columnists and reviewers. He wrote to Stein: "I assure you that even if we never succeed in making any great amount of money on this book, we appreciate the value of having your name on our list, and you may be sure that we shall not lose the opportunity offered by such an unusual book to get special publicity and comment."[40]

The press release sent to newspapers and periodicals explained that *Geography and Plays* contained "examples of each of [Stein's] experiences," an inaccurate but reassuring description of the eclectic pieces that make up the collection.[41] The text on the back cover further reveals how difficult the publisher found the book to classify:

> Gertrude Stein translates the rhythm of the spoken personality as directly as possible.... This new book, "Geography and Plays," is a book of examples in which she gives some of each of her experiences.... Gertrude Stein is still experimenting and still renewing her realization of peoples, people, and things, ways of revealing something. Out of her early experiments has sprung all modern writing.

Nor did Anderson's introduction, "The Work of Gertrude Stein," provide many clues for readers. As Kate Buss points out in her review of the book: "He explains nothing."[42] Anderson's primary goal seemed to be recasting Stein's public persona. Attentive to the impression that Americans, who had surely read parodies of *Tender Buttons* in the newspaper and were familiar with representations of expatriate writers in Pairs, may have had, Anderson deliberately paints a picture of Stein at odds with stereotypes of radical, effete, European artists. First, Anderson explains that Stein is "a woman of striking vigor, a subtle and powerful mind . . . a charmingly brilliant conversationalist." His analysis emphasizes the great attention Stein pays to ordinary language, as she attempts to "recreate life in words."[43] In fact, Anderson's description goes so far that he suggests that her work is not difficult at all, since she confines herself to expressions of the everyday:

> Here is one artist who has been able to accept ridicule, who has even forgone the privilege of writing the great American novel, uplifting our English speaking stage, and wearing the bays of the great poets, to go live among the little housekeeping words, the swaggering bullying street-corner words, the honest working, money saving words, and all the other forgotten and neglected citizens of the sacred and half forgotten city.[44]

Stein is presented as non-literary, unlike intellectual writers who alienate the average reader by using an obscure and difficult vocabulary. Anderson does not mention that, despite the preponderance of "housekeeping words," much of *Geography and Plays* would seem incomprehensible to everyday readers. In a piece for the *New Republic*, he continued to domesticate her writing process:

> In my own boyhood in an Ohio town I went about delivering newspapers at kitchen doors, and there were certain houses to which I went—old brick houses with immense old-fashioned kitchens—in which I loved to linger. . . . Something got into my mind connected with the great, light kitchens and the women working in them that came sharply back when, last year, I went to visit an American woman, Miss Gertrude Stein. . . . In the great kitchen of my fanciful world in which I have, ever since that morning, seen Miss Stein standing, there is a most sweet and gracious aroma. . . . Miss Stein is a worker in words with the same loving touch in her strong fingers that was characteristic of the women of the kitchens of the brick houses in the town of my boyhood.[45]

Anderson concludes that Stein "represents something sweet and healthy in our American life." Some critics have argued that Stein was considered a threatening writer because of her radical, androgynous persona, but it is clear that promoters like Anderson presented Stein as a warm, maternal figure that was unlike the "new woman" associated with the younger generation. But Anderson was not simply inventing an image that he thought might be palatable to American readers; others described her in similar terms. In fact, "Van Wyck Brooks . . . saw her popularity [among expatriates] as being based in the 'Middle Western' writers, heavily dependent on her maternal bearing ('the mature Gertrudian bosom') and her ability to give them a sense of community."[46]

Furthermore, *Tender Buttons* and *Three Lives* had both specifically addressed domestic themes, although in very different ways. Many of the pieces in *Geography and Plays* explore life in the home, suggesting that readers must rethink the implications of book's title. What does the domestic life have to do with geography? As the reviewer for the *Bookman* joked: "the title has about as much relevancy to the whole as the words have to the sentence structure."[47] One play is titled "Counting Her Dresses," and in "Turkey and Bones and Eating and We Liked It," a section titled "Genevieve and Cotton" explains: "I do not like cotton drawers. I prefer wool or linen. I admit that linen is damp. Wool is warm. I believe I prefer wool."[48] The poem "Sacred Emily," in which the famous "rose is a rose is a rose" appears, includes numerous lines that might be construed as referring to cooking or the home: "So great so great Emily./ Sew grate sew grate Emily." Or: "Sweeter than peaches and pears and cream./ Wiped wire wiped wire . . . Nursed./ Dough."[49]

Even contributions that directly relate to "Geography" focus on household concerns, such as culinary habits. In "England," for example, Stein suggests that the national character of that nation is directly related to the food its citizens eat:

> A pleasant taste and plenty of butter, a pleasant drink and plenty of water, tea and more fruit than in winter, bread and more eaten than ever this is so sad and every one sees that it is to be cheerful. Any one sees cheerful weather, every one eats cheerful potatoes, they are large and there is water and there is butter, a whole city is not subdued it is iniquitous, it is so soon to see the plant that is not buried showing more white tail than ever.[50]

Even if much of Stein's subject matter was not intimidating, her writing continued to baffle reviewers.

Although it had been almost ten years since the release of *Tender Buttons*, columnists assumed that readers were already familiar with Stein's work. Without directly naming *Tender Buttons*, the *New York Globe* declared, "Gertrude Stein has gone and done it again, reinforced by Sherwood Anderson."[51] Don Marquis was disappointed with *Geography and Plays* and noted in his new syndicated column with the *New York Tribune* that "We do not find in it, we regret to say, the first fine, careless rapture that made 'Tender Buttons,' issued almost a decade ago, such a delight."[52] San Francisco readers were also expected to remember Stein's previous book: *Geography and Plays* was described by the Chronicle as "more of the same as her former 'Tender Buttons.'"[53]

In the Providence *Journal*, F. H. Young revived the idea that Stein's writing may be a hoax, explaining that:

> We have never been able to understand just what sort of game Gertrude Stein tries to play with words. For the sake of convenience in approaching the subject we here refer to Gertrude Stein as if she were a

real person. It is quite possible that she is real, but we have always been inclined to have our doubts in spite of frequent reference to her. She has written books, or is alleged to have written them, and has achieved some fame as the inventor of a new prose style. But what if this whole Stein business were a gigantic hoax? . . . Anyway, there was a book called "Tender Buttons" which was published some years ago, or was alleged to have been published, and it caused considerable excitement and no small amount of mirth. . . .Now there are very definite reports of a new volume called "Geography and Plays," and judging by a few published extracts we have seen it is a masterpiece as unique as "Tender Buttons."[54]

This is not, of course, a review. Young admits freely that he has not seen a copy of the book (nor is he even certain that it exists!), and his comments exclusively refer to quotations that he has seen in other newspapers. Nor has he seen an actual volume of *Tender Buttons*; he is simply aware of the publicity generated by "Gertrude Stein." Similarly, a lengthy review in the *Philadelphia Public Ledger* confessed: "There was a time when I doubted the existence of any such person. Don Marquis quoted her in his column in the New York Evening Sun, and what he printed was so ridiculous that I assumed that she was a character of his own creation."[55]

Geography and Plays was not treated as an isolated phenomenon, and reviewers frequently connected the book to other recently published modernist works. The *New York Globe* noted that:

In the literary world especially life is one laugh after another. The present season of books has been an unusually merry one. We have not only had Mr. T. S. Eliot's poem, "The Waste Land," and Sherwood Anderson's novel, "Many Marriages," and Gertrude Stein's "Geography and Plays," (which we have not as yet read), but we have had reviews of these books which have been the most amusing of all.[56]

A review of *The Waste Land* on the *Chicago Daily Tribune's* "Books" page complained that Eliot's poem "seems to us a bad example of the thing that Gertrude Stein did years ago and that Dorothy Richardson and James Joyce do now to the despair of the plain clothes sleuth of literature."[57] In Iowa, the Des Moines *Register* also connected Stein with Eliot, asking readers "Do You Like the New Poetry?" The article warns: "Now don't think we are referring to the work of such old-timers as Amy Lowell, H. D., and the other vers libres artists. Among the really new poets of the present day are T. S. Eliot, Elinor Wylie, A. E. Housman and Gertrude Stein (though it is safe to say that none of them would care to be 'grouped') and the wildest of these is Gertrude Stein."[58] Donald Willard of the *Boston Globe* also thought Stein's work was representative of the literary cutting edge:

A new type of literature has burst upon the more or less erudite American public. It is a variety of prose narration, featured by short sentences, unusual punctuation, frequent repetitions of ideas, and the stressing of certain words till they run through the mind of the reader like the whisperings of a guilty conscience. Miss Gertrude Stein is the person who has let loose this new brain-teaser.[59]

The *Detroit News* credited Stein with initiating this new "style." "As a matter of fact, her writings are charged with meaning and purpose and they have had, beyond dispute, a tremendous influence on modern writers of fiction concerned with the psychology of the unconscious—James Joyce and Waldo Frank, to name only two of the most conspicuous examples."[60] Another article in the *Detroit News* explained: "You know, of course, who Gertrude Stein is. She is the mother of all modern style; the inspiration of the Joyces and Lawrences and May Sinclairs."[61]

Mary M. Colum's more lengthy exploration of "The Moderns" in *The Freeman*, a serious weekly review edited by Francis Neilson and Albert Jay Nock from 1920–1924, similarly characterized Stein as part of a literary movement. In a review of Waldo Frank's *City Block*, Virginia Woolf's *Jacob's Room*, and *Geography and Plays*, Colum expresses frustration with Frank and Stein, complaining that "Mr. Frank is too often merely eccentric; he too often appears to believe, with Gertrude Stein, that words have a form and shape apart from their significance in a sentence." By contrast, the "nimble-witted" Virginia Woolf "shows herself to be possessed of one of the most entertaining minds among contemporary writers—witty, subtle and ironic." According to Colum, Stein lacks Woolf's subtly and originality, because "she thinks one can express some beauty or significance in rows of words arranged regardless of their accepted meaning."[62]

Instead of taking Stein's work seriously, others saw *Geography and Plays* as a bizarre experiment, completely without sense. Stuart P. Sherman's review in the *Literary Review* of the New York *Evening Post* was an especially popular notice to discuss. Sherman explains to readers that he attempted produce writing that resembled Gertrude Stein's by writing a number of words down on paper, cutting them apart, and then mixing them up. He may have gotten the idea from the discussion of *Ulysses* and *The Waste Land* that appeared in the first issue of *Time* a few months before, which remarked that Joyce had shaken random words up in a "colossal hat" and then "laid them end to end."[63] But, much to Sherman's surprise, the sentences his experiment created actually made a certain amount of sense! He decided that Stein must be grouping words in a concerted effort to eliminate meaning. "Now, we know on the high testimony of Mr. Anderson that Gertrude Stein possesses intelligence of this order. The work before us leads us to believe that she has attempted precisely the difficult feat which my scissors and shuffled parts of speech failed to accomplish."[64]

The *Chicago Post* described Sherman's experiment in "Prof. Sherman Invents a New Game," and the Detroit *Free Press* mocked Sherman for admitting that, before coming across *Geography and Plays*, "I had never seen a line of Gertrude Stein's work nor had I even heard a whisper of her name." They commented: "We wonder where this 100 per cent young critic has been spending his time."⁶⁵ And, in "Two Futile Attempts to Rival the Style of Gertrude Stein," the *Indianapolis News* detailed Sherman's review as well as an unsuccessful attempt by a reader to copy Stein's style.⁶⁶ The commentary of respected book reviewers like Sherman was considered news in itself, as the many references to this review in other papers shows. Sherman was satisfied enough with his valuation of Stein that he reprinted the review in *Points of View*, a collection of essays that appeared the following year, and advertisements for the book declared that readers would find "the jumbled word experiment which the author makes in his discussion of Gertrude Stein."⁶⁷ Reviewers of the book commented on Sherman's "recipe for Steinesque literature" with amusement.⁶⁸

Some reviewers echoed Sherman's initial reaction to Stein's writing—that it was nothing more than a random scattering of words. The *Outlook* asked readers: "Have words virtue and beauty and inspiration of their own when used without apparent connection—shaken out of a pepperbox, as it were? Miss Gertrude Stein thinks so."⁶⁹ And a poem in the *Chicago News* offered another variation on this theme:

> Suppose a cyclone took and split
> The book that Noah Webster built
>   Across the county line;
> Conceive those words so neatly listed
> By some fierce brainstorm wrecked and twisted,
>   Class, that is Gertrude Stein!⁷⁰

Many reviewers remarked that Stein's writing was incomprehensible, but there was no suggestion that Stein's work was difficult, high-brow, or sophisticated. Instead, reviewers believed that Stein's aim had been to purge writing of recognizable meaning, possibly for comic effect. Another critic in the *Outlook* argued that "The task she is attempting is the use of words for the creation of sound patterns without regard to their meanings.... The basic material she seeks is not to be found in words, but in arrangements of vowels and consonants without relation to their accepted place in a spoken language."⁷¹ The *Bookman* similarly suggested that "it would seem that Gertrude Stein has used her language to conceal her thoughts." This reviewer emphasized that Stein's book could be read for mindless pleasure, rather than intellectual stimulation: "we will say this: the book is good reading when one seeks relief from present day high pressure literature."⁷²

The idea that *Geography and Plays* might be a great source of amusement was common. Just as *Tender Buttons* was frequently read aloud to entertain, John Crawford suggested that Stein's new book could be used to elicit dramatic reactions from listeners:

> Reading aloud from Geography and Plays to almost any gathering is to experience an electric charging of the room; none is able to sit quiet, none is able to keep silent. Everyone shouts at once. They become more and more angry, more and more exhilarated, more and more tickled in their larger, more internal risibles until they guffaw. She comes alive, unquestionably, when she is read aloud.[73]

While most reviewers were amused, such as the writer for the New York *Evening Post's Literary Review*, who threatened to publish his own unintelligible collection titled "The Universe and Vegetables," others had no patience for the book.[74] The *Baltimore Sun* complained that "The book is downright blather of the worst sort. Probably Miss Stein isn't to blame. Persons ready for occupational therapy usually aren't. The publishers are the ones who really belong in the stocks."[75] Probably the most scathing review came from the influential, iconoclastic H. L. Mencken in *Smart Set*:

> "Geography and Plays," by Gertrude Stein, is 419 pages of drivel. In the days before the war, when Miss Stein printed her "Tender Buttons," there was at least some charm of novelty in her ponderous prancing. That was also the time of the first Freud uproar, and I remember putting in an amusing evening with a distinguished American poet, examining the Stein dithyrambs in the light of the new revelation. But Freud and the device of stringing meaningless phrases together are both now stale. "Geography and Plays" is dreadful stuff, indeed.[76]

Carl Van Vechten strenuously attempted to defend Stein in the *New York Tribune* against critics who refused to take her work seriously or who regarded appreciators of Stein as "snobs," defined by the *New York Morning Telegraph* as persons who believe "you must read Homer in the original, belong to the Theatre Guild or claim to understand Gertrude Stein."[77] Like Anderson, Van Vechten saw that his first challenge was to defend and reshape her reputation. He was well aware of Stein's treatment in newspaper columns:

> Probably few writers are better known in this country than the American Gertrude Stein, who lives in Paris but it has been the pleasant custom to smile over this lady condescendingly or to sniff at her. Young men and old ladies who compile columns for the newspapers and who probably have never read more that two or three quoted lines of Miss Stein's work are in the habit of lifting their fingers to their noses in no very pretty gesture whenever they refer to her. Nevertheless, it is with the most complete assurance that I rest firm in the belief that I shall live to see a reversal of this attitude.

Van Vechten explains that "Gertrude Stein is not only the founder of the modern movement in English literature, she is also at the present time far ahead of her boldest follower," as if Stein was simply so advanced that readers naturally found her work unusual. While this defense is not unexpected and was a view that Stein shared, Van Vechten's final comments about Stein's sense of humor at the end of this piece may have taken some by surprise.

> It may be added that Miss Stein is rich in one quality which her disciples and followers notoriously lack—that is, a sense of humor. It is pleasant to remember that when the world stops laughing at Miss Stein it can still laugh with her. Read aloud 'White Wines,' one of the plays in her new book, and see if you can't agree with me.[78]

To regard Stein as a witty writer, rather than a difficult, high-brow aesthete was not simply a mistake by the everyday columnist; Van Vechten, one of her closest friends and supporters, regarded her work as both significant and comic.

The *Detroit News* directly responded to Van Vechten's piece. Defending their right to grimace at Stein if they pleased, this paper argued that Stein was guilty of "taking the beauty out of life":

> Miss Stein does it when she discovers they world of fancy is flat; just as Columbus did when he discovered the world of fact is round—and thereby robbed us of the terrible joy of believing that by sailing far enough we might slide off into infinite space.[79]

Other serious reviews by well respected literary figures appeared, but none were as unequivocal as Van Vechten's. Edmund Wilson's assessment in *Vanity Fair* was probably the most positive, although he did not pretend to understand the entire contents of the book:

> Miss Furr and Miss Skeene . . . makes *Geography and Plays* worth while, even if you are not able to understand a word of two-thirds of the rest of the book. In this story, Miss Stein, like Henry James, has evolved the method necessary for her theme: if the story were not told in this queer way, it could not be told at all; there would be no story.

He goes on to assert that "Miss Stein is an extraordinarily interesting figure and deserves to be written of at length," but even this compliment is severely qualified; Wilson believes that, unfortunately, "she seems to have spun herself away into a cocoon and left us no clue to unravel it."[80] Despite these misgivings, Wilson, as literary editor at *Vanity Fair*, remained supportive of Stein, publishing three of her works in the magazine in 1923–24 and a detailed assessment of her significance in September 1923.

Kenneth Burke also had mixed feelings about *Geography and Plays*; in *The Dial* he argued that Stein's work showed "the appeal of significant form" but he was frustrated by the lack of content: "the satisfaction stops with the form itself. Even the nursery rhyme, by its semblance of a 'message,' goes farther in this particular than the quotations from Miss Stein."[81] Although *The Dial*'s readership was limited, reviewers and columnists were faithful readers and habitually commented on its contents in the mainstream press. The *New York Globe* presented Burke's assessment as evidence of the ridiculous respect paid to faddish literature by the elite and reminded readers of Don Marquis's habitual commentary about Stein in the 1910s:

> The Hermione school of criticism is busy these days. The young woman of Don Marquis' fantasy has appeared in the flesh and been made the high priestess of a widespread cult. . . . There is as much sense in the chatter of primates in the monkey house of the Bronx Zoo as in the best of Gertrude Stein, and yet it is accepted by Dial critics as important. [82]

Ben Hecht argued that parts of *Geography and Plays* were successful in a review written for his unconventional *Chicago Literary Times*, a book review which looked like a tabloid and printed such extreme headlines as "Bodenheim runs amuck; six killed, five injured" (actually a severe critique of eleven writers by Bodenheim). Hecht praised some of the book, but the majority of *Geography and Plays* disappointed him. After admiring several lines, he comments: "Unfortunately, this quotation and its companion are equally isolated in a huge book whose statements are usually more trivial and filled with complicated attenuations of thought."[83]

Kate Buss offered a much less enthusiastic appraisal than might be expected. She did attempt to dispel the idea that Stein might be a hoaxtress: "Is Gertrude Stein a sincere writer? This for answer: she is a student of people, an intellectual, therefore not a dilettante to be amused to play a lifelong joke upon herself. Added assurance: she was trained in the means of the conscious and unconscious minds by William James and received a degree in mental science at Johns Hopkins Medical School."[84] Even if Stein may be a serious writer, Buss freely admits that she does not appreciate her use of repetition in pieces like "Miss Furr and Miss Skeene," the story that was more often discussed by reviewers than any other. She explains Stein's use of repetition with bewilderment: "Miss Stein has wielded some form of 'cultivate' thirty-one times; 'gay,' one hundred and fourteen; and 'regularly' thirty-three times. This is six pages!"[85] Overwhelmed, Buss makes no attempt to analyze the effect of repeating these words. It was only Edmund Wilson who saw the deliberate method behind stories like "Miss Furr and Miss Skeene."

Stein's became so well-known that in May 1923 the *New York Times* printed her photo in their Sunday photo supplement of famous people and notable events; the picture of Stein in at 27 Rue de Fleurus (with Picasso's portrait of herself in the background) was captioned: "THE AUTHOR OF 'TENDER BUTTONS' AT HOME IN PARIS: GERTRUDE STEIN, Who Has Given English Words a New Value and Meaning, in Her Studio, on the Walls of Which Hangs the Portrait of Her Painted by Picasso."[86] In November, Djuna Barnes's caricature of Gertrude Stein, described as the 'spiritual mother of all the modernists," was printed on the cover of the *New York Tribune*'s Sunday book section, "Book News and Reviews" (figure 2). Further confirming Stein's influence, in 1927 the *Times* reprinted the 1923 photograph with this caption: "THE PIONEER OF THE NEW LITERARY CANONS: GERTRUDE STEIN in Her Home in Paris, Which Is Filled With Pictures by Picasso, Whom She Discovered. His Portrait of Her Hangs Above Her Head."[87]

Vanity Fair: "how to write vers-libre on your shirt-bosom"

Even before *Geography and Plays* was released, *Vanity Fair* reiterated their faith in Stein's work by nominating her for their "Hall of Fame," as they did several individuals each month who had distinguished themselves in literature, art, or other cultural fields. Some of the many others so honored include: Rebecca West (1924), Edna Ferber (1924), Carl Van Vechten (1927), Pablo Picasso (1928), Thomas Mann (1928), Ernest Hemingway (1928), S. M. Eisenstein (1928), Virginia Woolf (1929), Singrid Undset

Figure 2   Djuna Barnes caricature, *Herald Tribune*.

(1929), Henry Luce (1930), James Joyce (1932), Pearl S. Buck (1932). To be recognized in *Vanity Fair* was so valued that Margaret Anderson complained in her 1930 autobiography that the *Little Review* had failed to attract the editors' attention; the "magazine had persistently ignored our existence; refused later to speak of James Joyce and 'Ulysses' in the pioneer days when such action would have helped."[88] Certainly, James Joyce's nomination for the "Hall of Fame" in 1932 was overdue. Recognized in 1922, Stein was the first experimental modernist writer to be acclaimed by the magazine, no doubt thanks to Edmund Wilson. The editors always included a blurb explaining their choices accompanied by a photograph of the chosen subject. Stein's nomination was justified as follows:

> Because she is entitled to write both L.L.D. and M.D. after her name; because she was instrumental in promoting the early fame of Matisse and Cezanne; because her Parisian salon is one of the most serious and interesting in the city of famous salons; and finally, because her experiments in style have already had an influence of the younger French writers.[89]

The first sentence is entirely false; Stein did not finish her medical degree at Johns Hopkins, although she was only one semester shy of graduating. The other claim is more mysterious, since Stein had no interest in law whatsoever. Furthermore, Stein's writing did influence young American writers, but probably not French writers. Like Kate Buss, *Vanity Fair* paints a portrait of a serious, highly educated woman—even more educated than she actually was—apparently to counter the charge that Stein was a "hoaxtress."

An advertisement for the February 1923 issue of *Vanity Fair* highlighted Stein's contribution to the magazine: readers were tantalized by the news that "Gertrude Stein has written a prose portrait of Jo Davidson."[90] When Stein's "A Portrait of Jo Davidson" was printed, just before reviews of *Geography and Plays* began to appear nationwide, Wilson's no-nonsense portrayal was further embellished. The lengthy editorial introduction briefly traces Stein's entire career, highlighting the connections between cubist art, which subscribers would have seen reproduced in the pages of *Vanity Fair*, and Stein's work: "The aim of Picasso and Braque was, by splitting the subject up and distorting it, to express the impression it produced more truly than could be done by a literal representation. Miss Stein's mysterious prose sketches were attempts to do the same thing with language."[91]

Further emphasizing the connection between Stein's work and modern art, the piece is accompanied by a picture of Jo Davidson working on a statue of Stein, a reproduction of Picasso's portrait of Stein, and picture of Jacques Lipchitz's bust of Stein. Wilson's sincere interest in promoting the work of new writers can be seen not just in his decision to treat Stein's "A Portrait of Jo Davidson" with such respect, but in his careful choice of other writers whose works he printed. An entire page of "Poems by Edna

St. Vincent Millay" appeared in 1920 that included "Wild Swans," "The Singin' Woman from the Wood's Edge," "Spring," and "Weeds." A similar page was dedicated to T. S. Eliot in 1923 with the following poems: "Burbank with a Baedeker: Bleistein with a Cigar," "The Boston Evening Transcript," "La Figlia Che Piange," and "A Cooking Egg." Although the attitude of *Vanity Fair* was light, chic, and urbane (always emphasizing that they provided material for dinner party conversations), Wilson expected the magazine's sophisticated readers to care enough about literature to appreciate these literary samples.

Vanity Fair's reprint of "Miss Furr and Miss Skeene" in July 1923 revealed a more humorous side of Stein and became so well known that it was considered a representative work. The magazine seemed to abandon its understanding of Stein's writing as solemn, complex, and European as Stein developed a more comic reputation among reviewers and columnists. Wilson's introductory note to "Miss Furr and Miss Skeene" reiterates his argument that the form is directly connected to the content of Stein's work:

> This amusing short story, in one of Miss Gertrude Stein's simpler manners, should convince those readers who have hitherto been baffled by her later and more telegraphic style that she is really a writer of remarkable abilities. It will be seen that the style, though queer, is exactly suited to the subject, which if it were not developed monotonously could scarcely be developed at all. [92]

Stein's deliberate formal innovation that Wilson describes can be seen in the following characteristic passage:

> They were quite regularly gay there, Helen Furr and Georgine Skeene, they were regularly gay there where they were gay. They were very regularly gay. To be regularly gay was to do every day the gay thing that they did every day. To be regularly gay was to end every day at the same time after they had been regularly gay. They were regularly gay. They were gay every day. They ended every day in the same way, at the same time, and they had been every day regularly gay.

This repetitive style was parodied for the rest of Stein's career, and in a short time, the definition of "Steinese" had changed; a typical Stein passage no longer consisted of a series of unrelated words, but instead was characterized by repetition. In fact, one of the earliest, lengthy, and most prominent parodies in this new style appeared in *Vanity Fair* in October 1923, the full page "When Helen Furr Got Gay With Harold Moos: A Narrative Written in the Now Popular Manner of Gertrude Stein." The piece was illustrated with a drawing of a man in a trench coat carrying a cane, with this caption: "Harold Moos, having regularly brained Helen Furr with his walking stick, feels a little more gay and comes to an eminently praiseworthy decision." This decision is presented in the last paragraph of the satire; Moos tells Helen that he has decided "to subscribe regularly to the gayest magazine in the world, which (if you had not been knocked regularly senseless) you would know is *Vanity Fair*."[93]

Although his own magazine did not hesitate to poke fun at Stein, Wilson continued to defend her efforts as significant literary contributions. He was a great admirer of *Three Lives* even if he was concerned about the direction of Stein's more recent work. Wilson's attempt to correct misconceptions about Stein in "A Guide to Gertrude Stein: The Evolution of a Master of Fiction into a Painter of Cubist Still-Lifes in Prose" meticulously details the ways Stein's writing developed from publication to publication, discussing *Three Lives*, what he calls "History of a Family" (which would be published in 1925 as *The Making of Americans*), "Portrait of Mabel Dodge," *Tender Buttons*, and *Geography and Plays*.[94] Like Stein's other promoters, Wilson's first task was to counter impressions of readers who were familiar with the attention *Tender Buttons* had received in 1914. He explains that:

> The first most of us heard of Gertrude Stein was when *Tender Buttons* was published in 1914 and was greeted with raucous guffaws as an example of exotic Greenwich Villagism. Yet Miss Stein had already published at this time, besides two curious and interesting brochures, one of the most distinguished works of fiction by any living American author. . . . If *Three Lives* were published today we should probably hear much more about it.

But, as Wilson argued in his review of *Geography and Plays*, he believes that her writing has become so removed from reality that readers can not fathom what she intends to portray or reference. In an early and unflattering comparison to James Joyce, Wilson articulates what he sees as the difference in these writers; in *Ulysses* "the queer devices are effective because we know what the author is trying to describe; but in [Stein] they go for nothing."

The other notable publicity Stein received in *Vanity Fair* that year was much more insulting. In August 1923, an exposé of the "Ten Dullest Authors: A Symposium: A Group of Eminent Literary Specialists Vote on the Most Unreadable of the World's Great Writers" was printed and Stein was featured on the lists of two celebrity writers, H. L. Mencken and Elinor Wylie.[95] The symposium may have been a response to the *Literary Digest International Book Review*'s May 1923 piece, "Choosing the New Century's Best Books."[96] Stein had only appeared on one list, Van Vechten's. The winner, with four votes, was Thomas Hardy's *The Dynasts*. Among those mentioned multiple times were Edgar Lee Masters' *Spoon River Anthology* (3 votes) and Lytton Strachey's *Eminent Victorians* (2 votes).

Most of *Vanity Fair*'s anti-lists were accompanied by explanations for each choice. Mencken explained that "It is hard for me to make up a list of books or authors that bore me insufferably, for the simple truth is that I can read almost anything." He then submitted his selections:

1. Doestoievski
2. George Eliot
3. D. H. Lawrence
4. James Fenimore Cooper
5. Eden Phillpotts
6. Robert Browning
7. Selma Lagerlöf
8. Gertrude Stein
9. Björnstjerne Björnson
10. Goethe

Mencken briefly justified each choice: "As for Lawrence and Miss Stein, what makes them hard reading for me is simply the ineradicable conviction that beneath all their pompous manner there is nothing but tosh."[97] Elinor Wylie's list included Shakespeare ("as a Comic Writer"), Dante, Whitman, George Eliot, Robert Louis Stevenson, Walter Pater, Selma Langerlöf, Henry James, Paul Claudel, and Gertrude Stein. Her reason for including Stein was: "Because." Naturally, Carl Van Vechten's list did not include Stein. He nominated Sigmund Freud, James Joyce, Edith Wharton, D. H. Lawrence and Amy Lowell, choices that reveal how similar Van Vechten's taste was to Stein's. Although she may not have enjoyed being included on two lists, thanks to her champion, two of Stein's least favorite writers, Joyce and Freud, suffered the same humiliation. And Stein, who was always interested in her American reception and saw the value of publicity of any kind, wrote to Edmund Brown optimistically: "It interests me to see how the general tone of the reviews has been changing. Though Mr. Menken [sic] includes me among his list of the ten dullest authors it is to be noted that several of them are accepted classics and the rest popular favorites."[98] Her logical conclusion seems to be that her work must fit into (at least) one of these established categories.

Amused by *Vanity Fair*'s feature, columnists nationwide reported on the results of the "Unreadable Writers" survey. The public valued the opinions of these celebrity judges and, as regular followers of news of books, would have been interested to discover which writers they could avoid without becoming culturally deficient. One writer clearly could be crossed off of reading lists. As the *New York Times* observed, "The prize, if there is one, must be awarded to D. H. Lawrence, whose name appears on five of the lists."[99] Because he was the most influential celebrity who participated, Mencken's list was reproduced most frequently by newspapers, including the Des Moines *Register*, the Pittsburg *Gazette Times*, and the New York *Evening Mail*. The *Columbus Dispatch* tallied the results of all the lists for readers: "Each of the following are on two lists: Walt Whitman, George Eliot, Gertrude Stein, George Meredith, Henry James, and Selma Lagerlof."[100] Other papers mentioned Stein in their discussion of the "winners," including the New York *Post*, the Indianapolis *News*, and the *Dallas News*.[101]

Stein's publications in *Vanity Fair* continued to receive attention by the daily newspapers. "If I Told Him," described as "A Completed 'Portrait' of Pablo Picasso, in an Eccentric Modern Manner," appeared in April 1924 and was extensively quoted in the *Boston Herald*. "Whiting's Column" was subtitled: "National Poet Needed and Nominated as Solver of Some Doubts: Quotations Assure Her Early Election: Gertrude Stein Interprets Accurately the National Political Situation"; the columnist pretended that certain lines from Stein's portrait of Picasso offer relevant political commentary. The idea that Stein was an able interpreter of nonsense and thus could be useful in Washington was a gag that had been introduced by Tracy Lewis in the New York *Morning Telegraph* in early March. The comic article, "Senate Enlists Gertrude Stein," reports that Stein was called in to interpret incomprehensible telegrams that were sent to the Senate:

> "Beautiful," she said, "It's the finest thing I have heard since J.S. Eliot's (sic) 'Wasteland.'"
> "But this isn't poetry," explained a Senator, kindly. "I'm afraid you don't understand."
> Miss Stein smiled patronizingly. "That's what a lot of persons tried to say about my stuff," she answered. "But they're still being printed, you'll notice," she added, with a bit more of venom in her voice."[102]

Stein was so well known that she was regularly used for comic effect in parodies, as in Ruth Lambert Jones's "'A Visit From St. Nicholas,' As it Might be Converted into Prose By Gertrude Stein" that appeared and was reprinted throughout the country in December 1923:

> If there were a Christmas three would be a Christmas mouseless dreaming in stockings and couchant red riots in the heavens jangled and pawed appellations uprisings not without chimneys and recognitions partridge-seeming pouter-pigeon perhaps floral fruition how else fillings until nasal-gesturing-accent of departure and vociferation if there were a Christmas there would be a Christmas unless there were not.[103]

Stein's work was not considered simply a joke by all; some reactionaries feared that Stein was a serious threat and discussed her work as a negative influence on contemporary literature. Theodore Dreiser was irritated by critics who were impressed by Stein and other modern writers, attending to "style" rather than "substance." In 1923 he complained that "Every young writer who wants to make a mark confines himself to form and lets the substance go. They strive after a quality of description, an alliterative feeling,

'Gertrude Stein' stuff that all the world considered a joke when it was born and now scrape to it so sedulously."[104] Although very little of Stein's work was available to the public in the early 1920s, thanks to the mainstream press, Americans not only easily understood jokes about Stein, but knew what Dreiser meant by "Gertrude Stein stuff."

It wasn't just Dreiser who was concerned about the new literary experimentation that was commonly associated with writers like Stein and Joyce. One Des Moines reader who was clearly familiar with discussions of both Anderson's introduction to *Geography and Plays* and Joyce's *Ulysses* complained in a letter to the editor:

> When Sherwood Anderson arises and blurbs to the effect that Gertrude Stein, by jotting down, in a row, the first twelve words that come to her mind, has thereby projected her soul upon the page, I grasp for air and make for the great open spaces. . .
>
> When James Joyce deposits his soul over a few hundred pages, any of which pages or any portion thereof may be deleted or rescrambled without injury to the whole, then —
> To sum up. All this soul-spilling, by the Incoherentsia, is at best, a bad habit.[105]

This letter reveals not only the writer's familiarity with modernist literature, but also the newspaper editor's confidence that his Des Moines readership would already be informed about the subject and find discussion about it interesting and relevant. Of course, some readers may have never seen a complete work by Joyce or Stein, but they would have at least seen excerpts, often accompanied by editorial comment—amused, shocked, baffled as it might be.

Little Magazines: "born to make verse free"

Just as readers who did not subscribe to *Vanity Fair* were likely acquainted with Stein's publications there thanks to the regular discussions of its contents in the daily paper and other periodicals, Americans who had never seen a copy of a little magazine were also familiar with the work that appeared in them. Some of these experimental publications received more publicity than others, but columnists were generally attentive to the daring literary experiments that were published in the more successful of these magazines, such as *The Little Review* and *transition*. While some of this work was radical and received attention because of its eccentricity, much of the poetry, fiction and essays in the little magazines was more accessible and debuted the early work of writers who would go on to have respected careers in the United States. Virtually all of the American writers who achieved critical notice in the modernist period published in these magazines; as Hoffman,

Allen and Ulrich observed in 1946, "[Little magazines] have introduced and sponsored every noteworthy literary movement or school that has made its appearance in America during the past thirty years."[106]

Americans did not confine themselves to books when searching for reading material; periodicals were a major source of literature in this decade, regularly printing short stories, essays and poems. In order to aid readers who wished to locate works by particular writers in the overwhelming number of magazines published, newspapers often described the contents of magazines. One consistent source was the weekly "Current Magazines" column in the *New York Times Book Review*, which not only listed the contents of popular and avant-garde periodicals but also included brief commentary and extensive quotations from some of the highlighted issues. In July 1922, for example, readers of the *Times* learned that: "After a long suspension the Little Review has appeared again. The current number, which is dated Spring, 1922, is put forward as a Picabia Number, and a group of that radical French artist's mathematical abstractions are reproduced. Just what their emotional appeal is, if they pretend to say, is a matter of conjecture." And the issue is described in even more detail. The same column also reported that "The New Republic for July 12 contains a full-page poem entitled "The Revenge," by Amy Lowell. It is written in regular quatrains, a style of technique that Miss Lowell does not often attempt."[107] Such evaluations were common. In 1921, before discussing the contents of the current issue of *Poetry*, the column noted: "Poetry, A Magazine of Verse, published in Chicago and edited by Harriet Monroe, usually contains at least one interesting piece in each number, and sometimes more."[108] And, because most literary works printed in newspapers or magazines were not copyrighted, they could often be found in various other publications in the week or month following the initial appearance. Entire poems were printed in "Current Magazines": Amy Lowell's "Portrait," which originally appeared in *Harper's*, was reprinted on 5 November 1922.

As discussions of little magazines and the experimental literature published there became more prominent in the mainstream press, Gertrude Stein's name was often linked with James Joyce's, almost as if the work of the two writers was interchangeable. Joyce received publicity for *Ulysses* as early as 1920 and 1921 when the editors of the *Little Review*, Margaret Anderson and Jane Heap, were arrested, put on trial, and fined $100 for publishing the "obscene" Nausicaa section of the book.[109] When Sylvia Beach published *Ulysses* in Paris in 1922, mainstream reviewers like the *Chicago Tribune*'s Fanny Butcher reminded readers of the controversy: "It was Ulysses that got the Little Review into trouble, you remember."[110] Modernist literature, if fact, was often effectively publicized as a result of accusations of obscenity. As Irene and Allen Cleaton observed in 1937: "When complaint of a book was made papers printed the news, and before the suppression became effective it was selling to a new alert public with redoubled speed.... Magazine editors, impressed by the notoriety, would pay top prices for stories they had previously rejected. Far from disgracing and impoverishing author and publisher, censorship brought them velvet."[111] *Broom* was conspicuous in the news in 1924, when the January issue was "declared undeliverable by the Post Office Department."[112] The *New York Times* observed that "many prominent writers have appeared in the magazine," including: "Alfred Kreymbourg, Amy Lowell, Carl Sandburg, Gertrude Stein, Sherwood Anderson, William Rose Benet, Louis Untermeyer, Edgar Lee Masters, John Dos Passos and Conrad Aiken." *Broom* and the *Little Review* both promoted Stein, contributing to her escalating public reputation and providing much needed space for other radical writers, even if neither could offer financial compensation for these efforts. In her memoir, Alice B. Toklas recalls that:

> Kate Buss brought Alfred Kreymborg to see Gertrude Stein. Kerymborg and Harold Loeb had come over from New York to publish some numbers of Broom in Paris. . . . Somebody said at the time, The Little Magazines were born to make verse free.[113]

The *Little Review* was the only little magazine to survive for an impressive fifteen years—from 1914 to 1929—and it often featured Stein's work. From her "Vacation in Brittany" in spring 1922, "B. B. or The Birthplace of Bonnes" in autumn 1922 to her "A Valentine to Sherwood Anderson: Idem the Same" and "Bundles for Them: A History of Giving Bundles" in spring 1923, subscribers regularly encountered Stein's most inventive work. Her intimate tribute to Alice in "Bundles" escaped notice of the censors (and thus failed to benefit from the publicity of an obscenity trial), who failed to recognize the same sex desire that has been celebrated by scholars in recent years:

> If you hear her snore
> It is not before you love her
> You love her so that to be her beau is very lovely
> She is sweetly there and her curly hair is very lovely
> She is sweetly here and I am very near and that is very lovely.
> She is my tender sweet and her little feet are stretched out well which is a treat and very lovely.
> Her little tender nose is between her little eyes which close and are very lovely.
> She is very lovely and mine which is very lovely.

In addition to creative submissions, the *Little Review* also printed debates about the value of modernist writing. Ezra Pound's important influence at the *Review* was often questioned by subscribers, many of whom failed to appreciate his contributions to modern literature and taste. Heap and Anderson printed a number of criticisms of Pound from readers, accompanied by positive assessments by Heap and Jean de Bosschère in one issue.[114] These lively discussions were an aid to mainstream reviewers and columnists in the United States, whose profession demanded that they keep abreast of such literary topics.

Journalists did not only read the *Little Review* to learn about modernism. As Mark Morrisson has shown, although the creative writing printed in the magazine was experimental, much of the advertising in the *Little Review* was dedicated to coffee table books, mass market fiction, and other mainstream publications. Morrisson suggests that these advertisements show that "American companies saw little 'highbrow'—'lowbrow' distinction between this little magazine of modernist literature and art and more obviously mass market publications" and that the *Little Review* was interested in "a broader audience than a tiny elitist coterie organ would desire."[115] It may also be that these advertisements targeted a select group of book columnists and reviewers who might potentially promote these works in the daily press.

The suppression of a little magazine for obscenity ensured publicity, but sometimes an issue or a particular piece of writing attracted the notice of the popular press for less obvious reasons. Heywood Broun chose to discuss Stein's "An Indian Boy," a poem which first appeared in *The Reviewer* in 1924, for comic effect in his enormously popular "It Seems to Me" column in the *New York World*, which was reprinted all over the country. He observed:

> Glancing through the Reviewer we came across a poem by Gertrude Stein. It is called "An Indian Boy," and it begins:
> Can the first one see me.
> Can the second one see me.
> Can the third one see me.
> At this point we almost desisted. We thought that we had grasped the story, and the plot seemed too absurdly simple.
> "Anybody could do the rest of that now," we thought.
> Fortunately, we did not stop, but went on with the poem, and to our great surprise we found that it continued as follows.
> Can the fifth one see me.
> Can the fourth one see me.
> Can the third one see me.
>
>
> That we had not anticipated. This undoubtedly is the touch which makes the poem, and yet we regret it. To us it seems the beginning of sophistication in the work of Miss Stein. . . . Just what the answer would have been given by the first, second, third and fifth ones we have no idea, but if Miss Stein is by any chance going to count up high enough to include us, we must reply, "Not at all."

Responding to this flippant dismissal of Stein, the *New York Times* discussed the poem in an editorial about an "inquiry" by M. Marcel Sauvage in the *Paris-Journal*: "Do you think that among the writers of the present day there are some too well known, who don't deserve by their writings either their glory or their situation and, consequently, for various reasons, exercise an unfortunate influence?" Implying that Stein might be such an author, the *Times* describes Stein's "prose poem," as "arresting, intriguing, palpitant, vibrant, scintillant, poignant." To illustrate this point, the *Times* printed these lines:

> Five Indians saw we said we know how to say five Indians as we said.
> We are amused when we say who is abused as we say.
> An Indian boy in Mexico.
> An Indian boy in India.
> An Indian boy in America.
> An Indian boy in Russia.
> Also an Indian boy in Georgia.
> An Indian boy in Italy.
> An Indian boy in India.
> An Indian boy in Africa.
> An Indian boy in America.

The *Times* finally declared: "Let the givers and takers-away and hunters of glory allot, despoil and grasp as best they can. The humble layman will not be presumptuous in regarding Gertrude Stein as one of the most original writers of all time." The quotation of Stein's poem was reprinted in other newspapers, including the *Bronx News*, with this editorial comment: "No doubt it will be contended that even 'Broom' has published nothing more original and that this wonderful Gertrude has all the great poets of all the ages on the hip."[116]

When *The Reviewer* had first printed "An Indian Boy," a note explained: "One of the editors of The Reviewer, meeting Gertrude Stein in Paris last summer, was asked by her if The Reviewer, like other magazines, was afraid of Miss Stein. To which the editor replied that The Reviewer was afraid of nothing. Whereupon Miss Stein rewarded him with the contribution in the present issue.... The editors refuse to enter into correspondence about An Indian Boy, so all questions will be quite useless." Clearly responding to an overwhelming reaction to piece, in April *The Reviewer* updated readers about Stein's current literary projects and then reiterated that: "all queries on the subject must be addressed to Miss Stein or Mr. Van Vechten."[117] In October, *The Reviewer* continued to discuss the controversy, noting that Stein's "Indian Boy" "elict[ed] startled inquiries from Heywood Broun and the New York Times, not to mention unprecedented local protest, even to a few cancellations of subscription by people who, happily for themselves, were without a sense of humor."[118] One reader who did have a sense of humor had written this response to the *New York Times*, where it appeared on March 2:

I read with interest the epic entitled "An Indian Boy," by Gertrude Stein. When I had recovered sufficiently to sit up I found myself muttering, "An Indian boy in Oshkosh, an Indian boy in Kalamazoo, and also and Indian boy in Brooklyn." Then I thought to myself: If Miss Stein will let me collaborate with her, we can have that Indian boy in every city and town in the United States by March 1!

"An Indian Boy" is certainly not one of Stein's well-known works today, but mainstream readers in the 1920s would have been acquainted with what seems an eclectic selection of her writing. Some surprising pieces appealed to columnists; Stein's 1925 reviews in *Ex libris* of two memoirs of her contemporaries, Sherwood Anderson's *A Story-Teller's Story* and Alfred Kreymbourg's *Troubadour*, were considered so amusing that they were discussed and reprinted in newspapers nationwide.[119] Anderson and Kreybmourg were both fashionable literary figures in the 1920s, which certainly intensified the interest in Stein's pieces, and both memoirs expressed admiration for Stein's work and influence. Isabel Paterson's comments in her tremendously popular "Turns With a Bookworm" column in the *Herald Tribune* may have started the conversation about the Anderson review, which focused on Stein's remark that "There are four men so far in American letters who have essential intelligence. They are Fenimore Cooper, William Dean Howells, Mark Twain and Sherwood Anderson." Paterson observes that the review

> hasn't got a thing in the world to do with Anderson's announcement last year that Gertrude Stein had been a great influence in his writing ... (The very idea!) ... It looks to us rather as if the influence had been exerted reciprocally ... Several of Gertrude's sentences almost seem to be intelligible. (ellipses in original)[120]

The *San Francisco Bulletin*, *Buffalo News* and the *New York Times* also commented on how uncharacteristically "intelligible" the review seemed to be. The conversation continued in the *Detroit News, Indianapolis Star, Boston Herald* and the [SC] *Columbia Record*, which emphasized how familiar Stein's unusual writing was to readers before reprinting the review: "Everyone knows Gertrude Stein and her experiments with the values of word sounds."[121] Confident that readers would be interested in Stein's peculiar style, an Oklahoma newspaper reprinted both the reviews of Anderson and Kreymborg.[122]

Stein's review of *Troubadour* attracted notice for its eclectic style rather than its conventionality. The *Providence Journal* asked readers: "Do you read Gertrude Stein? ... No, of course we know you don't. No one has time, and besides ... But this is so good, we can't keep it back" (ellipses in original).[123] The review was also discussed in the *Brooklyn Eagle* and the New York City *Telegram*. In addition to publicizing Stein herself, these reviews brought attention to the work of Anderson and Kreymborg, two memoirs which describe for mainstream Americans the development of American modernism in arts and letters. In his review of *Troubadour* in the *New York Times Book Review,* Lloyd Morris particularly admired the sections of the book that describe various efforts to revolutionize the arts: "The Stieglitz gallery, 'The Glebe' and 'Others', those hardy and courageous ventures of Mr. Kreymbourg's, the Provincetown Players and the rest down to the very recent 'Broom.'"[124] Thanks to Kreymbourg's memoir and the reviews that discussed its contents, these instigators of change were made visible to mainstream America. Kreymborg's modernist influence was most important in New York, rather than in Paris. But his decision to publish the work of writers including William Carlos Williams, Marianne Moore, and Wallace Stevens in *Others* significantly contributed to the contours of the popular understanding of modernism on this side of the Atlantic.

When *transition* first appeared in 1927, Americans would already have been familiar with the careers of Stein and Joyce, and would probably have been unsurprised to learn that the two would appear in the latest new magazine of experimental literature. The first issue of *transition* was discussed by reviewers all over America and became the subject of numerous jokes about incomprehensible modern literature. A cover story appeared in the *Saturday Review of Literature*, "Gyring and Gimbling (Or Lewis Carroll in Paris)," and focused on the contributions by "the half mythical James Joyce and that lesser mistress of experimental prose, the prophetic Gertrude Stein."

> The conception of "Ulysses" was clearly giant-like, the execution subject to controversy. Its details were praised by some of the discriminating, but by more who delight in art in proportion to its obscurity, and detest the very name of common sense. Gertrude Stein we knew in feats of word legerdemain which had strange powers since some minds were fascinated by her scrambled sentences and other driven to wails and cursings. Now, thanks to the midwifery of Mr. Elliot Paul, an American resident in Paris, where presumably one can take the English language without too much seriousness, and to the magazine "Transition," we can see Mr. Joyce in his latest work and Miss Stein "elucidated."[125]

Similarly, Helen Henderson's "Combining Art and Literature: Is Decidedly Being Done During These Modern Days in Paris; James Joyce and Gertrude Stein Are Explained by Ardent Devotees" in the *Philadelphia Inquirer* pokes fun at the works by Joyce and Stein in *transition*, but the article devoted enough space to the discussion that readers understood that their writing was considered significant literature by some critics. Henderson explains: "There are . . . many who take up the cudgels for Gertrude Stein most seriously and are ready to defend her prose with their lives."[126]

Some critics and reviewers were simply amused that Stein's "An Elucidation" had been printed in the first issue of *transition* with the pages out of order; the corrected version did not seem any more comprehensible to them.[127] Janet Flanner's mixed assessment of *transition* in the *New Yorker* quoted the entire first page of Joyce's "Work in Progress," the working title for *Finnegans Wake*:

> *transition*, the new magazine edited here by Elliot Paul and Eugène Jolas, in its initial number contains, if not a feast, some good food for thought, the tastiest plate being the German Carl Sternheim's "Busekow," an excellent story of an amorous Potsdammerplatz policeman—this in spite of excerpts from Ludwig Lewisohn's *The Defeated* and "Opening Pages of a Work in Progress," by James Joyce, which opens thus:[128]

This sample of Joyce's radical, new work was thus immediately known to a sizable American audience. James Thurber's parodies of Stein and Joyce in the *New Yorker* the next month, "More Authors Cover the Snyder Trial," suggest that, thanks to Flanner's lengthy excerpt, Thurber could assume that mainstream readers would be familiar with the style of *Finnegans Wake*.

> I
> WHO DID WE DID DID WE
> WE DID, SAYS MISS STEIN!
>
> By Gertrude Stein
>
> This is a trial. This is quite a trial. I am on trial. They are on trial. Who is on trial?..
> He says he did. He says he did not. She says she did. She says she did not. She says he did. He says she did. She says they did. He says they did. He says they did not. She says they did not. I'll say they did.
>
> II
> JOYCE FINDS SOCKSOCKING IS BIG ELEMENT IN MURDER CASE!
>
> By James Joyce
> Trial regen by trialholden Queenscountycourthouse w i t h tumpetty taptap mid socksocking with sashweights by jackals. In socksocking, the sashwiring goes: guggengaggleoggoggsnukkk . . . To corsetsale is to alibi is to meetinlovenkillenlove. *Rehab des arbah sed drahab!* Not a quart of papa's booze had poison booze vor the killparty for the snugglesnuggle. . .[129]

Thurber's joke uses the premise that if Joyce or Stein reported on the sensational, highly publicized Snyder trial, each would certainly write in his or her own sensational, highly publicized style of prose that Americans knew so well.[130]

Although the contents of the first issue may seem quintessentially modernist—abstract, difficult, and obscure—because many of the writers featured already were highly regarded and well-publicized, the magazine was virtually guaranteed a notable reception by critics and columnists. As Dougald McMillan reports, "Charls Boni of Boni and Liveright was passing through Paris at that time and paid a call on the Jolases. When he saw the table of contents, he remarked, 'But this is worth a fortune!' and suggested that the material should be exploited more commercially."[131] While *transition* proved to be an important outlet for modernism, the contours of the movement had already been established by other little magazines including the *Little Review*, and subsequently popularized in mainstream periodicals and newspapers.

The editors, Elliot Paul and Eugène Jolas, were so delighted with the attention the magazine received in the popular press that they began to print especially amusing blurbs in issues of the magazine under the heading "Some Opinions." One page of quotations in 1927 included the *New York Times*'s characterization of *transition* as "hopelessly muddled and unintelligible," the *Saturday Review of Literature*'s complaint that the publication consisted of "onslaught and ravage upon the English language," and the observation by the *Detroit News* that "Gertrude Stein, living in France, has apparently forgotten English—at least the kind of English this reviewer speaks."[132]

Two years later *transition* continued to be a popular topic in the mainstream press. On another page which sampled representative blurbs about the magazine, readers of *transition* learned that the *Baltimore Sun* had quoted a piece by Theo Rutra, then offered this advice: "after you have read it, call the doctor." Harry Salpeter observed in the *New York World* that *transition* was "generally unintelligble," adding: "Its unintelligibility is the result of intention not accident." Lewis Gannett's impatient response to the magazine was also quoted: he called *transition* "that irritating hodgepodge of genius and nonsense." But not all assessments were negative; Horace Gregory declared that *transition* was "the official organ of revolt in American today" and the conservative *Literary Digest* told its readers that "Foremost in leading . . . the present-day effort to remake the English language is the periodical called *transition* (Paris). Don't accuse us of a blunder; the lower case is elevated and capitals, as may be observed in much modern poetry, are left moldering in their cases."[133]

The mainstream press did occasionally report on the contents of *transition* in more detail. The *Washington Post* was especially interested in the survey that *transition* had circulated among its contributors, asking for the reasons each had chosen to live abroad. "U. S. Citizens Give Self-Exile Causes," the headline in the *Post* declared:

Transition, a publication boasting that it is a century ahead of contemporary literature, canvassed these American expatriates and asked why they prefer to live outside of America. "The United States is just now the oldest country in the world. There always is an oldest country and she is it; it is she who is the mother of twentieth century civilization," replied Miss Gertrude Stein, famous radical writer and author of "Tender Buttons," the work which fifteen years ago started the literary onslaught against the mechanized word.[134]

Stein continued to make appearances in other little magazines as they were established in the decade. *Close-Up*, a magazine devoted to themes related to film, printed several of Stein's short pieces in 1927 ("Mrs. Emerson" and "Three Sitting Here," in two parts). This innovative collaboration between H. D., Bryher and Kenneth Macpherson juxtaposed the writing of Stein, Dorothy Richardson and Marianne Moore with the work of filmmakers including Eisenstein. Macpherson explained to Stein that "The kind of thing you write is so exactly the kind of thing that could be translated to the screen."[135] Like *The Soil*, where Stein's work appeared in the previous decade, *Close-Up* suggested an intimate and profound connection between modernist writing and new technology, refusing to recognize categories of "high," "middle" or "low-brow" art or literature.

The most lengthy and, in her estimation, important contribution Stein made to little magazines in this decade was the serialization of sections of *The Making of Americans: Being a History of a Family's Progress* in Ford Madox Ford's *transatlantic review* beginning in April 1924 (these were printed in nine of the journal's total run of twelve issues). It was Ernest Hemingway, an assistant editor at the magazine, who convinced Ford to publish Stein's manuscript, probably by misleading him as to its length; Ford later claimed that he understood that the work was a "long short story." When Robert McAlmon finally agreed to publish an edition of 500 copies of the novel with his Contact Press in Paris, it came to almost 1000 pages. One hundred copies were then exported for an American edition published by Albert and Charles Boni in 1926.

As early as 1922, Van Vechten wrote to Stein: "What has become of The Family? It has occurred to me that the time is getting ripe for its publication now that you are a classic & have Imitators and Disciples!"[136] Stein's close friends were well aware that *The Making of Americans*, composed from about 1903 to 1911, had yet to find a publisher and they unsuccessfully labored to find a home for the book. Multiple avenues were pursued with disappointing results. Hemingway tried to persuade Horace Liveright to publish it, while Van Vechten attempted to place the manuscript with both Liveright and Alfred Knopf. After he wrote to Stein about his failed attempts, she replied:

> It is a shame because there seems no doubt of its market because everybody likes it in the Transatlantique even its worst enemies say it is like

Dostoievsky. . . . You see I don't understand yet why they hesitate. I see that a copy of Three Lives with my signature is selling to-day for $13 why then Knopf should hesitate so long, well it's not for me to understand.[137]

Meanwhile, Edith Sitwell asked Leonard and Virginia Woolf if they might be interested in publishing the lengthy manuscript with their Hogarth Press. They seriously considered publishing it, but when they learned how long the manuscript was and Stein understood that she would only be paid on commission, the negotiations ended.[138] Jane Heap contacted The Dial Press, B. W. Huebsch, and Boni and Liveright, who expressed interest but decided against the book.[139] Heap also failed in an attempt to arrange for *The Making of Americans* to continue its serialization in *The Criterion* when the *transatlantic review* ran into financial difficulties.[140]

Finally, Stein herself persuaded Robert McAlmon to publish *The Making of Americans* with his Contact Publishing Company in Paris, who believed her (as it turns out, overly optimistic) expectation that fifty copies of the book would immediately sell. Contact published an impressive list of modernist writers and Stein's book was an appropriate addition: Hemingway, Ezra Pound, H. D., Ford Madox Ford, William Carlos Williams, Mina Loy and Mary Butts all published books with Contact Editions. Generously financed by his father-in-law, McAlmon never felt pressure to make money with the small press which was, on the one hand, a positive aspect for some modernist writers whose work was not likely to find a large audience and thus live up to a commercial publisher's expectation of large profits; however, as Stein soon realized, a contract with Contact Editions also guaranteed no publicity or advertising, as McAlmon was content to simply print the (often very handsome) editions of modernist literature that were unable to find another home.

Frustrated that *The Making of Americans* seemed fated to a tiny distribution, Jane Heap and Stein took it upon themselves to arrange for 400 unbound copies to be sent to Stanley Nott, an English publisher, although McAlmon had only agreed to 200 copies. Before they were sent, an irate McAlmon was notified by the printer about the arrangement and the deal eventually fell through. The quarrel between Stein and McAlmon was exacerbated by financial details regarding the book's publication (such as printing costs) that each understood differently, not to mention almost nonexistent early sales. Stein's belief that the book might sell fifty copies does not sound particularly surprising, considering how well known she had become in America. But she does not seem to have considered how difficult it might be to sell the precious book to American readers; Kate Buss reported in *Boston Evening Transcript* that "Gertrude Stein's book is to be an expensive printing, and ranges from eight dollars to sixty a copy as it is bound in paper, in half leather, or on Imperial Japan, autographed, and covered in full vellum."[141] As Fanny Butcher noted in her review of the book, "'The Making of Americans' is one of those books which is eagerly sought by collectors, and has a phenomenal rise in value."[142] Not only was the price prohibitive; McAlmon struggled to export the book to the United States. As Hugh Ford observes, "books printed in Paris were automatically suspect and often confiscated simply because thy were believed to be obscene." Consequently, some copies of *The Making of Americans* were stopped by American customs. In the end, about 100 copies of the book sold in the first year after the book began to receive notice in the mainstream press.[143]

The Making of Americans: "a remarkably pleasing rhythm"

The Making of Americans focuses on members of the Hersland family: David and his wife, Fanny; their children, Martha, Alfred and David; and Alfred's wife, Julia Dehning. While the book does include some elements of plot, such as the marriage of Alfred and Julia or the death of the young David Hersland in the final section, the book is more concerned with defining the personalities of each family member until the conclusion, which shifts from the analysis of character to an extended meditation on death.

At times, Stein sets aside the Herslands, Dehnings and other peripheral characters to theorize more generally about character types for the reader. She asserts, for example, that "there are two kinds of women, those who have dependent independence in them, those who have in them independent dependence inside them; the first ones of them always somehow own the ones they need to love them, the second kind of them have it in them to love only those who need them."[144] But, according to Stein, this classification fails to complete the portrait. It is by observing the ways that, in all aspects of life, each individual repeats (gestures, speech, actions) with small variations that unique personalities emerge. "There are then many things every one has in them that come out of them in the repeating everything living have always in them, repeating with a little changing just enough to make of each one an individual being, to make of each repeating an individual thing that gives to such a one a feeling of themselves inside them."[145] While *The Making of Americans* is about a particular family, these characters are primarily a vehicle for Stein to test her theories about literary representations of character, personality, and individuality. As Leon Katz explains:

> [Stein] had labored at a single problem—with passion, with dedication, with monotonous persistence: the problem of describing "the last touch" of human being, or to put it another way, to pass beyond the practical acquaintance with human being that everyone has, to the total description of human being that no one had yet achieved.[146]

Stein's difficulty in writing the text is not concealed from the reader; about halfway through the book she seems to despair completing the project: "I am altogether a discouraged one. I am just now altogether a discouraged one. I am going on describing men and women."[147] For those who were frustrated by the repetitive, slow and even laborious style, Stein's comment may very well echo the reader's own frustration. As Janet Malcolm notes, "the anti-novel seems to be turning into a kind of nervous breakdown."[148]

Certainly, other modernists were experimenting with long, difficult novels at this moment. But Stein's character studies, unlike those of many other experimental modernists (Joyce, Proust, Woolf), failed to delve into the unconscious of her subjects, individual and cultural. Instead, her excessively detailed attempt to show the development of personality relies precisely on a conception of character that avoids the unconscious and specifically ridicules the idea of "repression," deliberately reporting and repeating only the surface actions and visible reactions of her subjects. It is Stein's understanding of personality in *The Making of Americans* and her reconsiderations of this concept throughout her career that ultimately separate her from other modernists and make her novel something very different from *Ulysses* or *Remembrance of Things Past*, two books that she felt had affinities with *The Making of Americans* because, as Stein explained, they all "do not tell a story."[149]

The Making of Americans has failed to achieve the monumental status of Joyce's *Ulysses*, although, like *Ulysses*, sections of this massive book first appeared in a little magazine and successfully attracted the notice of the mainstream press. Reviewers had some idea of what to expect from the *transatlantic review,* since it published many writers associated with the well-established *Little Review*: in addition to Stein, writers including Ezra Pound, James Joyce, Ernest Hemingway, Mary Butts and, of course, Ford Madox Ford, the magazine's editor, all published there.

Already familiar with Stein's reputation for obscurity, early notices emphasized the accessibility of the first installment of *The Making of Americans*. Fanny Butcher noted in the *Chicago Tribune* that:

> One of the most stimulating of all the magazines nowadays is the Transatlantic Review, only five volumes old, edited in Paris by Ford Madox Ford (who used to be Ford Madox Hueffer) and containing in each number something that is a special tidbit of culture. This month's issue, the May-June one, has a reproduction of a manuscript song by Erik Satie in it, for instance. There is also a story by Gertrude Stein which comes very near to the dangerous mark of being understandable.[150]

The New York *Herald* reported that "In an article 'The Making of Americans' in the transatlantic review, is something intelligible from the pen of Gertrude Stein." Even more complimentary, South Carolina's *Columbia Record* observed that:

> Gertrude Stein, author of "Tender Buttons," "Geography and Plays," "If I Had Three Husbands," [sic] etc., appears in the current issue of

The Transatlantic Review with "The Making of Americans," in which there is but a trace of the manner associated with her name. It is a piece of prose of distinction with something of significance to say.[151]

"If You Had Three Husbands" had appeared in three sections in *Broom*, January 1922, April 1922 and June 1922 and further reveals the assumption of the mainstream press that publications in little magazines were known by their readers. Not quite able to concede that Stein's new work was so conventional, the *Providence* [RI] *Journal* joked: "For the caviar taste there is the new transatlantic review (Yes, yes, they spell it without capitals.) Gertrude Stein has a very lucid article in it, but we don't know what about."[152]

The second issue of the *transatlantic review* was just as popular to discuss. *The New York Times* listed the contents of the issue in "Current Magazines" and the New York *Evening Post* offered a lengthy excerpt, explaining: "Gertrude Stein, who manages to make monotony somehow intense, is running a serial, 'The Making of Americans,' in the transatlatlatic review."[153] South Carolina's *Columbia Record* reiterated their support for Stein on June 8: "Attention must be called, however to 'The Making of Americans' by Gertrude Stein, the second installment of which appears in the May-June issue." Mary Crockett's appreciation in *Modern Quarterly* of the sections of *The Making of Americans* that appeared in *transatlantic review* was the most detailed and complimentary notice the serialization received. Defending Stein both personally and intellectually, Crockett insisted that "She is not a faddist."

> In "The Making of Americans," now appearing in "the transatlantic review," Miss Stein has gone back to the balance of sound and sense, producing a remarkably pleasing rhythm, and at the same time, telling a story. Perhaps her experimenting is over, and she has at last found her medium of expression.[154]

Much to Ford Madox Ford's irritation, when Hemingway had control of the magazine's submissions for the August issue of 1924, *transatlantic review* suddenly showed an interest in printing mainstream, even popular American writing alongside writers like Stein, disrupting Ford's intent of exclusively publishing international, radical work in his "intensely modernistic magazine," as California's *Fresno Republican* called it.[155] But Hemingway's editorial decisions suggest that he had no interest in promoting the kinds of high and low-brow distinctions that little magazines suggested to some readers. To Hemingway, Ring Lardner and Gertrude Stein both were representative American writers and could appropriately appear in the same publication.[156] The mainstream press took notice of the more inclusive list of contributors; the *Oakland Tribune* headlined its story: "Lardner Breaks Into Intelligencia Class."

> One looks for effusions from Ring Lardner in anything but so-called "highbrow publications" and therefore the joy is the more pronounced when the pursuer of the August number of the Transatlantic Review finds a three act play by the American humorist. It is done in typical Lardner fashion and is guaranteed to produce the merry chuckle. Other contributors are Paul Valery, Ludvig Nordstrom, Gertrude Stein, Ivan Beede and others of that class.[157]

Ford included an editorial note in the next issue explaining that Hemingway had been responsible for the previous issue's editorial decisions, but readers could not fail to consider the significance of juxtaposing the work of Stein with that of Ring Lardner—writers who, according to the popular press, could both be read as significant, comic American writers.

When *The Making of Americans* was released in 1925, reviews appeared gradually over several years, possibly since the book required such a time commitment for any reader. Early notices included Katie Hope Sternberg's "Gertrude Stein's 'Making of Americans' Is a New Year Offering of 1,000 Pages" in the Paris edition of the New York *Herald Tribune* in December.[158] Sternberg begins with a discussion of Stein's extraordinary reputation: "Whenever a discussion of Gertrude Stein arises, somebody is sure to exclaim: 'There is no such person! It's a legend!' Another will volunteer: 'No, it's a game, one of those cross-word puzzles!'" The article does include excerpts from the book, but no analysis of these passages. Sternberg appears to have been baffled by the selections, which seem to have been chosen at random as representative.

The reactionary editor of the *Saturday Review of Literature* had no patience for *The Making of Americans*; William Rose Benét freely admitted in his review that he had not read the book. He dared his readers: "We defy anyone to read [The Making of Americans] completely through. . . . It is appalling!"[159] This challenge was soon met by a contributor to the *Saturday Review*, Paul Rosenfeld. Never afraid to confront readers with a literary debate, the *Review* printed Rosenfeld's defense of Stein the following month.

> The writings of Gertrude Stein stand a massive doorpost in the entrance to the latest American literature. Her use of words which for a decade exhilarated the newspaper mind, has opened a way before the new writers and made them dare. . . . The second stage, clearer in its technique, is represented by the just published fifteen year old novel "The Making of Americans," indubitably the most monumental fiction to be given since the publication of "Ulysses."[160]

Not content to allow Rosenfeld the last word, the editors made clear that their refined tastes could neither accommodate Stein nor critics who celebrate her work. Indeed, Rosenfeld bears the brunt of the *Saturday Review*'s attack:

> Gertrude Stein and her disciples may be perfectly negligible phenomena, but the criticism that treats them not only with respect but as of enormous importance is a serious matter. It is the kind of criticism that is by the nature of the case militant rather than persuasive, that is supercilious to tradition, and scornful of standards. It is a proselytizing criticism that is dangerous since it makes a god of novelty and attaches to the bizarre inherent merit.

They added with scorn: "Surely such writing as Gertrude Stein's could not hold attention for a day if it were not for the smoke screen of importance which the critics have thrown about it."[161] The *Boston Transcript* also dismissed the book: "If one desires quantity in a book and ignores quality, I suggest that colossal work by Gertrude Stein."[162]

By contrast, the *Literary Digest*'s *International Book Review* printed a lengthy and admiring assessment of Stein by Willis Steell in February:

> Nothing is easier than to make fun of Gertrude Stein. Ridicule or something worse has been her bitter portion for thirty years. . . . But her mind has progressed. . . . Like Marcel Proust in his memories of times past, when a scent or a note of music would cause him to desert half-told a scene of passion in order to recall his grandmother's deathbed, so Gertrude Stein mixes up generations in a maddening way; but, also like the French genius, she never loses the clue which enables her to retrace her steps.[163]

Although the span of Stein's career is exaggerated, she was surely pleased to see a critic compare her long novel to Proust's. This review was quoted extensively in the weekly *Literary Digest*, usually a promoter of mainstream, conservative literary trends. But the *Literary Digest*, like the *Saturday Review*, found that Stein was such a prominent voice in the literary world that it could not be ignored. The *Digest* observed:

> She has been a conundrum to the literary world for a quarter of a century. Are her novels childish babble or works of genius? The answers are conflicting. And now Gertrude Stein has published in Paris a book called "The Making of Americans"—a book seven and one-half inches wide, nine and one-half inches long, and four and one-half inches thick! And the contents are as original as the format.[164]

Recognizing that Stein could now be counted as a serious writer with real influence, the Cincinnati *Commercial Tribune* observed that "for all the queerness of her style, Miss Stein is certainly not a fad or she would have been forgotten long ago. Instead, interest in her theories is greater than ever before."[165]

The most conspicuous positive response to *The Making of Americans* was Katherine Anne Porter's. Her "Everybody Is a Real One" appeared on the cover of the influential *New York Herald Tribune Books* in January 1927 and, although over a year had passed since the book's release, Porter's sensitive reading suggests that she had usefully spent that year making a genuine attempt to appreciate Stein's massive work. Porter observes that:

> [These pages] form not so much a history of Americans as a full description and analysis of many human beings, including Gertrude Stein and the reader and all the reader's friends; they make a psychological source book and the diary of an aesthetic problem worked out momently under your eyes. . . . I doubt if all the people who should read it will read it for a great while yet, for it is in such a limited edition, and reading it is anyhow a sort of permanent occupation. Yet to shorten it would be to mutilate its vitals, and it is a very necessary book.[166]

Looking at Stein's interest in characterizing personality types, Porter explains that: "Materials interest her, the moral content of man can often by nicely compared to homely workable stuff. Sometimes her examination is almost housewifely, she rolls a fabric under her fingers, tests it. It is thus and so. I find this very good, very interesting." This extensive, generous and domestic assessment on the cover of the *Herald Tribune*'s *Books* reached a large audience who might have been unsure for many years if Stein's experiments were serious. *The Making of Americans* was not widely available, but Porter's meaningful description of the book familiarized a large readership with her challenging work. That year, Elliot Paul's passionate defense of Stein, a two-part article in the *Chicago Tribune*, offered even more support for her difficult novel and more publicity came from Kate Buss, but not until 1928.[167] Her three-page "Gertrude Stein as a Writer and a Personality" in the *Boston Transcript* included a photograph of Stein and high praise for her work. She declared:

> "The Making of Americans" is direct thinking. Concerning Gertrude Stein, this statement may be startling. But it is true! . . . The sooner you read this word sonata of an American family, this Michael Angeleque structure of your native history, the sooner will be your realization that all the talk of the obscurity of the style of Gertrude Stein's writing is nonsense.[168]

Edmund Wilson, whose support of Stein in *Vanity Fair* was so important in building Stein's early reputation, expressed his frustration in a 1927 review of *The Making of Americans, Composition as Explanation,* and a new release of *Three Lives,* emphasizing his enthusiasm for Stein's early work and his uneasiness with her recent publications: "Except in her exasperating mode of interminable repetition, she writes with a good deal of distinction. . . . Yet, on the whole, it is impossible not to feel that she has somewhere gone off the track."[169]

Presenting a rosy interpretation of the early reception of *The Making of Americans*, Janet Flanner informed *New Yorker* readers in 1926 that Gertrude Stein "after the intellectual success of her The Making of Americans, is at work on Portraits and Prayers. A new verbal picture of Carl Van Vechten is to be included. No American writer is taken more seriously than Miss Stein by the Paris modernists."[170] But even if all critics and readers might not agree that *The Making of Americans* was an "intellectual success," as Flanner puts it, Stein's book did attract the notice of several influential cultural authorities at this moment in her career. Edith Sitwell, who had become an eager promoter of Stein in England, was certain that her already significant reputation in that country would be boosted by a live performance and she consulted with Cambridge about a possible lecture. In late 1925 Stein turned down Cambridge's invitation, but the following year Sitwell convinced her to rethink her decision and in 1926 Stein finally accepted invitations to speak at Cambridge and, thanks to another enthusiast, Harold Acton, an invitation from Oxford.[171] It was at Oxford that Stein first demonstrated her ability to amuse and impress audiences during the question and answer sessions after her lectures. As Alice recalls, after one man asked a question: "Another man, a don, next to him jumped up and asked something else. They did this several times, the two of them, jumping up one after the other. Then the first man jumped up and said, you say that everything being the same everything is always different, how can that be so. Consider, she replied, the two of you, you jump up one after the other, that is the same thing and surely you admit that the two of you are always different. Touchez, he said and the meeting was over."[172]

Both appearances were considered great successes and the talk, *Composition as Explanation*, was reproduced by Leonard and Virginia Woolf's Hogarth Press, a most distinguished English publisher of limited editions. Not only were initial sales of the book relatively strong (about 500 of the 1000 copies printed), the lecture was reprinted in the *Dial* in 1926 and soon became the subject of discussion in the American press.[173]

The *New York Times* was so taken with *Composition and Explanation* that they devoted an editorial to its contents. They explained:

> Professors of English and English Literature have an irritating habit of recommending young aspirants to study the classics, English and American, to follow the best models, and all that. There are many models, many classics; and some classics are not models for living usage.... Hitherto the "problem" has not been "attacked" in the right way. It is solved in The Dial by GERTRUDE STEIN, one of the most painstaking, original and creative of contemporary authors.... She erects a philosophical theory which, to those capable of the keen perception and reflection necessary to follow it, is irrefutable.[174]

Impressed with Stein's lecture, Marianne Moore solicited work for *The Dial*, and a short version of *A Long Gay Book* appeared there in September 1927. Stein also appeared in T. S. Eliot's *Criterion* after Jane Heap brought him to Stein's salon in 1924 and he asked for her "latest thing." As Alice recounts in *The Autobiography of Alice B. Toklas*, Stein immediately composed "The Fifteenth of November," the date of Eliot's visit, and sent it to him, but it did not appear until January 1926. These publications in *The Dial* and *The Criterion*, two elite, highly respected journals, suggest that Stein's work had broken out of the confines of little magazines and were taken seriously by a more academic readership. But, of course, these publications were not immune to the witticisms of the mainstream press. The *Louisville Herald* quoted from "The Fifteenth of November" and then remarked: "There is, alas, more where that came from. And it's art, if only one can be brought to believe it."[175] The *Saturday Review of Literature* commented that: "The New Criterion is liberal enough to print the work of Gertrude Stein, work which we shall never be able to regard as anything but futile."[176]

When Janet Flanner described the final issue of the *Little Review* in 1929, her *New Yorker* readers would have been well acquainted with the modernist writers and artists who had been so frequently discussed in the United States for over a decade. She observed that:

> Of the many illustrious and now salable writers whom [The Little Review] was the first in America to print, if not to pay—Sherwood Anderson, Ernest Hemingway, James Joyce, Gertrude Stein, Glenway Wescott, etc.—the greater number today live in France. Picasso, Léger, Picabia, Juan Gris, Miró—all were introduced in the States by the *Little Review*, and all are residents of Paris.[177]

For Flanner to call Stein, in the company of Joyce, Hemingway and Anderson "salable" in 1929 shows that she, at the very least, believed that the American public was not only attentive to modernist work, but interested in purchasing the publications of these writers. The final issue of the "Little Review" was a popular subject of columnists, including Harry Hansen, who enjoyed quoting from answers to the questionnaire that had been sent to its many contributors. As Hansen observed: "As for the questionnaires—well, this last number of the Little Review is going to be sought after and worn out by its eager readers."[178] Extensive quotations appeared in the *New Republic, New York Times, Boston Transcript*, and elsewhere.[179] *Dallas News*, for example, printed responses to the question "Why do you go on living?" by Sherwood Anderson, Brancusi, Emma Goldman, H.D., Aldous Huxley, Edith Sitwell, T. S. Eliot, William Carlos Williams, Havelock Ellis and others. Stein's succinct reply—"I am"—was of course mentioned.[180]

Anthologies: "a beneficent goose"

Since little magazines were unavailable to most Americans but interest in the writing published in them was high, the many anthologies that included modernist writing in the 1920s received much attention by the mainstream press. John G. Nichols observes that "from the mid-teens through the early 1920s ... literary compilations were the primary vehicle for circulating—and in the process, defining—contemporary, modernist verse" and it is certainly true that anthologies familiarized the American public with modernist prose as well.[181] Those compilations associated with little magazines and expatriate small presses, such as the *Contact Collection of Contemporary Writers* (1925) and *transition stories* (1929) further brought to the public attention writers who had published in the *Little Review, transatlantic review* and *transition*, although Stein and Joyce were the only writers to appear in both of these anthologies. These small, Paris publications were not available to the general public, but book reviewers and columnists discussed them and continued to acquaint Americans with modernist work.

In addition to these limited editions, Stein's work appeared in an astonishing array of collections in the 1920s; she was included in anthologies of representative American writing in the 1920s and, perhaps more surprisingly, collections of humor. That Stein appealed to such a wide range of editors demonstrates how pervasive her literary presence was in this decade. Anthologies were an especially popular and inexpensive publishing venture at this moment, since most work that had initially appeared in periodicals was not copyrighted. As Harvey Breit observed in his discussion of the massive profits earned by publishers who publish anthologies, "the modern anthology is a beneficent goose, and the publisher cannot be expected to kill it."[182] Stein's work in little magazines as well as more influential periodicals like the *Criterion*, the *Dial* or *Vanity Fair* were all available for any editor to exploit. These collections further publicized her name and writing; not only did many of these mainstream anthologies attract large audiences, they were also widely reviewed in the daily press and Stein's contributions were often singled out for mention.

Robert McAlmon's *Contact Anthology* appeared in 1925 and included previously unpublished work of many writers also associated with *transatlantic review*. The contents of the collection is a remarkable indication that the definition of "modernism" was actually established very early, and was easily recognized by mainstream reviewers. The collection includes work by Gertrude Stein, James Joyce, Ezra Pound, H. D., William Carlos Williams, Djuna Barnes, Bryher, Mary Butts, Ford Madox Ford, Ernest Hemingway, Mina Loy, Robert McAlmon, Dorothy Richardson, May Sinclair, and Edith Sitwell. One detailed review appeared in the [Columbus, OH] *State Journal*, with special criticism reserved for Stein:

> Much of the pioneering in this field of the publishing business has been done by Contact Editions, of Paris, and mainly distributed through the

bookshop of Sylvia Beach on the rue de l'Odeon. . . . Most of the new writers who have found their way into the public eye by sheer eccentricity are represented here—Gertrude Stein, William Carlos Williams, Djuna Barnes. . . . Alongside the exquisite fiction of Dorothy Richardson, you will find the erratic posturing of Gertrude Stein. . . . Reading it aloud at a party might be a good idea—if no one wants to play charades. Reading it to oneself is better than counting sheep jumping over a fence as a method of wooing sleep.[183]

The *transition* anthology included work that had previously appeared in the magazine, selected and edited by Eugene Jolas and Robert Sage. Unlike McAlmon, Jolas and Sage composed an elaborate introduction and biographical sketches of each writer to contextualize the contents of their collection. Their book could serve as an introduction to modernism for readers or reviewers who were less familiar with these writers. The editors described the philosophy behind *transition* as a corrective to what they saw as the homogenization of the arts, and sought to counter this threat by encouraging more complex and non-representational art. Jolas and Sage explained:

We are no longer interested in the bourgeois forms of literature. . . . We demand a sense of adventure that leads the individual towards a collective beauty, that is for every movement tending to demolish the current ideology, that seeks again the root of life in an impulse towards simplicity. For this reason we encourage the tendency to find new associations in theme as well as word.[184]

More specifically historicizing the development of modernism, the biographical descriptions detailed the progress of each writer's career. Stein's lengthy note focused on her American reception:

Her early book, *Tender Buttons* (a work which was unobtainable for years until it was reprinted in *transition* No. 14) first brought her to the attention of the critics, who unanimously found this work to be utterly nonsensical. Her ensuing writings, while occasionally attracting a penetrating critical appreciation, were greeted in print for the most part by the scoffs of the columnists. Despite this, however, she steadily gained a following until today she has a large number of readers who enjoy and appreciate her writing.[185]

Jolas and Sage were certainly aware that any reader would know Stein's name from the constant attention she had received in the newspapers for the previous fifteen years; their task was to defend Stein and, by extension, all experimental writing, against the flippant commentary known by virtually all literate Americans. The *New York Times Book Review* apparently took these defenses seriously, and opened its review by observing: "The world is not longer a simple place: one cannot laugh at Gertrude Stein. However ridiculous her lumpy rhythms may seem, there remains the indubitable fact that she had a salutary influence on the prose of Ernest Hemingway."[186]

The most obscure anthology of experimental writing to include Stein's writing was such a limited edition that it was did not attract much notice in the popular press, but it is a striking example of the ways some of the most innovative writers and publishers deliberately eschewed artificial distinctions between serious art and mass culture. Bob Brown's collection of "Readies" for his reading machine was published in 1931 by Roving Eye Press and, like other expatriate publications, was yet another characteristically modernist compilation, including writers such as Stein, Pound, Williams, and Kreymborg. *Readies for Bob Brown's Machine*, however, disrupts the conventional definitions of modernism by combining an interest in new technology with experimental writing of a wide range of artists who were by no means exclusively "high-brow." Brown himself started his career as a lucrative producer of pulp fiction, newspaper serials, Nick Carter detective stories and the best-selling *What Happened to Mary*, which was adapted into an early film. By his late twenties, Brown had "written myself out" but was then inspired by two things: Stein's *Tender Buttons* and the tape-tickers in Wall Street. Brown observes "At the time 'Tender Buttons' was published I had to read it because positively there was nothing else in America to read. No *transition* back in 1914, no Joyce, no Cummings, no Kay Boyle, just a peep of Sandburg, no tricky little playful magazines of word experiment." Frustrated with his own writer's block, "Gertrude Stein gave me a great kick. . . . I began to see that a story might be anything. . . . Thank God for that. Thank God for Gert Stein."[187]

Brown's reading machine, as Michael North has observed, "appears to have anticipated the microfilm reader."[188] The machine was intended to be "a method of enjoying literature in a manner as up to date as the lively talkies."[189] Books would be printed on a narrow tape and then viewed with an electronic machine that displayed the words by running them under a magnifying glass. Brown convinced himself the cumbersome machine was, in fact, more convenient than books. Concerned with the work of reading—moving the eye from line to line, and page to page—Brown believed that the speedy flow of text would relieve the reader of this burden, allowing for the text to be easily and quickly absorbed by the modern viewer.

Stein's work had already taken great steps toward the new literature Brown envisioned, and it was no surprise that he initiated a correspondence with her in 1929 after including Stein in the dedication to his *1450–1950*, printed by the Harry and Caresse Crosby's Black Sun Press.[190] In 1930, Stein sent an unpublished portrait of Brown, "Absolutely Bob Brown, or, Bobbed Brown," to him, a certain gesture of friendship, and requested a second copy of *The Readies*, his 1930 book about the philosophy behind his reading machine. "I am giggling over it quite pleasantly and read it to Alice," she wrote him. "Will you send another . . . there is an awful lot of good stuff in it and I want one to lend."[191] Her support was not even tempered by Brown's habit of equating her writing with Joyce's: "I repeat (having been set the example by our recentest writers) that I love every loveable Dublintender word James Joyce ever wrote an I gurgle with delight in the joyous jugfuls of Gertrude Stein (As a Wife Has a Cow—a Love Story, is a brimming pitcherful title)".[192]

Stein described her contribution to the *Readies* anthology, "We Came: A History," as "a study in movement." Brown's editorial policy appears to have been without prejudice; Stein's more serious piece was accompanied by Alfred Kreymborg's "Regrets": "Old man Kreymborg has grown too seedy / To write Bob Brown a speedy readie." Ezra Pound's poem specifically ridicules the idea of "high-brow" readers; his piece is titled "Highbrow's translation from Horace." William Carlos Williams's "Readie Pome" resembles a child's rhyme:

> Grace—face ; hot—pot ; lank—spank ; meat—eat ;
> hash—cash ; sell—well ; old—sold ; sink—wink ;
> deep—sleep; come—numb ; dum—rum ; some—bum.

Brown's anthologies may not have been known by most American readers, but they suggested that experimental writers of the 1920s were more open-minded and playful than is often assumed. Brown's eclectic literary background and taste accommodated both new technology and the most modern writing of the day, fundamentally challenging the hierarchical relationship between literature and mass culture often assumed by critics just as *The Soil* had in the 1910s. Most important, Brown seemed to find himself at home among the modernists, who encouraged his efforts by contributing to his various enterprises. When *transition* printed Brown's description of the reading machine in June 1930, there was some notice taken by the mainstream American press. Harry Hansen talked about the machine in his popular column, "The First Reader," while *Publisher's Weekly* and *Science and Invention* mentioned Brown's invention. Like *The Soil* or *Close-Up*, Brown saw that photography and film could change the way readers understood literature; his machine, however, failed to make the connection with audience that he anticipated.

Another limited edition, Leonard and Virginia Woolf's *Hogarth Essays* (1928), a collection of work previously published by the Hogarth Press, also included Gertrude Stein and was the subject of some comment in the mainstream press. The powerful, intellectual Woolfs juxtaposed Stein with Virginia Woolf, T. S. Eliot, Roger Fry, Leonard Woolf and E. M. Forster in the collection. Stein's visits to Oxford and Cambridge had solidified her reputation in the British Isles and brought about other evidence of a serious following there. The English publication of the popular *Georgian Stories*, usually considered a reactionary rather than an experimental annual publication, had included Stein's piece for T. S.

Eliot's *Criterion*, "The Fifteenth of November," in its 1926 volume. The appearance of Stein in this collection was so surprising that the *New York Times* printed an editorial about the subject, sarcastically suggesting that the following lines in Stein's piece contains "invaluable advice and directions":

> He said enough,
> Enough said,
> He said enough,
> Enough said.
> Enough said,
> He said enough,
> He said enough,
> Enough said.
> He said enough.

The *Times* used this quotation to berate politicians in Washington: "If the whole herd of Congressional yawpers, squawkers, wailers, weepers, bellowers, denouncers, defiers, taunters, could heed this invocation! Then the campaign of 1928 might be left to its sufficient day."[193]

One reader wrote to Harry Hansen about Stein's contribution to *Georgian Stories* and he reprinted the query in his popular column with the New York World News Service.

> Gertrude Stein's prose continues to bewilder readers who take their grammar seriously, as witness this: Dear Mr. Hansen: have you ever heard of Gertrude Stein and her short story, 'The 15th of November' in 'Georgian Stories—1926'? It was amusing to see what some of those Georgian authors had in mind, but when it comes to 'The 15th of November' I give up...
> --Frank Davis

> I have come to no conclusion, Mr. Davis, because I am waiting for the lady's collected works and should like to keep an open mind until then.[194]

On the American side of the Atlantic, Stein found a home in other collections whose editorial philosophies varied tremendously. The 1927 *American Caravan*, edited by Van Wyck Brooks, Lewis Mumford, Alfred Kreymborg, and Paul Rosenfeld, focused on creating a space for American writers whose work did not adhere to the conventional requirements of mainstream periodicals but still represented important aspects of modern American literature. Offended by "the many taboos of commercial and rubber-stamp policies [that] set limits not only to the length but on the character of literary work," the *American Caravan* promised to be more inclusive and representative. Certainly, the range of writers in the *Caravan* was impressive and introduced many and varied writers to the vast American public. In addition to Stein's "Mildred's Thoughts," modernism was represented by Hart Crane, William Carlos Williams, Ernest Hemingway, Edmund Wilson and John Dos Passos. A short story by the Marxist critic and editor of the radical *New Masses*, Mike Gold, as well as middle-brow poets Mark Van Doren and Robert Hillyer appeared in the anthology; Louis Untermeyer, Allen Tate, Robert Penn Warren were all included, as was the drama of Eugene O'Neill. Most surprising, the editors allowed the recognizable "W-tt-er B-nn-r" to print "Posthumous Poems of Emanuel Morgan"; the Spectra Hoax was still a memorable moment in the development of *vers libre* and the editors apparently felt that these verses did have a legitimate place in modern American literature. Indeed, the variety of material for the collection was in itself a difficulty for some reviewers; the *Los Angeles Times* noted that:

> A few good pieces are to be found here and there, to lend plausibility to the work. . . . But, then, there is Witter Bynner, the gentleman who did the delicious "Spectra" hoax; Kreymborg, who is forever playing pranks, and lastly, Miss Gertrude Stein, who is herself the very incarnation of hoax or praecox; surely these names are sufficient to let us know beyond peradventure that "The American Caravan" is laden with a Barnum show.[195]

The *American Caravan* was a selection of the Literary Guild, and this book club guaranteed an enormous distribution of the anthology. At this date "Mildred's Thoughts" was owned by a much larger audience than any other writing by Gertrude Stein, although her abstract portrait of Mildred Aldrich is by no means one of her most well known writings today. Reviews of the sizable, diverse anthology were plentiful, appearing nationwide in major periodicals and newspapers including the New York *Herald Tribune's Books*, the *New York Times*, the *Boston Herald*, the *Nation*, the *Saturday Review of Literature*, the *Dial*, and the *New Republic*. Stein's unusual contribution was often mentioned without sympathy. Jo Ranson noted that "Gertrude Stein is unintelligible and even a scribbler of gibberish"[196] while in Kansas, the *Wichita Beacon* complained that: "This reviewer, being somewhat orthodox, rather likes the simpler forms of expression. He never could understand what Gertrude Stein and her kind were driving at."[197] In Kentucky, the *Lexington Herald* noted that "'Mildred's Thoughts,' by Gertrude Stein is a trifle hard to digest" and the *Boston Herald* joked that "If Mildred's mental processes are really like that she should be taken to the psychopathic ward right away."[198] Henry Longan Stuart's review for the *New York Times* was no more enthusiastic: "Every caravan has its stragglers," they observed when discussing Stein's piece.[199] The *Boston Transcript* found room for extensive comment on Stein's contribution:

Some of the volume, to be frank, is so dreary, some so bleak, some so senseless! The Stein stuff, for instance. It leads nowhere, for it means nothing. It says nothing, for it seemingly is meant to say nothing. It is merely a few pages of perverted English. Perhaps it serves its purpose because of the contrasting light it throws.[200]

Unwilling to dismiss Stein altogether, the *New Orleans Times-Picayune* had this equivocal reaction: "'Mildred's Thoughts,' by Gertrude Stein, is a typical specimen of Miss Stein's absurd interpretation of fluid consciousness. It is awful stuff—by one of the most brilliant women alive."[201] Less critical, but still apparently skeptical, when Robert Ballou of the *Chicago News* listed the contributors, he commented after Stein's name: "you see the editors' tastes were all-embracing!"[202] Even Harry Hansen discussed Stein's contribution: "The boys still fall for Gertrude Stein on the ground that she is experimental. She is. But she composes in Esperanto and a translation would help a great many of us to find out whether she has anything besides tenacity."[203]

The 1925 edition of *Tom Masson's Annual*, a collection of humorous writing and drawings gathered from newspapers and periodicals, declared on its cover: "Pay $2.00 for this book and laugh it off." Stein's "If I Told Him," which had appeared in *Vanity Fair* in 1924, was apparently presented as comedy, although there is no indication that Stein herself is the subject of ridicule. Instead, Masson simply presents the work as one of many amusing literary tidbits without any editorial comment. Reviews appeared in such prominent publications as the *New York Herald Tribune Books* and the *New York Evening Post*'s supplement, the *Literary Review*.

Burton Rascoe's 1928 *Morrow's Almanack* was another humorous and eclectic hodge-podge of selections, organized according to each month of the year and accompanied by horoscopes, calendars and wood cuts. The collection was cheerfully applauded in numerous reviews, such as the *New York Herald Tribune Books*, who called it "an hilarious counterblast against owlishness . . . It is easily an event of the season"[204] They explained that:

> Nearly every one, from Aesop to Gertrude Stein, from Sam Johnson to Frank Sullivan, from Shakespeare to Ziegfeld, has contributed something to the volume, and no one, so far as our many ventures between the covers reveal, has anything to be ashamed of. Except, perhaps, Miss Stein, whose composition may be of her best or her worst, for all we know, or ever hope to find out. [205]

Rascoe chose Stein's "Van or Twenty Years After: A Second Portrait of Carl Van Vechten," which had appeared in *The Reviewer* in April 1924, and although the collection was lighthearted, there was no suggestion that her work was being ridiculed. Stein herself is seriously described as "an American born novelist now living in Paris whose work has had a great influence upon the younger writers. Author of Tender Buttons and The Making of Americans." Rascoe's own significant literary reputation, of course, suggested that the kind of diverting compilation he imagined might, unlike Masson's, actually improve the mind, as he happily predicted in his introduction: "We are offering for your consideration an almanack, from a serious and continued perusal of which we believe you will be considered very bright and that through and absorption of its contents you will grow great in wisdom."[206]

Although Stein did successfully find a place in these numerous anthologies in the 1920s (and would go on to appear in many more in the 1930s), since her work rarely fell into the conventional category of the "short story," she was unable to attract the notice of the most influential editor of anthologies in that decade, Edward J. O'Brien, who created the *Best Stories* anthology in 1915 and edited the series until he died in 1941, thus spanning the years many scholars define as the modernist period. Harry Hansen's *O'Henry Memorial Award Prize Stories* series was also influential, but O'Brien not only defined but also significantly altered the American conception of a successful, serious short story when the genre was a tremendously popular form of entertainment for many American periodical readers. Deliberately opposed to the formulaic stories routinely printed by the *Saturday Evening Post*, *McClure's*, *Collier's* and *Ladies Home Journal*, O'Brien instead looked for the most innovative work he could find, even in little magazines.[207]

Sherwood Anderson and Ernest Hemingway, two writers O'Brien championed and whose careers he successfully propelled into literary prominence, were his greatest and most important discoveries, as he freely admitted in the introduction to his complication of the *Fifty Best American Short Stories 1915–1939* (an immensely popular collection that was a selection of the Literary Guild).[208] Both writers had been unsuccessful in placing their early work with the mainstream magazines whose editorial policies O'Brien disliked, but thanks to the publicity he and other critics, such as Edmund Wilson, bestowed on them, both Anderson and Hemingway became known as masters of the short story in this decade and were soon able to place their work in popular publications; the style of Anderson and Hemingway quickly became mainstream. Stein's work was unrecognized by O'Brien, but the close relationship between Anderson, Hemingway, and Stein emphasized by many critics was familiar to readers. Even if Stein's writing was understood as difficult or even incomprehensible, the recurring observation that she had influenced and won the admiration of Anderson and Hemingway proved to some that she was serious and meaningful literary presence.

Ernest Hemingway: "an onion is an onion is an onion"

In 1937, *Time* magazine called the well-publicized tension between Hemingway and Stein "one of the most persistent literary squabbles of the generation" although their early friendship was also an important aspect of the public persona of each.[209] In March 1922, when Hemingway was 22 years old, he met Stein at the urging of Sherwood Anderson, who generously supplied Hemingway with letters of introduction to such Paris notables as Stein and Ezra Pound. A young journalist who aspired to be a successful fiction writer, Hemingway took seriously the advice he received from Anderson, Stein and Pound, although he would soon attempt to rid himself of the perception that the influence of Anderson or Stein could be detected in his work.

Hemingway's early career resembles that of Stein and other modernist writers in many respects. His first writing was published in little magazines although he unsuccessfully submitted his work to mainstream American periodicals. Stein, of course, had courted the *Atlantic Monthly* in the 1910s and 1920s, just as Hemingway tried without success to interest the *Saturday Evening Post* in his early writing. Hemingway's first unremarkable publications were with *The Double-Dealer*, a little magazine published in New Orleans. His short prose piece, "A Divine Gesture," was printed in May 1922 and in June a poem titled "Ultimately" appeared there. Faulkner also made his debut in the *Double-Dealer* that year with "Portrait," a poem which would appear in his volume, *The Marble Faun*, published with Four Seas Co., the publisher of Stein's *Geography and Plays*. Carlos Baker suggests that it was Sherwood Anderson who brought about the publication of both Hemingway and Faulkner in the *Double-Dealer*, whose modest circulation averaged about 1,500.[210]

Once Hemingway had made contact with Stein and the influential Ezra Pound in Paris, many more literary outlets were available to him. *Poetry* magazine printed six of Hemingway's poems in January 1923, and six short vignettes, which would later appear in *In Our Time* as italicized sections between the short stories, were published in the *Little Review* in spring 1923. That same year Robert McAlmon expressed interest in publishing *Three Stories and Ten Poems* with his Contact Publishing Company. William Bird's Three Mountains Press (soon to merge with McAlmon's Contact Press) then published 170 copies of the thirty-page *in our time*, a collection of "miniatures" including those that had appeared in the *Little Review*. After Hemingway published "Indian Camp" in the *transatlantic review* in April 1924, "Mr. and Mrs. Elliot" in the Autumn 1924—Winter 1925 issue of the *Little Review* and "Big Two Hearted River" in the first issue of *This Quarter* in summer 1925, Hemingway's resumé began to resemble that of many other experimental writers of that moment. The premiere issue of *This Quarter* was dedicated to Ezra Pound and also included Hemingway's "Homage to Ezra": Stein's "Capital Capitals," rather surprisingly, was also printed in this issue, although she never did appreciate the genius of Pound.[211] By the time he was included in McAlmon's 1925 *Contact Collection of Contemporary Writers*, Hemingway clearly had established a reputation for himself as a serious modern experimental writer whose work was on par with that of the other modernists who appeared in the anthology. It was no surprise that *transition* would also find Hemingway's work interesting; "Hills Like White Elephants" appeared there in August 1927.

Stein was close to Hemingway in his early career, personally as well as professionally. Hemingway asked her, with Alice B. Toklas, to be his son's godmothers in 1923, and that year Hemingway and Stein wrote reviews of each other's work for the Paris edition of the *Chicago Tribune*. Stein clearly assumed that she and Hemingway would mutually benefit from promoting the other, as she, Carl Van Vechten and Sherwood Anderson did. But Hemingway soon chafed at any obligation to unfailingly support the writing of any other writer and his March 1923 review, in fact, shows how early in his career he tried to distance himself from contemporary writers. Dedicating only limited space to Stein's *Geography and Plays*, ostensibly the subject of the review, Hemingway instead took the opportunity to poke fun at those who had already achieved public recognition and respect.

> Gertrude Stein is a sort of gauge of civilization. If you think Mr. Sinclair Lewis is a great writer and Babbitt a great book you probably won't like Gertrude Stein. . . . Gertrude Stein is probably the most first rate intelligence employed in writing today. If you are tired of Mr. D. H. Lawrence who writes extremely well with the intelligence of a head waiter or Mr. Wells who is believed to be intelligent because of a capacity for sustained marathon thinking or the unbelievably stupid but thoroughly conscientious young men who compile the Dial you ought to read Gertrude Stein. . . . There is an introduction to the book called "The Work of Gertrude Stein," by Sherwood Anderson. You ought to read that before you start the book and you ought to read her Three Lives. . . . Sherwood wrote the introduction soon after he won the Dial prize and the new respectability was still on him. It is a little restrained, the introduction. But the next to the last paragraph is a corker.[212]

In December, both Stein's review of *Three Stories and Ten Poems* and, her ultimate compliment, a short portrait of Hemingway, "He and They, Hemingway," appeared. The review, however, suggested that Stein thought that Hemingway had potential but she was unsure if it would be realized:

> Three stories and ten poems is very pleasantly said. So far so good, further than that, and as far as that, I may say of Hemingway that as he sticks to poetry and intelligence it is both poetry and intelligent. Rosevelt [sic] is genuinely felt as young as Hemingway and as old as Rosevelt. I should say that Hemingway should stick to poetry and intelligence and eschew the hotter emotions and the more turgid vision. Intelligence and a great deal of it is a good thing to use when you have it it's all for the best.[213]

It may be that the review is a response not just to his book, but also to his review of Stein; the "hotter emotions" that led him to disparage other writers would certainly not have pleased her. Her cryptic "He and They,

Hemingway: A Portrait" appeared in *Ex libris* and, like the review, fails to express any confidence in Hemingway's writing career. Neither the review nor the portrait of Hemingway elicited the extensive commentary in the mainstream press that Stein's reviews of Sherwood Anderson and Kreymbourg would in 1925, as Hemingway was relatively unknown at this early point in his career. He soon received an enormous publicity boost from Edward O'Brien's inclusion of "My Old Man" in *The Best Short Stories of 1923*, which also included contributions by Sherwood Anderson, Theodore Dreiser, Edna Ferber and others, but the volume had not yet been released when Stein's pieces appeared.[214]

Ezra Pound, an unfailing promoter of Hemingway in the 1920s, further expanded Hemingway's modernist circle by introducing him to Ford Madox Ford, who found use for Hemingway's talents at the *transatlantic review*. Not only did Hemingway suggest publishing Stein's *The Making of Americans* there, he was so enthusiastic about the project that when he learned that there was only one copy of the massive text, he graciously offered to copy it. His own work was also welcome at the *transatlantic review*, of course. The remarkable April 1924 issue of *transatlantic review* included, in addition to the first installment of *The Making of Americans*, Hemingway's untitled "Indian Camp" under "Works in Progress," a section that also included part of Joyce's *Finnegans Wake*, and Marjorie Reid's positive review of *in our time*.

Edmund Wilson was one of the first major critics to recognize that Hemingway was an important new voice, with only *Three Stories and Ten Poems* and the short *in our time* to support his view. Wilson's comparison of Hemingway to Anderson and Stein was common in the 1920s and, for the competitive Hemingway, most irritating:

> [Hemingway] must be counted as the only American writer but one—Mr. Sherwood Anderson—who has felt the genius of Gertrude Stein's Three Lives and has been evidently influenced by it. Indeed, Miss Stein, Mr. Anderson, and Mr. Hemingway may now be said to form a school by themselves. The characteristic of this school is a naiveté of language often passing into the colloquialism of the character dealt with which serves actually to convey profound emotions and complex states of mind. It is a uniquely American development in prose.[215]

This important recognition by Wilson in the *Dial* surely helped Hemingway obtain a contract with a major publisher. An expanded version of *In Our Time* was accepted by Boni and Liveright after the manuscript had been recommended by several allies: in addition to Edward O'Brien, Harold Loeb and Sherwood Anderson, both Boni and Liveright authors, endorsed the book. In October 1925, a small printing of 1335 copies was produced. Walking a fine line with the censors, *In Our Time* was marketed as a risqué book that dealt with intimate issues. The title page included this juicy bit of dialogue: "Tell us about the French women, Hank. What are they like?"[216]

Ignoring the publisher's attempt to generate publicity, reviews neglected to focus on the scandalous subject matter in the book. Allen Tate's review of *In Our Time* in *The Nation* praised Hemingway's "naturalistic" style, and Louis Kronenberger printed a positive review in the *Saturday Review of Literature*. Echoing Edmund Wilson's assessment of Hemingway, Paul Rosenfeld observed in the *New Republic*:

> There is something of Sherwood Anderson, of his fine bare effects and values coined from simplest words, in Hemingway's clear medium. There is Gertrude Stein equally obvious: her massive volumes, slow power, steady reiterations, and her intuition of the life of headless bodies. The American literary generations are learning to build upon each other.[217]

Assisting Hemingway in his attempt to distance himself from comparisons to Sherwood Anderson, F. Scott Fitzgerald's essay in the *Bookman* on current literary trends described Sherwood Anderson as primarily a writer of style rather than ideas; Hemingway was the new writer to watch, Fitzgerald contended.[218] But this effort was not enough to satisfy Hemingway. His 1926 parody of Anderson's *Dark Laughter*, *The Torrents of Spring*, not only pilloried Anderson, but poked fun at Stein as well. The title of part four is "The Passing of a Great Race and the Making and Marring of Americans"; and, even more directly, Hemingway seemed to dismiss the celebration of Stein by eager, superficial Americans: "There was a street corner in Paris named after Huysmans. Right around the corner from where Gertrude Stein lived. Ah, there was a woman! What were her experiments in words leading her? What was at the bottom of it? All that in Paris. Ah, Paris!"[219]

Not many were amused by Hemingway's joke. Even Harry Hansen discussed *The Torrents of Spring* negatively in his syndicated column, but he indicated that he did admire Hemingway's short stories.[220] Stein, who valued the loyalty of friends and fellow writers, was especially incensed at Hemingway's rebellion. His association with Stein and Anderson had effectively launched his career; but at this early stage, he risked alienating his mentors.

Hemingway's other major publication in 1926, however, suggested that the parody was meant in good fun; by including Stein's quotation "you are all a lost generation" as an epigraph for *The Sun Also Rises*, the association between the two writers was again affirmed. *The Sun Also Rises* was not hailed by all as a literary masterpiece, but it was certainly recognized as a sensational scandal. The book was too controversial for both the Book-of-the-Month Club and Hollywood, essential promoters of the most popular fiction of the decade.[221] Hemingway, whose literary ambition was certainly willing to embrace these commercial industries, wrote to Max Perkins at Scribner's in December 1926: "As for movie rights [for the *The Sun Also Rises*] please get the best you can i.e. the most money," but the project was eventually blocked by censors.[222]

In addition to the explicit sexual nature of *The Sun Also Rises*, readers were fascinated to learn that the characters were based on real people who knew and drank with Hemingway. Those who lived in Paris had no trouble identifying the main characters; for others, there were clues in many major publications as to these identities. Janet Flanner, for example, explained in her "Paris Letter" for the *New Yorker* that:

> "The Sun Also Rises" has stirred Montparnasse, where, it is asserted, all of the four main characters are local and easily identifiable. The titled British declassée and her Scottish friend, the American *Frances* and her unlucky *Robert Cohn* with his art magazine which, like a broom, was to sweep esthetics clean—all these personages are, it is to be maintained, to be seen just where Hemingway so often placed them at the Select. Not being amorously identified with the tale, it should be safe to say that Donald Ogden Stewart is taken to be the stuffed-bird-loving *Bill*. Under the flimsy disguise of *Braddocks*, certainly Ford Madox Ford is visible as the Briton who gives, as Mr. Ford does, dancing parties in the *bal musette* behind the Panthéon.[223]

Readers who had followed the many notices of Harold Loeb's *Broom* in the mainstream press, of course, could easily identify him from Flanner's unsubtle hint.

Some scholars have suggested that Hemingway's contribution to the *New Yorker* the following year that includes a section with the heading "The True Story of My Break with Gertrude Stein" in fact details a rift between the writers, but this piece is a humorous parody, as the title makes clear: "My Own Life" is the title of the piece, subtitled: "After reading the second volume of Frank Harris' 'My Life.'" Frank Harris, who had been the editor of London newspapers including the *Evening News*, the *Fortnightly Review* and the *Saturday Review*, had been publishing his multi-volume, sexually explicit memoir, "My Life and Loves" privately in Paris to avoid the censors.[224] Rather than acknowledging the controversial content of the book, Hemingway instead pokes fun at Harris for his incessant name-dropping and the numerous abrupt ends to friendships detailed in the book. Hemingway's sections include: How I Broke With John Wilkes Booth; The True Story of My Break With Gertrude Stein; How I Broke with My Children; How I Broke with Benchley. And the piece concludes with this teaser: "(Next Installment—How I broke with Dos Passos, Coolidge, Disraeli, Lincoln and Shakespeare.)"[225]

Hemingway had no quarrel with controversial content, and did not heed Gertrude Stein's advice to avoid what she called *"inaccrochable"* subjects in his work. Thus, when the first sections of *A Farewell to Arms* were serialized in *Scribner's Magazine* in 1929, issues of the magazine were found "salacious" and banned by the Boston police, ensuring that the book would be even more popular when it was released.[226] Not only did *A Farewell to Arms* become a bestseller, it also became a Broadway theater production in 1930 and a hit movie in 1932 starring Helen Hayes and Gary Cooper. The movie was nominated for Academy Awards for best picture and best art direction, and won for best cinematography and best sound recording. These developments not only made Hemingway financially secure, but they assured that he need not publish in little magazines with limited circulations any more. In the 1930s, Hemingway instead contributed to periodicals like *Esquire* and, instead of writing more characteristic "hard boiled" fiction, composed chatty letters about the exotic locations in which he lived or vacationed: Spain, Key West, Cuba, Paris. By 1940, Hemingway's work confidently embraced by the mainstream. The rights to *For Whom the Bells Tolls* were purchased by Paramount soon after the book was published for a record $100,000 with an additional ten cents for the first 500,000 copies of the book that were sold. Rumors even circulated that Hemingway might be cast in the movie.[227]

It was not until the publication of Stein's *Autobiography of Alice B. Toklas* that the real "break" with Hemingway took place. Alice observes in the book:

> Gertrude Stein and Sherwood Anderson are funny on the subject of Hemingway. The last time that Sherwood was in Paris they often talked about him. Hemingway had been formed by the two of them and they were both a little proud and a little ashamed of the work of their mind. . . . They admitted that Hemingway was yellow, he is, Gertrude Stein insisted, just like the flat-boat men of the Mississippi river as described by Mark Twain. But what a book they both agreed, would be the real story of Hemingway, not those he writes but the confessions of the real Ernest Hemingway. It would be for another audience than the audience Hemingway now has but it would be very wonderful.[228]

Numerous scholars have noted the many places in which Hemingway reacted to this insulting characterization.[229] Even Sherwood Anderson, who might have been expected to delight in this representation of Hemingway, was shocked by her cruelty and wrote to Stein that he was "a bit sorry and sad . . . when you took such big patches of skin off Hemmy with your delicately held knife."[230] After this date, negative references to Stein seemed to become something of an obsession with Hemingway, from his widely read series in *Esquire* in which he compared Stein's physique to that of a Buddha, to obscure periodicals like *Cahiers d'art*, where a reproduction of Miró's "The Farm" was accompanied by Hemingway's explanation of how he came to acquire the painting. He explained that:

> No one could look at [The Farm] and not know it had been painted by a great painter and when you are painting things that people must take on trust it is good to have something around that has taken as long to make as it takes a woman to make a child (a woman who isn't

a woman can usually write her autobiography in a third of the time) and that shows even fools that you are a great painter in terms that they understand.... If you have painted "The Farm" ... and then keep on working very hard afterwards, you do not need an Alice B. Toklas.[231]

This non sequitur was noticed by the mainstream press and June Provines alerted her *Chicago Tribune* readers to it. She claimed that "Those of you who read Gertrude Stein's The Autobiography of Alice B. Toklas ... will be amused at the parody of her style."[232] Obviously still irritated by Stein, almost half of the introduction to *This Must Be the Place: Memoirs of Jimmie the Barman* (1937) discusses her (although she is never named) and the relevance of Hemingway's rant is minimal. He opens his introduction:

> Once a woman has opened a salon it is certain that she will write her memoirs. If you go to the salon you will be in the memoirs; that is, you will be if your name ever becomes known enough so that its use, or abuse, will help the sale of the woman's book.... Literary ladies like them young or famous; and not too famous and famous in some other line. Literary salon women do not like Mr. James Joyce for instance. They would be happier if there had not been any Mr. James Joyce. However, if you go to the salon you must expect to be in the memoirs.[233]

Stein was not the only target of this introduction; Margaret Anderson had recently published her own memoirs, *My Thirty Years' War* (1930), and in it she included Jane Heap's description of Hemingway as a rabbit with a "white and pink face, soft brown eyes that look at you without blinking. As for his love for boxing and bull-fighting—all that is thrashing up the ground with his hind legs."[234] In fact, Hemingway was so sensitive to negative publicity that he attacked any writer who threatened his masculine persona. After Virginia Woolf's unenthusiastic review of *Men Without Women* (1927) appeared in the *New York Herald Tribune*, she became a target as well. In a description of bullfighting in *Death in the Afternoon* (1932), Hemingway sniped that "The females that are used in amateur fights almost invariably make for the man rather than the cape ... but they do this not because of any innate superior intelligence in the female, as Virginia Woolf might suppose."[235]

Publishing such petty remarks about Stein was apparently irresistible for Hemingway and he continued to do so for years. In 1935 he included this conversation in *Green Hills of Africa*:

> "Yes, and he doesn't have to read books written by some female he's tried to help get published saying how he's yellow."
> "She's just jealous and malicious. You never should have helped her. Some people never forgive that."
> "It's a damned shame, though, with all that talent gone to malice and nonsense and self-praise. It's a god-damned shame, really. It's a

shame you never knew her before she went to pot. You know a funny thing; she never could write dialogue. It was terrible. She learned how to do it from my stuff and used it in that book. She had never written like that before. She never could forgive learning that and she was afraid people would notice it, where she'd learned it, so she had to attack me. It's a funny racket, really. But I swear she was damned nice before she got ambitious. You would have liked her then, really."

"Maybe, but I don't think so."

One review of the book observed that Hemingway "went all the way to Africa to hunt, and then when he thought he had found a rhinoceros, it turned out to be Gertrude Stein."[236] As late as 1940, Hemingway continued to reference Stein; in *For Whom the Bell Tolls* he included this exchange:

"What hast thou against the onion?"
"The odour. Nothing more. Otherwise it is like the rose."
"Like the rose," he said, "Mighty like the rose. A rose is a rose is an onion."
"Thy onions are affecting thy brain," Augustin said. "Take care."
"An onion is an onion is an onion," Robert Jordan said cheerily and, he
  thought, a stone is a stein is a rock is a boulder is a pebble.

Hemingway even composed a vicious parody of *The Autobiography of Alice B. Toklas* titled "The Autobiography of Alice B. Hemingway," but it was never published.[237] But the last and certainly most well-known attack on Stein appeared in Hemingway's posthumous memoir, *A Moveable Feast* (1964), in a homophobic anecdote which exposes the romantic relationship between Stein and Toklas to the general public and emphasizes his own disgust. Of course, he was not the only individual who was incensed by the *Autobiography of Alice B. Toklas*. Certainly, the publication of the book brought about an end to the relationships Stein had with many writers and artists in Paris. The "Testimony Against Gertrude Stein," printed in *transition*, with negative responses from Matisse and others, suggests how disconcerting it was for these artists to be described in flippant, unflattering or dismissive anecdotes. But only Hemingway fostered his grudge for a lifetime.

Useful Knowledge: "a sumptuous literary curiosity"

On Christmas Day 1927, the *New York Times Book Review* printed this erroneous notice, prompting comment from columnists and reviewers for the next several weeks.

> Gertrude Stein has written "A Novel." The quotes are there because that is what the book is to be called. Apparently even Miss Stein herself is stumped when it comes to giving a name to what she writes. The

book is to be published in Paris by Edward W. Titus, whose establishment is at the Sign of the Black Mannikin, near the Dome, where the literary folks gather. As an added attraction of the book will be a portrait of the author by Picasso.[238]

A Novel was eventually titled *A Novel of Thank You* and did not appear until 1958, over a decade after Stein's death. Stein had considered placing the book with Titus, but negotiations had failed. This early notice was considered news enough for quips to appear throughout the nation. In Nebraska, the *Lincoln Journal* noted that: "Gertrude Stein has written 'A Novel.' That is the name of it. If you have read any of Miss Stein's writings you will not be surprised to learn that she is at a loss to know what to call anything she has produced."[239] Similar comments appeared in the *Savannah Press*, the Philadelphia *Public Ledger*, and Spokane Washington's *Spokesman Review*.[240] The Seattle *Times* simply observed: "There is a certain arresting succinctness to the title which Gertrude Stein has chosen for her new novel. It is simply 'A Novel.'"[241]

Stein's next book was actually *Useful Knowledge*, which, like *Geography and Plays*, was a compilation of various short pieces and published by an obscure press. Payson & Clarke, Ltd. expressed interest in publishing just the kind of innovative work that Stein produced and in 1926, the firm's Joseph Brewer actually approached Stein for a manuscript, a thrilling first experience for her. Although Brewer wanted to print Stein's book in a new series of limited editions, suggesting that he realized that Stein's work would only attract a small audience, he did hope to profit from the venture. The back cover of *Useful Knowledge* explains that:

> It is the happy lot of the publisher to entertain from time to time a manuscript which because of its inherent significance or its literary importance he feels to have a special and perhaps a permanent value for the world, but which he also feels is not likely to appeal in the first instance to the wider reading public.

Stein, who continued to struggle to find publishers willing to take a financial risk with her intimidating manuscripts, again discovered that although the American press enjoyed discussing her newest publications, most readers were still unwilling to purchase her esoteric writing; only 226 copies of the 1500 printed sold and, since the firm ultimately lost a thousand dollars on *Useful Knowledge*, Brewer was forced to reject her next manuscript, *Lucy Church Amiably*.[242] Some critics cynically assumed that obscurity of Stein's art was a deliberate play for attention; the *Christian Science Monitor* observed that "Publicity is a great art" while the *Saturday Review of Literature* speculated that: "the publishers are probably laughing in their sleeves, having decided that a little humor is an excellent ingredient (my goodness! We've caught the contagion) of any list."[243]

The *Providence Journal* and the *Portland Telegram* both worried about the sanity of the proofreaders. Portland's reviewer admitted that he "has never opened a book nor read a poem by Gertrude Stein—since he first read her immortal verses upon the entry into the World War, in the Metropolitan some ten years ago—without feeling that somebody is getting away with a hoax, and making it profitable." He went on:

> The only sad element in connection with the contemplation of Gertrude's volume of "Useful Knowledge" is the realization that innumerable printers and proofreaders must have gone gibbering mad and gained permanent homes in padded cells, as a result of their association with Miss Stein's "Useful Knowledge."[244]

The *Argonaut* was amused by Stein's title: "Gertrude Stein has written a new book, and—of all the titles in the world—has chosen to name it 'Useful Knowledge.'" Other notices characterized the book as a "sumptuous literary curiosity" or a sedative: "It is no doubt a criticism of myself as of Miss Stein, but a page or two of hers at first makes me a little cross-eyed, and then puts me quite conclusively to sleep."[245] Harry Hansen expressed wry enthusiasm for the book: "This is much better than many of the songs that come over the radio. Miss Stein has found her métier at last. She is headed for Tinpan Alley. We knew she had something in her if only she could get her words placed in suitable combinations."[246]

Katherine Anne Porter, who did admire Stein and had written such a positive review of *The Making of Americans* for the *Herald Tribune*, joined the company of many reviewers in the 1920s by producing a clichéd parody. She wrote:

> In this book you will look for sex to vex. There is no sex to vex. Look visibly. Stimulation is one and irritation is another. Another to smother Americans, who wear glasses and read if a hat is dropped suddenly. They send white wedding cake too in painted boxes. We are told this is being American, but it is not pleasant. She says it is pleasant.[247]

The tenor of this discussion was finally improved by Edmund Wilson, who defended Stein's kind of "nonsense" in the *New Republic* in February 1929. He called her "A Patriotic Leading" "one of the most amusing of her nonsense pieces" and quoted it in full.[248] He explained that:

> I have described this production as nonsense, and I have therefore no doubt led the reader to suppose that I regard it with contempt. To characterize something as nonsense is usually to throw it out of court as literature, and there are always a great many people who are ready to dispose of new and unconventional poets, playwrights or novelists in this way. Yet our ordinary use of the word "nonsense" in English, in

connection with matters of literature, is based upon a complete misconception of the nature of literature, and of human experience itself.

Instead, Wilson viewed Stein's nonsense as meaningful literary experimentation, not to be dismissed by readers. As he was well aware, Stein's name continued to crop up in the daily press; some journalists even implied that her writing was about as comprehensible as the ravings of a drunken man. The *New Yorker*, for example, printed the following anecdote (which was then reprinted in newspapers):

> We are told of a gentleman who, at a recent bachelor dinner, suspected himself of intemperance and slipped off to a guest room. Reaching the chamber he hit upon a plan to test his condition. He would, he said to himself, pick up a magazine, open it and read the first paragraph he saw. If it made sense all was well. If not, a nap. Friends found him sound asleep a few minutes later, a nearby periodical opened to a poem by Gertrude Stein.[249]

Similarly, as early as 1926 a *New York Times* columnist told an anecdote about a drunken man who accidentally strangled an ostrich in the Franklin Park Zoo. He explained: "McGuire's speech became as clear as the writings of Gertrude Stein. What he saw Dadaist painters strive to convey. What he heard has been faithfully recorded by some modern composers."[250]

Despite these unserious references to Stein, there was a genuine attempt by many columnists and reviewers to assess her work and that of other experimental writers. As early as 1922, Fanny Butcher argued in the *Chicago Tribune* that Stein, Joyce and Dorothy Richardson share the same method. She explains:

> Unless I am mistaken, Gertrude Stein was the first person in the generation to throw into her sentences all of the conflicting vagaries of the mind that derail the old fashioned train of thought. Anyway, what they do, in words of one syllable, is to dump everything out of the minds of their characters on to the paper, with no selection whatever. The result is a realistic muddle of impressions and thoughts which is, to some, extremely stimulating and significant but which is, to others, merely a confusing muddle.[251]

In 1926, Harry Hansen emphasized for his mainstream readers that literature of the 1920s was notable for its experimentation:

> Inventiveness in styles belongs particularly to our generation. Gertrude Stein, Dorothy Richardson, James Joyce all presented their tales in a new way. Miss Stein's is a monologue and is taken by some to be a form

of spirit-communications, hence not taught in any Berlitz school. Miss Richardson has put editors and proofreaders to sleep for days at a time. Mr. Joyce has been more fortunate. He has become a prophet.[252]

This syndicated column, appearing from coast to coast, ensured that mainstream readers were reminded of the newest, most innovative modernist writing as it was published throughout the 1920s.

Indeed, becoming familiar with these modern trends in literature and culture was not difficult to accomplish thanks to popularizers like Hansen and that more elite, trusted taste-maker, *Vanity Fair*. In 1927, *Vanity Fair* tested its reader's cultural intelligence by printing a quiz of 50 questions taken from Alfred Barr's course on modern art at Wellesley. Barr would go on to be the first director of the Museum of Modern Art in New York. Readers were asked to identify "the significance of each of the following in relation to modern artistic expression" including: Henri Matisse, *The Hairy Ape*, James Joyce, Alfred Stieglitz, The Imagists, Harriet Monroe, The Sitwells, Frank Lloyd Wright, George Gershwin, George Antheil, and Arnold Schoenberg. Another question asked: Who wrote this?

> Silence is not hurt by attending to taking more reflection than a whole sentence. And it is said and the quotation is reasoning. It gives the whole preceding. If there is time enough then appearances are considerable. They are in a circle. They are tendering a circle. They are a tender circle. They are tenderly a circle.

Gertrude Stein was identified as the author on the answer page.[253]

The publicity and comment surrounding modernism was so pervasive that some writers clearly felt threatened, and expressed discomfort, jealousy, and other negative reactions to Stein, Joyce and others. The famous Marxist critic Max Eastman, for example, was especially defensive in his reactionary analysis for *Harper's*, "The Cult of Unintelligibility." He complained:

> If you pick up a book by Hart Crane, E. E. Cummings, James Joyce, Gertrude Stein, Edith Sitwell, or any of the "modernists," and read a page innocently, I think the first feeling you will have is that the author isn't telling you anything. It may seem that he isn't telling you anything because he doesn't know anything. Or it may seem that he knows something, but he won't tell. In any case he is uncommunicative.[254]

The article was the subject of much comment, and was extensively quoted in the "Current Magazines" column in the *New York Times*, further familiarizing the public with the writers that Eastman denigrates. Other critiques of modernism were widely publicized, such as Wyndham Lewis's in *The Enemy* (yet another little magazine). Harry Hansen noted in his syndicated column in May 1929 that: "The attempts of

Gertrude Stein and James Joyce to separate English from its familiar connotations strike Lewis as uproariously funny."[255] And Isabel Paterson extensively quoted from Stein in a discussion of Lewis's criticism in the *Herald Tribune*.[256]

Later that year, Paterson detailed which modernist writers were and were not accessible. "We find no difficulty in Marcel Proust," she explains, "but André Gide's 'The Counterfeiters' was incomprehensible to us. . . . Virginia Woolf is easy enough," but Romer Wilson and Mary Butts are not; D. H. Lawrence and Luigi Pirandello are sometimes comprehensible, but not Stein: "we don't believe a word of it, and never shall," she declared.[257] Paterson proved her cultural sophistication by distinguishing between these writers, but the following year she offered a less hopeful assessment of experimental literature, concluding that: "It is optimistic and kind of the Modernists to continue hoping that we may some day rise to their level, but honestly, we fear the chances are infinitesimal." According to Paterson, "The Gertrude Stein—e. e. cummings—James Joyce method of using words" is too much like "falling down the cellar stairs with a lemon pie in our arms. . . . We have our mouth wide open to absorb a phrase, and it hits us on the nose or gets stuck in our hair."[258]

Paterson and other columnists who struggled to understand Joyce and Stein would surely not have bothered if so many critics and writers did not seriously regard the influence of modernist writing. Like Paterson, reviewers and columnists naturally grouped writers we now consider modernists together and struggled to understand or, at the very least, define this new literary movement. By the end of the 1920s, the "modernist" or "modern" style was so recognizable that references to the distinctiveness of modern writing regularly appeared in mainstream newspapers. In the *Galveston News*, Lloyd Morris observed that:

> Four modern writers seem to have profoundly influenced contemporary literature in the element of expression or "style." These writers are Marcel Proust, Andre Gide, James Joyce and Gertrude Stein. . . . Miss Stein has attempted to exploit the secondary qualities of words; she has dissociated words from their meanings, and used them as a musician might use notes for their emotional values of sound and color."[259]

Similarly, in the *Chicago Herald Examiner*, James Weber Linn explained to readers that Gertrude Stein, James Joyce, Virginia Woolf and May Sinclair are all exponents of the 'stream of consciousness' technique."[260] The *New Yorker* went further trying to explain what connected them: "The single uniting characteristic of these writers—Joyce, Gertrude Stein, Virginia Woolf, etc.—is that they have really lost interest in the plot entirely, or at least that they no longer depend on it explicitly as justification for their philosophizing or their poetizing."[261]

Stein's work might have been the equivalent to "futility" for many readers, as Charles Driscoll observed in Paterson New Jersey's *Call*; he defined futility as follows: "to try to learn the Russian language; to try to understand Einstein; to try to make sense out of Gertrude Stein; to try to reason with one disappointed in love; to try to make H. L. Mencken mad by criticizing his work."[262] But throughout the 1920s, the *New York Times* reminded readers of Stein's presence, even if their editorial comments were not always as complimentary as their 1925 "Injustice to Genius," a passionate defense of Stein. Following the common practice of discussing articles and reviews that appeared in other periodicals, the *Times* objected to a series of articles by Alan Porter on "The Present State of Literature" in the *Spectator*. The *Times* complained that Porter was "blind to one of the most striking literary manifestations of the present. . . . Miss Stein is but one of its most brilliant representatives."[263]

Newspapers outside New York also followed the careers of Joyce and Stein with interest. In 1929, a Louisville, Kentucky column wondered if they would ever be considered canonical:

> [We] had rather seek and find a lovely edition of [Puccini's] Manon Lescaut than the latest excursion of James Joyce, or Gertrude Stein, of any of that galaxy which, or who, lend brilliance to 'transition.' Are they stars . . . or will [they] flicker and fade . . . Who knows or who can tell?[264]

And the same year, with no real prompting, a columnist in the *Boston Transcript* asked readers: "And speaking of French, what news have we of those industrious Americans, Elliot Paul and Gertrude Stein who, aided by James Joyce, are sponsoring a new language in their spare moments?"[265]

The uncertain fate of Stein and other modernists plagued critics, columnists and readers in the 1920s. Would their experiments be considered important literary innovations or outrageous silliness in the future? It was unclear to most concerned Americans if Stein's work could ever be truly popular. A dubious Carl Sandburg commented in the *Chicago Daily News* that "There are people who enjoy reading Gertrude Stein as they enjoy a taste of gorgonzola cheese—occasionally."[266] Not until the 1930s did the vast American public cease wondering about the fate of modernism and end the suspense. In that decade, Stein and Joyce both became bestsellers, thereby ensuring that the future significance modernism was not a risky gamble, but a sure bet.

4 The 1930s
Bestselling Modernism

Just as reviewers and columnists published frequent assessments of modern literature in newspapers and periodicals, attempting to classify and explain the value of the experimental writing that invaded the American literary landscape in the 1920s, critics also began to include discussions of Stein and other modernists in books with similar goals. Stein had been mentioned in several widely reviewed books of the mid-1920s, such as the 1925 memoirs by Sherwood Anderson and Alfred Kreymbourg, and Stuart P. Sherman's collection of reviews, *Points of View* (1924). Including reviews of Stein in collections became more and more common; Edith Sitwell's review of Stein had been reprinted in *Poetry and Criticism*, published by Leonard and Virginia Woolf's Hogarth press in 1925 and then released by Henry Holt in America in 1926, and Katherine Mansfield's posthumous collection of reviews, *Novels and Novelists* (Knopf, 1930) also included a review of Stein that had initially appeared in England and thus became available to an American audience for the first time. These retrospective endorsements suggest that many writers and critics believed that Stein's work was significant, influential, and had longevity. By 1930 any critic who wished to discuss trends in American literature or influential writers of the 1920s was compelled to explain, celebrate or dismiss the importance of Stein. Mainstream publishers regularly printed analyses of recent literature that included lengthy discussions of modernism, clearly with the expectation that readers did care about the pervasive debates in the media about the value of modernist work.

Some of these analyses were severely critical, such as Horace M. Kallen's popular *Indecency and the Seven Arts* published by Liveright in 1930. In a passionate rant, Kallen berates Hollywood, literary critics (with special notice given to H. L. Mencken), and modernist writers. The review of Kallen's book in the *New York Times Book Review* observes that he "warns the 'modernists,' both poets and prose writers—like E. E. Cummings and Gertrude Stein—that their visual 'typography,' with sound, but without meaning, has no possibilities."[1] That Hollywood, modernist literature and H. L. Mencken could equally elicit Kallen's visceral reaction shows how pervasive and influential these developments were in the 1920s: all were new, modern developments dramatically affecting mainstream American culture.

Another mainstream commentary on modern literature used humor rather than hostility to suggest to readers that modernism was often no more than a surprising linguistic puzzle. Lyon Mearson's travel book about the Paris experience, *The French They Are a Funny Race* (1931), included what the *New York Times Book Review* called a "very good, though slightly irrelevant, satire on modern art and the school of James Joyce":

> "But about Joyce—"[I said], trying futilely to grasp the meaning of this modernism.
> "He's Gertrude Stein's father," said my companion.
> "Who is Gertrude Stein?"
> "She is Joyce's father." I looked blank, and it angered him. "Can't you see! It is not enough to break up the word. That is only the beginning"...
> "By the way," I said, "You don't happen to be Joyce yourself, do you?"
> "No," he said slowly. "I'm his father."[2]

The *New York Times* review suggests that it would have been best if Mearson had left out this story and "let the Transition writers go" since most tourists would probably not have such an encounter, but the anecdote was so amusing that the reviewer reprinted it.

Harcourt, Brace published Wyndham Lewis's widely reviewed *Time and Western Man* in 1928, further familiarizing the public with his argument first published in *The Enemy* that the simplicity of Stein could be usefully compared to that of best selling Anita Loos, whose *Gentlemen Prefer Blondes* was one of the most popular books of the 1920s. Another serious writer who emphasized the simplicity of Stein, Laura Riding, published her appraisal of modern literature and poetry in *Contemporaries and Snobs* (1928) with Doubleday. Her lengthy chapter "T. E. Hulme, The New Barbarism, & Gertrude Stein" suggests that the modern artist's interest in the barbaric has only been successfully achieved by Stein. "None of the words Miss Stein uses have ever had an experience. They are no older than her use of them, and is herself no older than her age conceived barbarically," Riding explained.[3] For Riding, the rare consistency of Stein's artistic vision and execution proves its contemporary importance.

Paul Rosenfeld's more obscure *By Way of Art* suggested in 1928 that:

> Gertrude Stein has not led on the new American literature. Rather it is the new American literature that has discovered her.... Sport for fifteen years of the journalistic mind, her vision is patently the common one. Despite the late hilarity, words are no longer realities for Sherwood Anderson and Wallace Stevens, E. E. Cummings and Waldo Frank, Hart Crane, Alfred Kreymborg, William Carlos Williams and Marianne Moore, no more than for the dumb grotesque of the journalists.[4]

Like Lewis and Riding, Rosenfeld never suggests that Stein's relationship to language and literature is elitist or even difficult. Rather, her vision is simple and individual, leading Rosenfeld to argue that Stein is, in fact, democratic, a direct contrast to T. S. Eliot. Williams Carlos Williams's passionate defense of Stein in the little magazine *Pagany* (1930) also emphasizes Stein's simple and democratic method, one of Williams's own poetic goals, and shows that she avoids the pitfalls of Eliot's academic poetry. "To be democratic, local (in the sense of being attached with integrity to actual experience) Stein, or any other artist, must for subtlety ascend to a plane of almost abstract design to keep alive," Williams explains.

Williams's ardent defense was unconvincing to Harry Hansen, who asked readers in his chatty column: "Won't somebody tell the young man of Manhattan, Paris, and Rutherford N.J. that Gertrude Stein is no longer news?" To prove Stein's unfashionable status, Hansen cheerfully quotes from the Fall 1929 issue of *Modern Quarterly* dedicated to "The Revolution of the Word." Eugène Jolas and others contributed to the discussion of Joyce, Stein and various modernists; S. D. Schmalhausen submitted a severe critique of Gertrude Stein. As Hansen observes: "Dr. Schmalhausen gets really violent on the subject of Gertrude Stein." Millions of readers were offered this tidbit of his argument: "Gertrude's mental age is 12, her emotional age is 14, her artistic age is 7."[5]

Although modernists including Stein, Eliot, and Joyce were often linked by columnists and reviewers in the 1920s, serious literary critics were less assured that these writers should be appropriately compared. Riding, Rosenfeld and Williams all stress the importance of Stein's democratic simplicity and her radical difference from T. S. Eliot. These distinctions—not usually interesting to the mainstream press—were of vital importance to writers like Williams, who lamented what he saw as the destructive ascendance of Eliot in the world of poetry. Just as Eliot feared a future in which Stein's "barbaric" writing would become normative, Williams was tormented by the possibility that Eliot's learned style might eventually define the modernist movement in poetry.

By contrast to Williams, perhaps the most influential American critic to creatively assess the contours of modern literature did link the work of Stein, Eliot and Joyce. Edmund Wilson's critically acclaimed *Axel's Castle* (1931) suggests that the modern writing of W. B. Yeats, Paul Valéry, T. S. Eliot, Marcel Proust, James Joyce, Arthur Rimbaud and Stein is connected by the strong influence of French symbolist poets of the nineteenth century, most importantly Mallarmé. The brief chapter on Stein is not so long nor detailed as the others; although Stein is committed to "reminding people of the true nature and function of words," unfortunately she has taken her work in an extreme, disappointing direction.[6] However much Wilson might have championed Stein at the beginning of her career, he had lost patience with her by the time *Axel's Castle* was published and he offered this mixed assessment:

> Most of us balk at her soporific rigmaroles, her echolaliac incantations, her half-witted-sounding catalogues of numbers; most of us read her less and less. Yet, remembering especially her early work, we are still always aware of her presence in the background of contemporary literature. . . . And whenever we pick up her writings, however unintelligible we may find them, we are aware of a literary personality of great distinction.[7]

Despite his misgivings, Wilson affirmed the connection between Stein, Joyce and Eliot, even if many others found these writers to have very different goals and methods.

The lively conversation about Stein, Joyce and other modernists was so pervasive that when both Stein and Joyce appeared in the July 1932 *Hound and Horn*, a new little magazine, this literary news was reported by Harry Hansen, in a *New York Times* editorial, and elsewhere. "A Great Stylist Reappears," the editorial was headlined. "After too long a silence Miss GERTRUDE STEIN, most original of American authors, speaks with most miraculous organ. She enriches Hound and Horn with a masterpiece entitled 'Scenery and George Washington: a Novel or a Play.' Strictly speaking, it is neither. It is a stein."[8]

Not so enthusiastic about Stein's reappearance, the *New York Sun* explained that: "James Joyce contributes to the current 'Hound and Horn' prose impressions of the Paris Opera singer O'Sullivan in various roles. Gertrude Stein blurts out a characteristic thing which she calls 'Scenery and George Washington—A Novel or a Play.'"[9] This description of the contents was reprinted in the *Worcester Telegram*; other notices appeared in papers including the *Washington D. C. News*, the *Tulsa Tribune*, the *Newark News* and the *Boston Herald*.[10] Although the *New York Times* and the *New York Sun* disagree as to the value of Stein's experiments, both clearly display their familiarity with her "characteristic" writing, and both emphasize that her radical work continued to be news.

Plain Edition

Since Stein was unable to attract commercial publishers, nor could she find a more obscure publisher willing to take on more than one of her works, she and Alice B. Toklas finally decided to start their own private publishing company in Paris. Joseph Brewer of Payson & Clarke initially considered publishing Stein's next novel, *Lucy Church Amiably*, but the short abstract of the book she submitted for consideration did not inspire confidence in the publisher, who had already lost money on *Useful Knowledge*.[11] With no other immediate options available, *Lucy Church Amiably* was the first of five books printed in quick succession by Plain Edition; after *Lucy Church* appeared in 1930, *Before the Flowers of Friendship Faded Friendship Faded* and *How to Write* were printed in 1931, *Operas and Plays* in 1932; and *Matisse Picasso and Gertrude Stein, with Two Shorter Stories* in 1933.

Stein and Toklas were disappointed with the copies of *Lucy Church*, and Maruice Darantière, who had printed *Ulysses* in Dijon, was hired to produce the other books. Not only was *Lucy Church* full of errors, the poorly constructed spine either broke or failed to keep the covers closed. Thus Darantière's imprint on modernist literature was once again affirmed, as was the connection between the writing of Joyce and Stein.[12]

To stimulate interest in *Lucy Church*, Stein and Toklas sent order forms to bookshops and review copies to some bewildered journalists, who could always be depended upon to advertise Stein's efforts, no matter how small the possibility that readers could actually acquire the limited editions. William Bradley, Stein's new literary agent who was unsuccessfully trying to place *The Making of Americans* with a commercial publisher, and Bob Brown helped publicize the book by distributing subscription blanks to booksellers and, indeed, some prepaid orders did arrive before one thousand copies of *Lucy Church* were printed.

Stein's friend Robert Coates noted the publication of *Lucy Church* in the *New Yorker*, although his attempt to defend Stein against the habitual teasing of the daily press proved ineffective. He observed

> One thing that has always amused me about Miss Stein is that she is more often talked of, argued about, than almost any other writer today by people who have never read a line of hers. By making her work again available, this printing, if it does nothing else, ought to help do away with a lot of this futile pointing at her, either with pride or the finger of scorn.[13]

Contrary to Coates's optimistic suggestion that *Lucy Church* might reduce the "pointing at" Stein encouraged by the mainstream press, instead her new book brought about a new round of witticisms in papers from coast to cost. A columnist for the *Providence Journal* commented to readers: "As a matter of fact I don't quite know why Miss Stein DID send me her book. . . . I have never done anything but make fun of her, and I never shall (unless something cracks up top and I go out and shoot her)."[14] The *Christian Science Monitor* joked that "What interests us most is that occasionally in 'Lucy Church Amiably' you come across a sentence that seems to mean something. Not in connection with the surrounding sentences, but just in itself."[15] The *Kansas City Star* wryly observed that "Holding the book in front of a mirror doesn't seem to help."[16] And the *Boston Transcript* explained to readers that "Gertrude Stein's latest published work is a 'novel' of refined irony; so refined, in fact, that most persons who look at it will not get the point at all, and most of the rest will not be interested even if they do get it."[17] The *Spokane Review* sensitively suggested that the problem was with readers, who expected a novel and instead found that *Lucy Church* was "more like a book of poetry than a work of fiction. Miss Stein has a hard time pleasing the public." They went on to observe: "Still, the

Stein method has its advantages. No one has yet indignantly accused Gertrude of having used real persons in her books."[18] It was only a short time, of course, before *The Autobiography of Alice B. Toklas* changed all of that; many of the real persons in that book were indeed indignant.

A more lengthy and mostly respectful review, accompanied by a photograph of Stein, appeared in the *Chicago Tribune* and was even highlighted in the index on the front page of the newspaper. Despite the teasing tone of the article, Ellen Du Poy expresses admiration for Stein's peculiar antinovel. "The book teems with poetry," she observes, quoting from the book: "it is not easy to be seen wishing when the water is noisy." Never revealing to readers if she really is serious, Du Poy declares: "There's a whole essay on psychology in that sentence."[19]

It wasn't until 1932 that *Lucy Church* received two significant notices in the American press. Louis Bromfield included the book on the summer list of recommended reading for the *New York Daily Tribune* after Robert Coates had educated his *New Yorker* readers as to the significance of *Lucy Church* in February, attempting to dispel the often expressed idea that Stein's writing was simply random words, and thus some kind of lazy attempt at writing rather than a concerted effort to revolutionize literature. His commentary appropriately introduces any reader who might be resourceful enough to actually obtain a copy of the book:

> May I say once more, however, that I think a good part of the confusion is due to the reader's expecting to find what was, by the author's design, deliberately left out: a connected narrative? . . . One may read [*Lucy Church*] for the intricate delicate embroidery of its style. One may read it for the peculiar evasive beauty of some of its passages, or for one's interest in the author's way of probing the oddities of words. But one should never read it—or for that matter the writings of any other of the "moderns"—for its plot.[20]

This prudent advice is prefaced by a striking, prescient observation. Coates notes that Stein "has attained the curious position of being more talked about by more people who have never read a line of hers than any other author, and if all the witlings who have mauled her name about were some day to decide to buy one of her books and see what it was actually like, her sales would put her on the best-seller lists immediately."[21]

The mutual support Coates and Stein displayed for each other repeats a pattern she established with Carl Van Vechten and Sherwood Anderson. In each of these friendships, Stein's work was prominently mentioned by the well-known writer, and Stein made her admiration for the writer clear in her own way. The American press was so interested in these kinds of literary friendships that the smallest item could become a national story. When the Macaulay Company sent out a questionnaire to writers asking what books they remembered reading as children, Coates's response was reprinted in newspapers throughout the Midwest, including the *Cincinnati Star*, *South Bend News Times*, *Portsmouth* [Ohio] *Sun*, and *Sioux Falls Leader*. The papers reported that "Gertrude Stein is the only person [Coates] knows who lends books properly. When she found he displayed an interest in her copies of Anthony Trollope, she had the whole set boxed and sent to him, rather than have him borrow one at a time."[22] Stein considered this anecdote so familiar that when Alice refers to Stein's Trollope collection in the *Autobiography*, she notes without further explanation: "it is of this collection that Robert Coates speaks when he tells about Gertrude Stein lending books to young writers."[23] Stein's gesture meant so much to Coates that he mentioned it in the 1959 introduction to a reprint of his first novel, *The Eater of Darkness*, first published by Robert McAlmon's Contact Editions in 1926. That introduction expresses considerable gratitude to Stein for her role in generating interest in his novel; as Coates puts it, she "read it, and liked it, and immediately set about getting it published."[24] This warm tribute to Stein not only corroborates the reports of many younger writers who associated Stein with profound generosity, but also shows how clearly Stein's interest in modern literature blurred boundaries between what might be classified as high- and low-brow writing.

The Eater of Darkness is, as Coates remarks in the introduction, modeled after the Nick Carter detective stories, but his experimental style can more usefully be compared to the other modernists that McAlmon regularly published. Coates shifts from conventional narrative to experimental passages or chapters, which include lists, numbered events, or present only limited, stream-of-consciousness style perspectives. But the most unusual aspect of the book to today's readers is certainly the plot. The book concerns Charles Dograr, a young man renting a room New York, whose elderly neighbor calls him into his room and demonstrates the power of his great invention: an "x-ray" machine that passes through walls and, as Dograr accidentally discovers, kills people from a great distance by cooking their brains. Once he has become a murderer, there is no turning back, and Dograr and the neighbor set about terrorizing the city.

Like Carl Van Vechten, Coates paints the cultural scene in his novels with lists: as our hero first aims the "x-ray", it "progressed swiftly through" a number of items including a copy of the *New Yorker*, a sheaf of Shulte Cigar Store coupons, a pack of Luckies and notable people (including Laurence Vail, Peggy Guggenheim, Theodore Dreiser, H. L. Mencken, Kenneth Burke, Julian Levi, Malcolm Cowley).[25] None of these prominent artists or critics is the victim of Dograr, and each simply appears as part of the landscape in the 1920s. Others were less lucky: soon, New York City panics after, as a headline puts it, "Nine Prominent Critics Die By X-Ray Bullet." Harry Hansen, Heywood Broun, Waldo Frank, Henry Canby, James Thurber and George Jean Nathan are all victims of the x-ray machine. The juxtaposition of the many seemingly incongruent aspects of the novel are most unsettling for the reader: the fantastic criminal plot (which relies on a futuristic, technologically advanced weapon), the modernist style, the literary and artistic cultural references, not to mention a racy seduction scene. Certainly, *The Eater of Darkness* defies traditional categorization and instead might be simply called "modern." This strange jumble of contemporary culture may now be forgotten, but it appealed to Stein: as Coates observed, "she liked it," and she wasn't the only one. Janet Flanner called the novel "a bright blague," and noted in her "Paris Letter" column for the *New Yorker* that the book was so controversial that it "stirred the American quarter to dispute, with A. K. Small (*Herald*) against and Elliot Paul (*Tribune*) violently for."[26]

Like *The Eater of Darkness*, Stein's breakthrough book, *The Autobiography of Alice B. Toklas*, can also be considered a radical reworking of a popular and familiar genre, in this case the autobiography. Memoirs of writers, artists and other cultural figures were popular in the modernist period; these personal, anecdotal, descriptions of modern art and culture effectively educated mainstream Americans without suggesting that the newest literary or artistic developments were too sophisticated or "high-brow" for the average reader to appreciate. Sherwood Anderson's *Story Teller's Story* (1925), Alfred Kreymbourg's *Troubadour* (1925), Janet Scudder's *Modeling My Life* (1925), Violet Hunt's *The Flurried Years* (1926), Isadora Duncan's *My Life* (1927), Margaret Anderson's *My Thirty Years War* (1930), Mabel Dodge Luhan's *Lorenzo in Taos* (1932), Violet Clifton's *The Book of Talbot* (1933) all were widely discussed in the daily press (and many were commercial successes), and each contributed to the interest in Stein's contribution to this compelling genre. Indeed, Margaret Anderson and Mabel Dodge had already introduced readers to many of the individuals who figure prominently in Stein's book, including Stein herself. As Loren Glass observes, "the entire modernist 'lost generation' was absorbed into American mainstream culture through a bombardment of gossipy memoirs."[27]

In her memoir, Margaret Anderson's portrait of Stein confirms that she should not be characterized as a typical intellectual, and emphasizes the influence of Sherwood Anderson's promotion of her work and personality.[28]

> Gertrude Stein to-day is noted for her hospitality, her laughter, her clothes, her comfortable talk, as well as for her "incomprehensible" literature and her acumen in buying the modern painters before they became old masters. Since Sherwood Anderson introduced her to American readers her first legend as a decadent aesthete has evaporated in view of the facts.... She is now known to be a healthy, robust, amusing woman dressing in brilliant flowered chintz and heavy men's shoes, [who] drives a battered Ford to her farm and likes to sit about swapping talk with the garage man before she composes addresses to the students of Oxford.[29]

Further establishing the contours of this literary group in the public's mind, reviewers of *Lorenzo in Taos* and the next book in Dodge's multi-volume memoir, *Intimate Memories* (1933), were quick to point out that Dodge had been the inspiration for Carl Van Vechten's Edith Dale in his enormously successful *Peter Whiffle* (1922).[30] Kreymbourg and (Sherwood) Anderson, of course, had also mentioned Stein in their 1925 memoirs. This public awareness of Stein's literary friendships certainly paved the way for her own remarkable success with *The Autobiography of Alice B. Toklas* in 1933. That year, Harcourt, Brace published Dodge's *Intimate Memories*, Stein's *Autobiography of Alice B. Toklas*, Lincoln Steffens's *Autobiography* and Virginia Woolf's *Flush*, which were all classified by the publisher as "biography." Woolf's book was a deliberate parody of Lytton Strachey's modernist biography, *Eminent Victorians*, and the creative license she takes in recreating the subjective impressions of Elizabeth Barrett Browning's dog, Flush, might suggest that her book would be more accurately called "fiction." But Harcourt, Brace not only advertised the book as a "biography," it also appeared on bestseller lists under the heading "non-fiction," as did *The Autobiography of Alice B. Toklas*. (figure 3)

The *Chicago Tribune* printed a similar advertisement that featured the prominent heading "*biography.*"[31] On the same page where this advertisement appeared, Fanny Butcher reprinted part of a warm letter Stein sent to

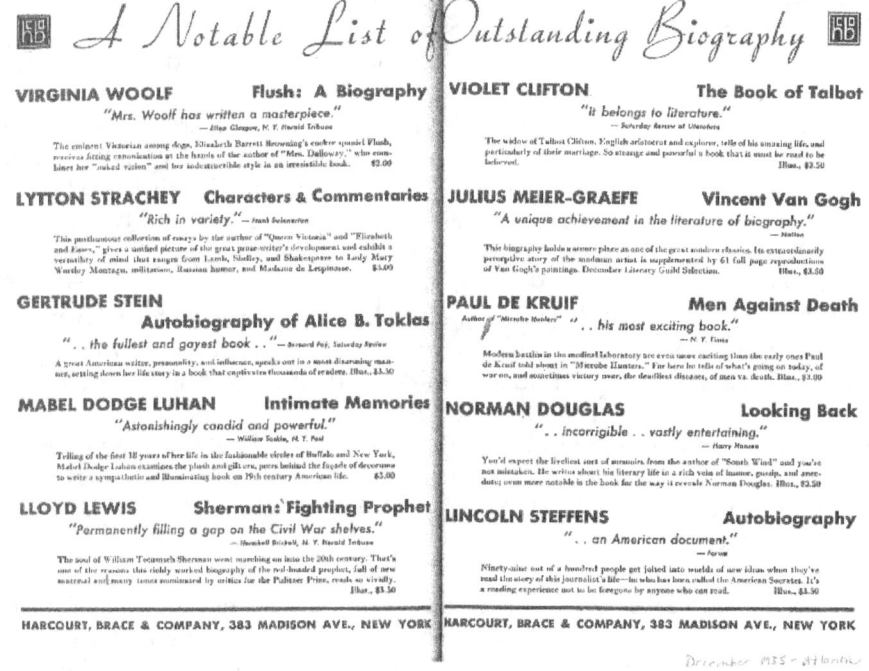

Figure 3 *Atlantic* advertisement (December 1933): "A Notable List of Outstanding Biography."

her that expressed pleasure at the success of her book and Butcher's own role in helping to promote it. "Thanks to you all America is very near these days. I am enjoying more than I can say my close touch with the American public. I have always wanted it and now I have it and it makes me content very very content."[32]

The Autobiography of Alice B. Toklas subverts so many autobiographical conventions that, like *Flush*, it also could be accurately categorized as "fiction," unlike most of the other memoirs published in the period. Kreymbourg related the story of his own life in the third person, but this unusual narrative choice was neither so radical nor amusing as Stein's decision to write Alice's autobiography for her, using Alice B. Toklas as the narrator of this "memoir." Thus *The Autobiography of Alice B. Toklas* is not, in fact, Alice B. Toklas's autobiography; instead it is Gertrude Stein's idea of what such a book might look like. Many readers have remarked that, because the book describes Gertrude Stein more than any other person, the book is actually Stein's autobiography of herself. The *Autobiography* does, however, begin in an almost conventional way with a brief chapter about Alice's childhood in San Francisco, "Before I Came to Paris." It is also true that much of the book describes Stein's life before she knew Toklas, including childhood memories: chapters three and four, "Gertrude Stein in Paris, 1903–1907" and "Gertrude Stein before she came to Paris" give extensive accounts of events that Toklas did not witness, but has apparently heard described by Stein. In these sections, Stein suggests that Toklas subjectively interprets and imperfectly recalls the stories that she has heard about Stein's past.

The Autobiography of Alice B. Toklas can also be described as a selective history of artistic and literary developments in Paris in the 1910s and 1920s. The book tells witty stories of how Stein and her brother Leo began to collect early paintings by Paul Cézanne, Henri Matisse, and Pablo Picasso, who were all unknown artists at the time, and became close friends with Matisse and Picasso. We hear her first-hand accounts of numerous social gatherings, including the famous banquet for Rousseau given by Picasso and his wife, Alice's and Gertrude's travels in Spain, meetings with Clive and Vanessa Bell (Virginia Woolf's brother-in-law and sister), Roger Fry, T. S. Eliot, Ezra Pound, F. Scott Fitzgerald, and Ernest Hemingway; a visit to London to meet with John Lane to discuss the publication of Stein's *Three Lives*; and so forth. Stein's ventriloquism of Alice is not revealed until the last page of the book, which effectively contains the punch line of the narrative:

> About six weeks ago Gertrude Stein said, it does not look to me as if you were ever going to write that autobiography. You know what I am going to do. I am going to write it for you. I am going to write it as simply as Defoe did the autobiography of Robinson Crusoe. And she has and this is it.

Alice in the Atlantic: Alice B. Toklas is Gertrude Stein and Gertrude Stein is Alice B. Toklas

Although he was unable to find a commercial publisher for *The Making of Americans*, William Bradley had no trouble with *The Autobiography of Alice B. Toklas*. Bradley, who Alice describes as "the friend and comforter of Paris authors," and his wife Jenny ran the literary agency in Paris that most frequently represented American expatriate writers and they also hosted a literary salon, where writers including Joyce, Fitzgerald, and Hemingway were likely to meet one another.[33] Bradley is probably most remembered for his success in placing *The Autobiography of Alice B. Toklas* with Harcourt, Brace, but he also famously arranged to have Henry Miller's controversial *Tropic of Cancer* published by the Obelisk Press in Paris in 1934. Jenny Bradley, who was a close friend of Joyce, translated his *Exiles* into French in 1950.

From May to August 1933, four sections of *The Autobiography of Alice B. Toklas* appeared in the *Atlantic Monthly* and Harcourt, Brace released the complete book in August of that year. Periodically, Stein had continued to send her work to Ellery Sedgwick at the *Atlantic* in the 1920s and had received disappointing but conscientious rejection letters from him. In 1927 she submitted "Portrait of Cézanne" and Sedgwick confessed to Stein that "[t]he little rhythms which ripple through your picture do not, to my heavy wit, call up the faintest suggestion of the exciting impression of a Cézanne." Sedgwick suggested that it was his own deficiency that prevented him from appreciating Stein, and he encouraged her to continue their correspondence. He wrote to her:

> You have taken a friendly interest in my training, and as an example of adult education it is an experiment worth trying! Perhaps you would some day write to me an entirely intelligible comment upon these paragraphs of yours. I ask this in all seriousness, for as I near my second childhood, I yearn increasingly to be educated.[34]

The open-minded Sedgwick maintained interest in Stein's literary development and when he read the first sections of the *Autobiography* in 1933, he expressed his delight that Stein's opaque vision had apparently cleared. He wrote to her with enthusiasm:

> There has been a lot of pother about this book of yours, but what a delightful book it is, and how glad I am to publish four installments of it! During our long correspondence, I think you felt my constant hope that the time would come when the real Miss Stein would pierce the smokescreen with which she has always so mischievously surrounded herself. . . . Hail Gertrude Stein about to arrive![35]

The sections of the *Autobiography* appearing in the *Atlantic* became a favorite topic of columnists, thus immediately acquainting readers with Stein's new, accessible style and virtually guaranteeing the book's overwhelming success. Marshall Maslin's syndicated "All of Us" column, for example, explained to readers that "Gertrude Stein is writing her life for the Atlantic Monthly in quite intelligible English, but as you read her you have a terrible feeling that she will drop off any moment into such sentences as Gertrude is a stein. Stein is a stone . . . But Gertrude doesn't go steinish once."[36] Maslin followed his remarks with an anecdote from Dodge's *Intimate Memories*, showing readers that Stein presented another view of the literary and artistic groups that Dodge frequented.[37] Positive commentary about the *Autobiography* in the *Atlantic* also appeared in the *Chicago Herald*, Washington D. C. *Herald*, Philadelphia *Public Ledger*, and elsewhere.[38]

The *New Yorker* assumed that readers would be familiar with Stein's latest publication and printed this response from Frank Sullivan:

> I got the idea for writing this autobiography from a very interesting series of articles now appearing the Atlantic Monthly, called "The Autobiography of Alice B. Toklas." My name being also "Alice B.," I naturally read them. One of the many interesting things about "The Autobiography of Alice B. Toklas" is that it was not written by Alice B. Toklas at all. It was written by Gertrude Stein. Another interesting thing about the autobiography is that there is practically nothing in it about Alice B. Toklas. It is all about Gertrude Stein. I said to myself, "Well, if Alice B. Toklas can have her autobiography written, I guess Alice B. Sullivan can, too," so I called up my very dear friend, Frank Sullivan, and asked him if he would come directly over and write my autobiography. He did and this is my autobiography, by Frank Sullivan.[39]

Sullivan suggests that Stein's narrative choice deserves at least gentle criticism and, indeed, some irritated reviewers found that Stein's decision to use as Alice the narrator of her own autobiography to be largely driven by Stein's unchecked ego. The *Torrington* [CT] *Register* remarked that: "Anybody reading this autobiography might gain the impression that Miss Stein is one of the greatest women who ever lived. Perhaps she is but her enthusiastic self-eulogism scarcely adds to any greatness which she may have achieved."[40] But other readers found the chapters in the *Atlantic* inspiring. One eager reader wrote to the *Atlantic*:

> Dear Atlantic—
> A certain limerick runs: —
> There's a notable family named Stein:
> There's Gert, and there's Ep, and there's Ein:
> Gert's poems are punk,

Ep's statues are junk –
Can't make head nor tail out of Ein.

These lines recurred to me as I read Gertrude Stein's delightful autobiography. Years ago I puckered my brain over Tender Buttons and The Making of Americans. But now I understand. It isn't Gertrude Stein who is out of step—it is I. The May Atlantic had not been out two days before every copy in our town had been bought up by members of a modern art society to which I belong. Even then there were not half enough to go round.
All of us think that 'Alice B. Toklas' is as refreshing a piece of writing as we have ever come across—free, unrestrained, original. Many be the chapters!
--Anna Work Shawkey
Charleston, West Virginia[41]

This West Virginian shows how easy it was for readers to follow news of arts and literature, even outside of urban centers. Did this woman actually own, or had she seen, copies of *Tender Buttons* and *The Making of Americans*, as she suggests? Perhaps she had attended art lectures that quoted from these works. But even if she had only seen excerpts in the daily press, her tone suggests an intimate and sure knowledge of modernism, and her enthusiasm echoed that of many other American readers. Furthermore, the limerick quoted in the letter shows how recognizable Stein's name was by mainstream Americans. *Time* magazine would reprint the poem in Stein's cover story that fall, surely assuming that readers were already familiar with the dismissive lines. As with any joke, of course, the rhyme is only funny if audiences are already acquainted with the subject matter.

Stein's use of Alice as the narrator of her autobiography interested readers and critics, but another aspect of the book occupied the mainstream press for many months. Today's readers are often surprised that the romantic nature of the relationship between Stein and Toklas was invisible to contemporary readers, but this possibility did not appear to occur to any reviewers or columnists. In fact, the identity of Alice B. Toklas was not at all certain; first readers of the *Autobiography* doubted her existence, and speculated that Alice was a literary invention. Harry Hansen may have planted the doubt in the minds of some readers, but he seems to have expressed a common suspicion. As soon as the first issue of the *Atlantic* appeared, Hansen observed:

> Another literary convention goes by the board when Gertrude Stein writes about herself in the third person, in prose that readers of the Atlantic Monthly can understand. . . . Alice poses as a lady who has lived with Gertrude Stein for twenty-five years and knows all about her. She admires her very much.[42]

After receiving numerous corrections to his blunder, Hansen filled an entire column with various reprisals from readers, including Carl Van Vechten's: "Whadya mean by Alice poses as a lady who has lived with Gertrude Stein for twenty-five years? Alice has lived with Gertrude for twenty-five years and does presumably know a great deal about her." On May 1, Van Vechten wrote to Stein about the sensation the first issue of the Atlantic created, and mentioned Hansen's misreading of Alice's identity: "Wherever one goes—and I have just gone to Baltimore—one hears about your paper in the Atlantic. Everybody loves it. Even Harry Hansen who made some asinine remarks about it really loves it. Anyway, it seems the whole town rose to write and correct him."[43]

Many readers continued to wonder about Alice's existence. Isabel Paterson, always more savvy and sardonic in her column than Hansen, implied that attempts to defend Alice's identity only cast more doubt. She noted in July that:

> There is a persistent rumor or theory that Gertrude Stein is the actual author of the "Autobiography," and we are told, though not authoritatively, that Alice B. Toklas is a real person, but that is not her real name; so the question of authorship is doubly obscure. It seems to be two other fellows.[44]

The following week, Paterson repeated Hansen's device of reprinting a letter from an authority on Alice, but further added to the mystery by deliberately choosing an unconvincing piece of evidence:

> So much confusion has been caused by the prominence of Gertrude Stein in "The Autobiography of Alice B. Toklas" that Lucy Goldthwaite writes to assure us "Alice B. Toklas is a real name and not the result of an anagram gone wrong." . . . . Yes we did try it backward! The girl is a mindreader . . . "At least," Lucy continues "that's what some one who knew her in Paris years ago tells me."[45]

Obviously, it would have been easy for Paterson to confirm Alice's existence if she chose to do so. But the ambiguity appealed to columnists, who continued to perpetuate this constructed topic for debate and discussion. As Edward Kingbury noted in his review of the book for the *New York Times*, "Some heartless and incurable skeptics have ventured to express doubt or denial of the existence of Alice B. Toklas.[46]

Attentive to the persistent, real doubts as to Alice's actual presence in the Stein household expressed by readers and reviewers, Harcourt, Brace emphasized in its advertisements for the *Autobiography* that Alice was a "real person." In *Publishers' Weekly*, an ad explained that: "Alice B. Toklas really exists. She has been Gertrude Stein's intimate companion for 25 years, and she appears in this book as 'I.' But you find out on the last

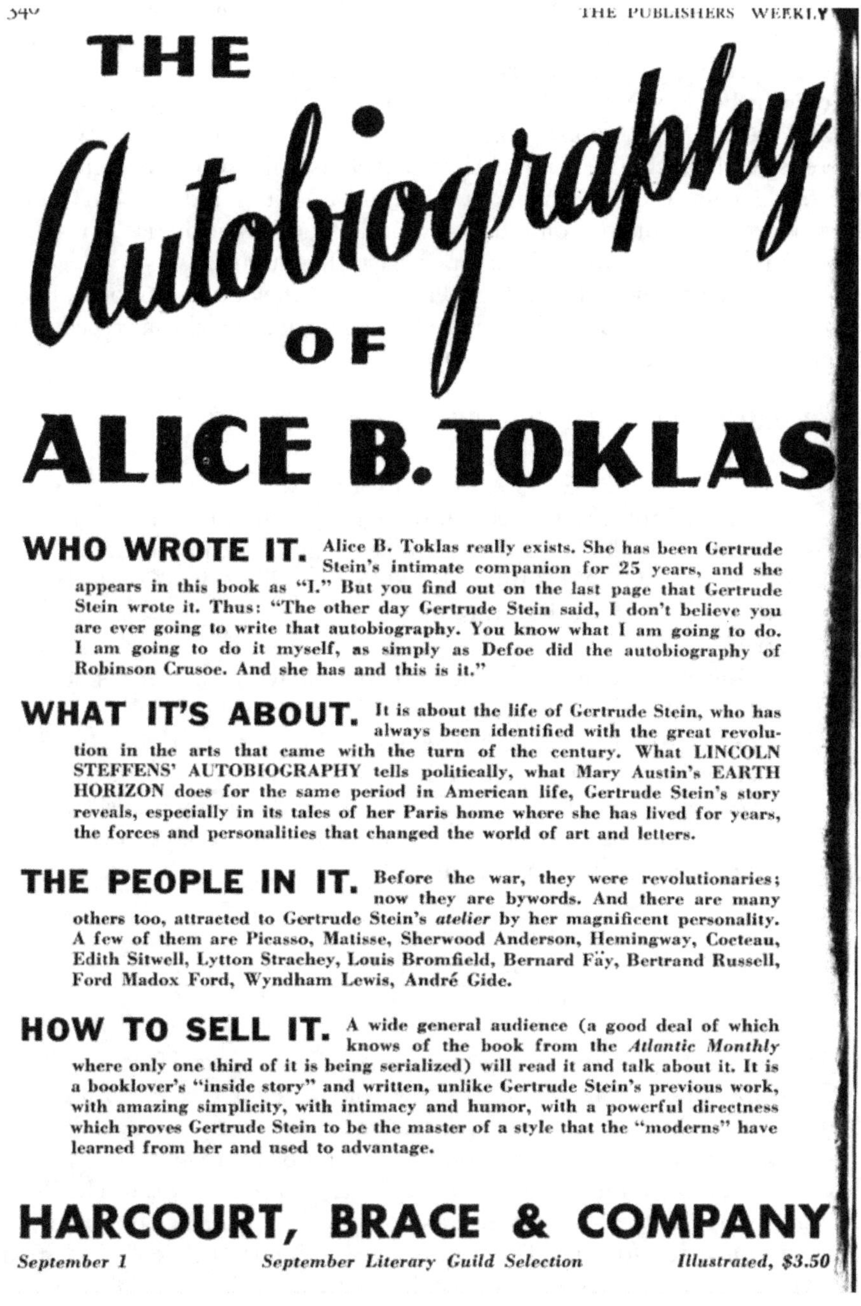

THE Autobiography OF ALICE B. TOKLAS

WHO WROTE IT. Alice B. Toklas really exists. She has been Gertrude Stein's intimate companion for 25 years, and she appears in this book as "I." But you find out on the last page that Gertrude Stein wrote it. Thus: "The other day Gertrude Stein said, I don't believe you are ever going to write that autobiography. You know what I am going to do. I am going to do it myself, as simply as Defoe did the autobiography of Robinson Crusoe. And she has and this is it."

WHAT IT'S ABOUT. It is about the life of Gertrude Stein, who has always been identified with the great revolution in the arts that came with the turn of the century. What LINCOLN STEFFENS' AUTOBIOGRAPHY tells politically, what Mary Austin's EARTH HORIZON does for the same period in American life, Gertrude Stein's story reveals, especially in its tales of her Paris home where she has lived for years, the forces and personalities that changed the world of art and letters.

THE PEOPLE IN IT. Before the war, they were revolutionaries; now they are bywords. And there are many others too, attracted to Gertrude Stein's *atelier* by her magnificent personality. A few of them are Picasso, Matisse, Sherwood Anderson, Hemingway, Cocteau, Edith Sitwell, Lytton Strachey, Louis Bromfield, Bernard Fäy, Bertrand Russell, Ford Madox Ford, Wyndham Lewis, André Gide.

HOW TO SELL IT. A wide general audience (a good deal of which knows of the book from the *Atlantic Monthly* where only one third of it is being serialized) will read it and talk about it. It is a booklover's "inside story" and written, unlike Gertrude Stein's previous work, with amazing simplicity, with intimacy and humor, with a powerful directness which proves Gertrude Stein to be the master of a style that the "moderns" have learned from her and used to advantage.

HARCOURT, BRACE & COMPANY

September 1   September Literary Guild Selection   Illustrated, $3.50

Figure 4   Publishers' Weekly advertisement.

page that Gertrude Stein wrote it" (figure 4).[47] Another advertisement in the *Saturday Review of Literature* informed readers that: "Alice B. Toklas is a real person, an intimate friend of Gertrude Stein's. But Gertrude Stein wrote this book, speaking of herself in the third person and of Miss Toklas as 'I.'" In the *Minneapolis Journal*, Bess Wilson declared that: "Whether there is really such a person as Alice B. Toklas, alleged house comrade of Gertrude Stein, is one of the moot questions of critics and it doesn't in the least matter."[48] But for columnists around the country the issue was not moot, and continued to intrigue (or at least fill columns).

Fueling the publicity the debate generated for the book, Harcourt, Brace changed tactics and issued this amused press release, which was repeated as "news" in papers throughout the nation:

FOR IMMEDIATE RELEASE, November 1, 1933

ROSE IS A ROSE IS A ROSE

In Halle Brothers, Cleveland, there is on exhibition an actual letter signed by the real Alice B. Toklas. One of the Cleveland readers of Gertrude Stein's THE AUTOBIOGRAPHY OF ALICE B. TOKLAS wrote to Miss Stein and received this answer:
Dear Sir:
Miss Gertrude Stein desires me to thank you for your letter of September 18, in which you express your appreciation of her book
The device rose is a rose is a rose is a rose means just that. Miss Stein is unfortunately too busy herself to be able to tell you herself, but trusts that you will eventually come to understand that each and every word that she writes means exactly what she says, for she says exactly what she means, and really nothing more, but of course, nothing less.

                    Very sincerely,
                    ALICE B. TOKLAS (signed)
                    Secty.

Columnists' interpretation of this letter may have surprised Harcourt, Brace (or perhaps they anticipated it); the style of the letter seemed to resemble Stein's so closely that this press release was consistently used as evidence that Alice was, indeed, an invention.[49] It did not occur to anyone that Stein had deliberately imitated Toklas's style for the *Autobiography*. The *Tulsa World* referred to the "'actual letter' signed by the 'real Alice B. Toklas.'"[50] In the *Milwaukee Journal*, Floyd Van Vuren explained that: "Miss Stein, incidentally, is more or less exposed in a letter which Miss Toklas wrote to a woman in Cleveland, Ohio, in reply to a letter asking the meaning of the device that appears on the cover of The Autobiography of Alice B. Toklas."[51] The *Providence Journal* did not even entertain the possibility that the letter might have been written by Alice:

Miss Stein is right in assuming that each word she writes is right and write and right and that the meaning is exactly what she says for she says exactly nothing more, but of course it is nothing less, than that Alice B. Toklas is Gertrude Stein and Gertrude Stein is Alice B. Toklas—really nothing more but of course nothing less. [52]

The Watertown [New York] *Times* reprinted the letter on display, then quipped: "Does that make it clear? Well, some think that it means that Toklas is Gertrude is Gertrude is Gertrude, and means just that and no more and no less."[53] Nor could the San Francisco *Call Bulletin* resist the temptation to parody Stein's repetitive style. They noted that Alice's letter was: "clear as mud clear as mud clear as mud clear as mud is clear."[54] The humorless *Boston Post* simply noted in its discussion that: "Of course readers of the Atlantic Monthly recognize that Alice B. Toklas is simply a pseudonym used by Gertrude Stein in her autobiography in that magazine when she made use of another idiosyncrasy by portraying her own story as if written by her secretary."[55]

The Autobiography of Alice B. Toklas: "the real Gertrude Stein"

Interest in Stein's memoir was so great that when *The Autobiography of Alice B. Toklas* was released on September 1, the entire first printing of 5,400 copies had already been sold.[56] The *Autobiography* was the September selection of the Literary Guild, the Book-of-the-Month Club's largest competitor, and thus a second printing was automatically distributed to homes throughout the United States. The book ran to four printings by 1935 and a French translation by Bernard Faÿ was published in 1934.[57] The publication of the *Autobiography* was considered such news that Stein appeared on the cover of *Time* magazine on September 11. "My sentences do get under their skin. . ." the cover picture of Stein was captioned. At the age of fifty-nine years old, Stein finally had produced a commercial and critical success; she was not only a literary celebrity, but also a bestselling author.

Although the popularity of Stein's book was no surprise to supporters including Robert Coates, Sherwood Anderson, and Carl Van Vechten, demand for the book was not simply the natural, effortless outcome of a widespread public interest in Stein's personality and her writing. The enterprising Harcourt, Brace regularly sent press releases detailing new items of interest to columnists and reviewers and, like the lively discussion about Alice in the mainstream press, discussion of the book was gently shaped by this media blitz. As Florin McDonald noted in a 1936 study of book reviewing:

> [Press releases] come to the editor's desk constantly, and the publicity agent's hope is that this news will either find its way unchanged into the review pages or that it will be translated into the reviewer's own words

and become a part of his review. Because such news often makes the reviewer's work lighter and facilitates his work during rush hours, he often finds it convenient to make use of book news.[58]

Indeed, reviewers were well aware of each publisher's attempt to promote authors and titles. Harry Hansen observed in 1930 that

> Practically every important publishing house today has its publicity man (or woman) who promotes its books by writing interesting copy about authors and their work, by apprising editors of publications and arranging for interviews with authors. This man sees that authors are properly introduced, arranges meetings with persons in key positions, plans talks over the radio, and cooperates with the advertising and sales departments. In modern merchandising such an effort is almost indispensable.[59]

Stein's book was promoted with just the verve described by Hansen. When the *Autobiography* was first released, the Jacksonville [FL] *Times Union* remarked in its review that: "This is Gertrude Stein Week. At least so it appears from the voluminous press-notices that are following the appearance of 'The Autobiography of Alice B. Toklas.'"[60] Some of these releases did not report any real "news," but, as McDonald suggests, contained phrases that Harcourt, Brace clearly hoped might find their way into reviews or columns. The publisher framed the book as a direct blow to "literature aesthetes" who produce obscure, precious works that would never appeal to mainstream readers:

> FOR IMMEDIATE RELEASE, September 29, 1933
>
> HARD- AT- WORK DEPARTMENT
>
> ... Trouble in the Paradise of Literature Aesthetes is caused by the fact that Gertrude Stein has written a book that's a best-seller because it is brilliant, intelligible, informative (the rule being among Literary Aesthetes that no member of the club can write a book that is brilliant, intelligible and informative.) Ordering the second printing in two weeks, when the first was 5,500 (exclusive of the Literary Guild) is Big Excitement.

Early reviewers certainly emphasized Stein's accessibility. But even more, the barrage of press releases conditioned reviewers to regard the publication of Stein's book as important literary news. Her appearance on the cover of *Time* magazine the week of the *Autobiography*'s publication assured that America was alerted to its significance, and probably the two most influential reviews, the *New York Herald Tribune*'s *Books* and the *Saturday Review of Literature*, featured cover stories about *The Autobiography of Alice B. Toklas* by two of her admirers, Louis Bromfield and Bernard Faÿ. Bromfield's "Gertrude Stein, Experimenter With Words" was prominently subtitled: "Louis Bromfield Hails Her 'Autobiography' as a Literary Event."

Bromfield, whose *The Farm* was a bestseller at the time, expressed his admiration for not only Stein's writing, but also her personality, setting the agenda for many other reviews.

> Gertrude Stein has an extraordinary power of personality and it is my impression that she has the clearest intelligence I have ever encountered. . . .Throughout her life as an experimenter with words and sentences, I suspect that Gertrude Stein the writer has been plagued by being Gertrude Stein the individual, Gertrude Stein the person. She is forever coming between her work and the public.[61]

Perhaps until the publication of *The Autobiography of Alice B. Toklas*, only those who had come to Stein's salon and were themselves directly affected by her personality were able to truly appreciate her significance. Bromfield explained that: "Her influence upon American writing, so much greater than is known or conceded, has always been an intensely personal one. It has been achieved as much by Gertrude Stein the person as by Gertrude Stein the writer."

Bernard Faÿ also expressed his admiration for Stein's character, as if to counter the many reviewers and columnists who had suggested in the 1910s and 1920s that Stein might either be perpetuating a hoax or, equally appalling, was an obscure, intellectual snob. Following in Sherwood Anderson's footsteps, Faÿ celebrates her down-to-earth honesty and integrity:

> Her writings are not tricks, but life, and I have been sure of it since I met her and since I have read her books, and everybody will see it in reading the "Autobiography of Alice B. Toklas." . . . Miss Stein is a great relief in a world where everybody is pompous, and particularly in literary circles.[62]

Lewis Gannett, unlike Bromfield and Faÿ, was not a personal friend, but he still suggested that the *Autobiography* could be read as an introduction to Stein's riveting personality and thus a personal relationship with Stein could be achieved for all readers. He argued that the book anecdotally shows how strongly her vivid and appealing character affected others.

> Gertrude Stein must be one of the great personalities of our day. . . . I suspect that the influence of her writing has been less than she believes; and that the influence of her personality has been immense. . . . One emerges from this book with a new respect for Gertrude Stein. You realize why those who have met her never cease talking about her.[63]

Gannett put the *Autobiography* in the context of other recently published memoirs, observing that Stein's book "has something of that unforgettable quality of Mabel Dodge Luhan's 'Lorenzo in Taos,' which I think will be remembered when the bestsellers of 1932 are forgotten." By contrast, Mina Curtiss suggested in the *Atlantic* that Stein's work was not only superior to Luhan's because of her more democratic worldview; she was praised as a genuine artist. Stein "differs in many important ways from, for example, so well known an autobiographer as Mabel Dodge Luhan. In the first place, Miss Stein herself is an artist. . . . Her relationship with the artists of whom she writes has never been one-sided or leech-like."[64] John Selby's popular, syndicated column for the Associated Press, appearing in newspapers from coast to coast, "The Literary Guidepost," similarly characterized Stein's book as an especially successful biography, "a book that most unbiased readers will feel deserves to hang very high in the biographical firmament, perhaps, indeed, out of sight."

Edmund Wilson's review in the *New Republic* explained that Stein's memoir was, in fact, unlike other popular autobiographies of the day. Emphasizing that her triumph in the book was to write about life with Alice as if it were a novel, he observed that: "When you have read it, you take away an impression of Miss Stein and Miss Toklas in Paris, not in the least like anything you get from the memoirs, say, of Margot Asquith or of Isadora Duncan, but, rather, like your recollection of one of the households of Jane Austen." Apparently revising his equivocal assessment of Stein in *Axel's Castle*, Wilson not only praised the book, but also emphasized Stein's literary significance.

> Let us hope that "The Autobiography of Alice B. Toklas," with its wisdom, its distinction and its charm, will have the effect of causing the general public to recognize Gertrude Stein for what she is: one of the remarkable women of her time and if not "in english literature the only one" at least one of the genuinely original ones.[65]

Wilson was only one of many critics and reviewers who were acutely aware of the perceptions of the "general public" and recognized that the parodic understanding of Stein might finally be corrected. Certainly, a caricature of Stein was familiar to mainstream readers from coast to coast, so widely recognized that a Denver newspaper noted that Stein's name is "part of the folklore whose origin . . . [has] been entirely lost. You say 'Gertrude Stein' as you would say in ordinary conversation, 'Knock on wood.'"[66]

James Agee's cover story in *Time* reiterated this popular understanding of Stein before attempting to revise it. He opens with a slight variation on the familiar limerick reported by the West Virginia reader of the *Autobiography* in the *Atlantic*, which now appears in Bartlett's *Familiar Quotations*:

> There is a notable family named Stein:
> There is Gert, and there is Ep, and there is Ein:

> Gert's poems are bunk,
> Ep's statues are punk—
> And nobody understands Ein.[67]

Rather than endorse the sentiments of these dismissive verses, *Time* argued that: "Plain readers ... after reading *Alice B. Toklas* will find their faith in the limerick verdict sadly shaken [and] may begin to understand why Gertrude Stein's importance as a writer has received so many testimonials from writers of accredited sanity." Other misconceptions or rumors are dispelled; Alice is described as "no fancy figment but a real live companion-secretary ... who has lived with Gertrude Stein for the last 26 years." And, like other reviews, *Time* emphasizes Stein's accessible personality: "though she has lived among artists and pictures all her life there is nothing precious or arty about her." The most insightful aspect of Agee's piece is his recognition that, as revealing as the *Autobiography* might be, Stein's personal life receives little attention in the book:

> Two subjects which bulk large in ordinary lives—money and love—she hardly mentions in *Alice B. Toklas*. It is a strangely impersonal book. . . . [I]f curious readers wonder why she passes over these matters so lightly, they may answer themselves by reflecting that no doubt Gertrude Stein, like everybody else, has autobiographical passages which she does not choose to run.

Certainly, most of the gossip in the book focuses on the lives—often the romantic lives—of other people. The obvious reason for Stein's reticence in the book was never mentioned, and was missed by readers. Alice was hardly understood to be a real person, and was never even covertly presented as Stein's love interest by the mainstream press.

Many reviews opened by acknowledging Stein's notoriety. A Memphis newspaper remarked: "We take it that you know who Gertrude Stein is, was and has been; and if you don't you should and reading 'The Autobiography of Alice B. Toklas' will be a good way of finding out."[68] In Salt Lake City, readers who were unfamiliar with Stein were severely disciplined: "Any little boy and girl in class who doesn't know who Gertrude Stein is, (and who is still awake) may now stand in the corner, bumping his nose into the wall until it hurts."[69] Or, as a Topeka, Kansas newspaper explains to its readers: "Gertrude Stein is a paradox—a name in letters known to everyone but whose work is obscure and mysterious to all but a select group of the 'precious.'"[70]

Other critics—who were not only aware of the scorn that was often directed at Stein's writing but certainly had contributed to this national understanding—found that Stein was vindicated by her brilliant book. As William Troy wrote for the *Nation*, Stein "makes ridiculous all those who have ridiculed her for the last twenty-five years with the charge that she has had 'nothing to say.' . . . And the deepest interest of the book lies in the insight it gives us into the genesis of the mind and sensibility reflected in Gertrude Stein's other and more characteristic books."[71] The headline of Fanny Butcher's review clearly reveals the assumptions that mainstream readers were expected to hold about Stein: "Gertrude Stein Writes a Book in Simple Style: Readers Can Understand Her Autobiography," the article declared, since the publication of a comprehensible book from Gertrude Stein was news in itself.[72] Emphasizing that radical artists can easily become mainstream, Butcher astutely observed that "Gertrude Stein was the first appreciator, the first intelligent critic of many of the young painters (who are today as accepted as cellophane) [which] linked her in the minds of the unknowing with 'those crazy moderns.'" Even Harry Hansen admitted the value of Stein's contribution to modern literature in his review of the book. "Gertrude Stein comes out from behind her barrage of disassociated words today and writes her autobiography in newspaper English. . . . This extraordinary character, whose personality has had a wide influence on writers, has been writing prose for 20 years that no one could make head or tail out of save as a psychological exercise."[73]

Newspapers both in and outside of urban centers could assume that readers were familiar with Stein's reputation and had interest in her literary activities. As the *Augusta* [GA] *Herald* noted: "A book from the pen of Gertrude Stein is always an event and when that book happens to be her own autobiography, well—it should mean something." This notice compliments the Literary Guild for choosing the *Autobiography* for its September selection, and notes that the book club has selected several other notable and fascinating memoirs:

> The Literary Guild is to be congratulated on some of its selections. It has brought out the "Autobiography of Lincoln Steffens," "Earth Horizon," the autobiography of Mary Austin, "The Journal of Arnold Bennett," which is practically an autobiography, and now "The Autobiography of Alice B. Toklas," or really Gertrude Stein.[74]

Certainly, this Georgia newspaper's emphasis on the Literary Guild's choices reveals how much book clubs defined the reading lists of Americans, especially for those with limited access to bookstores.

The Literary Guild's endorsement of Stein was considered evidence that Stein's book would have widespread appeal, and that her notorious reputation must be revised. Samuel Putnam's syndicated column in the New York *Sun*, "A Book a Day," noted that: "This is an Age of Last Things, no doubt of that. Gertrude Stein first of the Atlantic Monthly, and then a book-club selection for September!" But he conceded that the book was not a surprising choice for the Literary Guild after all. It is, he noted . . . "a work which will be perfectly at home on any American club-lady's drawing room table . . . They should eat it up and cry for more."[75] As the *American Magazine of Art* noted:

With the publication of this autobiography first in the pages of the Atlantic Monthly, subsequently in book form by the un-radical firm of Harcourt, Brace, Gertrude Stein can be said to have come home to her people. That her people were ready for her seems indicated by action of the Literary Guild in selecting this work as its September title.[76]

The Guild's choice of such a large number of biographies also shows the strong interest in biographies of literary and artistic subjects in the early twentieth century. Stein's autobiography, like Virginia Woolf's "biographies" *Flush* and *Orlando*, were understood by many readers as whimsical variations on the traditional biographies and autobiographies that dominated the non-fiction best-seller lists rather than as radical or subversive experiments.

Indeed, the public proved extraordinarily attracted to literary personalities, whether they were presented in biographies, autobiographies, or fiction. Stuart Sherman identified himself as representative of the mainstream attitude when he declared in his column: "What I like is personality. It seems to me the very marrow of literature, and I am ready to quarrel with all the highbrows and high hats who try to banish it."[77] Dorothy Canfield Fisher considered what literary qualities seemed to attract current readers and similarly concluded that:

> By and large, what readers seem to like to find in a book is the feeling of contact with living, vital personalities. The traditional classification by subject matter—biography, travel books, humor, fiction, and so on—may be quite irrelevant, since apparently what people enjoy in a book is the meeting with a fellow man who interests them.[78]

Reviews emphasized that *The Autobiography of Alice B. Toklas* necessitated a reappraisal of Stein's personality as much as her writing style. For many critics, Stein emerged as the antithesis of the effete literary stereotype that many had associated with her for so many years. As the *Buffalo News* noted:

> Gertrude Stein is the most intelligent of living American writers and the least intellectual—the most completely civilized of them all.... It is a constant amazement to her that she has become a cult of the precious; for, as she says, she is "good friends with all the world and can know them and they can know her."[79]

Or, as the *Los Angeles Times* succinctly put it: Stein "is here revealed as a humorous and kindly old lady."[80] The *Washington Post* agreed that readers would "find the book wholly likable, as they will, at last, find Miss Stein herself."[81] The review in *America* noted: "For those who are not acquainted with the immensity of Gertrude Stein's mind and personality, a real treat is in store for them."[82] And in the newsletter for the Book-of-the-Month Club, which was, of course, competing with the Literary Guild, Amy Loveman's positive review observed that "there seems to be a universal consensus of opinion as to the force of her personality."[83] Both the *Chicago Herald-Examiner* and *News-Week* compared her influential personality to Samuel Johnson's.[84] Stein's personality appeared to be so unlike that of other modern writers that some reviewers were convinced that she should no longer be compared to them; the *Dallas Times-Herald* noted that "Miss Stein is really not a member of the so-called school of unintelligibility. . . . She is utterly sincere and much of her work breathes a beauty which will some day be appreciated as it deserves."[85]

Not all critics were charmed by Stein's portrait of herself, and some prominent reviewers wondered how appropriate it was for Stein to exploit Alice, who identifies Stein as a "genius" in the book. In his *New Yorker* review, Clifton Fadiman stubbornly refused to find Stein's personality to be exceptional or refreshing. Instead Fadiman classified Stein as an irritating "type" of intellectual: "She is the Radcliffe aesthetic bluestocking, very arty, very snobbish, totally sheltered from life . . . with a dilettante passion for the 'advanced,' pathetically reminiscent of the most artificial gestures of the nineties." Apparently offended by Stein's choice to use Alice's voice to compliment herself, Fadiman complained, "Gertrude has always conscientiously done justice to Gertrude, but this book is a high-water mark in the delicate art of self-appreciation."[86] Some readers considered the classification of herself as a genius to be most impudent, rather than amusing. A headline in the *New York Times* declared: "News of Books: Gertrude Stein Calls Herself, Picasso and Whitehead the Only Geniuses She Has Met." One reviewer in Oklahoma, who entirely missed the humor of the book, objected to Stein's playful use of Alice as a subjective narrator:

> Gertrude Stein's writing the autobiography of someone else seems like a childish publicity stunt. And then to write the book (after having urged Miss Toklas to do it herself) and fill it full of Gertrude Stein to the almost exclusion of its putative author—well, it's just too much.[87]

But others praised Stein's narrative experiment as a creative strategy to present herself in the most positive light. Mary Colum, who followed Stein's work with interest, found the book interesting for this reason:

> I commend the ingenuity of it to any one who wants to write a book praising himself and making himself the unabashed hero. It would have been difficult for Gertrude Stein without being accused of lunacy to have said in the first person that she herself is one of the three great modern geniuses, but it is simple to make Alice say it naively.[88]

Like Colum, Isabel Paterson failed to reject the book even if its presentation of Stein was obviously self-congratulatory, contending that there was no contradiction between finding Stein an egoist and a charming woman. She remarked:

> We get into fruitless arguments by remarking that the book is a wonderful self-portrait of a perfect egotist . . . The objectors protest that Miss Stein has innumerable devoted friends and is a most interesting person . . . Why not? Egotists are not necessarily unamiable, and are frequently very interesting . . . Babies are complete egotists, and they possess a naïve charm . . . If a baby could write a book it would resemble "The Autobiography of Alice B. Toklas." (ellipses in original)[89]

If Stein's arrogance impeded the enjoyment of some readers, others still recommended the book for its literary excellence. A columnist in the *San Francisco Chronicle* conceded that "No doubt she is a poseur and an awful exhibitionist. But I think her talent for writing is remarkable."[90] Isaac Goldberg disagreed; he explained that "Miss Stein is undoubtedly a remarkable personality; her salon in the Rue de Fleurus is undoubtedly a rendezvous of the arts and sciences. She is not, however, simply not, a writer, and her work has grown steadily worse since the artificial simplicity of the Three Lives."[91] The *Christian Century* similarly expressed skepticism as to the lasting value of her work: "one gets the impression that Gertrude Stein is a very remarkable personality. She must be, to do such writing and yet make such friends."[92]

By contrast to these few negative reviews, the American press overwhelmingly celebrated Stein's charming personality and emphasized her significant influence on modern literature. Even reviewers who admitted that Stein's early work was baffling to them acknowledged that Stein had changed the literary landscape. In the *Cleveland News*, for example, Mary Rennels observed that in the *Autobiography*, "[Stein] has had a great influence on all modern writers"[93] and in the *Chicago Daily News*, Sterling North declared that Stein "profoundly influenced the entire second and third generations of 20th Century American writers. Her prose rhythms reverberate through Sherwood Anderson, Ernest Hemingway, and William Faulkner to mention only a few." This aspect of Stein's value was frequently stressed in headlines. The *New York Post* titled its review "Gertrude Stein's Excellent Autobiography—Her Lasting Influence on Modern Writers."[94] Throughout the country, Stein's "influence" was celebrated: *Scribner's* noted that [Stein's] prose and poetry have influenced most of our important modern writers," the *Des Moines Register* observed that Stein "has exerted a profound influence on the growth of the new art, music and literature during the great revolution in the arts which came in the twentieth century," the *Florida Times Union* called Stein "the creator of modern American writing," and the *Mason [GA] Telegraph* declared that "she has had more influence, perhaps, on modern artists and writers than any other living person."[95]

In addition to appearing on numerous bestseller lists around the country, *The Autobiography of Alice. B. Toklas* also was cited in lists of books recommended by authors or celebrities. Not surprisingly, Bernard Faÿ included the *Autobiography* on his October list of favorite new titles in the *Herald Tribune*, noting Stein's book is "first on my list; I put it far ahead of all the other ones. It is witty, intelligent, original and deeply human."[96] In the *Herald Tribune*'s regularly reported "Recent Books I Have Liked" column, *The Autobiography of Alice B. Toklas* appeared on the lists of James Weldon Johnson and Kay Boyle.[97]

The popularity of Stein was not considered an isolated or exceptional event by critics. Her success was part of a much larger trend; in the years 1933—1934, modernism generally became known as mainstream, rather than elitist or inaccessible. As Harry Hansen observed in an article for *Publishers' Weekly*:

> In 1933 a number of events, such as repeal, were concerned not with opening new vistas but closing old accounts. These included: Return to America of T. S. Eliot . . . decision to admit "Ulysses" free of censorship . . . emergence of Gertrude Stein as the favorite of the Atlantic Monthly reader and subsequent collapse of her reputation among those who championed her unintelligible prose.[98]

Hansen's extreme description of a mutiny among Stein's early admirers does not appear to be accurate. Instead, Random House's release of a new edition of *Three Lives* in September reaffirmed the importance of the experimental Stein for her more ambitious readers; the introduction by Carl Van Vechten further attracted a new audience. Van Vechten was thrilled by the dual publications of the *Autobiography* and *Three Lives* and the recognition that Stein had finally achieved. He wrote to her: "I am so excited! You are on every tongue like Greta Garbo!"[99]

Four Saints in Three Acts

Just at Hansen was impressed by the remarkable coincidence of Stein's success with the *Autobiography of Alice B. Toklas* and the publication of Joyce's *Ulysses* in America, *Vanity Fair* celebrated these literary developments, adding yet another modernist triumph to the list: Stein's sensational opera, *Four Saints in Three Acts*.

> There may have been a few far-seeing souls who were prepared for the lifting of the governmental ban on *Ulysses*, and the consequent huge sale of the master-work; but we doubt if any one—even Miss Stein herself—ever envisaged a time when a Stein book would, month after month, grace the best seller lists, and a Stein opera run four solid weeks

at a Broadway theatre, to re-open three weeks later at *popular demand*. But this is 1934, and the twin miracles have happened.[100]

Stein's libretto was set to music by Virgil Thompson, who arranged with A. Everett (Chick) Austin, Jr., the director of the Wadsworth Atheneum, Hartford's art museum, for the premiere of the opera to take place there. The performance coincided with the opening of the museum's new modern art wing and an impressive Picasso exhibition. Produced by John Houseman, who went on to have a well-known career as a film producer and actor, and with costumes and brightly colored cellophane sets designed by Florine Stettheimer, an idiosyncratic New York artist who hosted an avant-garde salon, the production could not fail to create an original effect. Furthermore, as if these elements weren't enough to attract the notice of journalists and critics, Thompson decided to cast African Americans in the opera, attracting even more comment and interest in the performance.

Four Saints in Three Acts opened in February of 1934; the preview on February 7 was the social event of the season.[101] The press commented on the show extensively and a live fifteen-minutes of act three were broadcast by Columbia radio nationwide, creating such interest that the *March of Time* rebroadcast three minutes of the opera, immediately popularizing Stein's phrase: "pigeons on the grass, alas."[102] The radio may have democratized the performance, but those who actually attended the premiere were decidedly of the social elite, many of whom came from New York in limousines or in special New Haven parlor cars designated for the event. *News-week* explained that the "fashionably esoteric . . . opening night audience was full of enthusiastic cosmopolites, in silks and ermines, or tall coats and toppers."[103] Stein's friend William Rogers similarly reports that: "A perfumed air of chi-chi pervaded the famous premiere in Hartford. . . . The best people sponsored the event and held pre- and post- performance cocktail parties and suppers, and many tickets to the theatre were bought in the hope they meant admission to the right houses."[104]

Although gossip columnists were more interested in the appearance of Buckminster Fuller, Clare Boothe, and Dorothy Hale, many writers and artists also attended the Hartford performance.[105] Marianne Moore called the premiere "a blasphemous but talented thing" and said that Saint Teresa's was the only soprano that she had ever admired.[106] Muriel Rukeyser, Carl Van Vechten, Henry McBride, and Alexander Calder all attended.[107] Wallace Stevens's reaction in a letter to Harriet Monroe is frequently quoted, for obvious reasons:

> While this is an elaborate bit of perversity in every respect: text, settings, choreography, it is most agreeable musically, so that, if one excludes aesthetic self-consciousness from one's attitude, the opera immediately becomes a delicate and joyous work all round.

There were, however, numerous asses of the first water in the audience. New York sent a train load of people of this sort to Hartford: people who walked round with cigarette holders a foot long, and so on. After all, if there is any place under the sun that needs debunking, it is the place where people of this sort come to and go to.[108]

The musical community was also represented; Alfred Harcourt reported to Stein that Arturo Toscanini (who was conductor of the New York Philharmonic Orchestra at the time) "applauded vigorously."[109]

The opera then moved to one of Broadway's largest theaters and became the "longest running opera in Broadway history." Audiences in New York were just as impressive. George Gershwin, Robert Benchley, Dorothy Parker, and Cecil Beaton (who was apparently reduced to tears by the performance), *Vanity Fair*'s Frank Crowninshield, and sculptor Jo Davidson all attended. Reaction was so overwhelming that Olin Downes reported in the *New York Times* that: "Debussy and the poor old Met were buried last night, buried to shouts of joy and hosannas of acclaim for the new dawn of the lyric drama."[110]

Paul Bowles sent Stein clippings from the New York newspapers after the opening, but finally gave up because "there were so many references to it."[111] He wrote to Stein that "People walking on Broadway and sitting in Automats talk of 'the Saints play' and usually sound doubtful as to whether it would be worth while to try to get tickets for it."[112] According to *Variety*, the opera was discussed by the press more than any production "in the previous ten years."[113] George Gershwin commented that *Four Saints* was "refreshing as a new dessert" but a skeptical FPA wrote in his celebrated column, "The Conning Tower," that "Our conviction is that he can't spell."[114] Unimpressed by the popular response, FPA declared that he had an "unyielding . . . opinion of the libretto. I say it is spinach."[115]

The windows and advertisements of New York merchants were immediately influenced by the opera's success: Bergdorf Goodman, John Wannamaker, Elizabeth Arden and Gimbel's all were inspired by the production. Bergdorf's named a gown "Saint," claiming that "it looks like one of the thrilling costumes in the much-talked-of Four Saints opera," Wanamker's advertised evening wear, with the caption "Four Wraps in Cellophane," and Saint Teresa appeared in Elizabeth Arden's Easter window.[116] Van Vechten photographed Gimbel's window and sent a copy to Stein: "Four Suits in Three Acts," the display declared. Gimbel's also produced tablecloths named after phrases in the opera, including "Instead of," "After a While," and "Have to Have."[117]

Although *Four Saints in Three Acts* is generally considered to be consistent with other experimental literature and art of this period, like Stein's other works it defies easy categorization. Her libretto is commensurate with other writing that had appeared in the little magazines or *Geography and Plays*, but Thomson's pleasant score and the brightly colored cellophane sets rendered the production somewhat difficult to define. In a letter, Henry McBride complimented "Virgil's really adorable music" but there was nothing shocking or radical about it.[118] William Carlos Williams was one of the only writers to comment that Thomson's music was a "doubtful aid to Stein's prose" which was notable for "smashing every connotation that words heave ever had, in order to get them back clean."[119] Indeed, the sentimental, even anti-modernist score has nothing in common with music we now associate with modernism, such as the atonal work of Stravinsky. Van Vechten wrote to Stein that: "I haven't seen a crowd more excited since Sacre du Printemps, but in this case, pleasurably excited," and certainly this more congenial reception was partly due to the fact that Thomson's score was so conventional or, as Olin Downes put it, "syrupy."[120] Indeed, the most accurate description of the production *Four Saints in Three Acts* would not be "avant-garde"; the opera can more appropriately be described as "camp."

Even Virgil Thomson justified the choice of Florine Stettheimer by recognizing this important aspect of the performance. He explained: "Florine's paintings are very high camp, and high camp is the only thing you can do with a religious subject. Anything else gets sentimental and unbelievable, whereas high camp touches religion sincerely and its being at the same time low pop."[121] The choice of these gaudy, extravagant visuals to accompany the opera certainly did aid the overall popular success of the opera, as Thomson and Stein had hoped. As late as 1938, when Stein and Thomson began to discuss a new project, she wrote to him that "Neither you nor I have ever had any passion to be rare, we want to be as popular as Gilbert and Sullivan if we can, and perhaps we can."[122] *Four Saints* may not have made them quite this popular, but the production was certainly that season's great success.

Rather than the music, the most radical element of the production was the African American cast. As Steven Watson observes: "Never before had African Americans been cast in a work that did not depict black life. Never before had they been paid for rehearsals. And never before had an all-black cast performed in an opera before white audiences."[123] Although the press consistently praised the performances, with special notice for Beatrice Robinson-Wayne, Bruce Howard and Edward Matthews, the compliments often included the racist implication that only black singers could have performed the strange lyrics without displaying confusion (since they were apparently accustomed to singing words they did not understand). Olin Downes noted that Thompson thought that "Negroes could recite the Stein text without being troubled by self-consciousness because of its apparent senselessness, as white singers, perhaps already inured to operatic and textual traditions, could not do."[124] A reviewer in the African American periodical, *Opportunity*, observed: "Just how these simple children were able to memorize the highly complicated, intellectualized libretto in the first place, was never explained."[125] One student at Howard University, Ulysses G. Lee, Jr., was so offended by the insulting reviews that he wrote to Stein. She described the letter to Van Vechten:

> I have just had a charming letter from a colored boy all about the opera, his feelings were hurt because it would appear they said in the newspapers they chose the Negroes as singers because they would not giggle and he said that of course they would not because why should they giggle since of course they would understand. Very sweet of him.[126]

Stein maintained a correspondence with Lee, who went on to praise Stein's Melanctha in another letter. He found it difficult to understand "how any young white woman could have known enough about Negroes to draw such different people as Rose, Jane, and the Herberts. To me, 'Melanctha' is one of the most inviting studies I have read."[127]

Even as Stein continued to impress such serious admirers, the opera primarily attracted attention as a spectacle. *Four Saints* was considered escapist entertainment, but not lasting, serious art. As one reviewer noted: "'Four Saints in Three Acts' is a success because all its elements—the dialogue, the music, the pantomime, and the sparkling cellophane *décor*—go so well with one another while remaining totally irrelevant to life, logic, or common sense."[128] It was not until Stein was able to speak for herself in the United States that Americans learned that "common sense" was one of her most marked and endearing traits.

Arrival in America: "Salute to Gertrude Stein (Who Needs No Press Agent)"[129]

As the question and answer session after Stein delivered "Composition as Explanation" in 1926 had been the most amusing part of her performance for her English audiences, this aspect of her American lecture tour in 1934 and 1935 proved to be most important for establishing a new, comic reputation and solidifying a warm relationship with the public and the press. Before the tour, Stein had the opportunity to refresh her ability to banter with audiences in January 1934, when she lectured in Paris in place of Bernard Faÿ, who had been unable to return to the city in time for his talk. An American woman declared that Stein and other artists only cared to "create a sensation" and Stein answered simply: "Don't be silly. Have you read my latest book?" The woman admitted that she had not. "Well, you better go read it!" Stein commanded, adding that:

> Present day geniuses can no more help doing what they are doing than you can help not understanding it, but if you think we do it for effect and to make a sensation, you're crazy. It's not our idea of fun to work for thirty or forty years on a medium of expression and then have ourselves ridiculed.[130]

Perhaps this experience contributed to Stein's anxiety about the reception she might expect in the United States if she agreed to lecture there. It was finally William G. Rogers who convinced Stein that her return would be triumphant. Rogers was an American doughboy Stein had met during World War I who, after recognizing her photograph in American newspapers, re-established contact with Stein and Toklas in the 1920s. Although he expressed confidence that she would be warmly received, privately Rogers feared that Stein might not meet with the respect and appreciation she deserved. He later recalled: "In my mind's eye I saw Miss Stein squeezed insultingly into half-inch fillers at the bottom of all the back pages. I was afraid I should have kept my mouth shut."[131]

Lecture tours did often boost the reputation of writers in the United States and could be lucrative if the writer proved to be an entertaining or otherwise stimulating speaker. Amy Lowell's tours were wildly successful in the 1920s, while in the 1940s and 1950s Robert Frost and E. E. Cummings were certainly the most celebrated and profitable American writers on the lecture circuit. Great success with audiences was not assured, and the press that followed each appearance could dramatically affect the turnout at later engagements. As one critic observed in 1931, "Lecture tours are, of course, a form of news creation and are subject to the same limitations and uncertainties as other news. There is no doubt, however, unless it is overdone, that the lecture tour of an author with the necessary platform and other social graces can do much for his books."[132]

Rogers, who was a newspaper editor in Massachusetts at the *Springfield Union*, was acutely aware that any tour might flop if reporters were unimpressed, but he was unable to predict how this sensitive and influential audience might respond to Stein's usually remarkable presence. Stein too understood that attracting the interest of journalists was of the highest importance. The summer before she sailed for America, the young James Laughlin, who later became a distinguished editor at New Directions, wrote abstracts of her lectures. She sent the work of the "Harvard boy," as she called Laughlin, to Rogers, explaining that he might be able to use them "as the basis of some articles and they would probably help a lot."[133] Harcourt, Brace then sent out press releases advertising the titles of the lectures with brief descriptions based on these abstracts.

Just as Stein anticipated, newspapers immediately commented on the titles of the lectures. One reporter for the *St. Paul Dispatch* who thought that "It will be an extraordinary privilege to study this extraordinary American phenomenon at closer range" expressed some concern that Stein would be unfairly mocked for these titles: "Lectures' Titles Leave Opening for Punsters" was the subheading of one section of the lengthy article.[134] Most journalists did not use the titles for laughs, however and instead reported Stein's upcoming tour with eagerness; as the Iowa City *Press Citizen* noted in its headline: "Gertrude Stein, Coming From Paris, Promises to Create Literary Sensation."[135]

Vanity Fair also whetted the public's taste for Stein, publishing her own reaction to becoming a celebrated, bestselling author in September of 1934. Stein's mediation on the difficulty of maintaining her identity once she achieved such dramatic literary success was prefaced by an editorial note which described readers Stein's recent success with the *Autobiography* and *Four Saints*, highlighting *Vanity Fair*'s own early role in recognizing Stein's value as a writer. "Vanity Fair views all this with a certain smugness, for it has been publishing Miss Stein's work at various times for seventeen years," they observed.[136]

Not all of the mainstream press was certain of Stein's significance, of course. Months before Stein arrived in America for her lecture tour, B. F. Skinner published an article in the *Atlantic* titled "Has Gertrude Stein a Secret?" He argued that in *Tender Buttons* Stein had reproduced techniques that she and her partner, Leon Solomons, used in experiments to determine whether subjects could perform "automatic writing" at Harvard in 1896–98. According to Skinner, *Tender Buttons* was essentially the act of a secondary personality that wasn't very interesting. He explained that the conscious Stein had a fine, well-developed mind and could write very well, as in *The Autobiography of Alice B. Toklas*, but the secondary Stein who produced *Tender Buttons* was a failure. Stein responded to this accusation in *Everybody's Autobiography*: "I did not think it was automatic I do not think so now, I do not think any university student is likely certainly not under observation is likely to be able to do genuinely automatic writing, I do not think so, that is under normal conditions."[137] In a letter to Ellery Sedgwick she further explained that her writing technique "is not so automatic as [Skinner] thinks. If there is any secret it is the other way to. I think I achieve by xtra consciousness, xcess." Unlike the subjects whom she and Solomons observed, she was not distracted but instead unusually focused when writing.[138]

Other evidences of a skeptical public surfaced before she began her tour. The *Baltimore Sun* asked certain professors at Johns Hopkins to explain the meaning of an obscure passage from *Geography and Plays*, obviously hoping to baffle these scholars. The responses, however, were mixed. Ignoring the specific passage at hand, English Professor Dr. Raymond Dexter Havens responded that: "She is reaching for a new art form. . . . She doesn't seem so strange to us as Whitman and Wagner did to our forefathers in their time. Perhaps she is just pointing a new way, and it will be for some one else to perfect her method." But unable to resist an easy joke, a Professor in the French Department, James M. Beall simply commented: "I think the word 'nuts' in the passage is very expressive."[139] Also representing both sides of the debate, *News-week* reported in October that "one of the most-talked-about authors in the world returns to America this week. . . . Some people call her the 'most intelligent American woman alive today'; others say she is crazy."[140]

New Yorker readers were always informed about Stein's latest activities thanks to Janet Flanner, whose "Paris Letter" column consistently referred to her writing and influence with respect. Flanner explained in early October that "Paris figures and their products slated for New York this autumn include Miss Gertrude Stein in a series of lectures about grammar, poetry and pictures or, as she says, lectures about herself, and 'Who knows more about that than I do?'"[141] Following up on this brief notice, a lengthy exposition about Stein appeared in the "Talk of the Town" section the next week. The piece notes the titles of the lectures, then quickly moves on to gossip: "In case you're interested, we have learned a few things about her that she may not tell in her lectures." Painting Stein as the most eccentric and absurd character, the *New Yorker* explained that Stein and Toklas drive in the county looking for cows to inspire Stein's writing. If the first cow fails as muse, they get back in the car and look for another one. Concluding with a ridiculous description of Stein's wardrobe, the *New Yorker* includes this embarrassing anecdote: "She also wears extraordinary blue - and - white striped knickers for underdrawers. This came out when she lost them once at a concert given by Virgil Thomson at the Hotel Majestic. She just stepped out of them somehow and left them lying there on the floor. She thought it was very funny and laughed loudly."[142]

Although Flanner remained Stein's ally, other writers at the *New Yorker* failed to take her seriously. Clifton Fadiman's review of *The Autobiography of Alice B. Toklas* was one of the only prominent, negative notices printed in the United States. Other staff writers seemed to share his skepticism. E. B. White contributed a parodic poem that was printed the week of Stein's arrival in New York, "Is a Train," subtitled "The strange systemic recession of a punctual lyricist in a railroad station waiting to meet not to meet Gertrude Stein." The poem begins: "One november two november three no trumps is not a rose./ The train the train hat I would meet is one that I have known alas. . ."[143] And so on. White's knowledge of Stein seems to consist of "An Indian Boy," "The Fifteenth of November," and Stein's well-known phrases: "a rose is a rose is a rose" and "pigeons on the grass, alas" and is really more representative of the American understanding of Stein before the appearance of the *Autobiography*. But the *New Yorker* refused to revise its impression of her. Melville Cane's poem appeared the following week, after Stein had arrived in New York, requesting that she explain "In communicable prose/ What a rose a rose a rose."[144]

Cane's sarcastic verse appears not to have been influenced by Stein's presence in New York. Journalists who actually met her ceased to present Stein as incomprehensible. But these *New Yorker* writers collectively decided not to give her a chance. When Harold Ross's friend Bennett Cerf asked him to a party celebrating Stein's arrival, he declined. Ross wrote to Cerf, "Nuts to Gertrude Stein. If you want to play backgammon tonight telephone me."[145] The presentation of Stein in the *New Yorker* may have been very different if she had been able to meet the eminent Ross and, as she usually did with her detractors, win him over.

When Stein and Toklas arrived in New York on the Champlain on 24 October 1934 they were greeted by a throng of reporters who were eager to interview the most notable passenger aboard the ship. Before Stein could touch land and greet her trusted friends, Carl Van Vechten, William Rogers, and Stein's new promoter, Random House's Bennett Cerf, she was thrust into a candid performance that effectively defined the reception she would receive throughout her extensive tour in the United States. The lengthy descriptions of Stein's warm, pleasant demeanor in the mainstream press suggest that these journalists expected to have a very different impression of this enigmatic writer, but Stein charmed them all.

If some reporters set out to challenge Stein with pointed questions, her unaffected and humorous responses soon showed who controlled the conversation. Her engaging confidence disarmed her audience, who were unable to accurately remember the apparently profound banter described by the *Chicago Tribune* as "lucid, strong-voiced and mellow-toned."[146] A survey of the numerous reports, many appearing on the front page accompanied by large photographs, shows that although the reporters did use quotation marks as if they had accurately recorded Stein's remarks, they all actually remembered or heard slightly different answers. To the question: "Why don't you write as you talk?" Stein was credited with saying:

"I write as words come up naturally to me. I think I write as a talk ... I do talk as I write, but you can hear better than you can see" (*Saturday Review of Literature*)

"I do! It's all in learning how to read my works. I do, really." (*New York Post*)

"I do," she said. "I'll have to insist on that. You are accustomed to seeing with your eyes a different thing from what you hear with your ear. Youngsters see it better than older people who are set in their ways." (*New York World Telegram*)

"I write as words come up naturally to me.... I think I write as I talk. I am very insistent about that. I do talk as I write, but you can hear better than you can see. You are accustomed to see with your eyes differently to the way you hear with your ears, and perhaps that is what makes it hard to read my works for some people." (*New York Herald Tribune*)

"I do talk as I write, but you can hear better than you can see. You are accustomed to see with your eyes differently to the way you hear with your ears, and perhaps that is what makes it hard to read my works for some people." (*The Nation*)

"My writing is nearer to human speech than ordinary writing. I write just as I talk. It's all in the way you hear it. . . . It is a matter of being used to seeing different things with the eyes than one hears with the ears." (*Chicago Tribune*)

"But you don't write the way you talk, either. I write the words just as they come to me, and if you can't get out of them what I put into them, I can't help it. But maybe you'd better not mention it. You might misquote me." (*Chicago Herald*)

And, finally, the *New York Times* dramatized the exchange with the reporter, the *Herald Tribune*'s Joseph Alsop, Jr., who had asked "Why don't you write as you talk?" According to the *Times*, Stein replied: "Oh, but I do. After all it's all leaning how to read it."

The reporter sighed.

"It's a matter of perception," she continued, relentlessly. "Youngsters with the least education get it quicker than those not in set in their ways."[147]

Alsop may have expressed impatience at this first encounter with Stein, but he wrote extensive stories for the *Herald Tribune* throughout her visit and was eventually so taken with her that he arranged for Stein to meet his mother in Springfield, Massachusetts. He wrote to Stein before she left the country: "Your lectures have been a revelation to me in many ways. The chief revelation has been yourself. You may possibly have gathered from my reports, if you have troubled to read them, that I have conceived a real admiration for you and for your work."[148] Perhaps only *Time* magazine was disappointed in Stein's performance. Below a picture of her arrival in New York, a caption read: "Expatriate Stein: She was disappointingly intelligible."[149]

In addition to Stein's witty remarks, reporters also focused on one unusual item of clothing in these early reports: her hat. The *New York Times* described it as "a gay hat which gave her the appearance of having just sprung from Robin Hood's forest" and Rogers recalled that:

Her hat was called variously a braumeister's cap, a jockey's cap, a deerstalker's cap and a grouse-hunter's cap. It was a small gray tweed, it was mannish, its brim turned down "visorlike so that it gave a squirrel-like appearance to her face." One observer explained: "A strange article, apparently a compromise between feminine toque and male cap; black and white tweed, with visor in front and coy upcurl at rear."[150]

According to Rogers, Miss Stein said: "It's just a hat." Or, as the New York *World Telegram* reported, she said: "It's just a cap." But, of course, it wasn't just a cap. It had been copied from a Louis XIII hat in the Cluny Museum, but Stein's accessible persona could not have revealed that kind of eccentric origin.[151] Discussion of the hat was so prevalent that the *New Yorker* printed a cartoon of a custom's inspector saying to another inspector: "It begins like this: gertrude says four hats is a hat is a hat. Now what the hell can you make out of a declaration like that, chief?"[152]

Not surprisingly, the appearance of Alice B. Toklas was also an important aspect of the story for some journalists who had never believed in her existence. Evelyn Seeley headlined her article for the *World Telegram*: "Alice Toklas Hides in Shadows of Stein." According to Seeley, Stein was asked: "Is there an Alice Toklas?" " 'Well, of course!' replied Miss Stein. 'There she is!'"[153] The *Nation* opened its report: "Looking like a benevolent Viking, Miss Gertrude Stein on October 24 returned to her native land, bringing Miss Alice B. Toklas with her in tangible form to quiet any doubts that may have been harbored or her existence."[154]

The response to Stein was a great relief to Rogers, who discovered the morning after Stein's arrival that journalists had not only been impressed with Stein, but they also faithfully delivered lengthy and complimentary stories to their newspapers. He recalls, "Even if I had been too sleepy to glance at the newsstand in the lobby, the headlines would have shrieked up at me. There were Miss Stein and Miss Toklas on every single front page.... The give and take aboard ship had been sharp and entertaining, and not only Miss Stein but also the reporters had had the time of their lives."[155] As Brinnin explains: "In this aura of good feeling they wrote more copy than they had planned, and turned in engaging accounts of the woman they had expected only to jeer.... A number of these stories were carried throughout the country on newsservice wires. Local papers took the cue and when she turned up in one city after another she was nearly always front-page news."[156]

Stein on the Radio and in the Movies: or "How Gertrude Stein Has Mark Twain Backed Off the Map"

The national interest in Stein's lecture tour sparked by her triumphant session with the New York reporters might have ensured a respectable reception throughout the tour, but her popularity was further boosted by two other strategic promotions. Thanks to Bennett Cerf, she was interviewed over NBC's nationally broadcast New York station, WJZ, and she was filmed for a Pathé newsreel that was shown in movie theaters nationwide. Stein's willingness to utilize these important technological developments suggests that she understood her writing to be at home with modern, advanced America, and not all opposed to contemporary culture.

As soon as *The Autobiography of Alice B. Toklas* began appearing in the *Atlantic*, Cerf contacted Stein in Paris, offering to publish *Three Lives* and *The Making of Americans* as Modern Library titles. Stein regretted that she had already arranged for Harcourt, Brace to release an abridged version of *The Making of Americans*, but the reissue of *Three Lives* appeared in September, Cerf agreed to publish a collection titled *Portraits and Prayers* in November 1934 and, when her lectures proved to be popular, he published *Lectures in America* in the spring of 1935.[157] The reissue of *Three Lives* was such a success that Cerf wrote to Stein in December that "I sent out a publicity note to the effect that THREE LIVES was the best selling book in the Modern Library in November, and that has caused a great deal of comment."[158] Cerf understood his role as publisher to include generating Stein-related news; after he arranged for the Pathé newsreel, he introduced Stein's interview with William Lundell on the radio and hosted Random House's well-publicized, fashionable New York party to celebrate the tour.[159]

One segment of Stein's newsreel resonated with audiences and introduced a new catch-phrase, even superceding "rose is a rose is a rose."[160] As Stein explains: "When we first arrived in New York I did make an actuality of reading the Pigeons On The Grass and taking off my glasses and putting them on again while I was doing that thing, and it was given in the cinema theatres everywhere and everybody said everybody liked it."[161] Numerous columnists reported that Stein's explication of "pigeons on the grass, alas," first heard in the radio broadcasts of *Four Saints in Three Acts*, was the most memorable aspect of the performance even if she failed to clarify the lines. James Thurber was inspired to counter Stein's claim that pigeons were "alas" in a satirical piece for the *New Yorker*, "There's an Owl in my Room." "I saw Gertrude Stein on the screen of a newsreel theatre one afternoon and I heard her read that famous passage of hers about pigeons on the grass, alas," he explained. "It is neither just nor accurate to connect the word alas with pigeons. Pigeons are definitely not alas."

> Pigeons come closer to a zero of impingement than any other birds. Hens embarrass me the way my old Aunt Hattie used to when I was twelve and she insisted I wasn't big enough to bathe myself; owls disturb me; if I am with an eagle I always pretend that I am not with an eagle; and so on down to swallows at twilight who scare the hell out of me. But pigeons have absolutely no effect on me. They have absolutely no effect on anybody.[162]

The newsreel, filmed the first day Stein was in New York, confirmed her fame and further promoted the upcoming lectures. One New Yorker was inspired to write a letter to the editor that was printed in the *New York Times*:

> It was interesting to hear Gertrude Stein in the news reel express her reaction to "pigeons in the grass, alas!" (sic) May I suggest that Miss Stein throw a handful of seeds to the pigeons? It would then be still more interesting to note her reaction. I'm sure it would be far less doleful and might even end up with "hooray!" Think how pleased the pigeons would be![163]

Stein's approachable demeanor on film reassured those who may not have been convinced by the reports in the daily newspaper, and easily showed that her charisma could be appreciated by all. But it was in her highly publicized radio interview that Stein was given an opportunity to present her celebrated personality, since the question and answer format highlighted her characteristic sense of humor.

The radio was an especially important new medium for promoting books in the late 1920s and 1930s. Although publishers had expressed much concern that the radio would compete with literature and depress book sales, these fears proved unfounded. Some publishers advertised specific titles on the air with radio programs like the National Home Library's "Fireside Hour," a show that invited actors to perform sections of certain books.[164] In addition, programs that reviewed, read, or analyzed literature became useful promotion tools for publishers and authors. One especially popular reviewer on radio was Harry Hansen, who had already developed a national reputation with his syndicated column, "The First Reader." In the late 1920s he was a weekly book reviewer on the Mutual Broadcasting Network and from 1931 to 1935 his program "Women's Radio Review" was broadcast Tuesday nights on NBC.[165] In 1935 *Publishers' Weekly* reported that he would begin a new show on NBC every Monday afternoon, and cautioned booksellers that Hansen was "responsible for selling a considerable number of books through the bookstores."[166]

The radio voice most capable of influencing book sales was clearly Alexander Woollcott. His first radio show, "The Early Bookworm," exclusively focused on books but it was his enormously popular, twice-weekly "Town Crier," a program that debuted in 1933, in which Woollcott discussed a variety of topics that established Woollcott's national fame. Indeed, the *Literary Digest* observed that "his voice was familiar to every one in America who owned a radio," and recalled the astonishing outcome of Woollcott's mention of James Hilton's *Goodbye Mr. Chips* on the air.[167] The book became an overnight bestseller.

Woollcott was one of the celebrities invited to dine with Stein as she stayed in New York at the Algonquin Hotel. They became fast friends after she disagreed with him and he declared: "People don't dispute Woollcott." "I'm not people," she replied. "I'm Gertrude Stein."[168] They also shared a love for poodles, and Woollcott solicited a piece from Stein about her dog, Basket, for a collection he put together titled "The Brotherhood of the French Poodle."[169] Woollcott maintained a lively correspondence with Stein and visited her in France in 1936. He was such an important new acquaintance that Stein wrote to Thornton Wilder that Woollcott "sort of replaces Mildred Aldrich in our life a necessary thing to have in one's life." Aldrich had died in 1928.[170]

During the lecture tour, Woollcott expressed his admiration for Stein on the air; one newspaper agreed with his comment that she is a "very beautiful woman."[171] Delighted by her lack of pretension, Woollcott made a point of recalling a conversation he had with Stein in his "Shouts and Murmurs" column in the *New Yorker*. Defending his right to read Proust's *Remembrance of Things Past* in translation, Woollcott explained that Stein "reads even the more obscure novels of Dumas (to which she is unexpectedly addicted) in English." She had explained to him: "I prefer reading books in translation." Woollcott was so pleased with this response that he declared: "Bless the good and candid lady."[172] If the public was not aware that the two celebrities were friends, several years later the relationship was further publicized by George Kaufman and Moss Hart in *The Man Who Came to Dinner*, a wildly successful play about a character based on Woollcott. While stranded at a Midwestern home at Christmas, he gets a "trans-Atlantic" call from Gertrude Stein: "Hello, Gertie! How's my little nightingale? . . . How'd you know I was here? . . . I see. Well, it's wonderful of you to call . . . Yes. Yes, I'm listening." He explains to his surprised hosts: "Miss Stein calls me every Christmas, no matter where I am, so that I can hear [the bells of Notre Dame.] Two years ago I was walking on the bottom of the ocean in a diving suit with William Beebe, but she got me."[173] A film, with Bette Davis in a starring role, was released in 1942. This was not the only mention of Stein in a Moss Hart production; his 1935 musical, *Jubilee!*, also mentions Stein.[174]

In addition to scheduling book reviews or shows that might include book recommendations such as Woollcott's, radio stations also broadcast literary programs which highlighted poetry. As Milton Kaplan observes: "By 1930 many stations reported that their schedules included readings of excellent verse. WNYC, the New York City Municipal station, offered the work of Robinson Jeffers, T. S. Eliot, Walt Whitman, Emily Dickinson, Ezra Pound, Carl Sandburg, Vachel Lindsay, and many others."[175] The hosts of certain programs became celebrities; Ted Malone, who had his first show in Kansas City, became one of the most popular with programs including "Between the Bookends" and "Pilgrimage of Poetry," a show in which he broadcast from the homes of various poets including Amy Lowell, Emily Dickinson, Walt Whitman and Francis Scott Key. Readers could also buy a short book with facts about these writers and the poems Malone had read on the air.[176] Literary programs often issued related books or anthologies; David Ross began broadcasting poetry in 1926, and his anthology, *Poet's Gold*, included E. E. Cummings, Emily Dickinson, Robert Frost and Carl Sandburg.[177] These programs were so popular that some writers believed radio offered extraordinary possibilities for entertaining large audiences and wrote dramatic verse explicitly for this medium. Original scripts were produced by writers including Carl Sandburg, W. H. Auden, Edna St. Vincent Millay, Sherwood Anderson, Pearl S. Buck and Archibald MacLeish.

With radio listeners demonstrating such interest in literary subjects, Bennett Cerf's inspired suggestion that Stein participate in a radio interview was no surprise. Newspapers nationwide mentioned the upcoming broadcast, sometimes as a separate news item and in other papers highlighted at the top of the day's programs as "recommended." Harcourt, Brace had sent out a press release on November 1 about the interview to journalists and this release was often simply reproduced: "Those who are unable to get seats for Gertrude Stein's lectures will be glad to know that she is going to broadcast on the evening of November 12 over WJZ and the Blue Network. William Lundell will interview her." The interview was highlighted with other special programs of interest on the page with the day's radio schedule in most newspapers, and W. G. Rogers's Springfield newspaper included a photograph of Stein headlined "On Air Is On Air Is On Air" with the caption "Gertrude Stein: the mighty matron of modern art and literature will be interviewed by William Lundell over an NBC network, including Springfield's WBZA, tomorrow night at 8:30." The *New Yorker*'s "On the Air" listing commented: "You'd better listen in."[178] A more detailed advertisement for the program appeared in the New York *World Telegram*, which reported Lundell's reaction to a preliminary meeting with Stein: "After making arrangements for the radio appearance Mr. Lundell returned with the verdict:— 'She's not so crazy. She's smart.' The interview, he says, will settle it."[179]

The scripted interview included many of Stein's impressions of America and Americans that were then repeated in an article for *Cosmopolitan* in February 1935, "I Came and Here I Am," and again in *Everybody's Autobiography*. Thrilled to find herself a celebrity, Stein emphasized how frequently she was approached by strangers:

> Why even at the football game a little boy came up to me and bowed and said please Miss Stein may I have an autograph. I said how old are you and he said twelve and we were both pleased, then everybody handed me their programs and it was perfectly charming, simply charming. Why when I first arrived off the boat the first evening I took a walk and I wanted an apple and I went into a little fruit store on Sixth Avenue to buy it, and the clerk said how do you do Miss Stein did you have a pleasant trip over.

Having established both her legitimate fame and her gracious response to it, Stein attempted to distance herself from any association with intellectual elites. After she discussed her favorite "most vigorous" American expression— "and how"— Lundell suggested that Stein's "study in these slang phrases, it would seem to me, must be rather limited. In your literary circles you don't meet much new and vigorous slang." She countered: "O, don't I. How do you know I do not. And what makes you think I only talk to literary circles. I talk to and listen to anybody."

As much as Stein attempted to show her democratic and open-minded understanding of Americans, her discussion of punctuation and, most important, her reaction to the Yale-Dartmouth football game that she and Alice attended with Alfred Harcourt might have suggested that her perspective was not so ordinary after all. She explained to Lundell that: "The thing that interested me was that the Modern American in his movements and his actions in a football game so resembled the red Indian dance and it proves that the physical country that made the one made the other and that the red Indian is still with us. They just put their heads down solemnly together and then double over, while on the side lines the substitutes move in a jiggly way just like Indians." Lundell observed: "But those jiggles are warming up exercises." Stein found this comment irrelevant: "It doesn't make any difference what they are doing it for, they are just doing it, like the way the Indian jiggles in the Indian dance and then there is that little brown ball they all bend down and worship."[180]

Harcourt, Brace had sent out a press release about Stein's invitation to the Yale-Dartmouth game, and newspapers had dutifully reported the event; the *Herald Tribune* explained that "Miss Stein and Miss Toklas will cheer for Dartmouth."[181] After the game, the *New York Times* considered what Stein's reaction might be:

> Last Saturday, by way of a break in her program, [Stein] and Miss Toklas went with Alfred Harcourt to see the Yale-Dartmouth game. I wonder what she made of it? When Tommy Curtin had two kicks blocked on two successive plays, she must have felt at home in a continuing present very like her prose. And when Roscoe flipped his shovel pass to Stratford Morton for the tenth time, and the tenth gain, it must have seemed like home. There may be something to this repetition of effects.[182]

This reporter could not know that Stein's amusing analysis would be broadcast to the nation later that week.

Her unexpected interpretation of American football was only one aspect of the interview that listeners found amusing. Stein's final remark was especially popular for columnists to quote. She asserted: "But after all you must enjoy my writing and if you enjoy it you understand it. If you did not enjoy it why do you make a fuss about it? There is the real answer." Theodore Hall found Stein's humor so winning that his headline in the *Washington Post* declared: "Gertrude Stein Has Mark Twain Backed Off the Map." It was not only her closing remark that tickled this listener; he especially liked her response to Lundell's query about how books should be judged. "The function of a book reviewer is to review books and they do," she replied. Hall reported that "One of her audience, at least, nearly rolled out of his chair at that." Perfectly willing to reassess his impression of Stein, he told readers that: "Miss Gertrude Stein, I now see, is one of our prime humorists."[183]

Although Harry Hansen thought the interview was funny, he failed to understand that Stein intentionally scripted the interview to entertain. In his syndicated column, he wrote that the exchange was "a gorgeous piece of unconscious humor."[184] Robert Strunsky was also disappointed. He complained in the *New York Sun* that: "Few people are better off now than before, and many people are worse off."[185] Certainly, the interview was calculated to amuse and charm audiences rather than educate them. The stodgy *New York Times* responded with a wry editorial, also expressing frustration. They found Stein's strong opinion that "question and quotation marks are uninteresting" and that commas are "positively degrading,'" was inconsistent, and wanted to know why apostrophes and periods escaped her critique.[186] The *Birmingham News* extensively quoted from the interview, highlighting many of Stein's most amusing remarks.[187]

The most creative response to the interview appeared in the *New Yorker*. Irma Brandeis's lengthy anecdote describes a visit to her apartment by a radio repairman, just in time for the highly anticipated Stein interview. "I'm rather anxious to hear a program that begins in ten minutes," she explains to him. Much to her surprise, after successfully completing his task the man sits and stays for the interview, smiling and nodding at all of the appropriate moments. The classist description of this common man, whose suit "gleamed brightly at the shoulder-blades, the jacket hem, and the seat of the trousers," and his appreciative response to Stein is only one of many examples of her real, coveted connection with ordinary Americans. As Brandeis points out: "Miss Stein was unassuming and yet authoritative, and at the same time conclusively American; and the young man, unaware of any oddness in his staying without being invited, and yet so nicely unaware, was unanswerably American too."[188]

One consequence of the association between Stein and radio was an advertisement later that month in the *Chicago Tribune* for RCA radios that asserted, after this apology: "(with a bow to Gertrude Stein)" that "an RCA Victor ... is an RCA Victor ... is an RCA Victor."[189] Another unexpected result was an introduction to William Saroyan, who heard the radio broadcast and immediately sent a telegram followed by a letter to Stein from California. "I cannot tell you what a fine thing it was to hear you talking so naturally and easily and sensibly over the radio," he wrote to her. "Some critics say I have to be careful and not notice the writing of Gertrude Stein but I think they are fooling themselves when they pretend any American writing that is American and is writing is not partly the consequence of the writing of Gertrude Stein."[190] Saroyan's new collection of stories, *The Daring Man on the Flying Trapeze*, had just received positive notice in the *New Yorker* with the exception of one remark, surely thanks to Clifton Fadiman: "When Mr. Saroyan goes Gertrude Stein or Sherwood Anderson, he is not so good; but speaking in his proper voice, he makes you sit up. The title story is a dazzler, and so are half-dozen others."[191]

Stein herself seemed to regard exposure on the radio to be evidence of certain celebrity. In the *Autobiography*, her former cook, Hélène, observes "isn't it extraordinary, all those people whom I knew when they were nobody are now always mentioned in the newspapers, and the other night over the radio they mentioned the name of Monsieur Picasso."[192] The massive publicity surrounding Stein during her first weeks in the United Sates including the announcement in lights circling Times Square that "Gertrude Stein has arrived in New York," the numerous reports in newspapers and periodicals, the radio interview, and the Pathé newsreel increased her fame so that she was constantly recognized by Americans wherever she went. Looking back on the tour, Stein recalls that

> I used to say that was long ago in between I never had thought of going, I used to say that I would not go to America until I was a real lion a real celebrity at that time of course I did not really think I was going to be one. But now we were coming and I was going to be one. In America everybody is but some are more than others. I was more than others.[193]

This measured response contrasts with the breathless excitement Stein felt when she first realized how famous she had become. In a letter to Rogers, who had returned to Massachusetts after her meeting her in New York, she wrote: "It is unbelievable, you know I did a news reel for the Pathe people [sic] . . . and everybody knows us on the street, and they are all so sweet and kind it is unimaginable and you go into a store anywhere to buy anything and they say how do you do Miss Stein and Alice goes anywhere they say how do you do Miss Toklas and they so pleasantly speak to us on the street, its unbelievable. . . . I too thought I might be news but not like that."[194] When Rogers accompanied Stein and Toklas on part of her tour in New England, he found that in was not only New Yorkers who knew her. He recalls that:

> When we entered public dining rooms, in Pittsfield, Northampton, Providence, some one would recognize her, introduce himself or send a note by a waiter asking for her autograph. . . . Even taxi drivers knew her. One of them led me into a corner, asked if she was the famous Stein, said he missed Four Saints in Hartford and guessed he'd "wait till it gets in the movies, because the movies make them easier."[195]

Rogers liked the anecdote about the taxi driver so much that he printed it in the *Springfield Union*.[196]

The overwhelming American response to Stein delighted her friends. Her tour was not just a success. It was, as the *Iowa City Press Citizen* had predicted, a "literary sensation." Bernard Fäy was so pleased and impressed with Stein's effect on audiences that he wrote to her:

> I feel that what is going on now in America—what this trip of yours is doing is tremendously important in the mental life of America. What you bring them, nobody had brought them since Walt Whitman. . . . And they know it, they feel it. You know I have watched them very closely since 1919—and seen them get excited over all kinds of things: the new Ford cars, Mr. Hoover, Al Smith, air-travel, the Queen of Rumania, speak-easies, etc.; but I have never seen them act as they do now with you.—It is something deeper and more personal. What your work and yourself stir up in them had not been stirred up for decades.[197]

Even more noteworthy evidence of Stein's genuine success came from the White House. Since she could not attend Stein's lecture in Washington D. C., Eleanor Roosevelt invited Stein and Toklas to tea. On December 30 they joined her on a busy afternoon. Stein explained in an interview: "My visit to the White House was very funny. Everything was confused. They were preparing the message to Congress, so naturally everything was confused."[198] Despite the disorder she and Toklas witnessed, Stein certainly recognized the honor attached to the meeting.

Stein on Tour: "The Boop-a-Doop Girl of Modern Literature"[199]

Although reports of Stein's lectures often used parodic, repetitious headlines, the articles themselves offered much greater and more respectful insights into her ideas and, most importantly, personality. The silly headlines were so prevalent that they irritated several communists, including two of the most famous, Robert Benchley and Heywood Broun. Benchley explained that "the running gag which has got me down this season is the burlesque of Gertrude Stein." He went on to say: "All of the news-writers and headline-writers who handled the story of her arrival felt that it would be comical to burlesque the Stein style in their treatment . . . as I read nine newspapers in New York every day, I had had almost enough Gertrude Stein parodies the very first day."[200] Heywood Broun was similarly motivated to defend Stein. He observed that "journalistic commentators are fond of parodying the style of the visiting author. The trick, they seem to feel, is nothing more than a repetition of some key word. . . . I doubt that the cadences which Miss Stein seeks are quite as simple as all that. . . . After all, I am aware of the fact that Sherwood Anderson has acknowledged his debt to the school of Gertrude Stein."[201] An advertisement from Bergdorf Goodman further exploited the popular stereotype of Stein's work (figure 5).[202]

Not all advertisements resorted to easy puns. Stein also appeared on the cover of a brochure advertising Ford automobiles: "Gertrude Stein and Her Fords" was printed next to a drawing of Stein, who was standing next to a car with Alice sitting inside.[203] For Stein to appear on the anti-Semitic Henry

Figure 5 Bergdorf Goodman advertisement.

Ford's advertisement is particularly striking. Ford's *Dearborn Independent* had printed the notorious anti-Semitic document *Protocols of the Elders of Zion* and numerous articles about the threat of "International Jews" in the 1920s.[204] But Stein's anecdotes in the *Autobiography* about driving a Ford during the war made her a patriotic, all-American spokesperson. Indeed, reporters emphasized her striking "Americanism" throughout the tour.

Even if lazy headline writers resorted to repetitious puns, the descriptions of Stein's lectures presented a mush more sensitive and appealing picture of the writer. As Stein observed in an interview in Michigan with Olivet College's school newspaper:

> The headlines still say the same thing, because as a general rule, that is all that people read, and people can glance at them and maintain an unshattered calm. The stories underneath are beginning to change, however, and sometime, when the public has been eased into it, the headlines also will change.[205]

T. S. Matthews's representation in the *New Republic* is characteristic:

> The first glimpse you get of her, as she trudges resolutely up on the lecture platform, is reassuring. . . . Her short-cropped hair doesn't look queer, it looks as right as a cap on a grandmother. . . . Foreign parts of speech have not affected her at all: she talks in as flatly sensible an American tone as any Middle Western aunt. We also notice with approval that she indulges in no gestures—except the natural, grandmotherly one of taking her pince-nez off and putting them on. . . . As she looks out over the audience and thanks us, with a quick low hoot of laughter, for "controlling yourselves to 500," we laugh too, in appreciative relief, and settle back in our seats to give her the once-over.[206]

The *Washington Post* was similarly enthusiastic about Stein's good humor and winning personality. Like Matthews, Ralph Renaud quotes Stein's candid remarks as evidence of her genuine and, most important, her anti-intellectual demeanor:

> Gertrude Stein . . . is undoubtedly the most popular and accepted visitor New York has had this winter. . . . She is certainly an attractive old lady . . . [with] a grand, infectious laugh and a well-developed sense of humor. When some one asks her, "Did you write the autobiography of Alice B. Toklas as a literary concession?" and she answers, "I never concede. I wrote it to make a heck of a lot of money," the effect is irresistible.[207]

In Pittsfield, Massachusetts, another reporter emphasized Stein's captivating effect on her audience: "Gertrude Stein made a great many new friends last night. . . . There are two human characteristics which are irresistible, kindliness and sincerity. And Miss Stein has both. They are written all over her deep-lined, virile face, and they are mirrored in her smile and in her hearty, infectious laugh." Like other reporters throughout the tour, this writer included an extensive report of the question and answer session after Stein's scripted talk as evidence of her humor. When asked what Stein thought of artist Thomas [Hart] Benton, she answered that she'd never heard of him, but that "The chances are he's not great."[208] Benton was one of the most well-known and celebrated American artists at the time, and had just appeared on the cover of *Time* magazine on 24 December 1934.

As soon as Stein began to lecture, this kind of report dominated the press and presented the American public with an entirely new understanding of her personality. It was not only her likeability that was so consistently emphasized; Stein emerged as a distinctly anti-intellectual, down-to-earth woman who was, like the majority of American journalists and their readers, unimpressed by artifice and highbrow posturing. Even at book signings Stein charmed reporters. The *New Yorker* reported that during a signing at Brentano's,

> one confused man somehow found himself standing in front of Miss Stein without a book, so he shouted at a clerk, "Three Saints!" "Three Saints!" he said. "Give me a Three Saints!" The right title is "Four Saints," a clerk corrected the gentleman coldly. Miss Stein just laughed. She doesn't get peeved about things like that. . . . People who hear her always like her as a person. After her lectures she will answer any questions—if they are sensible.[209]

Joseph Alsop was quickly converted to distinct admiration after attending Stein's first lecture at New York's Colony Club. He observed on the first page of the *Herald Tribune* that: "It was a curious thing that even though many in the audience had certainly come to stare, there was a definite quality of affection in their applause. They liked Miss Stein at first sight whether they liked what she said or not."[210] The New York's *Evening Journal* also found that "Miss Stein captured her audience by her frankness, humor and total lack of artificiality . . . she talked to everyone just as if they were intimate friends."[211] Or, as the *Art Digest* reported that month: "Whether it was her good natured ruddy face, her hearty and spontaneous laugh or her scintillating observations, the audience immediately liked and applauded her."[212]

The usually cautious *Saturday Review of Literature* even printed one of Stein's complete lectures, "Plays and Landscapes," on the front page of the November 10 issue, which includes Stein's description of *Four Saints in Three Acts* as a "play" which "really is a landscape." The audience for this perplexing lecture was thus immediately increased to well over the usual 500. One reader, the extraordinarily named Gussie Cholmondely-Tinklepaugh, wrote a heartily amused letter to the editor: "You have done the world a service in printing the article by Gertrude Stein, 'Plays and Landscapes.' When I was younger, I used to play question games, and one of the queries which we could never answer was 'When is a saint not a saint?' Now Miss Stein (*laus deo!*) has given us an inkling of the answer."[213]

In December, the *Saturday Review* followed up this ambivalent reader's response by printing a letter to Amy Loveman, who regularly addressed inquiries of readers, from "Mrs. T. W. J. of Minneapolis, Minn.," who "wants to know where to get material on Gertrude Stein, that is, where to get discussion of her work and artistic ideals." Loveman helpfully suggests Edmund Wilson's *Axel's Castle*, Stuart P. Sherman's amusing "A Note on Gertrude Stein" in *Points of View*, and Paul Rosenfeld's *By Way of Art*.[214] Even if Loveman's own assessment of Stein is somewhat tempered, her response suggests that the reader's query is easily answered by numerous influential critics.

The *New York Times*, the one New York paper that consistently downplayed Stein's importance, conceded that "According to some members of the audience, Miss Stein's straightforwardness and amiability largely disarmed those who had come to find fault. At the outset of her lecture she laughingly tested the carrying power of her voice, asking if she could be heard in the rear of the room."[215] This may have surprised readers, appearing after the misleading headline: "Miss Stein Speaks to Bewildered 500." Unwilling to believe the evidence reported in its own pages, the *Times* suggested that Stein's popularity was only the result of a savvy "publicity man" in a parodic editorial the following day, but this sarcastic response only proved their own provinciality.[216]

One other dissenting voice was Isabel Paterson, who admitted to Stein's charm but refused to re-evaluate her literary importance. Paterson attended the Random House celebration for her, as did numerous personalities who happened to be in New York at the time, including George Gershwin, Mary Pickford and Lewis Gannett. Although Paterson thought "Bennett Cerf's party for Gertrude Stein and Alice B. Toklas was a great success," she complained that "her only readable writing is the 'Autobiography of Alice B. Toklas,' and the rest is very tiresome nonsense." Nevertheless, "we could see why everybody likes Miss Stein herself; she's likable . . . She doesn't talk as she writes . . . We can't understand why people are impressed by nonsense."[217] Surely Paterson's belief that Stein's work should be evaluated on its own, rather than as an extension of her character, is valid. But the public sentiment was so strongly in support of Stein that Paterson was compelled to reiterate her impatience with the charming Gertrude Stein the following week:

> Most people want to know: "is Gertrude Stein genuine? Does she herself believe in that gibberish she writes?" . . . And we say, sure she believes in it; they say, then it must mean something. . . . When we reply to this, that the rubbish is rubbish nevertheless, they say: "But she is a very pleasant woman, you can't help liking her." . . . Certainly . . . We don't mind Miss Stein publicizing herself; it's a good show, and she has a good time, and why not?[218]

Stein and Toklas made a special, brief visit to Chicago to see a production of *Four Saints in Three Acts* on November 7 before returning later that month for an extended visit. Reporters and photographers greeted their arrival by plane and, as in New York, Stein gave refreshing replies to the many questions directed at her. The *Chicago News* reported that when asked "Now Miss Stein, can you tell us just when buttons are tender?" she happily answered: "I don't know, you will have to ask the buttons." This satisfying exchange was followed by a skeptical query from another journalist, but:

> She would not admit that, as one put it to her bluntly, she is "pulling the public's leg." Rather she said, "I don't know anything about the public's leg and I'm too old to pull a leg if I wanted to." Gracious, abounding in kindliness, sly humor and lots and lots of laughter, she gave of herself in ready repartee.[219]

The *Tribune* had printed a picture of Stein, Toklas and Basket (Stein's poodle) on November 3 titled "The Toklas Family Complete" in anticipation of this visit.[220] A glowing review of the opera was then printed in the *Tribune*: "'This is how they do not like it,' sang a dusky belle in red sequins in the prolog of 'Four Saints in Three Acts' last night; but she was wrong, for they did like it!" Stein's cryptic reaction to seeing the opera live for the first time was the highlight of the report: "I am completely satisfied with it. Before it was inside me and now it is outside me."[221]

Just as Joseph Alsop proved to be Stein's important ally and promoter in New York, Fanny Butcher, who was already her friend and admirer, informed Chicagoans of Stein's lectures, book signings and other activities in late November and early December. Butcher predicted that "Stein Lectures May Clear Up Thick Writing" and, when she finally appeared at the Arts Club of Chicago, reported that the "exclusive and intellectual" audience was rewarded: "To their prolonged and vociferous applause, [Stein] replied smilingly, 'is that what you wanted?'"[222] Stein's lectures were such a sensation in Chicago that other touring writers found difficulty attracting the public's notice. June Provines reported in her column for the *Tribune*, "Front Views and Profiles," George Murray's complaint that Robert Hillyer, who had won the Pulitzer Prize in poetry that year, could not compete with Stein. "Gertrude Stein comes out here preaching the gospel of obscurity and is a riot. And here's Hillyer, writing beautiful, limpid, lucid prose, coming to read his poetry, and I can't make anybody care. . . .You can't get near Stein, but I've got plenty of tickets for Hillyer."[223]

Only the occasional audience failed to elicit Stein's usual good-natured responses to questions after her lectures. Two newspapers in Philadelphia agreed that Stein was impatient with her questioners; the *Philadelphia Record* reported that she "spent just ten minutes squelching the befuddled questions of her audience" while the *Philadelphia Inquirer* thought one member of the audience "was treated by Miss Stein like a none too intelligent school boy. While her questioner fumbled in confusion she upbraided him for using words which, she said, he didn't know the meaning of himself, among others, 'meticulous' and 'cosmic.'" But, lest readers might come away with the impression that Stein had alienated her listeners with these remarks, the *Inquirer* explained that "then, R. Sturgis Ingersoll, well-known Philadelphia attorney and art connoisseur, informed Miss Stein that 'I hope you come back often, because you are a damn good thing for Philadelphia.' That remark was wildly applauded and evoked loud laughter and cheers." Even the *Record* admitted that "it was a great show."[224]

Stein's question and answer sessions were soon known to be the highlight of each performance and when she was unable to accommodate questions after her Providence lecture, the newspapers not only expressed regret at this omission, but clearly inspired by her radio interview and other reports, imagined what Stein might have said. "If she had been able to talk," the reporter speculated, "she probably would have marveled, as she has elsewhere, about how American automobiles and traffic lights understand each other so well, how football players look to her like Indians doing tribal dances, and how she was astonished, on her first airplane ride, to discover that the air 'is solid.'"[225]

Stein's humor was also emphasized by one reporter who saw her speak at Radcliffe. Her claim that she never used repetition elicited the most laughs from the audience; according to Stein, it was the tedious newspaper columnists who were guilty of this sin, reusing "the same old theme . . . over and over again in their clever stories about me." Completely won over by Stein's attitude and good humor, this reporter admitted that "Simply because Miss Stein does not try to carry it off in such a high-handed way, you begin to think that there may be something in her work after all."[226] Similarly impressed by Stein's accessibility, the headline in the *Toledo Blade*, "Gertrude Stein Just Folksy, Reporter Finds," represents not only that city's reaction to Stein, but her reception throughout the Midwest. Stein's candid remarks were the highlight of the stories about her in every city. At the University of Wisconsin, a student paper reported that when she got off of the train she immediately said: "What university is this?" The student went on to report that: "A few minutes later when it developed that the students had met two other trains, not knowing on which she was to arrive, she said it never occurred to her that there was more than ONE train to Madison or she would have let them know."[227] This article also reported that Stein conceded to one private meeting with an admirer: Frank Lloyd Wright.

She emphasized throughout the tour that she did not like to associate with intellectuals or "high-brows," and specifically worked to counter the impression that, since she considered herself a genius, she could not relate to everyday people. In Cleveland she addressed this issue directly: "I'm a person of great common sense," she said. "You must use common sense. Most people have it, but if they are intellectual they are afraid to use it. I suppose a good definition of a genius would be a person who uses his common sense."[228] A front-page story in the *Daily Oklahoman* explained

Stein's desire to be understood by mainstream America: "Her speech, her accent is like that of your next door neighbor. She prides herself on being the most ordinary American, though she is the most extraordinary woman of letters."[229]

Stein's laughter and the "mischievous twinkle in her eye" was reported in Columbus; in Toledo the report that Stein was "just folksy" described her as "cheerful-mannered, good-humored, wholesome-appearing, her gray hair clipped mannishly short, her dark, discreetly-figured dress belonging to no definite era of fashion."[230] The suggestion by some recent critics that Stein's androgynous appearance was intimidating to audiences is not supported by any reports I have found.[231] Although many newspapers described Stein's haircut as "masculine," the overall impression she gave was comforting rather than threatening; indeed, Stein was consistently domesticated by the mainstream press. Certainly the romantic nature of Stein's relationship with Toklas was invisible to American audiences. Stein was confident enough that their secret was safe that in her "Poetry and Grammar" lecture she read one of her love poems to Alice, "Bundles for Them," which had appeared in the *Little Review*. Furthermore, although photographs and drawings tended to make Stein look unusually large, she was, as Linda Wagner-Martin observes, "surprisingly small in stature."[232] At about five feet tall, many reporters were reassured by her unthreatening physical presence.

The only negative press Stein received was unrelated to her appearance or sexual identity. When Stein and Toklas toured in California in the spring of 1935, reporters failed to warm to Stein, but this negative response seems to be a direct consequence of her folksy persona and pointed rejection of the high-brow elites she was expected to embrace. Mabel Dodge Luhan telephoned Stein and expressed her wish to introduce her to Robinson Jeffers, but Alice, who answered the call, declined the invitation to meet either Luhan or Jeffers. Alice recalls that Luhan said, "Hello, when am I going to see Gertrude? And I answered, I don't think you are going to. What? Said she. No, said I, she's going to rest. Robinson Jeffers wants to meet her, she said. Well, I said, he will have to do without."[233]

Stein and Toklas had not heard from Luhan in recent years, possibly because, as Luhan believed, Toklas was uncomfortable with the past friendship of the two women. Whatever the reason for the rejection, newspapers soon reported Stein's shocking refusal to meet Jeffers, a highly regarded poet at the time. "A Snub, a Snub, a Snub: Gertrude Stein Gives Carmel's Highbrows the Go-By," the *San Francisco Examiner* declared.[234] Explaining her decision to decline Luhan's invitation to meet her at an artist's colony, Stein explained to a reporter that "I like ordinary people who don't bore me. Highbrows do, you know, always do."[235]

Although it might seem that in California, and glitzy Hollywood in particular, Stein's social choices should not affect her reception, in fact it was in this community most anxious about designations of status and class in which Stein's fluid understanding of high- and low-brow culture offended her audiences. Her anti-intellectual pose, so refreshing in New York, New England, or the Mid-West, was used by Californians as evidence that she was not capable of making important and obvious distinctions between writers, artists and culture. Much to this self-conscious community's surprise, Stein was particularly interested in meeting Harry Leon Wilson, a popular novelist whose *Merton of the Movies* was a bestseller in 1922 and was, according to Stein, "the best book about twentieth-century American youth that has yet been done. I always give it to every one to read who reads English and always have done ever since I first read it." Dashiell Hammett also attended a party in honor of Stein at her request; like Wilson, Hammett was considered by Stein to be singularly American and modern in his depictions of contemporary life. Another guest at this dinner, Charlie Chaplin, proved to be a kindred spirit who, like Stein, attracted the notice of a varied audience of mainstream and intellectual Americans, including Edmund Wilson.

Although California newspapers did comment on Stein's everyday accent and abundant laughter, these reports seemed to find her speech and manner more evidence of her failure to understand the valued high-brow, intellectual world. Alma Witaker seemed critical of Stein's answer to a question in Pasadena "How come you lived thirty years abroad—to acquire the American tempo?" According to Witaker, Stein answered: "I'm 'Amurrican.'"[236] The report in the *Los Angeles Sunday Magazine* by her old acquaintance David Edstrom similarly failed to take any aspect of Stein's personality or influence seriously and presented her as a curiosity. Edstrom first related a telephone conversation he had with Stein:

> Gertrude Stein, the literary enigma of an age, answered my telephone call immediately and after we had opened our first conversation in twenty years with the customary incoherent gasps of excitement, she called out:
>
> "David! David! Are you fat?" . . . She sounded it all in the same breath so that it had the poetic plow of rhythm; and she most certainly would never have punctuated it as I did when I wrote it here. . . . Then Gertrude's voice came over the telephone again: "David, I am driving one of those 'drive-yourself cars." She chortled, "What a name, 'drive-yourself! Where do you live when can I see you?"[237]

Indeed, the California press consistently treated Stein's visit as gossip rather than serious news, and no reporter seemed to be impressed by Stein's lectures. In San Francisco Stein's lectures were ridiculed by the press. The *San Francisco News* reported that "Baffled Literati Hears Gertrude Stein," explaining that the audience, "amazed at the outset by her strange composition, snickered, then sat back in their seats with an air that it was to be an evening of fun." Even more critical, Annie Laurie wrote that "Now Miss

Stein is not only so-called and she really is a celebrity, but Thursday night she just talked the most absolute rubbish on earth."[238]

This negative reaction may also have been influenced by a new dimension of Stein's tour. Just before Stein reached California, "I Came and Here I Am" appeared in *Cosmopolitan,* an article that recounted her arrival in the United States, and when Stein was in California, her series of weekly articles that discussed various impressions of the United States were appearing in the *New York Herald Tribune* (these were later incorporated into *Everybody's Autobiography*). The first, "American Newspapers," appeared on March 3 and was followed by "The Capital and Capitals of the United States of America" (March 9), "American Education and Colleges" (March 16), "American Newspapers (continued)" (March 23), "American Crimes and How They Matter" (March 30), "American States and Cities and How They Differ from each Other" (April 6) and "American Food and American Houses" (April 13). These humorous but obscure reflections were not only known to *Tribune* readers, of course; Van Vechten reported to Stein that they were "syndicated no end. Reports roll in from coast to coast."[239] The hostile reaction to Stein may have been a response to these unconventional anecdotes and observations which were certainly written for a mainstream, rather than elite, readership. Furthermore, her hosts may have been acutely aware, as her earlier audiences were not, that they themselves might be the subject of her next piece. Whatever the precise reason for the unenthusiastic press she received, Stein's relentless failure to respect the boundaries of high- and low- culture that California's artistic community apparently revered seems to have been a significant factor.

In this decade, distinctions between high- and low- culture were certainly acknowledged by American critics throughout the country, but not all arbiters of taste assumed that low culture was toxic. *Vanity Fair* emphasized in 1933 that "The low-brow is worthy of attention—Walter Winchell, Minsky Brothers burlesque, comic strips, dance marathons—though no longer as fresh as when discovered by Gilbert Seldes."[240] Following this view, in her report of the lecture tour in *Everybody's Autobiography*, Stein recalled her impressions of a dance marathon in Chicago and she delighted in other unexpected artifacts of American culture. Rogers reports that during the tour:

> On an auto trip to Providence, Rhode Island, we sang songs to while away the time. Among them was Gertrude Stein's favorite, "On the Trail of the Lonesome Pine." We sang the wartime "Madelon" and "Sur le Pont d'Avignon." Mrs. Kiddie contributed a popular radio ditty which advertised a bakery product: "Yo ho yo ho yo ho yo ho for we are the makers of Wonder Bread." That song got into subsequent Stein prose, too.[241]

Despite Stein's frequent assurances that she was interested in mainstream culture rather than high-brow art and literature, evidence of this truth was still surprising to some journalists. A short article in the *New York World Telegram* reported an anecdote from A. A. Van Duym, who had fulfilled Stein's literary requests worked at the American Library in Paris in 1922.

> Strangest of all and a mystery to be solved by Stein devotees, she always reserved ahead of time the forthcoming novels of Harold Bell Wright, James Oliver Curwood, Rex Beach. Whether this was to get close to the real 'soul' of the American people or merely to get books intended for the consumption of Alice or some other member of her household I cannot tell.[242]

This "mystery," of course, is not a mystery at all. Stein did enjoy these popular writers, just as she read Dashiell Hammett and Harry Leon Wilson. During World War II, Stein struggled to convince Thornton Wilder that she really did want for him to send her popular mysteries to read. She wrote to him in 1941:

> And now Thornton about my literature not that that I write but that I read. Could you instead of sending me books well thought of by historians could you go to a railway station or to the nearest drug store and send me every few weeks or once a month four or five of the mystery stories that the man in charge recommends as the best, everybody when they send me reading matter consult not my tastes but my education, I suppose even when I give you the detail of the method of pleasing me you won't because after all to a good American principles are more important than pleasure.[243]

Indeed, Stein's belief in the pursuit of "pleasure" significantly contributed to her enthusiastic American reception. She emphasized the delight she took in becoming reacquainted with the United States to the *New York Times* before leaving the country in May of 1935: "I am already homesick for America. I never knew it was so beautiful. I was like a bachelor who goes along fine for twenty-five years and then decides to get married. That is the way I feel—I mean about America." Even Charles Hanson Towne, a celebrity editor, journalist and poet who had written for the *Smart Set*, *McClure's*, and *Harper's Bazaar*, wrote in his popular, conservative column for the hugely popular New York *American*, "Allow Me to Say," that her charm was irresistible, even to the most skeptical:

> I confess that I had loathed with a deep loathing everything the lady had written—except one book. . . . Her esoteric statements annoyed—even angered me. . . . Then a friend asked me to dine with her. Out of a curiosity that could no longer be controlled I went. And instantly, as if by some magic I have no means of telling about, a spark burst forth, and the small room where we sat was filled with

wonder. . . . Personality! How it gushed forth! How it surrounded us, how it floated all about us![244]

Dissent: The fault I'm sure is solely mine/ But I cannot root for Gertrude Stein

Stein's unquestionable status as a literary celebrity was not appreciated by all Americans. The enormous attention given to the tour by the press annoyed Ogden Nash, who refused to be convinced by Charles Towne's tribute and penned a response that was printed in the next month's *American*: "The fault I'm sure is solely mine,/ But I cannot root for Gertrude Stein. . ." he explained.[245]

Since lecture tours were known to create publicity hype for certain writers, it was not only Ogden Nash who wondered about the value of this sensational attitude towards visiting writers. Reflecting on the lectures of T. S. Eliot in 1933 and Stein in the fall of 1934, Arthur Tourtellot observed in the *Boston Transcript* that "it is probable, almost certain, that these visits are occasions less for the encouraging of literary criticism about the visitors' work than for the circulation of literary gossip about their personalities."[246] Even so, the corresponding publicity increased the public's interest not only in the lives but also the work of these writers. Random House published Stein's abstract *Portraits and Prayers* during the tour in November of 1934 and it appeared on the *New York Times* bestseller list on 26 November although the book was greeted with almost universal scoffing from critics and reviewers.

The *New York Times* declared baldly: "On one point it seems impossible to waver. There is nothing in this book to merit more than five minutes' attention of a reasonably honest and intelligent mind." Joseph Alsop, who became such an admirer of Stein's lectures, wrote in the *Herald Tribune* that: "This seems to be an excellent place for me to confess quite frankly that I found hardly a comprehensible paragraph in all of 'Portraits and Prayers.' And so the book gave me less than no pleasure." Henry Seidel Canby even pronounced the book unreadable; or, at least, he could not read it: "I have never before reviewed a book I have not read. I have always tried to read Gertrude Stein since her earliest publications and I have always failed. I have tried in this book, though not so hard as before, because I anticipated failure."[247] In St. Louis, Reed Hynds explained in a headline that "Gertrude Stein . . . Provides a Further Study of the Art of Unintelligibility," while John Woodbun's headline in the *San Francisco Chronicle* also gave away the thesis of his review: "Aloft With Miss Stein in Verbal Fog."[248]

This nationwide condemnation did not seem to deter the public's interest in the book. In the *New York Post*, Hershel Brickell noted with astonishment that "'Portraits and Prayers' . . . is selling so fast Random House, the publishers, are having a hard time keeping it in stock." To account for this,

Brickell suggests that Americans had been brainwashed by the publicity surrounding Stein's tour. "Obviously, the fuss that is being made over her is without any conceivable relation to her importance or to the merit of her work; we just needed a spell of ballyhoo and she happened along at the proper moment."[249] Similarly, John Chamberlain argued in the *New York Times* that Stein could be defined as a spectacle more than as a legitimate writer with literary significance. He snidely asked readers:

> Have you ever watched a crowd staring into an excavation? Have you ever dropped in on a dance marathon as it staggers into the fifteenth day? Have you ever seen a group of people looking up at Shipwreck Kelly as he sits motionless in a chair that is balanced on the top of a flagpole? Have you ever listened to some one as he or she tried to explain Yoga? If you can elucidate what these people get out of their goggling, gaping and gazing, then you may be able to explain why Americans flock to hear Gertrude Stein.[250]

Perhaps most disgusted with Stein's warm reception was Clifton Fadiman, who titled his scathing review of *Portraits and Prayers* "I am not amusing." In his opinion, "the interesting thing about *l'affaire Stein* is the way in which the newspaper boys, who followed their finer instincts some years ago when they made loud noises at Gertrude, are now discovering there is something to it after all."[251] In the following issue the *New Yorker* listed *Portraits in Prayers* under their general recommendations, describing the book with some sarcasm: "Various mumblings, in the Simon-pure, pre-Toklas manner, about Miss Stein's artist and writer friends. Tastefully bound, for the most part, in a large photograph of the author."[252] Despite his enthusiasm for the *Autobiography*, Edmund Wilson concurred with Fadiman's judgment of *Portraits and Prayers*, reporting with disappointment in the *New Republic* that: "there is nothing new to say about Miss Stein. She is a first-rate literary talent to whom something very strange and probably unfortunate has happened—perhaps it is the basic emptiness of the life of the artistic foreigner in Paris."[253]

Stein's contribution to the first issue of *Story* magazine that month also perplexed some reviewers; the *Little Rock Gazette*, for example, explained that some of the stories printed there "are entirely understandable while others (we recall one by Gertrude Stein) are crammed with such a lot of art, as it is termed, that they go completely over our proletarian heads."[254] The following month, *America and Alfred Stieglitz*, an anthology edited by Waldo Frank, Lewis Mumford, Dorothy Norman, Paul Rosenfeld and Harold Rugg, appeared and Stein's piece, "Stieglitz," elicited many impatient comments from reviewers.[255] Clifton Fadiman, for example, simply noted that: "one regrets it cannot be excised."[256] The Literary Guild chose the book as its December selection, creating an enormous readership for the anthology.

A much more highly publicized reaction against Stein came in February of 1935, when many of Stein's Parisian friends who had been described in the *Autobiography* at Rousseau's banquet and in other anecdotes decided to retaliate. Offended writers and artists including Henri Matisse, Eugene and Maria Jolas, André Salmon, Georges Braque, and Tristan Tzara published "Testimony Against Gertrude Stein" as a supplement to *transition*, a publication that still maintained a tiny subscription list but, thanks to this hostile protest, was mentioned by the popular press. While the artists do point out numerous factual errors, it is clear that none understood Stein's use of Alice as narrator. The *Autobiography*, of course, never claims to be "true" and instead is presented as what Toklas remembers.

The *New Yorker* called the "Testimony Against Gertrude Stein" the "Latest Dirt on Gert" and various publications quoted from the supplement. The New York *World Telegram* printed Jolas's claim that "These documents invalidate the claim that Miss Stein was in any way concerned with the shaping of the epoch she attempts to describe. There is a unanimity of opinion that she had no understanding of what really was happening around her."[257] Stein, who always appreciated the value of publicity, cheerfully wrote to Van Vechten on March 7:

> what I enjoyed was Salmon's statement that he was drunk only in appearance to impress the American ladies and so he ought to be happy that he fooled them instead of complaining that they were fooled, apparently paris is amusing itself greatly about it all it seems to have made them forget politics for a brief moment and my french publishers are naturally very pleased.[258]

Fanny Butcher's report for the *Chicago Tribune* similarly emphasized the positive effect that the protest would have on the reception of Stein's *Autobiography*, not to mention *transition* magazine, which had been nearly ignored by the mainstream press since Stein and Joyce had ceased publishing there.

> [The controversy] has done much to revive the public's interest in [transition], which began its career with a small 't' in 1927 and still more to requicken its interest in "The Autobiography of Alice B. Toklas," by Gertrude Stein. . . . They do this sort of getting worked up over literature so well in Paris![259]

The positive side of this unexpected publicity did not appeal to the libeled painters. According to Henry McBride, Matisse was horrified. "Henry McBride . . . said all the painters should be delighted because I had revivified them at a moment when everybody was not thinking about painting. Henry McBride wrote that as he said these words Matisse shuddered." Stein was forced to concede that, unlike most of the writers she discussed,

"Braque and Marie Laurencin and Matisse they did not like it and they did not get used to it."[260]

The other appalled reaction to Stein's rise in fame came from Marxist critics. Stein's politics had never been a focus of mainstream critics, but as leftist intellectuals gained prominence in the 1930s some readers did begin to consider her work through a new, partisan lens. Not surprisingly, the most famous Marxist personality in the United States, Mike Gold, was unimpressed with Stein and found her work dangerous. He published a scathing assessment of Stein in his *New Masses* by Isador Schneider and attacked her in his 1936 *Change the World!* According to Gold, Stein was "a literary idiot" with absolutely no interest in changing the world; indeed, Stein's work perpetuates a bourgeois, isolated perspective. "In Gertrude Stein, art became a personal pleasure, a private hobby, a vice.... She had no responsibility except to her own inordinate cravings.... In this light, one can see that to Gertrude Stein and to the other artists like her, art exists in the vacuum of a private income."[261]

Gold's reaction may have been partly the result of his awkward meeting with Stein in 1934. According to Bennet Cerf, he invited Gold to the Algonquin to interview Stein and she was not only impatient with him, but really rude. She said to him:

> As far as the general public is concerned, you foolish Communists—and all other people who waste their time with politics—are like janitors. When my flat is warm and clean, and the elevator is running regularly, and the garbage is collected twice a day, I never give a thought to the janitor in the cellar. But—let the hot water fail to run, or the mail be undelivered, and I begin to think, "that darn janitor doesn't know his job." If things continue to go wrong, I see that the old janitor is fired and a new one gets the job. It's the same way in government. Let my own life go on undisturbed, and my private affairs prosper—and I don't give a continental whether the government is being run by a Communist, or a Seventh Day Adventist, or a Hottentot. When they start interfering with my own business, however—by heaven, I, and all the other people in the country, suddenly become aware of the men who are mismanaging it. We just go out and get ourselves a new janitor.

Gold said angrily, "Miss Stein, I came here to discuss your books and your views on literature, not to be called a janitor." But she persisted: "Nevertheless," said Miss Stein, "that's what you are—a janitor. Now run along and get yourself a worth-while job and stop filling your head with a lot of nonsense."[262]

Gold was correct in his assumption that Stein's politics were conservative. Several clues emerged to alert American audiences to Stein's political sympathies after she returned to France if, up to this point, they had been obscure. An interview published in the *New York Times Magazine* in

May 1934 had offered a vague impression of her politics: Lansing Warrren highlighted her surprising comment that "Hitler should have received the Nobel Peace Prize" at the beginning of the article, but when the context for this statement was revealed, her tone seems to have been sardonic. She explained: "By driving out the Jews and the democratic and Left elements, he is driving out everything that conduces to activity. That means peace." Later in the interview, Stein emphasizes the positive value of "stimulation" and "activity" arguing that "that is the reason why I do not approve of the stringent immigration laws in America today. We need the stimulation of new blood."[263] By contrast to these pronouncements, Stein's 1936 *Saturday Evening Post* "money" series and her responses to a *Partisan Review* symposium in 1939 are decidedly conservative.[264] More evidence of her political views has emerged recently in Stein's previously unpublished "Introduction to the Speeches of Maréchal Pétain," but Americans would not have known about this piece.[265]

Stein's series of five articles about "money" in the *Saturday Evening Post* (1936), the most popular magazine in America, clearly demonstrate her failure to comprehend the significance of the depression that devastated American life during her lecture tour and the concomitant American leftist intellectual turn. In "Still More About Money," the third in the series, Stein observes that: "One of the funny things is that when there is a great deal of unemployment you can never get any one to do any work." Stein had discussed the situation in France with her domestic employee, "a Chinaman" named Trac. According to Stein, he explained that unemployment becomes a motivation for people not to work:

> Why he said it's like this. They get ten francs a day as unemployed. Now a Chinaman can live on five francs a day and that gives him five francs to gamble. The rest of the time he puts on his hat and goes out. He takes a temporary job, which still leaves him unemployed, and buys a new suit of clothes. Then by and by he catches cold, he goes to a hospital, free, and then he dies, and has a free coffin. All the Indo-Chinamen in Indo-China want to come to Paris to live like that. They call that living like a Frenchman.[266]

Stein clearly suggests that the unemployed are lazy and only encouraged to be more lazy by such government "handouts," failing to recognize devastating effects of the depression on many who wished very much to work but could not.

We might assume that Stein's choice to publish a conservative critique in this mass-produced periodical would diminish her literary status among intellectuals. Most modernist writers who published in the *Post*, such as F. Scott Fitzgerald and William Faulkner, did so deliberately to make money and saw these literary ventures as separate from their serious work, just as the writing that both Fitzgerald and Faulkner produced in Hollywood was calculated to pay bills rather than contribute to their canonical position. Stein eschewed such conventional hierarchies of taste and, indeed, had always regarded publishing in the *Post* and in the *Atlantic* as particular goals. Furthermore, she was correct that publishing in *Cosmopolitan*, the *Herald Tribune* and the *Saturday Evening Post* did not signal an end to her status as a significant American writer nor did these publications close doors in the publishing world.

During and after the tour, Bennett Cerf was most active in promoting Stein's canonical status and solidifying her identity as one of Random House's most valued writers. In addition to publishing a Modern Library edition of *Three Lives* in 1933, Cerf chose from it "The Good Anna" for his 1936 anthologies, co-edited with Angus Burrell, *An Anthology of Famous American Stories* and *The Bedside Book of Famous American Short Stories*, a book that was given to new subscribers to the Book-of-the-Month Club as a promotion in 1936. In these nearly identical anthologies, Stein's work is accompanied by stories that have retained a place in the American canon by Washington Irving, Nathaniel Hawthorne, Edgar Allan Poe, Mark Twain, Henry James, Stephen Crane, Willa Cather, Sherwood Anderson, F. Scott Fitzgerald, Ernest Hemingway, William Faulkner, and so forth. Cerf's choice of Stein for his anthologies might seem self-serving since he was, of course, promoting one of his own authors. But William Rose Benét and Norman Holmes Pearson also included selections of Stein's work in their 1938 *Oxford Anthology of American Literature*, another endorsement of her canonical status. All of the American writers now associated with modernism are significantly represented, including T. S. Eliot, Ezra Pound, William Carlos Williams, Wallace Stevens, Marianne Moore, E. E. Cummings, H. D., William Faulkner, John Dos Passos, Ernest Hemingway. *Tender Buttons* was considered, but "How Writing is Written," "The Life of Juan Gris," and excerpts from "A Long Gay Book" finally appeared in the collection.[267] Nor did Stein's relationship with the *Atlantic* suffer. Two excerpts from *Everybody's Autobiography* appeared in the *Atlantic* in 1937: "Butter Will Melt" and "Your United States."

In December 1937, when Stein had published in the most extensive range of magazines imaginable, including *Life*, the *Saturday Evening Post*, *Cosmopolitan*, the *Atlantic*, *Vanity Fair*, and the *Dial*, Van Vechten wrote to her with admiration: "I guess by now you have appeared in every kind of magazine in every possible country. Your bibliography will be an eye-opener to that small part of the public that is unaware of your writing. I guess it will even surprise your admirers."[268] And, in the next decade she would go on to publish in such diverse periodicals as *Poetry* (1940), *Collier's* (1944) and *Vogue* (1945).[269] Indeed, Stein's admirers continue to ignore not only the kinds of publications that printed Stein's work and the range of audiences Stein attracted but also the importance she attached to this literary range.

Conclusion
Stein and Hollywood

In 1943, Edmund Wilson lamented the rise of what he called "the two great enemies of literary talent in our time: Hollywood and Henry Luce."[1] Wilson's hostility was certainly not shared by Gertrude Stein, whose relationships with Hollywood and *Time* magazine were solidified in the 1930s. Not only did she appear on the cover of *Time* before her tour in September 1934, become friends with Henry and Clare Boothe Luce in the late 1930s, and arrange social encounters with Charlie Chaplin and Dashiell Hammett and other Hollywood celebrities while she was in the United States, Stein was mentioned in two popular films in 1935: *Top Hat*, starring Fred Astaire and Ginger Rogers, and *The Man on the Flying Trapeze*, starring W. C. Fields.[2]

Both references to Stein in these comedies suggest that her lecture tour had not only created a mainstream public awareness of her, but also showed that the most celebrated form of popular culture, Hollywood movies, found Stein an appropriate subject. In *Top Hat*, a telegram is read to Dale (Ginger Rogers) by her friend Alberto. "Come ahead stop stop being a sap stop you can even bring Alberto stop my husband is stopping at your hotel stop when do you start stop," he reads, and then comments with bewilderment: "I cannot understand who wrote this." Dale declares brightly "Sounds like Gertrude Stein!" It is the only literary reference in the film. In *The Man on the Flying Trapeze*, a depressed W. C. Fields slowly nibbles a piece of toast at breakfast while his annoying "literary" wife tortures him by dramatically reading aloud a selection from a poem printed in the daily newspaper, an obvious parody of *Tender Buttons*. Not at all offended by this representation, Stein wrote to Carl Van Vechten with enthusiasm: "Georges Maratier has just come in and says the cinema where they read a poem by me out loud while the toast burns is right around the corner."[3]

Vanity Fair, too, connected the celebrity of Stein with Hollywood and printed an invented "interview" of Stein, conducted by Gracie Allen in January 1935. In addition to her fame as a radio personality, Allen had recently found great success on film; she and George Burns had appeared with Bing Crosby in *The Big Broadcast* (1932), *College Humor* (1933) and *We're Not Dressing* (1934); and the comic team also had supporting roles in *International House*

(1933) and *Six of a Kind* (1934) with W. C. Fields. *Vanity Fair* combined the signature styles of these two celebrities to produce a comic effect of its own.[4] Stein and Allen were both known for creating a certain linguistic confusion. In Allen's case, her humor relied on her consistent misinterpretation of what people say; she would choose the wrong meaning of any word or phrase that might have two meanings, when the true meaning should never have been in doubt. Or, she hilariously understood only the most literal interpretations of everyday expressions. By contrast, Stein's characteristic style was to create confusion by introducing no clear meaning. As "Allen" observes: "Now Gertie, don't you start to make sense, or people will begin to understand you, and then you won't mean anything at all. If you or I ever made sense, we wouldn't last two minutes, would we?"

Stein demonstrates in *Everybody's Autobiography* her fascination with American contemporary culture, and emphasizes that she believed her work reflected it. Stein thought that she was both the most American writer and the most modern, explaining further that:

> I am always trying to tell this thing that a space of time is a natural thing for an American to always have inside them as something in which they are continuously moving. Think of anything, of cowboys, of movies, of detective stories, of anybody who goes anywhere or stays at home and is an American and you will realize that it is something strictly American to conceive a space that is filled always filled with moving and my first real effort to express this thing which is an American thing began in writing The Making of Americans.[5]

The comparison of Stein's work with movies and detective stories certainly suggests that Stein organized cultural products in an entirely different way than conventional literary critics. But even if Stein succeeded in producing a "space filled with moving" in her writing, her enthusiasm for the possibilities for adapting her work to film took some time to evolve during the 1930s.

The conversation with Charlie Chaplin that Stein reports in *Everybody's Autobiography* about the formal possibilities and restrictions of film, both with and without sound, suggests that she found the medium to be too confining. It was always a problem for Stein to write any dramatic work for performance because she found that the audience's experience of watching the drama unfold diminished the significance of each moment of the piece, as the audience always lagged behind the action by a step, attempting to follow a logical sequence and missing the present moment. Still, Stein attempted to solve this problem with her many unconventional plays that disregarded or subverted traditional plots, characters and settings. She even began experimenting with movie shorts in the 1920s. As Alice explains in the *Autobiography*, after World War I Stein and Toklas watched the celebratory military procession through the Arc de Triomphe and Stein described this event in her own way:

> All the nations marched differently, some slowly, some quickly, the French carry their flags the best of all, Pershing and his officer carrying the flag behind him were perhaps the most perfectly spaced. It was this scene that Gertrude Stein described in the movie she wrote about this time that I have published in Operas and Plays in the Plain Edition.[6]

This experiment was produced before Stein toured the Untied States, visited Hollywood, and began seriously considering the possibilities of film. Although she did find the movies an essential component of American popular culture, it took her some time to become enthusiastic about the medium's potential for her own life and work. Stein heard many positive reports of her appearance on the Pathé newsreel, but did not actually see it until the spring of 1935 and this experience seems to have been disconcerting. As Stein explains:

> there it was and when I saw myself almost as large and moving around and talking I did not like it particularly the talking, it gave me a very funny feeling and I did not like that funny feeling. I suppose if I had seen it often it would have been like anything you can get used to anything if it happens often but that time I certainly did not like it and so when the Warners asked us to come and lunch we did not go.[7]

Stein must have regretted her decision to decline this lunch invitation with the Warners, since as soon as 1936 she began thinking seriously about the possibilities of writing, producing, or starring in a Hollywood movie and began pitching ideas to her well-connected friends.

Stein's closest friend with the most promising ties to Hollywood was Thornton Wilder. His Pulitzer Prize winning *Bridge of San Luis Rey* (1928) was produced by MGM in 1929 and he was one of the writers who worked on an adaptation of Tolstoy's *Resurrection* for screen (renamed *We Live Again* for the 1934 Samuel Goldwyn production). Wilder would go on to write, with several other screenwriters, Hitchcock's *Shadow of a Doubt* (1943). In 1936, Stein heard Wilder was leaving his usual post at the University of Chicago to do some work in Hollywood and immediately began to write him letters about the possibility of filming a version of the *Autobiography of Alice B. Toklas*, suggesting the idea somewhat tentatively:

> I am pleased on the whole that you are giving up the U of C for a bit, and going to Hollywood, I wish we could be there together, it would be fun, listen Thornton, couldn't they do the Autobiography of Alice B. Toklas at Hollywood, that might make a lovely film, I do not know what makes lovely films but that might and they could shoot the background here and in Paris and we could be taken in Hollywood including the puppies Basket and Pepe and we would have enough money to make a leisurely trip across the continent.... I'd love you to put us on

the Hollywood map, but don't think about it twice only perhaps there is something in it.⁸

This is the first indication Stein gave to her friends that a film of the *Autobiography* appealed to her. She and Wilder had already discussed the idea of adapting her "Benjamin Franklin" for film, but the more she considered the possibilities for the *Autobiography* the more enthusiastic she became. In September she wrote to Wilder:

> Is there not way of changing Benjamin Franklin into Pablo Picasso and Alice B. Toklas if I do not make money there I may be driven to do a cigarette advertisement they have just asked me, we will like to travel around and not lecture, can't Hollywood do something about it, someone once dreamed of doing the Gentle Lena there but I never did quite see that but they seemed to think so.⁹

As Stein suggests here, Lillian May Ehrman, a friend of Carl Van Vechten, had talked to Stein when she was in Hollywood about the possibility selling the rights of "The Gentle Lena" to a studio, and wanted to arrange a meeting with an agent, but at the time Stein hesitated. As Marsha Orgeron reports, Stein finally signed an "agreement" with Ehrman's brother, but no studio expressed interest in the project.¹⁰ Still, encouraged by this attention, once she returned to France Stein seems to have decided that Hollywood interest in her work might be an unexpected, exciting, and lucrative new development. An article in the *Herald Tribune* about P. G. Wodehouse's enormous salary with MGM greatly increased her interest in the idea and prompted this letter to Wilder:

> I just read in this morning's paper that Wodehouse says they give him $104 000 for doing nothing at Hollywood they keep him there but they do not use what they ask him to do, now that would suit us just fine, we want a payed which is à la mode here now, of course we are not valuable like he is, but for considerably less would we write dialogue and titles that they do not want to use, not at all do we insist that they use our words printed or unprinted not at all, we just want to run around and do nothing and be payed largely for it, that is as everything they do not want, it is a pleasant xtravagance and we are just pining for pleasant xtravagance, so keep your eyes and ears open, if they want us we will come, we would love to be payed largely and we are kind of tired of just staying here.¹¹

As Orgeron puts it: "the economic lure of Hollywood was irresistible."¹²

This was not the only movie idea percolating in 1936. Harry Dunham and Paul Bowles had suggested that two of Stein's plays, *Ladies Voices* and *What Happened*, could be adapted for film, accompanied by music written by Bowles. Stein expressed interest in the project in February of 1936, but nothing came of the project.¹³ In 1937 Stein wrote to Van Vechten with an entirely different, fabulous idea: she thought her "Daniel Webster" might be produced as some sort of musical—comedy—ballet , with a musical score by Virgil Thomson or Gerald Berners and choreographed by Freddie Ashton.

> I am awfully happy that you like Daniel Webster, I have a dream of its being done in Hollywood, with Virgil or Gerald [Berners] or somebody to do the music not xactly an opera, and Freddie Ashton who could make it go funny and real and it would be lots of fun, and give us an xcuse to go to America, to put it on, and it might be a great success . . . and I think all of us together out there could have a wonderful time and do something, is there any producer, I could write to out there and tell him he ought to have us, you know Carl I do think we could do something there together.¹⁴

It was just at this time that Thompson had begun to write musical scores for film. His music accompanied Pare Lorentz's *The Plow That Broke the Plains* (1936) and *The River* (1937); in 1949 his score for Robert Flaherty's documentary, *Louisiana Story*, won the Pulitzer Prize for music.¹⁵ Freddie Ashton was not only a great success as a choreographer but also as a dancer in his hilarious role as one of the ugly stepsisters in annual performances of Sergei Prokofiev's *Cinderella* for many years. He choreographed Berners's ballet, *A Wedding Bouquet*, inspired by Stein's *They Must. Be Wedded. To Their Wife.* which premiered in London in April 1937. Stein's imagined production of Daniel Webster would clearly have been directly linked to *Four Saints in Three Acts*, a fanciful, experimental work that, like *Four Saints*, would surely have been accurately classified as "camp," competing with the hugely successful Busby Berkeley films of this decade.

Perhaps most surprising, Stein's next Hollywood inspiration came from Francis Rose, who had illustrated the English edition of her 1939 children's book, *The World Is Round* and thought it would be perfect material for a children's movie (Clement Hurd illustrated the American version). The book made a splash in the United States with a review on the cover of the *New York Herald Tribune's Books*, which observed: "It is not often that a child's book makes the front pages on the day of publication."¹⁶ Before the book was released, Stein wrote to Van Vechten in November of 1938: "Francis Rose wants to use it as a film he says it just is a film as it is but that is easy for him to know and not so easy to make the film people know it, however we all live in hope."¹⁷ Later that month she gushed with excitement: "There is a cinema project, a real one this time":

> Everybody seems to be xcited about the World is Round, the Harpers people seem to think it will make a very successful film I have kept all the movie rights for myself so I hope somebody will be interested,

somebody said Walt Disney but of course I do not know anybody do you know anybody who does, I would like to make a lot of money off of it, now that it is written, I am so glad you like it I do think it kind of lovely.[18]

A camp Hollywood musical of "Daniel Webster" or a Walt Disney movie of *The World is Round* would have created huge publicity and each would have added a new dimension to Stein's already complex and multidimensional artistic reputation. Disney, of course, was not opposed to modernism and effectively popularized the experimental music of Stravinsky's controversial "Le Sacre du Printemps" in *Fantasia* (1940). Stein and Toklas had attended the concert in Paris and Toklas claims in *Autobiography* that it was the first occasion that Stein saw Carl Van Vechten, a musical backdrop most appropriate for that literary introduction. The homogenous signature style of today's Disney films betrays the radical possibilities that Disney's early animators explored; a film of a Gertrude Stein book might have been a serious creative project as well as a commercial success in the early 1940s.

Indeed, *The World is Round* became especially fashionable in the United States. It first appeared in *Harper's Bazaar* in June 1938 and Clement Hurd's illustrations inspired a set of rugs designed for children's nurseries sold at the exclusive W & J Sloane's on Fifth Avenue. The advertisement, titled "Nursery Steins: Sloane's New Group of Children's Rugs," explained:

> Those bewitching Clement Hurd illustrations of Gertrude Stein's first children's book, "the World Is Round," started it all. Whimsical, impish . . . they flashed on us as perfect naturals for the designs of children's rugs. Now we have ready . . . just when your youngster is clamouring for the lyric nonsense of "The World Is Round" . . . a group of six scatter rugs. They're hand hooked, genuine wool. They'll clean like lambs. While there are no pigeons in the grass, alas . . . you can choose "Rose Is a Rose," "Eyes a Surprise," "Willie and His Lion," "Is a Lion Not a Lion," "There" or "The World Is Round," $14.50.

Despite Rose's creative brainstorming and persistence, he never succeeded in generating interest for the project. When Stein saw that neither *The World is Round* nor "Daniel Webster" would be realized, she began to rethink the potential for a film version of the *Autobiography*. Wilder, Van Vechten, and others had been urging her to make another trip to the Untied States to escape the war and she began to consider the possibility of a lecture tour combined with work in Hollywood on a movie. Samuel Steward had explicitly asked Stein what she would do in the case of war, and she had answered: "Who knows . . . We might stay here, we might go again to America and lecture, or we might go to Hollywood and make a movie about the first autobiography. That, I think that would be really and truly exciting."[19]

When Wilder failed to turn up any leads, Stein considered other influential contacts. In February, she brought up her interest in making a movie of the *Autobiography* to Van Vechten for the first time and asked him to mention the idea to Bennett Cerf. She hesitantly wrote to Van Vechten: "I do not like to ask [Cerf], you can always make him do anything you think he ought to do so if you think he ought to do this then you make him, it is just a dream."[20] The eager Van Vechten replied with enthusiasm in March:

> I talked to Bennett about the motion picture possibilities of The Autobiography which are ENORMOUS, but the motion picture people are peculiar. You can't approach them. They must approach you. I think the time to take this up is when you are lecturing in Hollywood. Of course you both would have to appear in the picture. Even Greta Garbo and Lillian Gish couldn't be you and Alice. I can't wait for this! It will be wonderful![21]

This rather strange response might suggest that Cerf had reservations about the project, but Stein believed Van Vechten's characterization of the "motion picture people" and mentioned to Wilder in May that "I understand Hollywood is never suggested to, they must have the idea themselves."[22]

Stein began negotiations with several lecture agents about touring the United States, and was brave enough to mention her idea of working in Hollywood to them. Colstein Leigh of the Colstein Leigh lecture Bureau especially appealed to her because he suggested a limited schedule of only 15 lectures, and most important, Stein wrote to Van Vechten that he "is also connected with the cinema and seems very taken with the idea of the Auto A. B. T. as cinema material, in which case we would be over this fall and be photoed in color but then always of course nothing may come of it all."[23] Word of Stein's interest in making a movie of the *Autobiography* began to spread, and thanks to Steward, June Provines reported in the *Chicago Tribune* that

> Gertrude Stein wrote a friend in Chicago the other day that she wants to go into the movies, appearing herself in the Autobiography of Alice B. Toklas. Well, Hollywood ought to put her on celluloid, and with a little imagination an interesting documentary picture might be evolved.[24]

Despite these attempts, Stein never did make her Hollywood film, nor did she return to the United States. Unable to leave France after the German occupation, she and Toklas endured the war at their summer home at Bilignin, walking miles every day to obtain food, growing what they could in an extensive garden, negotiating the black market, and even on one frightening evening, giving their home up to German soldiers who failed to notice that the women were American, lesbian, and Jewish.

Even if Stein's Hollywood ambitions were not realized, the appeal of the project signifies how modern, American and mainstream her tastes and artistic goals were. On the lecture tour she had seen the possibilities that Hollywood offered to artists, especially artists who were not bound by conventional and arbitrary designations of status or worth. Indeed, Stein's democratic attitude towards art might have given her a new and fertile outlet in Hollywood if she had been able to make another trip there. To Stein, making movies did not diminish the significance of an artist's creation. Indeed, she began to romanticize the effect of transforming the work of great artists into Hollywood productions; what might this juxtaposition or conjunction create? She observes in *Everybody's Autobiography*:

> Well anyway Lascaux did think that the cheapest thing being made of the costliest material was romantic. It was romantic to him and it is, that the cheapest thing is made with the most care and the highest-paid creators are those that make that thing. It is romantic. Perhaps Hollywood too is that thing.[25]

There may be something "cheap" about Hollywood film—anyone can afford go see them—but they may also be made by the "highest-paid creators" and even the most respected artists. This most popular, accessible form retains the value of its elite creator. It is high art for everyone, or, to put it another way, popular modernism.

Although Stein's popularity after the war certainly was revived in the mainstream press, who emphasized her many enduring relationships with American soldiers in Paris and celebrated her new bestseller, *Wars I Have Seen* (1945), after her death in 1946 Stein's reputation suffered. Her living presence was vital to securing and maintaining the public's enthusiasm, and soon a caricature of her became institutionalized. Stein's radical conception of modern literature had broken not only conventional ideals of form and content, but also suggested a complete rethinking of the role of art and literature in everyday life that was soon forgotten. While mainstream American periodicals had endorsed this view and responded to this accessible Stein during her lifetime, after Stein's death a stratified, hierarchical literary landscape became normalized first in the academy and, subsequently, in American culture generally.

Notes

NOTES TO CHAPTER ONE

1. John Malcolm Brinnin, *The Third Rose: Gertrude Stein and Her World* (Boston: Little, Brown and Company, 1959), 307–08.
2. Edmund Wilson introduced the first phrase in *Axel's Castle* in 1931, and *Time* magazine repeated it in their cover story about Stein in 1933; the second was introduced in the 1933 *Time* story and now appears in the short biographical remarks about Stein at the beginning of the current Penguin edition of *The Autobiography of Alice B. Toklas*.
3. Catherine Turner, *Marketing Modernism: Between the Two World Wars* (Amherst: University of Massachusetts Press, 2003), 203.
4. "The Apotheosis of Miss Stein, 1934," *Vanity Fair* (May 1934), 21.
5. Loren Glass, *Authors, Inc.: Literary Celebrity in the Modern United States, 1880–1980* (New York: New York University Press, 2004), 8; Aaron Jaffe, *Modernism and the Culture of Celebrity* (Cambridge: Cambridge University Press, 2005).
6. See Kirk Curnutt, "Inside and Outside: Gertrude Stein on Identity, Celebrity and Authenticity," *Journal of Modern Literature* 23.2 (1999), 291–308; Susan M. Schultz, "Gertrude Stein's Self-Advertisement," *Raritan* (Fall 1992), 71–87; Bryce Conrad, "Gertrude Stein in the American Marketplace," *Journal of Modern Literature* 14.2 (1995), 215–33.
7. Glass, 2.
8. Theodore Greene, *America's Heroes: The Changing Models of Success in America's Magazines* (New York: Oxford University Press, 1970).
9. John Xiros Cooper, *Modernism and the Culture of Market Society* (New York: Cambridge, 2004), 3. Stein lived at 27 rue de Fleurus, not number 32.
10. Barbara Will, *Gertrude Stein, Modernism, and the Problem of "Genius"* (Edinburgh: Edinburgh University Press, 2000), 5.
11. Gertrude Stein, *The Autobiography of Alice B, Toklas* (London: Penguin Books, 1966), 83.
12. Sara Blair, "Home Truths: Gertrude Stein, 27 Rue de Fleurus, and the Place of the Avant-Garde," *American Literary History* 12.3 (2000), 420.
13. Stein, 78, 189.
14. *New York Herald Tribune* (7 April 1935), 1. Quoted in James R. Mellow, *Charmed Circle Gertrude Stein and Company* (New York: Praeger Publishers, 1974), 409.
15. Fredric Jameson, *Postmodernism: Or, the Logic of Late Capitalism* (Durham: Duke University Press, 1991); Andreas Huyssen, *After the Great Divide: Modernism, Mass Culture, Postmodernism* (Bloomington: Indiana University Press, 1986).

16. Jennifer Wicke, *Advertising Fictions: Literature, Advertisement and Social Reading* (New York: Columbia University Press, 1988); David E. Chinitz, *T. S. Eliot and the Cultural Divide* (Chicago: University of Chicago Press, 2003); Michael Coyle, *Ezra Pound, Popular Genres, and the Discourse of Culture* (University Park, PA: The Pennsylvania Sate University Press, 1995).
17. Maria DiBattista and Lucy McDiarmid, ed., *High and Low Moderns: Literature and Culture, 1889–1939* (New York: Oxford University Press, 1996), 4–5.
18. Jameson, 306.
19. Joan Shelley Rubin, *The Making of Middlebrow Culture* (Chapel Hill: University of North Carolina Press, 1992); Jancie Radway, *A Feeling for Books: The Book-of-the-Month Club, Literary Taste, and Middle Class Desire* (Chapel Hill: University of North Carolina Press, 1997).
20. Rubin, 81, 88.
21. Katherine Anne Porter, "Everybody Is a Real One," *New York Herald Tribune Books* (16 January 1927), 1; "Books for Young People," *New York Herald Tribune Books* (24 September 1939), 1; Janet Flanner, "History Tramps Down the Champs-Elysées," *New York Herald Tribune Books* (23 June 1940), 1.
22. See Harcourt, Brace and Company's advertisement in *Publishers' Weekly* (23 September 1933), 1046; the other selection was Thames Williamson's *The Woods Colt*.
23. "Gyring and Gimbling (Or Lewis Carroll in Paris)," *The Saturday Review of Literature* (30 April 1927), 1+.
24. For analysis of Random House's promotion of *Ulysses*, see Turner, 173–213.
25. For a discussion of the Woolf cover story, see Brenda Silver, *Virginia Woolf Icon* (Chicago: University of Chicago Press, 1999).
26. "Current Magazines," *New York Times Book Review* (8 June 1924), 26.
27. See *Tom Masson's Annual* (1925); *Contact Collection of Contemporary Writers* (1925); *Georgian Stories* (1926); *Morrow's Almanack* (1927); *The American Caravan* (1927); *The Hogarth Essays* (1928); *transition stories* (1929).
28. Benedict Anderson, *Imagined Communities: Reflections on the Origin and Spread of Nationalism* (New York: Verso, 1983).
29. Corrine E. Blackmur, "Selling Taboo Subjects: The Literary Commerce of Gertrude Stein and Carl Van Vechten," *Marketing Modernisms: Self-Promotion, Canonization, Rereading*, ed. Kevin J. H. Dettmar and Stephen Watt (Ann Arbor: University of Michigan Press, 1996), 244. Stein did not publish in *The Trend*, although Van Vechten's "How to Read Gertrude Stein" appeared there in 1914.
30. Lawrence Rainey, ed., *Modernism: An Anthology* (Malden, MA: Blackwell, 2005), 373.
31. Donald A. Stauffer, ed. *The Intent of the Critic* (Princeton: Princeton University Press, 1941).
32. John Tebbel, *A History of Book Publishing in the United States, Vol. II* (New York: R. R. Bowker Company, 1978), 700.
33. Wayne Gard, *Book Reviewing* (New York: Alfred A. Knopf, 1928), v.
34. Harry Hansen, "These Literary Lobbies," *North American Review* (August 1930), 162–68.
35. John Tebbel, *A History of Book Publishing in the United States, Vol. III* (New York: R. R. Bowker Company, 1978), 45. Interview for the New York *Herald* (13 November 1921).
36. Tebbel, Vol. III, 49.
37. Quoted in Harry Hansen, "Books Resist Commercialism," *Editor and Publisher* 67.1 (21 July 1934), 105.
38. For a state-by-state breakdown of literary periodical circulation, see O. H. Cheney's *Economic Survey of the Book Industry, 1930–31* (New York: R. R. Bowker Company, 1931), 27.

39. Florin I. McDonald, "Book Reviewing in The American Newspaper," Ph.D. Dissertation, University of Missouri, 1936, 11.
40. Harry Hansen, "Harry Hansen: Reviewer of Books," *Nation* (4 June 1924), 646.
41. Robert Morss Lovett, "The Function of Criticism," *New Republic* 28 (26 October 1921), 248; quoted in McDonald, 7.
42. Rubin, 62–65.
43. Tebbel, vol. II, 325; Rubin, 34–93.
44. McDonald, 16–17; Theodore Peterson, *Magazines in the Twentieth Century* (Urbana: University of Illinois Press, 1964), 209–10.
45. Turner, 31.
46. Newspapers located in cities with populations between 15,000 to 500,000 usually had weekly book pages that reached circulations from 5,000 to 150,000. Gard, 71.
47. John Farrar, "The Weekly Reviews: John Farrar Compliments Them All," *Time* (3 November 1924), 14.
48. "Survey Studies Review Readers," *Publishers' Weekly* (6 October 1934), 1276.
49. Peterson, 271.
50. See Faye Hammill and Karen Leick, "Modernism and the Quality Magazines: *Vanity Fair* (1914–36); *American Mercury* (1924–81); *New Yorker* (1925–); *Esquire* (1933–)," *Modernist Magazines: A Critical and Cultural History*, ed. Peter Brooker and Andrew Thacker (forthcoming, Oxford University Press).
51. *Ibid.*, 248.
52. Thomas Kunkel, *Genius in Disguise: Harold Ross of The New Yorker* (New York: Carroll & Graf, 1995), 308.
53. *Ibid.*, 407.
54. Linda Wagner-Martin, *"Favored Strangers": Gertrude Stein and Her Family* (New Brunswick: Rutgers University Press, 1995), 124.
55. "Concerning everything knowable and various other things besides." Robert T. Elson, *Time Inc: The Intimate History of a Publishing Enterprise, 1923–1941* (New York: Atheneum, 1968), 5.
56. Joe Moran, *Star Authors: Literary Celebrity in America* (Sterling, VA: Pluto Press, 2000), 29.
57. Peterson, 327.
58. "Shantih, Shantih, Shantih: Has the Reader Any Rights Before the Bar of Literature?" *Time* (3 March 1923), 12.
59. Peterson, 210.
60. Dwight MacDonald, *Memoirs of a Revolutionist: Essays in Political Criticism* (New York: Farrar, Straus and Cudahy, 1957), 255.
61. Edmund Wilson, *Classics and Commercials: A Literary Chronicle of the Forties* (New York: Farrar, Strauss, 1950), 121.
62. Harry Hansen, "Literary Previews," *Writing Up the News: Behind the Scenes of the Great Newspapers*, ed. Miriam Lundy (New York: Dodd, 1939), 95.
63. *Ibid.*, 97.
64. Dorothy Canfield Fisher, "American Readers and Books," *American Scholar* (Spring 1944), 190.
65. See Hansen's *Midwest Portraits: A Book of Memories and Friendships* (New York; Harcourt, Brace and Company, 1923).
66. For a detailed account of Hansen's career, see William Henry Roba, *A Literary Pilgrim: Harry Hansen and Popular Book Publishing, 1915–1945*. Ph.D. Dissertation, University of Iowa, 1979.
67. Edwin Hoyt, *Alexander Woollcott: The Man Who Came to Dinner* (New York: Abelard-Schuman, 1968), 259.

202 Notes

68. "Alexander Woollcott Sells 'Lost Horizon,'" *Publishers' Weekly* (27 October 1934), 1575.
69. Louis Kronenberger, "Down With Woollcott," *Nation* (18 December 1935).
70. Hoyt, 304.
71. Herbert Bayard Swope, executive editor of the *World* from 1920–29, invented the idea of the brilliant op-ed page. Roba, 100–1.
72. Carl Dolmetsch notes that if the *Smart Set* "had a successor at all, it was *The New Yorker*, founded the following year when, at a Saturday night poker session in Manhattan, Harold Ross and Raoul Fleischmann fell to lamenting the passing of the old *Smart Set* . . . and decided to start a magazine of their own that would be like it, 'only better.'" "Mencken as a Magazine Editor," *Menckeniana* 21 (Spring 1967), 1–8.
73. Edmund Wilson, *Shores of Light: A Literary Chronicle of the Twenties and Thirties* (New York: Farrar, Straus and Young, Inc., 1952), 368.
74. Ernest Hemingway, *The Sun Also Rises*. 1926 (New York: Bantam Books, 1949), 33.
75. H. L. Mencken, "A Cubist Treatise: Baltimore Woman's Book Is As Comprehensible as Paintings," *Baltimore Sun* (6 June 1914). Stein lived in Baltimore briefly with her maternal aunt from 1892–3 before she enrolled at Harvard Annex in 1894; she then lived in Baltimore as a medical student at Johns Hopkins from 1887–1901.
76. H. L. Mencken, Rev. of "Geography and Plays," *Smart Set* (October 1923), 144.
77. Patricia R. Everett, *A History of having a Great Many Times Not Continued to be Friends* (Albuquerque: University of New Mexico Press, 1996), 222.
78. Henry Seidel Canby, *American Memoir* (Boston: Houghton Mifflin Company, 1947), 263–64.
79. *Ibid.*, 103.
80. James Thurber, "There's an Owl in My Room," *New Yorker* (17 November 1934), 19.
81. Leslie Fiedler, *The Collected Essays of Leslie Fiedler* (New York: Stein and Day, 1971), 454.
82. Gertrude Stein, *Everybody's Autobiography*, 46.
83. Alyson Tischler, "A Rose Is a Pose: Steinian Modernism and Mass Culture," *Journal of Modern Literature* 26.3/4 (2004), 14.
84. Huyssen, 17, 47.
85. Thomas Kunkel, ed., *Letters from the Editor: The New Yorker's Harold Ross* (New York: Modern Library, 2001), 89.
86. Andreas Huyssen, "High/Low in an Expanded Field," *Modernism/Modernity* 9.3 (2002), 370–71.
87. Daniel Boorstin, *The Image: A Guide to Pseudo-Events in America* (New York: Atheneum, 1980), 57.
88. Isaac Rosenfeld, "Pleasure and Troubles," *New York Times Book Review* (21 September 1952), 6.

NOTES TO CHAPTER TWO

1. New York *Evening Globe* (16 March 1916).
2. Stein, *Autobiography*, 70.
3. Robert Bartlett Hass, "Gertrude Stein Talking: Transatlantic Interview," UCLAN Review (Summer 1962), 8.
4. Donald Sutherland, *Gertrude Stein: A Biography of Her Work* (New Haven: Yale University Press, 1951), 41.

5. Marianne De Koven, *A Different Language: Gertrude Stein's Experimental Language* (Madison: University of Wisconsin Press, 1983), 38.
6. Delta M. Bell, "'Melanctha' and Metonomy," *delta* 10 (May 1980), 21.
7. Brinnin, 120.
8. Donald Gallup, ed., *The Flowers of Friendship: Letters Written to Gertrude Stein* (New York: Alfred A. Knopf, 1953), 31–32.
9. May Bookstaver was Stein's first romantic interest. Their troubled relationship was the inspiration for Stein's posthumously published *QED*, or *Things as They Are*.
10. Stein, 123.
11. Kirk Curnutt, ed., *The Critical Response to Gertrude Stein* (Westport, CT: Greenwood Press, 2000), 10.
12. *The Nation* (20 January 1910).
13. New York *Post* (22 January 1910).
14. Brooklyn *Eagle* (2 March 1910); Cleveland *Plain Dealer* (28 February 1910).
15. "Notable Piece of Realism," *Boston Evening Globe* (18 December 1909).
16. (8 January 1910).
17. (29 January 1910).
18. (14 August 1910).
19. (15 October 1910).
20. *Philadelphia Booknews* (1 February 1910); *Philadelphia American* (6? January 1910); "Curious Fiction Study," *Chicago Record Herald* (22 January 1910).
21. (25 December 1909).
22. (17 January 1910).
23. *Washington* (D.C.) *Herald* (12 December 1909). Curnutt, 8.
24. (24 December 1909).
25. Brinnin 118–19.
26. Sherwood Anderson, *Winesburg, Ohio: Authoritative Text Backgrounds and Contexts Criticism*, ed. Charles Modlin and Ray Lewis White (New York: W. W. Norton, 1996), 154.
27. Raymond Weaver, "What Ails Pegasus?" *Bookman* (September 1920), 50.
28. Jennifer Parchesky, "'You Make Us Articulate' Reading, Education, and Community in Dorothy Canfield's Middlebrow America," *Reading Acts: U. S. Readers' Interactions with Literature, 1800–1950*, ed. Barbara Ryan and Amy M Thomas (Knoxville: University of Tennessee Press, 2002), 234.
29. "A Zolaesque American," N.Y. City *Press* (13 February 1910).
30. No date or source. Gertrude Stein and Alice B. Toklas Papers. Yale Collection of American Literature. Beinecke Rare Book and Manuscript Library.
31. Mellow, 147.
32. Gallup, 74.
33. Wagner-Martin, 109.
34. See Robert Crunden, *American Salons: Encounters with European Modernism, 1885–1917* (New York: Oxford University Press, 1993), 328.
35. Debra Bricker Balken, *Debating American Modernism: Stieglitz, Duchamp, and the New York Avant-Garde* (New York: American Federation of the Arts, 2003), 42–43, 66–70.
36. Stein, *Autobiography*, 17.
37. Mellow, 171.
38. Milton W. Brown, *The Story of the Armory Show* (Greenwich, Conn.: The Joseph H. Hirshhorn Foundation, 1963), 95, 173, 187.
39. *Ibid.*, 86–88.
40. Jo Davidson, "The Extremists: An Interview with Jo Davidson," *Arts and Decoration* (March 1913), 170.

41. *Ibid.*, 180.
42. Brinnin, 185.
43. "Futurist Literature" *Chicago Daily Tribune* (16 March 1913), 4.
44. Frank Crane, "Drawing the Line: The Three Card Monte Literary School," *Chicago Daily Tribune* (24 March 1913), 8.
45. "The Cubist Costume Milady in Crazyquilt," *Chicago Daily Tribune* (6 April 1913), G1.
46. Everett, 178.
47. (22 March 1913); *Everett*, 179.
48. "Flat Prose," *Atlantic Monthly* (September 1914), 430–32.
49. Mellow, 189.
50. *Ibid.*, 189.
51. Gallup, 92.
52. Steven Conn, *Museums and American Intellectual Life, 1876–1926* (Chicago: University of Chicago Press, 1998).
53. "Making Art Popular," *Saturday Evening Post* (24 May 1913), 24.
54. Walt Kuhn, *The Story of the Armory Show* (New York, 1938), 24.
55. See Shelley Staples, "Marketing Modern Art in America: From the Armory Show to the Department Store," May 2001 <http://xroads.virginia.edu/~MUSEUM/Armory/marketing.html>.
56. Brinnin, 184.
57. Brown, 110.
58. *Ibid.*, 111; See also "Lines Inspired by a View of the Cubist Paintings Followed by a Late Supper," *Chicago Daily Tribune* (26 March 1913), 6.
59. Mary Mills and Earl Harvey Lyall, *The Cubies A B C* (New York: G. P. Putnam's Sons, 1913). Five paintings by Morton Livingston Schamberg were exhibited. See Brown, 288.
60. Harriet Monroe, *A Poet's Life* (New York: Macmillan, 1938), 215
61. Joan Shelley Rubin, "'They Flash upon That Inward Eye': Poetry Recitation and American Readers," *Reading Acts,* 260.
62. Monroe, 251.
63. *Ibid.*, 259.
64. *Ibid.*, 287, 291.
65. "A Line-O'-Type or Two," *Chicago Daily Tribune* (12 October 1912), 8.
66. Monroe, 311.
67. Margaret Johns, "Free-footed verse is danced in Ridgefield, New Jersey," *New York Tribune* (25 January 1915).
68. "The Business of Poetry," New York *Sun* (12 September 1915), 8.
69. Amy Lowell, "The New Manner in Modern Poetry," *New Republic* (4 March 1916), 124.
70. Monroe, 387.
71. "A Birdseye View of 'The New Poetry,'" *New York Times Book Review* (11 March 1917), 1; "The Latest Books," *Life* (12 April 1917), 644.
72. "'Poetry' Has Its Sixth Birthday," *Chicago Daily Tribune* (14 July 1917), 7.
73. Jayne E. Marek, *Women Editing Modernism: "Little" Magazines and Literary History* (Lexington: University Press of Kentucky, 1995), 58.
74. Monroe, 386. For a discussion of "Trees," see Joan Shelley Rubin, *Songs of Ourselves: The Uses of Poetry in America* (Cambridge: Harvard University Press, 2007), 336–39.
75. To cite just one example, the *Washington Post* regularly printed poems from *Poetry*, including: Owen F. Aldis, "To a Mockingbird," *Washington Post* (3 November 1913), 6; Rabrindranath Tagore, "The Infinite Love," *Washington Post* (24 December 1913), 6; Grace Fallow Norton, "Oh Hush, My Heart!" *Washington Post* (10 January 1914), 6; Grace Fallow Norton,

"Heart's Holiday," *Washington Post* (2 February 1914), 6; Harriet Monroe, "A Love Song," *Washington Post* (17 March 1914), 6.
76. Harriet Monroe, "The Christmas Motive and Its Relation to Art," *Chicago Daily Tribune* (21 December 1913), 4.
77. Brinnin, 152.
78. Stein, 170.
79. Elinor Hope Warner, *"Officer, She's Writing Again": Gertrude Stein's American Readers*. Diss. University of Virginia, 1994. Ann Arbor: UMI, 1994. 9424456, 45.
80. Rev. of *Tender Buttons. Pittsburgh Dispatch* (6 June 1914); "Tender Buttons," Louisville *Courier Journal* (6 July 1914).
81. Leonard Diepeveen "The Newspaper Response to *Tender Buttons*, and What It Might Mean," *Emerging Media, Emerging Modernisms*, ed. Ann Ardis and Patrick Collier (forthcoming, Palgrave Macmillan, 2008).
82. Note in *Boston Transcript* (23 December 1914).
83. "Public Gets Peep at Extreme Cubist Literature in Gertrude Stein's 'Tender Buttons,'" *Chicago Daily Tribune* (5 June 1914), 15.
84. "Steinese Literature," Chicago *Evening Post* (7 August 1914); "Cubist Poetry," *Chicago Advance* (18 June 1914); "When the White Hunter Hunts," *New York Sun* (21 June 1914); "For Thoughts Like These," *New York World* (13 June 1914); "Frenzied Futurisms," *Philadelphia Press* (13 June 1914); "New Outbreaks of Futurism," *Boston Transcript* (11 July 1914); "A Cubist Treatise," *Baltimore Sun* (6 June 1914); "Cubist Literature," *San Antonio Light* (14 June 1914); "Dr. Lowes Finds 'Tender Buttons', Poetic Asparagus," St. Louis *Post Dispatch* (29 March 1916).
85. Stein, *Autobiography*, 70.
86. "Time to Show a Message," *Omaha Herald* (7 June 1914).
87. Gallup, 95–97.
88. Mellow, 179.
89. "News of Books," *New York Times Book Review* (5 April 1914), 179.
90. *Boston Evening Transcript* (23 September 1914).
91. "Public Gets Peep at Extreme Cubist Literature in Gertrude Stein's 'Tender Buttons,'" *Chicago Daily Tribune* (5 June 1914), 15.
92. Bridgman, 125.
93. See Dana Watson, *Gertrude Stein and the Essence of What Happens* (Nashville, TN: Vanderbilt UP, 2005), 36, 41; Michael J. Hoffman, *The Development of Abstractionism in the Writings of Gertrude Stein* (Philadelphia: University of Pennsylvania Press, 1966), 183–84; Michael Edward Kaufmann, "Gertrude Stein's Re-Vision of Language and Print in *Tender Buttons*," *Journal of Modern Literature* 15 (Spring 1989), 448; Marguerite S. Murphy, "'Familiar Strangers': The Household Words of Gertrude Stein's *Tender Buttons*," *Contemporary Literature* 32 (1991), 389; Lisa Ruddick, *Reading Gertrude Stein: Body, Text Gnosis* (Ithaca: Cornell University Press, 1990), 190–91; Catharine R. Stimpson, "Gertrude Stein and the Transposition of Gender," *The Poetics of Gender*, ed. Nancy K. Miller (New York: Columbia University Press, 1986), 14.
94. Robert Bartlett Haas, "Gertrude Stein Talking—A Transatlantic Interview," *UCLAN Review* (Summer 1962), 10.
95. Robert Bartlett Haas, "Gertrude Stein Talking—A Transatlantic Interview," *UCLAN Review* (Spring 1963), 48.
96. "Gertrude Stein Plagiary," New York *Evening Sun* (13 June 1914).
97. "Public Gets Peep at Extreme Cubist Literature in Gertrude Steins' Tender Buttons" *Chicago Daily Tribune* (5 June 1914), 15.
98. "A Line-O'-Type or Two," *Chicago Daily Tribune* (8 June 1914), 6.
99. N. P. D., "Books of the Week," *New York Commercial Advertiser* (6 June 1914); reprint in the *New York Call* (7 June 1914).

206 Notes

100. "The Amazing Gertrude Stein," *St. Paul Pioneer Press* (5 July 1914).
101. Robert Emons Rogers, "New Outbreaks of Futurism: 'Tender Buttons,' Curious Experiment of Gertrude Stein in Literary Anarchy." *Boston Transcript* (11 July 1914).
102. Rev. of *Tender Buttons*, *Buffalo Times* (15 November 1914).
103. "Literary Notes," St. Joseph (MO) *Press* (8 August 1914).
104. "When the White Hunter Hunts," New York *Sun* (21 June 1914).
105. Rev. of Tender Buttons, *Pittsburg Dispatch* (6 June 1914).
106. "What?" *Boston Herald* (29 August 1914).
107. "Futurist Literature," Detroit *Free Press* (11 June 1914), *Columbus Dispatch* (14 June 1914).
108. "Books and Writers," St. Joseph MO *News* (23 July 1914); "Gertrude Stein as Literary Cubist," Philadelphia *North American* (13 June 1914); Rev. of *Tender Buttons*, *Pittsburgh Post* (4 July 1914); *Smart Set* (Oct 1914).
109. "Futurist Essays," *Los Angeles Times* (9 Aug 1914).
110. N.P.D., New York City *Call* (7 June 1914); Curnutt, 15.
111. "Officer, She's Writing Again," *Detroit News* (6 June 1914).
112. George Cram Cook, "New York Letter," (12 June 1914).
113. Charles Ashleigh, "Steinese Literature," *Chicago Evening Post* (7 August 1914); "New Books," New York City *Press* (7 June 1914); Rev. of *Tender Buttons*, *Louisville Courier* (6 June 1914).
114. H. L Mencken, "Cubist Treatise: Baltimore Woman's Books Is As Comprehensible As Paintings," *Baltimore Sun* (6 June 1914).
115. G.V.S., Rev. of *Tender Buttons*, *Pittsburgh Sun* (17 July 1914).
116. "Words," *Chicago Evening Post* (6 November 1914).
117. "Futurist Poetry," *Chicago Daily Tribune* (16 August 1914), D9.
118. Fanny Butcher, "News in Brief of Authors and of Their Books," *Chicago Daily Tribune* (18 May 1918), 11.
119. Carl Van Vechten, "How to Read Gertrude Stein." *The Trend* (August 1914), 553.
120. *Ibid.*, 554.
121. Boston *Evening Transcript* (23 Sept. 1914).
122. "Words," *Chicago Evening Post* (6 November 1914).
123. Don Marquis, "The Sun Dial," New York *Evening Sun* (18 August 1914), 8.
124. Richard Burton, "Posing," Minneapolis [MN] *Bellman* (17 October 1914).
125. Alfred Kreymborg, "Gertrude Stein—Hoax and Hoaxtress: A Study of the Woman Whose 'Tender Buttons' Has Furnished New York With a New Kind of Amusement." New York *Morning Telegraph* (7 March 1915).
126. Sherwood Anderson, *A Story-Teller's Story* (Garden City, NY: Garden City Publishing Company, 1924), 5.
127. Kay Boyle, ed. *Being Geniuses Together*, by Robert McAlmon (Baltimore: Johns Hopkins University Press, 1984), 19–20.
128. Brinnin, 213.
129. Smith, 19.
130. *Ibid.*, 112.
131. Turner, 13.
132. Canby, 313.
133. Curtis D. MacDougal, *Hoaxes*. 1940 (New York: Dover Publications, Inc., 1958), 272.
134. William Jay Smith, *The Spectra Hoax* (Middletown, CT: Wesleyan University Press, 1961), 9.
135. Witter Bynner, "The Spectric Poets," *New Republic* (18 November 1916), 13.
136. Smith, 11–12.
137. Monroe, 408.

138. Smith, 15.
139. Thomas Ybarra, "Soulful Spectrism Nothing But a Hoax," *New York Times Magazine* (2 June 1918), 11; Smith, 35.
140. Smith, 37, 42. See also Suzanne W. Churchill, "The Lying Game: Others and the Great Spectra Hoax of 1917," *Little Magazines and Modernism: New Approaches*, ed. Suzanne W. Churchill and Adam McKible (Burlington, VT: Ashgate, 2007), 177–95.
141. *Ibid.*, 44.
142. Randolph Bourne, "Traps for the Unwary," *The Dial* (28 March 1918), 277–78.
143. MacDougal, 271.
144. Robert Bartlett Haas, "Gertrude Stein Talking—A Transatlantic Interview," *UCLAN Review* (Winter 1964), 44.
145. McBride arranged to have "M. Vollard et Cézanne" printed in the *Sun* on 10 October 1915 (section 5, page 12), accompanied by analysis by himself that included a letter from Stein explaining her relationship to Vollard, the picture dealer who sold Leo and Gertrude Stein their first Cézannes.
146. Stein, 133.
147. *Ibid.*, 35.
148. Mellow, 194.
149. Lynn Lee, *Don Marquis* (Boston: Twayne Publishers, 1981), 9.
150. E. B. White, *The Second Tree from the Corner* (New York: Harper & Brothers Publishers, 1954), 185–89.
151. Tischler, 12–27.
152. F. H. Young, "Topics of the Day" Providence RI *Bulletin* (29 June 1914).
153. "Line-O'-Type or Two," *Chicago Tribune* (20 November 1914), 6; "Line-O'-Type or Two," *Chicago Tribune* (26 April 1915), 6.
154. Lee, 61.
155. Don Marquis "The Sun Dial: Thoughts of Hermione," New York City *Evening Sun* (13 March 1915).
156. Don Marquis, "The Sun Dial," New York *Evening Sun* (8 July 1914), 10.
157. Don Marquis, "The Sun Dial: Gertrude Stein's Hints for the Table," New York *Evening Sun* (28 August 1914), 6.
158. Don Marquis, "The Sun Dial," New York Evening Sun (16 September 1914), 10. See also (16 September 1914), 10; (17 September 1914), 10; (18 September 1914), 12; (1 October 1914), 10; (4 February 1915), 10.
159. Don Marquis, "The Sun Dial," New York *Evening Sun* (23 December 1914), 12.
160. Don Marquis, "The Sun Dial: The Sweets of Earth Come Slowly, Drop by Drop," New York *Evening Sun* (5 October 1914), 10.
161. Don Marquis, "The Sun Dial: A Week More of It and You Would Have Been Lost," New York *Evening Sun* (17 June 1914), 12.
162. Don Marquis, "The Sun Dial: Anyhow, We Were Getting So We Thought It Meant Something," New York *Evening Sun* (13 November 1914), 14.
163. Don Marquis, "The Sun Dial: The Gertrude Stein Club," New York *Evening Sun* (26 September 1914), 6.
164. Don Marquis, "The Sun Dial: There Is, But We Don't Know Why," New York *Evening Sun* (11 July 1914), 6.
165. Don Marquis, "The Sun Dial: Aphasia, the Muse of Futurist Literature," New York *Evening Sun* (25 July 1914), 4.
166. Don Marquis, "The Sun Dial: Recipe for a Futurist Drink," New York *Evening Sun* (3 August 1914), 10.
167. Don Marquis, "The Sun Dial: The Gertrude Stein Club Grows," New York *Evening Sun* (18 September 1914), 12.

208   Notes

168. Don Marquis, "The Sun Dial: A Sermon in a Stein," New York *Evening Sun* (9 June 1914), 12.
169. Don Marquis, "The Sun Dial: C'est Magnifique, mais ce n'est pas la Gertrude," New York *Evening Sun* (16 October 1914), 14.
170. Don Marquis, "The Sun Dial: Blond Beer: Or Brunette? Why?" New York *Evening Sun* (16 July 1914), 10.
171. Don Marquis, "The Sun Dial: Blond Beer: Or Brunette? Why?" New York *Evening Sun* (17 July 1914), 6.
172. Don Marquis, "The Sun Dial: One Woman Who Prefers Light Beer," New York *Evening Sun* (21 July 1914), 8.
173. White, 186.
174. Max Eastman, "Lazy Verse," *New Republic* (9 September 1916), 138–40.
175. Smith, 6.
176. Don Marquis, "The Sun Dial: To G. S. and E. P.," New York *Evening Sun* (3 October 1914), 6.
177. Don Marquis, "The Sun Dial: The Golden Group," New York *Evening Sun* (26 March 1915).
178. Don Marquis, "The Sun Dial: Gertrude Is Stein, Stein Gertrude," New York *Evening Sun* (15 October 1914), 10.
179. Don Marquis, "The Sun Dial," New York *Evening Sun* (30 September 1914), 12.
180. Don Marquis, "The Sun Dial," New York *Evening Sun* (13 July 1914), 8.
181. Don Marquis, "The Sun Dial," New York *Evening Sun* (14 January 1915), 12.
182. Don Marquis, "The Sun Dial," New York *Evening Sun* (22 June 1914), 10.
183. See Edmund Pearson, *Books in Black or Red* (New York: The Macmillan Company, 1923). The review in the *Detroit News* (23 September 1923) quotes this reference to *Tender Buttons*.
184. A. S. K., "The Same Book from Another Standpoint," *The Little Review* (July 1914); reprint in St. Joseph [MO] *News Press* (11 August 1914).
185. Kenneth L. Roberts, "Cubist Poems—After Gertrude Stein," *Life* (5 July 1917), 47.
186. Kenneth L. Roberts, "Cubist Poems—After Gertrude Stein," *Life* (16 August 1917), 317; *Life* (30 August 1917), 344.
187. Stein, *The Autobiography of Alice B. Toklas*, 186.
188. "Notes and Activities in the World of Art," New York *Sun* (11 February 1917).
189. Gertrude Stein, "Relief Work in France," *Life* (27 December 1917), 1076.
190. Stein, *The Autobiography of Alice B. Toklas*, 186.
191. Gertrude Stein, "A League," *Life* (18 September 1919), 496.
192. *Life* (26 April 1917), 746.
193. Roland Marchand. *Advertising the American Dream: Making Way for Modernity: 1920–1940* (Berkeley: University of California Press, 1985), 140.
194. Michael Murphy, "'One Hundred Per Cent Bohemia': Pop Decadence and the Aestheticization of Commodity in the Rise of the Slicks," *Marketing Modernisms: Self-Promotion, Canonization, Rereading*, ed. Kevin J. H. Dettmar and Stephan Watt (Ann Arbor: University of Michigan Press, 1996), 63–64.
195. *Vanity Fair* (June 1917), 55.
196. Gertrude Stein, "The Great American Army," *Vanity Fair* (June 1918), 31.
197. Conrad, 223.
198. "New Poems by Gertrude Stein," *Vanity Fair* (March 1919), 88b.
199. Everett, 240.
200. "Flat Prose," *Atlantic Monthly* (September 1914), 430–32.
201. Stein, 210.

202. Donald Gallup, "Gertrude Stein and the Atlantic," *Yale University Library Gazette* 28 (1954), 110.
203. *Ibid.*, 111.
204. *Ibid.*, 111–12.
205. Michael North, *Camera Works: Photography and the Twentieth-Century Word* (New York: Oxford University Press, 2005), 62.
206. Juan A. Suárez, "City Space, Technology, Popular Culture: The Modernism of Paul Strand and Charles Sheeler's Manhattan," *Journal of American Studies* 36 (2002), 91.
207. *The Soil* (December 1916), 3–4.
208. Frederick J. Hoffman, Charles Allen, and Carolyn F. Ulrich, *The Little Magazine: A History and a Bibliography* (Princeton: Princeton University Press, 1947), 31.
209. The first issue of *Rogue* included Stein and Wallace Stevens. The editor's note following Stein's piece stated: "*Rogue* threatens to publish Miss Gertrude Stein's History of a Family which is in nine volumes of five hundred pages each." Stein's "History" was eventually published as *The Making of Americans* in 1925.
210. "The Soil," *New York Herald* (3 March 1917).
211. "Periodical Notes," *Publishers' Weekly* (16 December 1916).
212. New York *Globe* (20 March 1915); "Magazine Features," Newark *Evening News* (27 March 1915).
213. "Publishers and Authors," *Los Angeles Times* (11 April 1915).
214. *Boston Times* (13 February 1915).
215. "Futurist Novel," Philadelphia *Public Ledger* (10 April 1915).

NOTES TO CHAPTER THREE

1. Brinnin, 264.
2. Myrtle Conger, "Investigations and Oil (After Gertrude Stein—With Apologies)," *Saturday Evening Post* (21 June 1924).
3. Rev. The American Caravan, New Orleans *Times Picayune* (18 September 1927).
4. Marjorie Reid, "Shopkeeper of Shakespeare and Company," New York *Times Book Review* (3 December 1922), 7.
5. Merle Schuster, "Paris, the Literary Capital of the United States," New York *Times Book Review* (23 December 1923), 13.
6. Mellow, 248.
7. Alyson Tischler, *Massive Modernism: Reading Gertrude Stein and Company*. Diss. University of Michigan, 2002. Ann Arbor: UMI, 2003. 3068982, 27.
8. Dougald McMillan, *Transition: The History of a Literary Era, 1927–1938* (London: Calder and Boyers, 1975), 23.
9. Terry Eagleton, "Nudge Winking." Rev. of *The 'Criterion': Cultural Politics and Periodical Networks in Interwar Britain* by Jason Harding. *London Review of Books* (19 September 2002).
10. Mellow, 283.
11. Tischler, *Massive Modernism*, 27.
12. Mellow, 283.
13. McMillan, 1; Irene and Allen Cleaton report that "*Life* printed a cartoon showing four drunken Americans in a Montparnasse bar, on their right hand a copy of *The Sun Also Rises* and on their left a copy of *transition*. One drunk is inquiring of the waiter, 'Garçon, what's that the orchestra's playing?' And the reply, 'Why, that's the Star Spangled Banner.'" *Books & Battles: American Literature, 1920–1930* (Boston: Houghton Mifflin Company, 1937), 39.

14. "Life's Birthday Party," *Life* (4 January 1923), 28.
15. Warner, 223–24.
16. Cleaton, 42.
17. Katie Hope Sternberg, "Gertrude Stein's 'Making of Americans' Is a New Year Offering of 1,000 Pages," *New York Herald Tribune—Paris Edition* (27 December 1925), 9.
18. Carl Van Vechten, *Peter Whiffle: His Life and Works* (New York: Alfred A. Knopf, 1922), 59.
19. Ibid., 121–22.
20. Gallup, 151.
21. Bruce Kellner, *Carl Van Vechten and the Irreverent Decades* (Norman: University of Oklahoma Press, 1968), 139.
22. *Ibid.*, 142.
23. Carl Van Vechten, *The Blind Bow-Boy* (New York: Alfred A. Knopf, 1923), 128.
24. *Ibid.*, 164.
25. *Ibid.*, 204.
26. Kellner, 195.
27. *Ibid.*, 198.
28. Carl Van Vechten, *Nigger Heaven*, 1926, intro. Kathleen Pfeiffer (Urbana: University of Illinois Press, 2000), 57–58.
29. Pfeiffer, xiii.
30. Gallup, 80.
31. "Gertrude Stein's 'Three Lives' Out in a New Edition," *Chicago Daily Tribune* (7 May 1927), 15.
32. Edward Burns, *Letters of Gertrude Stein and Carl Van Vechten*, Vol. 1 and 2 (New York: Columbia University Press, 1986), 146–47.
33. Pfeiffer, xvi–xvii.
34. Blackmur, 222.
35. Four Seas published *Studies in Chinese Drama* by Kate Buss in 1922.
36. Book published by Four Seas include: William Carlos Williams: *Al Que Quiere! A Book of Poems* (1917), *Kora in Hell: Improvisations* (1920), and *Sour Grapes* (1921); Conrad Aiken: *The Jig of Forslin* (1916), *Nocturne of Remembered Spring and Other Poems* (1917), *The Charnel Rose. Senlin: Biography and Other Poems* (1918), *The House of Dust* (1920); Richard Aldington: *Images Old and New* (1916), *War and Love: 1915–1918* (1919), *Images of War* (1921).
37. Gallup, 143.
38. Wagner-Martin, 167.
39. "Book News and Reviews," *New York Times* (1 October 1922), 7; "Latest Books," *New York Times* (27 May 1923), 31.
40. Gallup, 144.
41. Ulla Dydo, *Gertrude Stein: The Language That Rises*, 1923–1934 (Evanston: Northwestern University Press, 2003), 44.
42. Curnutt, 30.
43. Sherwood Anderson, Introduction, *Geography and Plays.* 1922. (New York: Dover Publications, Inc., 1999), 6–7.
44. Ibid., 8.
45. Sherwood Anderson, "Four American Impressions: Gertrude Stein, Paul Rosenfeld, Ring Lardner, Sinclair Lewis," *New Republic* (11 October 1922), 171.
46. Wagner-Martin, 156.
47. Rev. of *Geography and Plays, Bookman* (September 1923).
48. Gertrude Stein, *Geography and Plays.* 1922. (New York: Dover Publications, Inc., 1999), 239.

49. *Ibid.*, 182, 187
50. *Ibid.*, 83–84.
51. H. V. D., "Books and Viewpoints," *New York Globe* (19 May 1923).
52. Don Marquis, "Miss Stein's Latest," *New York Tribune* (19 May 1923).
53. "Angels Could Make Nothing of This Book," *San Francisco Chronicle* (1 July 1923).
54. F. H. Young, "Topics of the Day," *Providence* [RI] *Journal* (1 June 1923).
55. George W. Douglas, "Is Steinism Responsible for Modern Literature?" *Philadelphia Public Ledger* (29 May 1923).
56. N. P. D., "A Mumbo-Jumble of the New Books," *New York Globe* (19 April 1923).
57. Fanny Butcher, "Help! Help!" *Chicago Daily Tribune* (4 February 1923), 23.
58. "Book Gossip: Do You Like the New Poetry?" *Des Moines Register* (10 June 1923).
59. Donald B. Willard, "The Latest Thing in Prose Style," *Boston Globe* (31 October 1923).
60. Rev. of *Geography and Plays*, *Detroit News* (10 June 1923).
61. D. K., "Announcing the Discovery of a Great Prose Style," *Detroit News* (19 August 1923).
62. Mary M. Colum, "The Moderns," *The Freeman* (17 October 1923), 139–41.
63. "Shantih, Shantih, Shantih: Has the Reader Any Rights Before the Bar of Literature?" *Time* (3 March 1923), 12.
64. Stuart P. Sherman, Rev. of *Geography and Plays*, *New York Evening Post* (11 August 1923), 891.
65. "Prof. Sherman Invents a New Game," *Chicago Post* (15 August 1923); Rev. of *Geography and Plays*, *Detroit Free Press* (2 September 1923).
66. *Indianapolis News* (15 August 1923), Curnutt, 249.
67. *New York Times Book Review* (7 December 1924), 12.
68. Frances Price, "Sherman Takes a Liberal View of Literary Things," *San Francisco Chronicle* (14 December 1924).
69. "Words, Wonderful Words!" *Outlook* (6 June 1923), 117.
70. "Modern Masterpieces," *Chicago News* (11 April 1923).
71. H. T. Pulsifer, "The Book Table," Outlook (6 June 1923).
72. "Recent Books in Brief Review," *The Bookman* (September 1923), 84.
73. John W. Crawford, "Incitement to Riot," *New York Call* (19 August 1923); Curnutt, 27.
74. Kenelh Digby, "The Literary Lobby," *Literary Review* (19 May 1923); reprint *Duluth Herald* (27 May 1923).
75. G. E. K. "Miss Stein Applies Cubism to Defenseless Prose," *Baltimore Sun* (25 August 1923); Curnutt, 28.
76. H. L. Mencken, Rev. of *Geography and Plays*, *Smart Set* (October 1923), 144.
77. "Snobs," *New York Morning Telegraph* (2 September 1923).
78. Carl Van Vechten, "Medals for Miss Stein," *New York Tribune* (13 May 1923), 20.
79. *Detroit News* (10 June 1923).
80. Edmund Wilson, Jr., "A Selection of Bric-à-Brac: Disappearance of Miss Stein," *Vanity Fair* (June 1923), 18.
81. Kenneth Burke, "Engineering with Words," *The Dial* (April 1923), 408–09.
82. "Bedlam in Belles-Lettres," *New York Globe* (4 April 1923).
83. Ben Hecht, Rev. of *Geography and Plays*, *Chicago Literary Times* (1 July 1923), 2.

84. Stein attended medical school at Johns Hopkins from 1897–1901, but did not graduate.
85. Kate Buss, "The Writing of Gertrude Stein and Geography and Plays," *Voices: Journal of Verse* (Summer 1923), 133–36.
86. *New York Times* (13 May 1923).
87. *New York Times* (24 July 1927).
88. Margaret Anderson, *My Thirty Years' War: An Autobiography* (New York: Covici, Friede, 1930), 142.
89. "WE NOMINATE FOR THE HALL OF FAME: GERTRUDE STEIN." *Vanity Fair* (August 1922), 72.
90. *Chicago Daily Tribune* (24 January 1923), 10.
91. Gertrude Stein, "A Portrait of Jo Davidson: An American Revolutionary of Prose Sets Down Her Impressions of an American Sculptor," *Vanity Fair* (February 1923), 48.
92. Although Wilson's use of the word "queer" and Stein's repetition of "gay" throughout "Miss Furr and Miss Skeene" may suggest to today's readers that the story is about a homosexual affair, this interpretation would not have occurred to mainstream readers in 1923. See Perloff 202n1.
93. K. D., "When Helen Furr Got Gay With Harold Moos: A Narrative Written in the Now Popular Manner of Gertrude Stein," *Vanity Fair* (October 1923), 37.
94. Edmund Wilson, "A Guide to Gertrude Stein: The Evolution of a Master of Fiction into a Painter of Cubist Still-Lifes in Prose," *Vanity Fair* (September 1923), 60.
95. Poet and novelist Wylie had been in the public eye ever since her highly acclaimed 1921 book of poetry, *Nets to Catch the Wind*, was published. A major player in the New York literary scene, in 1923 Wylie married William Rose Benét, who became editor of the *Saturday Review of Literature* in 1924. The other "literary specialists" were: James Branch Cabell, Carl Van Vechten, Christopher Morley, Edna Ferber, Ernest Boyd, George Jean Nathan, Hugh Walpole, Thomas Beer and Burton Rascoe.
96. "Choosing the New Century's Best Books: A Discussion by Hilaire Belloc, Henry Seidel Canby, Gertrude Atherton, Van Wyck Brooks, Christopher Morley, William Lyon Phelps, Maurice Francis Egan, Carl Van Vechten, John Erskine, Richard Le Gallenene," *The Literary Digest International Book Review* (May 1923), 1–3.
97. "Ten Dullest Authors: A Symposium: A Group of Eminent Literary Specialists Vote on the Most Unreadable of the World's Great Writers." *Vanity Fair* (August 1923), 58.
98. Warner, 37.
99. "Current Magazines," *New York Times Book Review* (5 August 1923), 28.
100. "The Most Unreadable Authors," *Columbus Dispatch* (6 January 1924).
101. A.K. Tutler, "The New Curiosity Shop," *New York Post* (4 August 1923); Indianapolis News (25 July 1923); *Dallas News* (29 July 1923).
102. Tracy Lewis, "Senate Enlists Gertrude Stein," *New York Morning Telegraph* (2 March 1924).
103. Ruth Lambert Jones, "A Visit From St. Nicholas as it might be Converted Into Prose By: Harold Bell Wright, Gertrude Stein, James Branch Cabell, and May Sinclair," *New York Post* (22 December 1923).
104. "Mr. Dreiser Passes Judgment on American Literature," *New York Times Book Review* (23 December 1923), 7.
105. *Des Moines Register-Leader* (9 March 1924).
106. Hoffman, 2.
107. "Current Magazines," *New York Times Book Review* (16 July 1922), 28.
108. "Current Magazines," *New York Times Book Review* (10 April 1921), 27.

109. "Books and Authors," *New York Times Book Review* (26 December 1920), 29.
110. Fanny Butcher, "An Impressionistic Ulysses," *Chicago Daily Tribune* (1 October 1922), E17.
111. Cleaton, 57.
112. "'Broom' is Barred from Use of Mails," *New York Times* (15 January 1924), 17.
113. Alice B. Toklas, *What Is Remembered*, 1963 (San Francisco: North Point Press, 1985), 107–08.
114. Marek, 85.
115. Mark Morrisson, *The Public Face of Modernism: Little Magazines, Audiences, and Reception, 1905–1920* (Madison: University of Wisconsin Press, 2001), 135–36.
116. *Bronx News* (9 March 1924).
117. "Things in General," *The Reviewer* (April 1924), 233.
118. *The Reviewer* (October 1924), 410.
119. "A Stitch in Time Saves Nine," *Ex libris* (March 1925), 177; "Troubador: an Autobiography," *Ex libris* (June 1925), 278.
120. I. M. P., "Turns with a Bookworm," *New York Herald Tribune* (31 May 1925).
121. [SC] *Columbia Record* (7 June 1925).
122. *Tulsa World* (7 February 1926).
123. *Providence Journal* (13 September 1925).
124. Lloyd Morris, "History of American Artistic Revolt in an Autobiography," *New York Times Book Review* (29 March 1925), 7.
125. "Gyring and Gimbling (Or Lewis Carroll in Paris)," *The Saturday Review of Literature* (30 April 1927), 1.
126. Helen Henderson, "Combining Art and Literature: Is Decidedly Being Done During These Modern Days in Paris; James Joyce and Gertrude Stein Are Explained by Ardent Devotees," *Philadelphia Inquirer* (4 December 1927).
127. See, for example, "Talk of the Town," *New Yorker* (7 May 1927), 14; David Garnett "The Authors' Protest for Joyce—a 'Typo' In Gertrude Stein!" *New York Evening Post* (23 April 1927).
128. Janet Flanner, "Paris Letter," *New Yorker* (30 April 1927) 106–7. See also *Paris Was Yesterday: 1925–1939*, ed. Irving Drutman (New York: Popular Library, 1972), 20.
129. J. G. T., "More Authors Cover the Snyder Trial," *New Yorker* (7 May 1927), 69.
130. The *New Yorker* had published an article about the sensational Snyder trial the previous month; see Morris Markey, "Crime Passionel," *New Yorker* (2 April 1927), 36–40. Ruth Snyder and her lover, Judd Gray, had killed her husband, Albert Snyder, in order to collect his life insurance policy, but left numerous clues. They were electrocuted in 1928. James M. Cain incorporated elements of the case into *Double Indemnity* and *The Postman Always Rings Twice*.
131. McMillan, 23.
132. Noel Riley Fitch, ed., *In Transition: Writing and Art from transition magazine: 1927–1930* (New York: Doubleday, 1990), 195, 201, 152.
133. "Some Opinions," *transition* 18 (1929), 290–91.
134. "U. S. Citizens Give Self-Exile Causes," *Washington Post* (25 November 1928), R3.
135. Dydo, 165.
136. Gallup, 151.
137. Burns, 101.
138. Dydo, 107–08.

139. Marek, 96.
140. Mellow, 287.
141. Kate Buss, "English Books From Paris: The Three Mountains Press and Its Publishing Work," *Boston Evening Transcript* (18 July 1925). Buss quotes these prices from the subscription forms sent out by Contact Editions.
142. Fanny Butcher, "'Making of Americans' Is Not as Vivid as Was 'Three Lives,'" *Chicago Daily Tribune* (24 July 1926), 9.
143. Ford, 65–68.
144. Gertrude Stein, *The Making of Americans*, 1925 (Normal, IL: Dalkey Archive Press, 1995), 249.
145. Ibid., 191.
146. Leon Katz, *The First Making of the Making of Americans: a Study Based on Gertrude Stein's Notebooks and Early Versions of Her Novel*. Diss. Columbia University, 1963. Ann Arbor: UMI, 1967, iii.
147. Stein, *The Making of Americans*, 548.
148. Janet Malcolm, *Two Lives* (New Haven: Yale University Press, 2007), 127.
149. Gertrude Stein, "Portraits and Repetition," *Writings 1932–1946* (New York: Library of America, 1998), 298–99.
150. Fanny Butcher, "The Transatlantic Review," *Chicago Daily Tribune* (28 June 1924), 7.
151. [SC] *Columbia Record* (11 May 1924).
152. *Providence Journal* (4 May 1924).
153. "Current Magazines," *New York Times Book Review* (8 June 1924), 26; *New York Evening Post* (28 June 1924); reprint *Philadelphia Public Ledger* (29 June 1924).
154. Mary Crocket, "Gertrude Stein," *Modern Quarterly* 2.3 (1925), 233–37.
155. *Fresno Republican* (3 August 1924).
156. See Carlos Baker, *Ernest Hemingway: A Life Story* (New York: Bantam Books, 1970), 25; Kenneth Lynn, *Hemingway* (New York: Simon and Schuster, 1987), 234–35.
157. "Lardner Breaks Into Intelligencia Class," *Oakland Tribune* (3 August 1924).
158. Katie Hope Sternberg, "Gertrude Stein's 'Making of Americans' Is a New Year Offering of 1,000 Pages," *New York Herald Tribune*—Paris edition (27 December 1925), 9.
159. W. R. B. "We Cease Being Living," *Saturday Review of Literature* (12 December 1925).
160. Paul Rosenfeld, "Newcomers," *Saturday Review of Literature* (2 January 1926).
161. "The Virtue of Intolerance," *Saturday Review of Literature* (27 February 1926).
162. *Boston Transcript* (21 December 1925).
163. Willis Steell, "An American Novel That Paris is Talking About," *The Literary Digest International Book Review* (February 1926), 173.
164. "Gertrude Stein in Critical French Eyes," *The Literary Digest* (6 February 1926), 58–62.
165. [Cincinnati] *Commercial Tribune* (21 February 1926).
166. Katherine Anne Porter, "Everybody Is a Real One," *New York Herald Tribune Books* (16 January 1927), 1.
167. Elliot Paul, "From a Litterateur's Notebook," *Chicago Tribune* (15 May 1927), 7; "From a Litterateur's Notebook," *Chicago Tribune* (22 May 1927), 7.
168. Kate Buss, "Gertrude Stein as a Writer and a Personality," *Boston Transcript* (21 April 1928).
169. Edmund Wilson, *New Republic* (13 April 1927).

170. Flanner, 9.
171. Mellow, 293–96.
172. Stein, *The Autobiography of Alice B. Toklas*, 254.
173. Ford, 73.
174. "Composition as Explanation," *New York Times* (24 October 1926), sec. 2 p. 8.
175. *Louisville Herald* (6 March 1927).
176. *Saturday Review of Literature* (20 February 1926).
177. Flanner, 56.
178. Harry Hansen, "The First Reader," *New York World* (July 1929).
179. T. S. Matthews, "Peeling an Onion," reprint from the *New Republic* in *Boston Transcript* (16 July 1929); *New York Times* (21 July 1929); C. J. Bulliet, "Artless Comment on the Seven Arts," *Chicago Post* (9 July 1929); William Soskin, "Books on Our Table," *New York Evening Post* (3 July 1929).
180. "Life is Like That," *Dallas News* (30 November 1930), 2.
181. John G. Nichols, "Ezra Pound's Poetic Anthologies and the Architecture of Reading," *PMLA* 121.1 (January 2006), 170.
182. Harvey Breit, "The Anthologies: Of Remaking Many Books There is No End," *New York Times Book Review* (22 December 1946), 5, 12–13.
183. *Columbus Ohio State Journal* (28 March 1926).
184. Eugene Jolas and Robert Sage, ed. *transition stories* (New York: W. V. McKee, 1929), xi.
185. Ibid., 348–49.
186. "Latest Works of Fiction," *New York Times Book Review* (24 February 1929), 9, 14.
187. Bob Brown, *Readies for Bob Brown's Machine* (Cagnes-sur-Mer: Roving Eye Press, 1931), 161–62.
188. North, 75.
189. Brown, 177.
190. The dedication was to: "ALL MONKS WHO ILLUMINATED MANUSCRIPTS—ALL EARLY ORIENTAL ARTISTS—OMAR—GUTENBERG—CAXTON—JIMMY-THE-INK—BOCCACIO—RABELAIS—SHAKESPEARE—DEFOE—GOYA—BLAKE—STERNE—WHITMAN—CRANE—STEIN—JOYCE—PAGLIACCI—AND MYSELF."
191. "Letters of Gertrude Stein," ed. with an Introduction by Bob Brown in *Berkeley: A Journal of Modern Culture*.
192. Brown, *Readies*, 12.
193. "Golden Words," *New York Times* (13 December 1926), 20.
194. Harry Hansen "The First Reader," *New York World* (? October 1927).
195. Paul Jordan-Smith, "The Frowzy in Art and Letters," *Los Angeles Times* (4 December 1927).
196. Jo Ranson, "Varied Parade of Writers Provides Wealth of Reading" *Brooklyn Eagle* (29 October 1927).
197. D. S. L., "Literary Gifts Find Mart in New 'Caravan,'" Wichita [KS] *Beacon* (21 October 1928).
198. Rev. of *The American Caravan*, Lexington [KY] *Herald* (30 November 1927); *Boston Herald* (24 September 1927).
199. Henry Longan Stuart, "The First 'American Caravan' Comes to the Bazaars," *New York Times Book Review* (18 September 1927).
200. Karl Schriftgiesser, "The American Caravan Starts Its Journey," *Boston Transcript* (24 September 1927).
201. *New Orleans Times-Picayune* (18 September 1927).

216 *Notes*

202. Robert O. Ballou, "Travel Light or Heavy with the American Caravan," *Chicago News* (28 September 1927).
203. Harry Hansen, "The First Reader," *New York World* (17 September 1927).
204. *New York Herald Tribune Books* (27 November 1927), 20.
205. "The Lantern," *New York Herald Tribune* (7 November 1927).
206. Burton Rascoe, *Morrow's Almanack for the Year of Our Lord* (New York: W. Morrow and Co., 1927), 11.
207. See Jacquelyn S. Spangler, *Edward J. O'Brien: Best Short Stories and the Production of an American Genre.* Diss. The Ohio State University, 1997.
208. O'Brien, *Fifty Best American Short Stories* (Literary Guild of America, Inc., 1939).
209. "All Stories End," *Time* (18 October 1937), 84.
210. Carlos Baker, 10n; Hoffman, 12–13.
211. Hoffman, 279.
212. Ernest Hemingway, "Recent Publications," *Chicago Tribune* (Paris edition) (5 March 1923), 2; See Michael S. Reynolds, "Hemingway's Stein: Another Misplaced Review," *American Literature* 55.3 (October 1983), 432–34.
213. Gertrude Stein, "Recent Publications" *Chicago Tribune* (Paris edition) (27 November 1923), 4.
214. Lynn, 199.
215. Edmund Wilson, "Mr. Hemingway's Dry-Points." *The Dial* 82.4 (October 1924), 340.
216. Leonard Leff, H*emingway and his Conspirators: Hollywood, Scribner's and the Making of American Celebrity Culture* (Lanham, MD: Rowman & Littlefield, 1997), 16–18.
217. Paul Rosenfeld, *New Republic* (November 1925), 22.
218. F. Scott Fitzgerald, "How to Waste Material: A Note on My Generation," *Bookman* (May 1926), 262–65.
219. Ernest Hemingway, *The Torrents of Spring* (New York: Charles Scribner's Sons, 1926), 116.
220. Harry Hansen, *New York World* (30 May 1926), 4; quoted in Baker, 42.
221. Leff, 46, 63.
222. Leff, 171–72.
223. Janet Flanner (Genêt), "Paris Letter," *New Yorker* (18 December 1926), 90.
224. Volume one appeared in 1922; volume two (1925); volumes three and four (1927); volume five was published posthumously (1954).
225. Ernest Hemingway "My Own Life," *New Yorker* (12 February 1927), 23–24.
226. Leff, 106.
227. John Raeburn, *Fame Became of Him: Hemingway as Public Writer* (Bloomington: Indiana University Press, 1984), 104.
228. Gertrude Stein, 233–34.
229. Wanger-Martin, 234–35; Brinnin, 260–61; Raeburn, 62–63
230. Mellow, 355.
231. Ernest Hemingway, "The Farm," *Cahiers d'art* 9 (1934), 28.
232. June Provines, ""Front Views and Profiles," *Chicago Tribune* (6 July 1934), 15.
233. Ernest Hemingway, "Introduction," *This Must Be the Place: Memoirs of Jimmie the Barman* (New York: Lee Furman, Inc., 1937).
234. Anderson, 259–60.
235. Glass, 147–48.
236. Brinnin, 260.
237. Wagner-Martin, 201.
238. "Books and Authors" *New York Times Book Review* (25 December 1927), 19.
239. *Lincoln Journal* (1 January 1928).

240. *Savannah Press* (31 December 1927); *Philadelphia Public Ledger* (31 December 1927); *Spokesman Review* (2 January 1928).
241. *Seattle Times* (8 January 1928).
242. Ford, 235; Burns, xii–xv.
243. L. A. Sloper, "Bookmans's Holiday: Romance is Useful Knowledge," *Christian Science Monitor* (29 August 1928); *Saturday Review of Literature* (13 October 1928).
244. Providence RI Journal (26 August 1928); Rev. of "Useful Knowledge," *Portland Telegram* (3 December 1928).
245. "Gertrude Stein's Solemn Quest for Genial Obscurity," *Philadelphia Public Ledger* (5 January 1929).
246. Harry Hansen, "The First Reader" *New York World* (8 September 1928).
247. Katherine Anne Porter, "Second Wind," *New York Herald Tribune* (23 September 1928). See also Isaac Goldberg, "In the World of Books," *Haldeman Julius Weekly* [Gerary, KS] (1 October 1927); Neal O'Hara, "Top o' The Morning," *St. Paul Pioneer Press* (4 October 1929).
248. Edmund Wilson, "Nonsense," *New Republic* (20 February 1929), 21–22.
249. *Hartford Times* (22 November 1927).
250. S. T. Williamson, "Stranger Than Fiction: A Bird in the Hand," *New York Times* (25 April 1926), sec. 9, p. 2.
251. Fanny Butcher, "An Impressionistic Ulysses," *Chicago Daily Tribune* (1 October 1922), 17.
252. Harry Hansen "The First Reader," *New York World* (28 November 1926).
253. Steven Watson, *Prepare for Saints: Gertrude Stein, Virgil Thomson, and the Mainstreaming of American Modernism* (New York: Random House, 1998), 93–94.
254. Max Eastman, "The Cult of Unintelligibility," *Harper's* (April 1929), 632.
255. Harry Hansen, "The First Reader," *New York World* (4 May 1929).
256. Isabel Paterson, "Books and Other Things," *New York Herald Tribune* (17 February 1928).
257. I. M. P., "Turns With a Bookworm," *New York Herald Tribune* (17 June 1928).
258. I. M. P., "Turns with a Bookworm," *New York Herald Tribune* (14 April 1929).
259. Lloyd Morris, "Modern Style and Contemporary Writers," *Galveston News* (17 February 1929).
260. James Weber Linn, "Round About Chicago: Current Literature," *Chicago Herald Examiner* (13 February 1928).
261. Robert Coates, "Books, Books Books: A Brief Consideration of Some Aspects of Modern American Writing," *New Yorker* (20 February 1932), 71.
262. Charles Driscoll, "The World and All: Futility," *Paterson Call* (21 February 1928).
263. "Injustice to Genius," *New York Times* (10 February 1925).
264. "Mostly at Random," *Louisville Post* (15 December 1929).
265. *Boston Transcript* (20 May 1929). See also John Gunther, "Surrealism, Latest Fad of Parisians," *Hartford Times* (4 February 1929).
266. Carl Sandburg, "From the Notebook of Carl Sandburg," *Chicago Daily News* (9 January 1929).

NOTES TO CHAPTER FOUR

1. Dino Ferrari, "Mr. Kallen Berates Current Artistic Values," *New York Times Book Review* (15 June 1930), 2.
2. "Comic Paris," *New York Times Book Review* (26 July 1931), 6–7.

3. Laura Riding, *Contemporaries and Snobs* (New York: Doubleday Doran, 1928), 188–89.
4. Paul Rosenfeld, *By Way of Art* (New York: Coward McCann Inc., 1928), 111.
5. Harry Hansen, "The First Reader" *Chicago News* (23 January 1930).
6. Edmund Wilson, *Axel's Castle: A Study of the Imaginative Literature of 1870–1930* (New York: Random House, 1931), 276.
7. *Ibid.*, 286.
8. Harry Hansen, "The First Reader," *New York World Telegram* (11 July 1932); "A Great Stylist Reappears," *New York Times* (15 July 1932), 14.
9. *New York Sun* (11 August 1932).
10. *Worcester Telegram* (18 July 1932); *Washington D.C. News* (16 July 1932); *Tulsa Tribune* (29 July 1932); *Newark News* (16 July 1932); *Boston Herald* (13 July 1932).
11. Ford, 235–36.
12. *Ibid.*, 237–41.
13. Robert M. Coates, "Books, Books, Books," *New Yorker* (21 February 1931), 71.
14. B. K. H., "The Sideshow," *Providence Journal* (4 February 1931).
15. "Bookman's Holiday," *Christian Science Monitor* (7 February 1931).
16. Rev. of *Lucy Church Amiably*, *Kansas City Star* (7 February 1931).
17. Rev. of *Lucy Church Amiably*, *Boston Transcript* (11 March 1931).
18. Spokane [WA] *Spokesman Review* (15 May 1931).
19. Ellen Du Poy, "Gertrude Stein Writes Another Colorful Book: it's Called 'Lucy Church Amiably,'" *Chicago Tribune* (9 May 1931), 13.
20. Robert M. Coates, "Books, Books, Books," *New Yorker* (20 February 1932), 74.
21. *Ibid.*, 73.
22. *Cincinnati Star* (24 December 1929); *So. Bend*, [IN] *News Times* (24 December 1929); *Portsmouth* [OH] *Sun* (22 December 1929); *Sioux Falls* [SD] *Leader* (7 December 1929).
23. Stein, 93.
24. Robert Coates, *The Eater of Darkness* (1959), vii.
25. Laurence Vail ("the king of bohemia") and Peggy Guggenheim, whose name follows Vail's on the list, were married from 1922 to 1928.
26. Genêt, "Paris Letter," *New Yorker* (20 November 1926), 87.
27. Glass, 5.
28. *My Thirty Years' War* was published by Covici, Fried Publishers in New York, a firm that primarily published limited editions. Covici, Fried published Radclyffe Hall's *The Well of Loneliness* in 1928.
29. Margaret Anderson, 248–49.
30. See, for example, "Friend of Famous Writes Memoirs," Salt Lake City *Tribune* (14 May 1933).
31. *Chicago Tribune* (2 December 1933), 13.
32. Fanny Butcher, "Gertrude Stein is Pleased With Success In U. S.," *Chicago Tribune* (2 December 1933), 13.
33. Stein, 262
34. Mellow, 347.
35. *Ibid.*, 353; Ford, 248.
36. This column was reprinted in newspapers nationwide, including: *Aberdeen* [SD] *News* (9 July 1933); Wheeling [WV] *Register* (8 July 1933); Glens Falls [NY] *Post Star* (8 July 1933); Clinton [IA] *Herald* (8 July 1933).
37. Maslin, Marshall, "All of Us," Clinton [IA] *Herald* (8 July 1933).
38. Carolyn Wells, "Gertrude Stein," *Chicago Herald* (18 May 1933), reprint in Washington D. C. *Herald* (10 June 1933); Philadelphia *Public Ledger* (2 August 1933).

39. Frank Sullivan, "The Autobiography of Alice B. Sullivan," *New Yorker* (1 July 1933), 13.
40. "Autobiographic Bombast," Torrington [CT] *Register* (8 Jul 1933).
41. "Letters: On Understanding a Stein," *Atlantic Monthly* (Aug 1933), 20.
42. Harry Hansen, "The First Reader," *New York World* (25 April 1933) (syndicated).
43. Burns, 265; When the *Autobiography* was released, the *Philadelphia Record* repeated Hansen's initial remarks and the responses he printed in the subsequent column (3 September 1933).
44. Isabel Paterson, "Books and Things: Gertrude and Alice," *New York Herald Tribune Books* (11 July 1933).
45. I. M. P., "Turns With a Bookworm," *New York Herald Tribune Books* (23 July 1933).
46. Edward M. Kingsbury, "Gertrude Stein Articulates at Last: Her Autobiography, Written Simply, Is Thronged With Contemporary Figures in Literature and Art," *New York Times Book Review* (3 September 1933).
47. Advertisement for *The Autobiography of Alice B. Toklas*, *Publishers' Weekly* (5 August 1933), 340.
48. Bess M. Wilson, "New View of Gertrude Stein," *Minneapolis Journal* (15 October 1933).
49. I. M. P., "Turns With a Bookworm," *New York Herald Tribune Books* (12 November 1933), 31; *New York Times* (3 November 1933); "She Means," New York *Evening Post* (6 November 1933); New York *Sun* (6 November 1933); "That's All There is, Says Gertrude Stein," Fort Worth *Star-Telegram* (12 November 1933); Kansas City *Star* (18 November 1933); *Chattanooga* [TN] *Times* (19 November 1933); [Seattle] *Town Crier* (2 December 1933).
50. *Tulsa World* (12 November 1933).
51. Floyd Van Vuren, *Milwaukee Journal* (11 November 1933).
52. "Alice B. Toklas Explains," *Providence Journal* (8 November 1933).
53. "Shop Talk," *Watertown* [NY] *Times* (14 November 1933).
54. E. H. Suvdam, San Francisco *Call Bulletin* (18 November 1933).
55. "Gertrude Stein Says She Means Just What She Says She Means Just What She Says She Means," *Boston Post* (26 November 1933).
56. Mellow, 354.
57. See Mellow, 354–8, for further analysis of the book's reception.
58. McDonald, 27.
59. Harry Hansen, "These Literary Lobbies," *North American Review* (August 1930), 166–67.
60. [Jacksonville, FL] *Times Union* (10 September 1933).
61. Louis Bromfield, "Gertrude Stein, Experimenter with Words," *New York Herald Tribune Books* (3 September 1933), 1.
62. Bernard Faÿ, "A Rose Is a Rose," *Saturday Review of Literature* (2 September 1933), 77–78.
63. Lewis Gannett, "Books and Things," *New York Herald Tribune* (1 September 1933), 15; reprint in *Charleston* [WV] *Mail* (4 September 1933) and elsewhere.
64. Mina Curtiss, Rev. of *The Autobiography of Alice B. Toklas*, *Atlantic Monthly* (November 1933), 8.
65. Edmund Wilson, "27 rue de Fleurus," *New Republic* (11 October 1933), 246–7.
66. Caroline Bancroft, "Fantastic Absurdity Creates Demand for Story of Her Life," *Rocky Mountain News* (October 1933), 4.
67. The poem also appeared in the *Pittsburgh Press* (15 April 1934) with the first line: "I don't like the family Stein." In this article, various naives of Pittsburgh are asked if they knew the Stein family when they lived in the area. One woman responded: "Gertrude Stein? Oh yes. I accidentally tuned

in when they were broadcasting her opera. It was the most terrible drivel. No, I certainly didn't know she was born in this vicinity."
68. "The Book Boat," [Memphis] *Commercial Appeal* (10 September 1933).
69. "Stein Opus," [Salt Lake City] *Deseret News* (13 January 1934).
70. [Topeka, Kansas] *Capital* (10 September 1933).
71. William Troy, "A Note on Gertrude Stein," *Nation* (6 September 1933), 274–75.
72. Fanny Butcher, "Gertrude Stein Writes a Book in Simple Style: Readers Can Understand Her Autobiography," *Chicago Tribune* (2 September 1933).
73. Harry Hansen, "The First Reader," *New York World Telegram* (1 September 1933).
74. *Augusta* [GA] *Herald* (10 September 1933).
75. Samuel Putnam, "A Book a Day," *New York Sun* (2 September 1933).
76. F. A. W., Jr., "New Books on Art: The Autobiography of Alice B. Toklas," *American Magazine of Art* (November 1933).
77. Stuart Sherman, "Letter to a Lady in the Country," *New York Herald Tribune Books* (28 March 1926), 8; qtd. Rubin 79.
78. Dorothy Canfield Fisher, "American Readers and Books," *American Scholar* (Spring 1944), 179–191.
79. W.A. Martin, Rev. of *The Autobiography of Alice B. Toklas*, *Buffalo News* (9 September 1933).
80. Paul Jordan-Smith, "I'll Be Judge; You Be Jury," *Los Angeles Times* (10 September 1933).
81. Theodore Hall, "Miss Stein Looks Homeward," *Washington Post* (8 October 1933).
82. E.J.C., Rev. of "The Autobiography of Alice B. Toklas," *America* (28 October 1933).
83. Amy Loveman, Rev. of The Autobiography of Alice B. Toklas, *Book-of-the-Month Club News* (October 1933).
84. B.Y., "Gertrude Stein's Life," *Chicago Herald-Examiner* (16 September 1933); "Brain Anatomy: Miss Stein Does Friend's Autobiography," *News-Week* (9 September 1933).
85. "Gertrude Stein Reveals Herself in Autobiography," *Dallas Times-Herald* (24 September 1933).
86. Clifton Fadiman, "Books: 'I like being all alone with english and myself,'" *New Yorker* (2 September 1933), 50–51.
87. J.H. Leek, "It's Strange." *Daily Oklahoman* (28 January 1934).
88. Mary M. Colum, "Mr. Crane, Miss Stein, and Expression," *The Forum* (December 1933), 334.
89. I.M.P., "Turns With a Bookworm," *New York Herald Tribune Books* (1 October 1933), 19.
90. Alexander Fried, "Poking About. . ." *San Francisco Chronicle* (18 October 1933).
91. Isaac Goldberg, "A Stein on the Table," *Panorama* (April 1934), 8.
92. Rev. of *The Autobiography of Alice B. Toklas*, *Christian Century* (20 September 1933).
93. Mary Rennels, Rev. of *The Autobiography of Alice B. Toklas*, *Cleveland News* (9 September 1933).
94. Herbert Gorman "Gertrude Stein's Excellent Autobiography—Her Lasting Influence on Modern Writers," *New York Post* (1 September 1933).
95. Edna Lou Wilton, "Gertrude Stein," *Scribner's* (October 1933); Rev. of *The Autobiography of Alice B. Toklas*, *Des Moines Register* (5 November 1933); *Florida Times Union* (8 October 1933); "Toklas and Stein," *Mason Telegraph* (26 September 1933).

96. Lewis Gannett, "Books and Things," *New York Herald Tribune Books* (31 October 1933).
97. "Recent Books I Have Liked," *New York Herald Tribune* (3 December 1933); "Recent Books I Have Liked," *New York Herald Tribune* (18 December 1933). Boyle's list also includes Nathanael West's *Miss Lonelyhearts*, Virginia Woolf's *Flush* and William Faulkner's *Light in August*.
98. Harry Hansen, *Publishers' Weekly* (20 January 1934).
99. Burns, 277.
100. "The Apotheosis of Miss Stein, 1934," *Vanity Fair* (May 1934), 21.
101. Steven Watson has described in detail the entire history of the production of *Four Saints in Three Acts* in *Prepare for Saints*.
102. Watson, 278, 286.
103. "Stein Opera: First-Nighters Hear Four Acts of '4 Saints in 3 Acts," *Newsweek* (17 February 1934), 37–38.
104. Rogers, 49–50.
105. Mellow, 368.
106. Marianne Moore to John Warner Moore (1 March 1934); in *The Selected Letters of Marianne Moore*, ed. Bonnie Costello, Celeste Goodridge, and Cristanne Miller (New York: Alfred A. Knopf, 1997).
107. Watson, 268, 280.
108. Joseph Parisi and Stephen Young, ed. and compiled, *Dear Editor: A History of Poetry in Letters: The First Fifty Years, 1912–1962* (New York: W. W. Norton & Company, 2002), 312.
109. Mellow, 369.
110. Olin Downes, "Broadway Greets a New Kind of Opera," *New York Times* (21 February 1934), 22.
111. Mellow, 369.
112. Brinnin, 326.
113. Watson, 293.
114. *Ibid.*, 286.
115. Brinnin, 326.
116. Watson, 286.
117. *Ibid.*, 4–5.
118. *Ibid.*, 284.
119. William Carlos Williams, *Selected Essays* (New York: Random House, 1954), 161.
120. Downes, 22.
121. Watson, 74.
122. *Ibid.*, 12.
123. *Ibid.*, 6.
124. Downes, 22.
125. Watson, 288.
126. Burns, 290.
127. *Ibid.*, 303.
128. J. W. Krutch "Four Saints in Three Acts," *Commonweal* (9 March 1934), 525.
129. Helen Clanton, "Salute to Gertrude Stein (Who Needs No Press Agent)," *St. Louis Globe Democrat* (23 February 1934), sec. 3 p. 1.
130. Mellow, 371.
131. W. G. Rogers, *When This You See Remember Me: Gertrude Stein in Person* (New York: Rinehart, 1948), 90.
132. Cheney, 123.
133. Mellow, 376.
134. "Gertrude Stein's U. S. Visit in Fall Awaited Eagerly," *St. Paul Dispatch* (16 July 1934).

135. "Gertrude Stein, Coming From Paris, Promises to Create Literary Sensation," *Iowa City Press Citizen* (23 October 1934).
136. Gertrude Stein, "And now; And so the time comes when I can tell the story of my life," *Vanity Fair* (September 1934), 35, 64.
137. Stein, *Everybody's Autobiography*, 274–75.
138. *Ibid.*, 267; Bridgman, 135.
139. "'Nuts When Bloom Is On'—Gertrude Stein Is Coming," *Baltimore Sun* (8 October 1934).
140. "Gertrude Stein: Her Words 'Do Get Under Their Skin,'" *News-Week* (27 October 1934), 24.
141. Janet Flanner [Gênet], "Paris Letter," *New Yorker* (6 October 1934), 48.
142. "Talk of the Town," *New Yorker* (13 October), 22–23.
143. E. B. White, "Is a Train," *New Yorker* (27 October 1934), 26.
144. Melville Cane, "Appeal to Gertrude," *New Yorker* (3 November 1934), 84.
145. Thomas Kunkel, ed., *Letters from the Editor: The New Yorker's Harold Ross* (New York: Modern Library, 2000), 89.
146. "Reporter Tells in Stein Style the Stein Style," *Chicago Tribune* (25 October 1934), 17.
147. *Saturday Review of Literature* (3 November 1934); Norman Klein, "Gertrude Stein Barges In With a Stein Song to Stein," *New York Post* (24 October 1934), 1; "One Lecturer in Three Poses," *New York World Telegram* (24 October 1934), 1; "Gertrude Stein, Home Upholds Her Simplicity," *New York Herald Tribune* (25 October 1934), 3. "Gertrude Stein Arrives and Baffles Reporters by Making Herself Clear," *New York Times* (25 October 1934), 25.
148. Gallup, 298.
149. *Time* (5 November 1934).
150. Rogers, 98–99.
151. Mellow, 380.
152. *New Yorker* (27 October 1934), 14.
153. Evelyn Seeley, "Alice Toklas Hides in Shadows of Stein," *New York World-Telegram* (25 October 1934).
154. *Nation* (7 November 1934), 531.
155. Rogers, 96–97.
156. Brinnin, 343.
157. Mellow, 355, 393.
158. Gallup, 293.
159. The party was reported in "Book Notes," *New York Times* (27 October 1934), 13.
160. A manuscript titled "Pathe 1934" is reprinted in the *Letters of Gertrude Stein and Thornton Wilder*, 351. It does not specifically mention "pigeons on the grass, alas," but it does designate a moment for a quote (not identified) from *Four Saints* to be read.
161. Everybody's Autobiography, 288.
162. Thurber, 19.
163. "Gertrude Stein and the Pigeons," *New York Times* (8 November 1934), 22.
164. John Tebbel, *A History of Book Publishing in the United States, Vol. III* (New York: R. R. Bowker Company, 1978), 500.
165. Roba, 92, 100.
166. "Hansen Radio Reviews Pull," *Publishers' Weekly* (23 March 1935), 1232.
167. Rubin, 292.
168. Wagner-Martin, 210.
169. Burns and Dydo, 71.
170. *Ibid.*, 75.
171. Ernest Kirschten, "Stein Smile Wins Radcliffe and Words Bring Laugh," *Boston-American* (20 November 1934).

172. Alexander Woollcott, "Shouts and Murmurs," *New Yorker* (1 December 1934), 43.
173. George S. Kaufman and Moss Hart, *The Man Who Came to Dinner* (New York: Random House, 1939), 94–95.
174. The King, locked in a cage, says to the Queen: "Oh, no. There's nothing in here but me. I meant that it seemed like yesterday the Jubilee was next week and now its tomorrow." She replies: "There is someone in there with you and it's Gertrude Stein," Burns, 451.
175. Milton Kaplan, *Radio and Poetry* (New York: Columbia University Press, 1949), 3.
176. Ibid., 222–23.
177. Ibid., 212.
178. See, for example, "Leading Events of the Week," *New York Times* (11 November 1934), sec. 9 p. 14; "Today on the Radio: Outstanding Events on All Stations," *New York Times* (12 November 1934), 28; *New York World Telegram* (5 November. 1934); "On the Air," *New Yorker* (10 November 1934), 8.
179. Alton Cook, "Gertrude Stein to Settle All: Promises Microphone Interview for November 12—It Will Prove Her Style of Speech," *New York World Telegram* (31 October 1934).
180. Steven Meyer, "Gertrude Stein—A Radio Interview," *Paris Review* 116 (1990), 85–97; see *Everybody's Autobiography* for another discussion of football and "red Indians," 203–4.
181. "Notes on Books and Authors," *New York Herald Tribune* (3 November 1934), 9
182. "Playing the Stein Game," *New York Times* (7 November 1934), 19.
183. Theodore Hall, "Quips and Quiddities, or How Gertrude Stein Has Mark Twain Backed Off the Map," *Washington Post* (15 November 1934).
184. Harry Hansen, "The First Reader," *New York World Telegram* (17 November 1934).
185. Robert Strunsky, Rev. of *Portraits and Prayers*, *New York Sun* (17 November 1934).
186. "Perfecting Language," *New York Times* (19 November 1934), 16
187. "Literary Phenomenon Visits U.S.," *Birmingham News* (2 December 1934).
188. Irma Brandeis, "A Flair for Words," *New Yorker* (1 December 1934), 44, 46.
189. *Chicago Tribune* (25 November 1934), 3.
190. Gallup, 290–91.
191. "Also Out This Week," *New Yorker* (20 October 1934), 101.
192. Stein, 12.
193. Stein, *Everybody's Autobiography*, 172.
194. Rogers, 101.
195. Ibid., 110.
196. "The Carryall: Stein," *Springfield Union* (17 January 1935).
197. Gallup, 292.
198. "Gertrude Stein Gives Talk Before Century Club Here," *Springfield Union* (8 January 1935), 1.
199. George Jean Nathan, quoted in Ralph E. Renaud, "Foreign Lecturers Show a renewed Interest in America," *Washington Post* (27 January 1935), B5.
200. Robert Benchley, "The Running Gag," (no date/ source. 1935).
201. Heywood Broun, "It Seems to Me," *New York World* (7 November 1934).
202. Gertrude Stein and Alice B. Toklas Papers, Beinecke Rare Book and Manuscript Library, Yale University.
203. The picture is reprinted in Renate Stendhal's *Gertrude Stein: In Words and Pictures* (Chapel Hill: Algonquin Books, 1994), 141, courtesy of The Bancroft Library.

224   *Notes*

204. Neil Baldwin, *Henry Ford and the Jews: The Mass Production of Hate* (New York: Public Affairs, 2001), 141–45.
205. Wagner-Martin, 214.
206. T. S. Matthews, "Gertrude Stein Comes Home," *New Republic* (5 December 1934), 100–01.
207. Ralph E. Renaud, "Matinee Idols Find Spotlight Is Boring," *Washington Post* (1 December 1934), 9.
208. K. R. F., "Gertrude Stein Comes, Talks, Conquers Audience at Museum," no source (12 January 1935).
209. "Talk of the Town: Gtde," *New Yorker* (24 November 1934), 12–13.
210. Joseph W. Alsop, Jr., "Gertrude Stein Likes to Look at Paintings," *New York Herald Tribune* (2 November 1934), 1+.
211. "Captures Audience By Her Frankness," New York *Evening Journal* (17 November 1934).
212. "Quite Understandable," *Art Digest* (November 1934), 18+.
213. "Letters to the Editor," *Saturday Review of Literature* (24 November 1934), 308.
214. Amy Loveman, "The Clearing House," *Saturday Review of Literature* (22 December 1934), 388.
215. "Miss Stein Speaks to Bewildered 500," *New York Times* (2 November 1934), 23.
216. "Topics of the Times," *New York Times* (3 November 1934), 14.
217. I.M. P., "Turns With a Bookworm," *New York Herald Tribune Books* (11 November 1934), 36.
218. I.M. P., "Turns With a Bookworm," *New York Herald Tribune Books* (18 November 1934), 26.
219. "Gertrude Stein Gets Reporters That Way Too," *Chicago News* (8 November 1934).
220. "The Toklas Family Complete," *Chicago Tribune* (3 November 1934), 12.
221. "Audience Eyes a Simple Gown at Stein Opera: Author and Society Like New Work," *Chicago Tribune* (8 November 1934), 19.
222. Fanny Butcher, "Stein Lectures May Clear Up Thick Writing," *Chicago Tribune* (10 November 1934), 12; Fanny Butcher, "English Letters to Flower Next in U. S.: Gertrude Stein," *Chicago Tribune* (26 November 1934), 4.
223. June Provines, "Front Views and Profiles," *Chicago Tribune* (29 November 1934), 25. Hillyer is probably now most well known for his attacks on Ezra Pound in the *Saturday Review of Literature (*June 11 and 18, 1949), which appeared after Pound was awarded the Bollingen Prize for Poetry by the Fellows of the Library of Congress in 1949.
224. "Gertrude Stein Runneth Over and Over; Doesn't Understand What Audience Means," *Philadelphia Record* (16 November 1934); "Stein Is Stein and Art Is Art, Alas, Alas!" *Philadelphia Inquirer* (16 November 1934), 5.
225. "Miss Stein Class Question Mark Good Cattle Brander: Or It May be Used as Decoration, But It Is of No Use Otherwise As 'Anyone Who Reads Knows When Question Is Question,'" *Providence Evening Bulletin* (22 January 1935), 1.
226. Ernest Kirschten, "Stein Smile Wins Radcliffe And Words Bring Laugh," *Boston-American* (20 November 1934).
227. No date or source. The lecture in Madison was on December 6, 1934.
228. Ralph Kelly, "Miss Stein Calls This City a Mess," *Cleveland Plain Dealer* (21 December 1934).
229. "Ertsnay, Einstay: No Savvy Your Say: Gertrude Stein, Stein Is Here to Hear You Hear as She Talks, Talks She," *Daily Oklahoman* (26 March 1935), 1.
230. "Gertrude Stein Speaks of 'Poetry and Grammar' At Lecture Wednesday," *Columbus Dispatch* (18 December 1934), 14; "Gertrude Stein Just Folksy, Reporter Finds," *Toledo Blade* (20 December 1934), 6.

231. See, for example, Catherine R. Stimpson, "The Somagrams of Gertrude Stein," *Poetics Today* 6 (1985), 67–80.
232. Wagner-Martin, 208.
233. Toklas, *What Is Remembered*, 153.
234. "A Snub, a Snub, a Snub: Gertrude Stein Gives Carmel's Highbrows the Go-By," *San Francisco Examiner* (8 April 1935).
235. Mellow, 409.
236. See also *Los Angeles Illustrated Daily News* (30 March 1935).
237. David Edstrom, "Why Gertrude Stein Is What," *Los Angles Times Sunday Magazine* (14 April 1935), 3.
238. Annie Laurie, "Sound and Fury—La Stein Speaks," *San Francisco Examiner* (13 April 1935).
239. Burns, 411.
240. *Vanity Fair* (October 1933), 42; quoted in Watson, 180.
241. W. G. Rogers, *Gertrude Stein is Gertrude Stein is Gertrude Stein: Her Life and Work* (New York: Crowell, 1973), 164.
242. "Book Marks for Today," *New York World Telegram* (14 November 1934).
243. Burns and Dydo, 301.
244. Charles Hanson Towne, "Allow Me to Say: Portrait of A Triumphant Personality," *New York American* (February 1935).
245. Ogden Nash, *New York American* (22 March 1934).
246. Arthur Bernon Tourtellot, "A Backward Glance at Literary 1934," *Boston Evening Transcript* (29 December 1934).
247. "But a Stein Is a Stein Is a Stein," *New York Times Book Review* (18 November 1934), 10; Joseph W. Alsop, Jr., "In Words Gertrude Stein Finds Emotions: But This Critic Fails to Feel Them, and Wishes She Had Continued to Write Communicable Prose," *New York Herald Tribune* (25 November 1934); Henry Seidel Canby, "Cheating at Solitaire," *Saturday Review of Literature* (17 November 1934).
248. Reed Hynds, "Gertrude Stein in 'Portraits and Prayers': Enigma of Literary World Who Has Written 'That Way' for 20 Years Provides a Further Study of the Art of Unintelligibility," *St. Louis Star & Times* (16 November 1934); John Woodburn, "Aloft With Miss Stein in Verbal Fog," *San Francisco Chronicle* (20 January 1935).
249. Hershel Brickell, "Books on Our Table," *New York Post* (22 November 1934).
250. John Chamberlain, "Books of the Times," *New York Times* (7 November 1934).
251. Clifton Fadiman, "Books: 'I Am Not Amusing'—Gertrude Stein in 'Portraits and Prayers,'" *New Yorker* (17 November 1934), 106.
252. "Reader's Reminders List," *New Yorker* (24 November 1934), 112.
253. Edmund Wilson, "Review of *Portraits and Prayers*," *New Republic* (26 December 1934), 198.
254. *Little Rock Gazette* (19 November 1933); see also "Literary Topics," *Hartford Courant* (22 November 1933).
255. Edward Alden Jewell, "Alfred Stieglitz and Art In America: A Symposium Which Undertakes to Estimate His Cultural Contribution to Our Time," *New York Times Book Review* (23 December 1934), 4.
256. Clifton Fadiman, "Books," *New Yorker* (8 December 1934), 136, 138.
257. "Latest Dirt on Gert," *New Yorker* (16 March 1935); "Book Marks for Today," *New York World Telegram* (26 February 1935).
258. Burns, 407.
259. Fanny Butcher, "Paris Aroused Over Reply to Gertrude Stein: Six Declare 'Autobiography Is Inaccurate,'" *Chicago Tribune* (9 March 1935), 15.
260. Stein, *Everybody's Autobiography*, 32–33.

261. Isador Schneider, "Home Girl Makes Good," *New Masses* (27 November 1934), 21–22; Mike Gold, *Change the World!* (1936); reprinted in *Critical Essays on Gertrude Stein*, 76–77.
262. Bennett Cerf, "Trade Winds," *Saturday Review of Literature* (13 July 1946).
263. Lansing Warren, "Gertrude Stein Views Life and Politics," *New York Times Magazine* (6 May 1934), 9, 23.
264. "The Situation in American Writing: Seven Questions," *Partisan Review* (Summer 1939), 25–51.
265. The introduction was reprinted in *Modernism/Modernity* (September 1996); see Wanda Van Dusen's insightful analysis.
266. *The Previously Uncollected Work of Gertrude Stein*, ed. Robert Bartlett Hass (Los Angeles: Black Sparrow Press, 1973), 109.
267. William Rose Benét and Norman Holmes Pearson ed., *The Oxford Anthology of American Literature* (New York: Oxford University Press, 1938), 1446–53.
268. Burns, 584.
269. "Stanzas in Mediation" appeared in *Poetry* in February 1940, accompanied by Wendell Wilcox's explanatory piece, "A Note on Stein and Abstraction"; Gertrude Stein, "Liberation, Glory Be!" *Collier's* (16 December 1944), 14–15; Gertrude Stein, "Pierre Balmain—New Grand Succés of the Paris Couture Remembered from Darker Days," *Vogue* (1 December 1945), 126–27.

NOTES TO THE CONCLUSION

1. Edmund Wilson, *Classics and Commercials*, 118.
2. Burns and Dydo, 70*n*.
3. Burns, 452.
4. "Impossible Interview: Gracie Allen vs. Gertrude Stein," *Vanity Fair* (January 1935), 25.
5. Stein, *Writings*, 286.
6. Stein, *The Autobiography of Alice B. Toklas*, 208.
7. Stein, *Everybody's Autobiography*, 288–89.
8. Burns and Dydo, 106.
9. *Ibid.*, 112.
10. Marsha Orgeron, *Hollywood Ambitions: Celebrity in the Movie Age* (Middletown, CT: Wesleyan University Press, 2008), 160.
11. Burns and Dydo, 114, 115*n*; *New York Herald Tribune* (Paris Edition) (29 August 1936), 2.
12. Orgeron, 148.
13. *Ibid.*, 483.
14. Burns, 573.
15. Watson, 317.
16. "Books for Young People," *New York Herald Tribune Books* (24 September 1939), 1.
17. Burns, 615.
18. *Ibid.*, 627.
19. *Dear Sammy: Letters from Gertrude Stein and Alice B. Toklas*, ed. Samuel M. Steward (Boston: Houghton Mifflin, 1977), 37.
20. Burns, 667–78.
21. *Ibid.*, 670.
22. Burns and Dydo, 264.
23. Burns, 675.
24. June Provines, "Front Views and Profiles," *Chicago Tribune* (18 March 1940), 16
25. Stein, *Everybody's Autobiography*, 239.

Selected Bibliography

Anderson, Margaret. *My Thirty Years' War: An Autobiography.* New York: Covici, Friede, 1930.
Anderson, Sherwood. *A Story-Teller's Story.* Garden City, NY: Garden City Publishing Company, 1924.
———. *Winesburg, Ohio.* Ed. Charles E. Modlin and Ray Lewis Smith. New York: W. W. Norton & Company, Inc., 1996.
Anthony, Edward. *O Rare Don Marquis.* New York: Doubleday, 1962.
Ashton, Jennifer. *From Modernism to Postmodernism: American Poetry and Theory in the Twentieth Century.* Cambridge: Cambridge University Press, 2005.
Baker, Carlos. *Ernest Hemingway: A Life Story.* New York: Bantam Books, 1970.
Baldwin, Neil. *Henry Ford and the Jews: The Mass Production of Hate.* New York: Public Affairs, 2001.
Balken, Debra Bricker. *Debating American Modernism: Stieglitz, Duchamp, and the New York Avant-Garde.* New York: American Federation of the Arts, 2003.
Bell, Delta M. "'Melanctha' and Metonomy," *delta* 10 (May 1980): 19–31.
Benstock, Shari. *Women of the Left Bank: Paris, 1900–1940.* Austin: University of Texas Press, 1986.
Blackmur, Corrine E. "Selling Taboo Subjects: The Literary Commerce of Gertrude Stein and Carl Van Vechten," *Marketing Modernisms: Self-Promotion, Canonization, Rereading.* Ed. Kevin J. H. Dettmar and Stephen Watt. Ann Arbor: University of Michigan Press, 1996.
Blair, Sara. "Home Truths: Gertrude Stein, 27 Rue de Fleurus, and the Place of the Avant-Garde." *American Literary History* 12.3 (2000): 417–37.
Boorstin, Daniel. *The Image: A Guide to Pseudo-Events in America.* New York: Atheneum, 1980.
Bornstein, George. *Material Modernism: The Politics of the Page.* New York: Cambridge University Press, 2001.
Bourdieu, Pierre. *Distinction: A Social Critique of the Judgment of Taste.* Trans. Richard Nice. Cambridge: Harvard University Press, 1984.
———. *The Rules of Art: Genesis and Structure of the Literary Field.* Trans. Susan Emanuel. Stanford: Stanford University Press, 1995.
Bourne, Randolph. "Traps for the Unwary," *The Dial* (28 March 1918): 277–79.
Boyle, Kay. Revised and Ed. *Being Geniuses Together.* By Robert McAlmon. Baltimore: Johns Hopkins University Press, 1984.
Breit, Harvey. "The Anthologies: Of Remaking Many Books There is No End," *New York Times Book Review* (22 December 1946): 5, 12–13.
Breslin, James E. "Gertrude Stein and the Problems of Autobiography." *Georgia Review* 33 (1979): 901–13.

Bridgman, Richard. *Gertrude Stein in Pieces*. New York: Oxford University Press, 1970.
Brinnin, John Malcolm. *The Third Rose: Gertrude Stein and Her World*. Boston: Little, Brown and Company, 1959.
Brogan, Jacqueline Vaught. *Part of the Climate: American Cubist Poetry*. Berkeley: University of California Press, 1991.
Brown, Bob. *The Readies*. Cagnes-sur-Mer: Roving Eye Press, 1930.
———. *Readies for Bob Brown's Machine*. Cagnes-sur-Mer: Roving Eye Press, 1931.
Brown, Milton W. *The Story of the Armory Show*. Greenwich, Conn.: The Joseph H. Hirshhorn Foundation, 1963.
Burns, Edward. *Letters of Gertrude Stein and Carl Van Vechten, Vol. 1 and 2*. New York: Columbia University Press, 1986.
———. Forward. *Useful Knowledge*. By Gertrude Stein. New York: Station Hill Press, 1988.
Burns, Edward and Ulla Dydo. *The Letters of Gertrude Stein and Thornton Wilder*. New Haven: Yale University Press, 1996.
Canby, Henry Seidel. *American Memoir*. Boston: Houghton Mifflin Company, 1947.
Caramello, Charles. *Henry James, Gertrude Stein, and the Biographical Act*. Chapel Hill: University of North Carolina Press, 1996.
Cawelti, John G. "The Writer as a Celebrity: Some Aspects of American Literature as Popular Culture," *Studies in American Fiction* 5 (1977): 161–74.
Cerf, Bennett. *At Random: The Reminiscences of Bennett Cerf*. New York: Random House, 1977.
Cheney, O. H. *Economic Survey of the Book Industry: 1930–31*. New York: R. R. Bowker Company, 1931.
Chinitz, David E. *T. S. Eliot and the Cultural Divide*. Chicago: University of Chicago Press, 2003.
Churchill, Suzanne W. and Adam McKible, eds. *Little Magazines and Modernism: New Approaches*, Burlington, VT: Ashgate, 2007.
Cleaton, Irene and Allen. *Books & Battles: American Literature, 1920–1930*. Boston: Houghton Mifflin Company, 1937.
Conrad, Bryce. "Gertrude Stein in the American Marketplace," *Journal of Modern Literature* 19.2 (Fall 1995), 215–33.
Cooper, John Xiros. *Modernism and the Culture of Market Society*. New York: Cambridge, 2004.
Conn, Steven. *Museums and American Intellectual Life, 1876–1926*. Chicago: University of Chicago Press, 1998.
Coyle, Michael. *Ezra Pound, Popular Genres, and the Discourse of Culture*. University Park, PA: The Pennsylvania Sate University Press, 1995.
Crunden, Robert. *American Salons: Encounters with European Modernism, 1885–1917*. New York: Oxford University Press, 1993.
Curnutt, Kirk. "Inside and Outside: Gertrude Stein on Identity, Celebrity, and Authenticity," *Journal of Modern Literature* 23.3 (1999): 291–308.
———, ed. *The Critical Response to Gertrude Stein*. Westport, CT: Greenwood Press, 2000.
Davidson, Jo. "The Extremists: An Interview with Jo Davidson," *Arts and Decoration* (March 1913): 170+.
DeKoven, Marianne. *A Different Language: Gertrude Stein's Experimental Language*. Madison: University of Wisconsin Press, 1983.
———. "Gertrude Stein and the Modernist Canon," *Gertrude Stein and the Making of American Literature*. Eds. Shirley Neuman and Ira Nadel. London: Macmillan. 8–20.
———. "'Why James Joyce was Accepted and I was Not': Modernist Fiction and Gertrude Stein's Narrative." *Studies in the Literary Imagination* 25 (Fall 1992): 23–30.

Dettmar, Kevin J. H. and Stephen Watt, ed. *Marketing Modernisms: Self-Promotion, Canonization, Rereading.* Ann Arbor: University of Michigan Press, 1996.
DiBattista, Maria. Introduction. *High and Low Moderns: Literature and Culture, 1889-1939.* Ed. Maria DiBattista and Lucy McDiarmid. New York: Oxford University Press, 1996.
Diepeveen, Leonard. *The Difficulties of Modernism.* New York: Routledge, 2002.
Dupee, F. W. "General Introduction," *Selected Writings of Gertrude Stein.* 1962. New York: Vintage Books, 1990.
Dydo, Ulla. *Gertrude Stein: The Language That Rises, 1923-1934.* Evanston: Northwestern University Press, 2003.
Elson, Robert T. *Time Inc: The Intimate History of a Publishing Enterprise, 1923-1941.* New York: Atheneum, 1968.
Everett, Patricia R. *A History of having a Great Many Times Not Continued to be Friends.* Albuquerque: University of New Mexico Press, 1996.
Farrar, John, "The Weekly Reviews: John Farrar Compliments Them All," *Time* (3 November 1924): 14.
Ficke, Arthur Davison. *Spectra: A Book of Poetic Experiments*, by Anne Knish and Emanuel Morgan. New York: Mitchell Kennerley, 1916.
Fisher, Dorothy Canfield. "American Readers and Books," *American Scholar* (Spring 1944): 179-191.
Fitch, Noel Riley, ed. *In Transition: Writing and Art from transition magazine: 1927-1930.* New York: Doubleday, 1990.
Flanner, Janet. *Paris Was Yesterday: 1925-1939.* Ed. Irving Drutman. New York: Popular Library, 1972.
Ford, Hugh. *Published in Paris: American and British Writers, Printers, and Publishers in Paris, 1920-1939.* New York: Macmillan Co., Inc., 1975.
Gallup, Donald. *The Flowers of Friendship: Letters Written to Gertrude Stein.* New York: Alfred A. Knopf, 1953.
Gans, Herbert J. *Popular Culture and High Culture: An Analysis and Evaluation of Taste.* New York: Basic Books, 1974.
Gard, Wayne. *Book Reviewing.* New York: Alfred A. Knopf, 1928.
Gertrude Stein and Alice B. Toklas Papers. Yale Collection of American Literature. Beinecke Rare Book and Manuscript Library.
Gilbert, Sandra M. and Susan Gubar. *No Man's Land: The Place of the Woman Writer in the Twentieth Century, Volume 1.* New Have: Yale University Press, 1988.
Glass, Loren. *Authors, Inc.: Literary Celebrity in the Modern United States, 1880-1980.* New York: New York University Press, 2004.
Greene, Theodore. *America's Heroes: The Changing Models of Success in America's Magazines.* New York: Oxford University Press, 1970.
Hadas, Pamela, "Spreading the Difference: One Way to Read Gertrude Stein's *Tender Buttons.*" *Twentieth Century Literature* 24 (Spring 1978): 57-75.
Hansen, Harry. "Harry Hansen: Reviewer of Books," *Nation* (4 June 1924): 646-47.
———. "Literary Previews," *Writing Up the News: Behind the Scenes of the Great Newspapers.* Ed. Miriam Lundy (New York: Dodd, 1939).
———. "These Literary Lobbies," *North American Review* (August 1930): 162-68.
Hart, James D. *The Popular Book: A History of America's Literary Taste.* Berkeley: University of California Press, 1963.
Hegeman, Susan. *Patterns for America: Modernism and the Concept of Culture.* Princeton University Press, 1999.
Hemingway, Ernest. *The Sun Also Rises.* 1926. New York: Bantam Books, 1949.
Hoffman, Frederick J., Charles Allen, and Carolyn F. Ulrich. *The Little Magazine: A History and a Bibliography.* Princeton: Princeton University Press, 1947.

Hoffman, Michael J., ed. *Critical Essays on Gertrude Stein*. Boston: G. K. Hall & Co., 1986.
———*The Development of Abstractionism in the Writings of Gertrude Stein*. Philadelphia: University of Pennsylvania Press, 1966.
Hutchens, John K. "For Better or Worse, The Book Clubs," *New York Times Book Review* (31 March 1946): 1+.
Huyssen, Andreas. *After the Great Divide: Modernism, Mass Culture, Postmodernism*. Bloomington: Indiana University Press, 1986.
———"High/Low in an Expanded Field," *Modernism/Modernity* 9.3 (2002): 363–74.
Hyman, Stanley Edgar. *The Armed Vision: A Study in the Methods of Modern Literary Criticism*. New York: Vintage, 1955.
Jaffe, Aaron. *Modernism and the Culture of Celebrity*. Cambridge: Cambridge University Press, 2005.
Jameson, Fredric. *The Modernist Papers*. London: Verso, 2007.
———*Postmodernism: Or, the Logic of Late Capitalism*. Durham: Duke University Press, 1991.
Karl, Alissa. "Modernism's Risky Business: Gertrude Stein, Sylvia Beach, and American Consumer Capitalism," *American Literature* 80.1 (2008): 83–109.
Kaplan, Milton. *Radio and Poetry*. New York: Columbia University Press, 1949.
Kaufmann, Michael Edward, "Gertrude Stein's Re-Vision of Language and Print in *Tender Buttons*," *Journal of Modern Literature* 15 (Spring 1989): 447–60.
Kellner, Bruce. "Baby Woojums in Iowa." *Books at Iowa* 26 (1977): 318.
———*Carl Van Vechten and the Irreverant Decades*. Norman: University of Oklahoma Press, 1968.
Kostelanetz, Richard, ed. *Gertrude Stein Advanced: An Anthology of Criticism*. London: McFarland & Company, Inc., Publishers, 1990.
Kuhn, Walt. *The Story of the Armory Show*. New York, 1938.
Kunkel, Thomas, ed. *Letters from the Editor: The New Yorker's Harold Ross*, New York: Random House, 2000.
———*Genius in Disguise: Harold Ross of The New Yorker*. New York: Carroll & Graf, 1995.
Lee, Lynn. *Don Marquis*. Boston: Twayne Publishers, 1981.
Leff, Leonard. *Hemingway and his Conspirators: Hollywood, Scribner's and the Making of American Celebrity Culture*. Lanham, MD: Rowman & Littlefield, 1997.
Lyall, Mary Mills and Earl Harvey. *The Cubies A B C*. New York: G. P. Putnam's Sons, 1913.
Lynd, Robert S. and Helen Merrell. *Middletown: A Study in Modern American Culture*. New York: Harcourt, Brace & World, Inc., 1929.
Lynn, Kenneth. *Hemingway*. New York: Simon and Schuster, 1987.
McAlmon, Robert. *Being Geniuses Together: 1920–1930*. Revised with an afterword by Kay Boyle. Baltimore: Johns Hopkins University Press, 1984.
MacDonald, Dwight. *Memoirs of a Revolutionist: Essays in Political Criticism*. New York: Farrar, Straus and Cudahy, 1957.
MacDougal, Curtis D. *Hoaxes*. 1940. New York: Dover Publications, Inc., 1958.
McDonald, Florin I. "Book Reviewing in The American Newspaper," Ph.D. Dissertation, University of Missouri, 1936.
McMillan, Dougald. *transition: The History of a Literary Era, 1927–1938*. London: Calder and Boyers, 1975.
Malcolm, Janet. *Two Lives*. New Haven: Yale University Press, 2007.
Marchand, Roland. *Advertising the American Dream: Making Way for Modernity: 1920–1940*. Berkeley: University of California Press, 1985.
Marek, Jayne E. *Women Editing Modernism: "Little" Magazines and Literary History*. Lexington: University Press of Kentucky, 1995.

Masson, Thomas L., ed. *Tom Masson's Annual*. New York: Doubleday, Page & Co., 1925.
Mellow, James R. *Charmed Circle: Gertrude Stein and Company*. New York: Praeger Publishers, 1974.
Monroe, Harriet. *A Poet's Life*. New York: Macmillan, 1938.
Moran, Joe. *Star Authors: Literary Celebrity in America*. Sterling, VA: Pluto Press, 2000.
Mott, Frank Luther. *Golden Multitudes: The Story of Best Sellers in the United States*. New York: The Macmillan Company, 1947.
Morrisson, Mark. *The Public Face of Modernism: Little Magazines, Audiences, and Reception, 1905–1920*. Madison: University of Wisconsin Press, 2001.
Mott, Frank Luther. *American Journalism, A History: 1690–1960, Third Edition*. New York: Macmillan Company, 1969.
Murphy, Marguerite S. "'Familiar Strangers': The Household Words of Gertrude Stein's *Tender Buttons*," *Contemporary Literature* 32 (1991): 383–402.
Murphy, Michael. "'One Hundred Per Cent Bohemia': Pop Decadence and the Aestheticization of Commodity in the Rise of the Slicks," *Marketing Modernisms: Self-Promotion, Canonization, Rereading*. Ed. Kevin J. H. Dettmar and Stephan Watt. Ann Arbor: University of Michigan Press, 1996.
Nichols, John G. "Ezra Pound's Poetic Anthologies and the Architecture of Reading," *PMLA* 121.1 (January 2006): 170–85.
North, Michael. *Camera Works: Photography and the Twentieth-Century Word*. New York: Oxford University Press, 2005.
Orgeron, Marsha. *Hollywood Ambitions: Celebrity in the Movie Age*. Middletown, CT: Wesleyan University Press, 2008.
Parchesky, Jennifer. "'You Make Us Articulate'" Reading, Education, and Community in Dorothy Canfield's Middlebrow America," *Reading Acts: U. S. Readers' Interactions with Literature, 1800–1950*. Ed. Barbara Ryan and Amy M Thomas. Knoxville: University of Tennessee Press, 2002.
Parisi, Joseph and Stephen Young, Ed. and Compiled. *Dear Editor: A History of Poetry in Letters: The First Fifty Years, 1912–1962*. Forward Billy Collins. New York: W. W. Norton & Company, 2002.
Pease, Allison. "Readers with Bodies: Modernist Criticism's Bridge across the Cultural Divide," *Modernism/Modernity* 7.1 (2000): 77–97
Perelman, Bob. *The Trouble with Genius: Reading Pound, Joyce, Stein, and Zukofsky*. Berkeley: University of California Press, 1994.
Perloff, Marjorie. *21st-Century Modernism: The "New" Poetics*. Malden, MA: Blackwell Publishers Inc., 2002.
Peterson, Theodore. *Magazines in the Twentieth Century*. Urbana: University of Illinois Press, 1964.
Radway, Jancie. *A Feeling for Books: The Book-of-the-Month Club, Literary Taste, and Middle Class Desire*. Chapel Hill: University of North Carolina Press, 1997.
Raeburn, John. *Fame Became of Him: Hemingway as Public Writer*. Bloomington: Indiana University Press, 1984.
Rainey, Lawrence S. *Institutions of Modernism: Literary Elites & Public Culture*. New Haven: Yale University Press, 1998.
———, ed. *Modernism: An Anthology*. Malden, MA: Blackwell, 2005.
———. "The Price of Modernism: Reconsidering the Publication of *The Waste Land*," *Yale Review* 78.2 (Winter 1989): 279–300.
Ranson, Jo. "Varied Parade of Writers Provides Wealth of Reading" *Brooklyn Eagle* (29 Oct 1927).
Riding, Laura. *Contemporaries and Snobs*. New York: Doubleday Doran, 1928.
Roba, William Henry. *A Literary Pilgrim: Harry Hansen and Popular American Book Reviewing, 1915–1945*. Ph.D. Dissertation, University of Iowa 1979.

Rogers, William. *When This You See Remember Me: Gertrude Stein in Person.* New York: Rinehart, 1948.
———. *Gertrude Stein Is Gertrude Stein Is Gertrude Stein: Her Life and Work.* New York: Thomas Y. Crowell Company, 1973.
Rosenfeld, Paul. *By Way of Art.* New York: Coward McCann Inc., 1928.
Rubin, Joan Shelley. *The Making of Middlebrow Culture.* Chapel Hill: University of North Carolina Press, 1992.
———. "'They Flash upon That Inward Eye': Poetry Recitation and American Readers," *Reading Acts: U. S. Readers' Interactions with Literature, 1800–1950*, ed. Barbara Ryan and Amy M. Thomas. Knoxville: University of Tennessee Press, 2002.
Ruddick, Lisa. *Reading Gertrude Stein: Body, Text Gnosis.* Ithaca: Cornell University Press, 1990.
Ruland, Richard. *The Rediscovery of American Literature: Premises of Critical Taste, 1900–1940.* Cambridge: Harvard University Press, 1967.
Ryan, Judith. *The Vanishing Subject: Early Psychology and Literary Modernism.* Chicago: University of Chicago Press, 1991.
Scott, Bonnie Kime, ed. *The Gender of Modernism: A Critical Anthology.* Bloomington: Indiana University Press, 1990.
Steward, Samuel M., ed. *Dear Sammy: Letters from Gertrude Stein and Alice B. Toklas.* Boston: Houghton Mifflin, 1977.
Silver, Brenda. "Mis-fits: The Monstrous Union of Virginia Woolf and Marilyn Monroe," *Discourse* 16.1 (1993): 71–108.
———. *Virginia Woolf Icon.* Chicago: University of Chicago Press, 1999.
Simon, Richard Keller. "Modernism and Mass Culture," *American Literary History* 13.2 (2001): 343–53.
Smith, Barbara Herrnstein. *Contingencies of Value: Alternative Perspectives for Critical Theory.* Cambridge: Harvard University Press, 1988.
Smith, William Jay. *The Spectra Hoax.* Middletown, CT: Wesleyan University Press, 1961.
Spangler, Jacquelyn S. *Edward J. O'Brien: Best Short Stories and the Production of an American Genre.* Diss. The Ohio State University, 1997.
Stauffer, Donald A., ed. *The Intent of the Critic.* Princeton: Princeton University Press, 1941.
Stein, Gertrude. *The Autobiography of Alice B. Toklas.* New York: Harcourt Brace, 1933.
———. *Everybody's Autobiography.* New York: Random House, 1937.
———. *Four in America.* Intro. Thornton Wilder. New Haven: Yale University Press, 1947.
———. *The Geographical History of America Or The Relation of Human Nature to the Human Mind.* Intro. William H. Gass. Baltimore: Johns Hopkins University Press: 1973.
———. *Geography and Plays.* 1922. Intro. Sherwood Anderson. New York: Dover Publications, Inc., 1999.
———. *Last Operas and Plays.* Ed. Carl Van Vechten. New York: Rinehart & Co., Inc. 1949.
———. *The Making of Americans.* Foreword William H. Gass. Intro. Steven Meyer. Normal, IL: Dalkey Archive Press, 1995.
———. *Narration: Four Lectures by Gertrude Stein.* Intro. Thornton Wilder. Chicago: University of Chicago Press, 1935.
———. *Paris France.* New York: Charles Scribner's Sons, 1940.
———. *Selected Writings of Gertrude Stein, 1932–1946.* Ed. and Intro. Carl Van Vechten. New York: Random House, 1990.
———. *Stein Reader.* Ed. and Intro. Ulla E. Dydo. Evanston, IL: Northwestern University Press, 1993.

———. *Volume I of the Previously Uncollected Writings of Gertrude Stein*. Ed. Robert Bartlett Haas. Los Angeles: Black Sparrow Press, 1974.
———. *Volume II of the Previously Uncollected Writings of Gertrude Stein*. Ed. Robert Bartlett Haas. Los Angeles: Black Sparrow Press, 1974.
———. *Writings 1932–1946*. New York: Library of America, 1998.
Stendhal, Renate. *Gertrude Stein: In Words and Pictures*. Chapel Hill: Algonquin Books, 1994.
Stern, Philip Van Doren. "Books and Best-Sellers," *Virginia Quarterly Review* (January 1942): 44–45.
Stimpson, Catharine R. "Gertrude Stein and the Transposition of Gender," *The Poetics of Gender*. Ed. Nancy K. Miller. New York: Columbia University Press, 1986.
Suárez, Juan A. "City Space, Technology, Popular Culture: The Modernism of Paul Strand and Charles Sheeler's *Manhatta*," *Journal of American Studies* 36 (2002): 85–106.
Sutherland, Donald. *Gertrude Stein: A Biography of Her Work*. New Haven: Yale University Press, 1951.
Tebbel, John and Mary Ellen Zuckerman. *The Magazine in America: 1741–1990*. New York: Oxford University Press, 1991.
Tebbel, John. *A History of Book Publishing in the United States, Vol. II, III, and IV*. New York: R. R. Bowker Company, 1978.
Tischler, Alyson. "A Rose Is a Pose: Steinian Modernism and Mass Culture," *Journal of Modern Literature* 26.3/4 (2004): 12–27.
———. *Massive Modernism: Reading Gertrude Stein and Company*. Diss. University of Michigan, 2002. Ann Arbor: UMI, 2003. 3068982.
Toklas, Alice B. *What is Remembered*. 1963. San Francisco: North Point Press, 1985.
Turner, Catherine. *Marketing Modernism: Between the Two World Wars*. Amherst: University of Massachusetts Press, 2003.
Van Vecthen, Carl. *The Blind Bow-Boy*. New York: Alfred A. Knopf, 1923.
———. "How to Read Gertrude Stein." *The Trend* 7.5 (August 1914): 553–57.
———. *Interpreters and Interpretations*. New York: Alfred A. Knopf, 1917.
———. *Nigger Heaven*. 1926. Intro. Kathleen Pfeiffer. Urbana: University of Illinois Press, 2000.
———. *Peter Whiffle: His Life and Works*. New York: Alfred A. Knopf, 1922.
Veitch, Jonathan. *American Superrealism: Nathanael West and the Politics of Representation in the 1930s*. Madison: University of Wisconsin Press, 1997.
W., F. A., Jr. "New Books on Art: The Autobiography of Alice B. Toklas," *American Magazine of Art* (Nov. 1933).
Wagner-Martin, Linda. *"Favored Strangers": Gertrude Stein and Her Family*. New Brunswick: Rutgers University Press, 1995.
Warner, Elinor Hope. *"Officer, She's Writing Again": Gertrude Stein's American Readers*. Diss. University of Virginia, 1994. Ann Arbor: UMI, 1994. 9424456.
Watson, Dana. *Gertrude Stein and the Essence of What Happens*. Nashville, TN: Vanderbilt University Press, 2005.
Watson, Steven. *Prepare for Saints: Gertrude Stein, Virgil Thomson, and the Mainstreaming of American Modernism*. New York: Random House, 1998.
Weeks, Edward. "What Makes a Book a Best Seller?" *The New York Times Book Review* (20 December 1936): 2, 15.
Weinstein, Norman. *Gertrude Stein and the Literature of the Modern Consciousness*. New York: Frederick Ungar Publishing Co., 1970.
White, E. B. *The Second Tree from the Corner*. New York: Harper & Brothers Publishers, 1954.
White, Ray Lewis. *Sherwood Anderson / Gertrude Stein*. Chapel Hill: University of North Carolina Press, 1972.

Wicke, Jennifer. *Advertising Fictions: Literature, Advertisement and Social Reading*. New York: Columbia University Press, 1988.
Will, Barbara. *Gertrude Stein, Modernism, and the Problem of "Genius."* Edinburgh: Edinburgh University Press, 2000.
Williams, William Carlos. *Selected Essays*. New York: Random House, 1954.
Wilson, Edmund. *Axel's Castle: A Study of the Imaginative Literature of 1870–1930*. New York: Random House, 1931.
———. *Classics and Commercials: A Literary Chronicle of the Forties*. New York: Farrar, Strauss, 1950.
———. *I Thought of Daisy*. New York: C. Scribner's Sons, 1929.
———. *The Shores of Light: A Literary Chronicle of the Twenties and Thirties*. New York: Farrar, Straus and Young, Inc., 1952.
Wilson, Ian, Warwick Gould, and Warren Chernaik, eds. *Modernist Writers and the Marketplace*. New York: St. Martin's Press, 1996.
Wilson, Louis R. *A Geography of Reading: A Study of the Distribution and Status of Libraries in the United States*. Chicago: University of Chicago Press, 1938.

Index

A

Acton, Harold, 107
Adams, Franklin P. (F.P.A), 18, 19, 158
Agee, James, 150
Aiken, Conrad, 52, 75, 92
Aldington, Richard, 75
Aldrich, Mildred, 14, 63, 114, 169
Alighieri, Dante, 88
Allen, Gracie, 191–92
Alsop, Joseph, Jr., 165, 177, 179, 185
American Caravan (1927), 52, 67–68, 113–15
American Mercury, 18
Anderson, Benedict, 7
Anderson, Margaret, 68, 85, 91–92, 123, 138
Anderson, Sherwood, 8, 17, 29, 49, 61, 68, 69, 71, 73, 75–76, 79, 90, 95–96, 108, 116–20, 122, 131, 132, 136, 138, 147, 149, 155, 170, 172, 174, 190
Antheil, George, 128
Armory Show (1913), 5, 30–40, 44, 66
Arts and Decoration, 32–33, 61
Ashleigh, Charles, 46
Ashton, Frederick, 195
Asquith, Margot, 150
Astaire, Fred, 20, 191
Atlantic Monthly, 2, 8, 12. 13, 17, 19, 21, 35, 62–63, 117, 139, 141–44, 152–53, 156, 162, 167, 190
Auden, W. H., 15, 170
Austin, A. Everett, Jr., 157
Austin, Mary, 152

B

Baker, Carlos, 117
Barnes, Djuna, 6, 12, 61, 84, 109, 110

Barrymore, Ethel, 71
Beach, Rex, 184
Beach, Sylvia, 68, 91, 110
Beall, James M., 162
Beaton, Cecil, 158
Beede, Ivan 104
Bell, Clive, 140
Bell, Delta, 26
Bell, Vanessa, 140
Benchley, Robert, 12, 59, 158, 174
Benét, William Rose, 11, 92, 104, 190
Bennett, Arnold, 152
Benton, Thomas Hart, 177
Berkeley, Busby, 195
Berlin, Irving, 47, 71
Berners, Lord Gerald, 195
Bjørnson, Bjørnstjerne, 88
Blackmur, Corrine, 7–8, 74
Blackmur, R. P., 15
Blair, Sara, 4
Bodenheim, Maxwell, 64
Boni, Charles and Albert, 98
Book-of-the-Month Club, 2, 6, 16, 19–20, 120, 147, 153–54, 190
Bookstaver, May. *See* Knoblauch, May Bookstaver
Boorstin, Daniel, 22
Bosschère, Jean de, 92
Bourne, Randolph, 52
Bowles, Paul, 158, 194
Boyle, Kay, 49, 111, 156
Bradley, Jenny, 141
Bradley, William, 135, 141
Brancusi, Constantin, 32, 108
Brandeis, Irma, 172
Braque, Georges, 85, 187–88
Breit, Harvey, 109
Brewer, Joseph, 125, 134
Bridgman, Richard, 43

Brinnin, John Malcolm, 1, 26, 41, 67, 166
Bromfield, Louis, 6, 8, 71, 136, 149
Brooks, Cleanth, 41
Brooks, Van Wyck, 14, 67, 76, 113
Broom, 7, 68, 69, 92, 94, 96, 103, 121
Broun, Heywood, 8, 12, 18, 93–94, 174
Brown, Bob, 111–12, 135
Brown, Edmund F., 71, 75, 88
Brown, Milton, 33
Browning, Robert, 88
Bryher, Winifred (Annie Winifred Ellerman), 99, 109
Buck, Pearl S., 85, 170
Burke, Kenneth, 83, 137
Burns, George, 19
Burrell, Angus, 190
Burroughs, William S., 21
Burton, Richard, 48
Buss, Kate, 8, 68, 74–5, 83, 85, 100, 106
Butcher, Fanny, 8, 47, 91, 100, 102, 127, 139–40, 152, 179, 187
Butts, Mary, 100, 102, 109, 129
Bynner, Witter, 49–52, 114

C
Cabell, James Branch, 69
Calder, Alexander, 157
Camera Work, 7, 30–31, 35, 64, 65
Canby, Henry Seidel, 11, 15, 19, 50, 137, 185
Cane, Melville, 163
Cargill, Oscar, 43
Carroll, Lewis, 65, 96
Cather, Willa, 14, 190
Cerf, Bennett, 8, 20, 22, 163, 164, 166–67, 170, 178, 188, 190, 197
Cézanne, Paul, 25, 32, 65, 85, 140, 141
Chamberlain, John, 186
Chaplin, Charlie, 64, 71, 182, 191–92
Chicago Tribune, 8, 42, 187
Chinitz, David, 4
Churchill, Suzanne, 207n140
Claire Marie Press, 8, 42–3
Claudel, Paul, 88
Cleaton, Irene and Allen, 71, 91
Clifton, Violet, 138
Close-Up, 99, 112
Coady, Robert J., 64–65
Coates, Robert, 135–38, 147
Collier's, 21, 53, 116, 190
Colum, Mary M., 79, 154
Cone, Claribel, 35
Cone, Etta, 28

Conger, Myrtle, 67
Conn, Steven, 36
Conrad, Bryce, 3, 62
Conrad, Joseph, 14, 65
Contact Editions, 99–101, 109–110, 117, 137
Cook, George Cram, 46
Coolidge, Calvin, 71, 121
Cooper, Gary, 122
Cooper, James Fenimore, 88, 95
Cooper, John Xiros, 3, 199n9
Cosmopolitan, 13, 170, 183, 190
Coward, Noel, 14
Cowley, Malcolm, 137
Coyle, Michael, 4
Crane, Frank, 34
Crane, Hart, 114, 128, 132
Crane, Stephen, 25–26, 29, 190
Crawford, John, 81
Criterion, The, 18, 69, 100, 108, 109, 113
Crockett, Mary, 103
Crosby, Bing, 191
Crosby, Caresse, 111
Crosby, Harry, 111
Crowinshield, Frank, 71, 158
Cubies' ABC, The, 37–8
Cummings, E. E., 33, 61, 111, 128, 129, 131, 132, 161, 190
Curnutt, Kirk, 3
Curtiss, Mina, 150
Curwood, James Oliver, 184

D
Darantière, Maurice 135
Daring Young Man on the Flying Trapeze, The (Saroyan), 20, 191
Davidson, Jo, 33, 85, 158
Davis, Bette, 169
Defoe, Daniel, 140
DeKoven, Marianne, 26
Dial, The, 13, 52, 69, 73, 83, 107, 109, 114, 118, 119, 190
DiBattista, Maria, 4
Dickinson, Emily, 169
Diepeveen, Leonard, 42
Disney, Walt, 196
Dodge, Mabel. *See* Luhan, Mabel Dodge
Doolittle, Hilda (H. D.), 52, 78, 99, 100, 108, 109, 190
Doran, George, 9
Dos Passos, John, 14, 92, 114, 121, 190

Dostoyevsky, Fyodor, 88
Double-Dealer, The, 117
Downes, Olin, 158–59
Dreiser, Theodore, 25–26, 29, 89, 119, 137
Du Bois, W. E. B., 13, 74
Duchamp, Marcel, 32–33
Duffield, Pitts, 26
Dumas, Alexandre, 169
Duncan, Isadora, 138, 150
Dunham, Harry, 194
Du Poy, Ellen, 136

E
Eagleton, Terry, 69
Eastman, Max, 57, 128
Eater of Darkness, The (Coates), 137–38
Edstrom, David, 182
Ehrman, Lillian May, 194
Einstein, Albert, 130
Eisenstein, S. M., 84
Eliot, George, 88–89
Eliot, T. S., 1, 2, 12, 14–15, 29, 50, 68, 78, 86, 89, 108, 112, 133, 140, 156, 169, 185, 190; writings of: "The Love Song of J. Alfred Prufrock," 50; *The Waste Land* 2, 15, 78, 79, 89
Ellerman, Annie Winifred. *See* Bryher, Winifred
Ellis, Havelock, 108
Esquire, 20, 21, 122
Evans, Donald, 42, 47

F
Fadiman, Clifton, 163, 172, 186
Farrar, John, 10, 12
Faulkner, William, 14, 21, 75, 117, 155, 189, 190
Faÿ, Bernard, 147, 149, 160, 174
Ferber, Edna, 84, 119
Ficke, Arthur Davidson, 49–52
Fiedler, Leslie, 20–21
Fields, W. C., 20, 191–92
Fisher, Dorothy Canfield, 16, 29, 153
Fitzgerald, F. Scott, 18, 21, 68, 71, 120, 140, 141, 189, 190
Flaherty, Robert, 195
Flanner, Janet (Genêt), 6, 97, 107, 108, 121, 138, 163
Flaubert, Gustave, 25
Ford, Ford Madox, 99, 100, 102–03, 109, 119, 121

Ford, Henry, 71, 174–75
Ford, Hugh, 101
Forster, E. M., 112
Fortune, 14
Four Seas Company, 7, 71, 75
Frank, Waldo, 79, 132, 137, 186
Freud, Sigmund, 73, 81, 88
Frost, Robert, 14, 161
Fry, Roger, 140
Fuller, Buckminster, 157

G
Gannett, Lewis, 8, 12, 98, 149–50, 178
Garbo, Greta, 156, 197
Gard, Wayne, 9, 200n33
Gaugin, Paul, 12
Genêt, *See* Flanner, Janet
Gershwin, George, 128, 158, 178
Gide, André, 61, 129
Gilbert, Stuart, 6
Ginsberg, Allen, 21
Gish, Lillian, 197
Glass, Loren, 3, 138
Glebe, The, 96
Gogarty, Oliver, 35
Goodbye, Mr. Chips (Hilton), 17
Goethe, Johann Wolfgang von, 88
Gold, Mike, 114, 188
Goldberg, Isaac, 155
Goldman, Emma, 108
Gregory, Horace, 98
Gris, Juan, 108
Guggenheim, Peggy, 137

H
Hadden, Britton, 14–15
Hale, Dorothy, 157
Hale, Phillip, 27
Hall, Theodore, 171
Hammett, Dashiell, 182, 184, 191
Hansen, Harry, 7, 8, 9, 10–11, 16–17, 108, 113, 115, 116, 120, 126, 127–29, 133, 134, 137, 143–44, 148, 152, 168, 172
Hapgood, Hutchins, 26, 34
Harcourt, Alfred, 158, 171
Harding, Warren G., 67, 69
Hardy, Thomas, 87
Harper's, 91
Harris, Frank, 121
Hart, Moss, 20, 169
Hartley, Marsden, 31, 35
Havens, Raymond Dexter, 162
Hawthorne, Nathaniel, 190

Hayes, Helen, 122
H. D. *See* Doolittle, Hilda
Heap, Jane, 51, 68, 91–92, 100, 108, 123
Hecht, Ben, 17, 69, 83
Hemingway, Ernest, 8, 13, 14, 18, 21, 68, 71, 84, 99, 100, 102–03, 108, 109, 111, 114, 116–24, 140, 141, 155, 190; writings of: *Death in the Afternoon,* 123; *A Farewell to Arms,* 121–22; *For Whom the Bell Tolls,* 122, 124; *Green Hills of Africa,* 123–24; *In Our Time,* 119–20; *Men Without Women,* 123; *A Moveable Feast,* 124; *The Sun Also Rises,* 18, 120–21; *The Torrents of Spring,* 120
Henderson, Alice Corbin, 40
Henderson, Helen, 96
Hilltop on the Marne, A (Aldrich), 14
Hillyer, Robert, 114, 179
Hilton, James, 17, 168
Hitchcock, Alfred, 193
Hitler, Adolf, 189
Hogarth Press, 8, 100, 107, 112, 131
Holly, Flora, 26
Hound and Horn, 134
Houseman, John, 157
Housman, A. E., 78
Howard, Bruce, 159
Howells, William Dean, 64, 95
Hoyt, Helen, 41
Hughes, Langston, 73, 74
Hunt, Violet, 138
Hurd, Clement, 195–96
Huxley, Aldous, 108
Huyssen, Andreas, 4, 21–22
Hynds, Reed, 185

I

Irving, Washington, 190

J

Jaffe, Aaron, 3
Jeffers, Robinson, 169, 181
James, Henry, 13, 88–89, 190
Jameson, Fredric, 4–5
Johnson, James Weldon, 74, 156
Johnson, Samuel, 115, 154
Jolas, Eugène, 97–98, 110, 133, 187
Jones, Ruth Lambert, 89
Joyce, James, 1–2, 6, 7, 13, 14, 21, 22, 35, 68, 69, 78, 79, 85, 88, 90–91, 96, 97, 102, 109, 111, 112, 123, 127–28, 130, 132, 133, 134, 141, 187; writings of: *Dubliners,* 18; *Ulysses,* 2, 15, 68, 73, 79, 85, 90–91, 96, 102, 104, 135, 156, 200n24; *Finnegans Wake,* 7, 97, 119
Jubilee!, 20, 169

K

Kallen, Horace M., 131
Kandinsky, Wassily, 32
Kaplan, Milton, 169
Katz, Leon, 101
Kaufman, George S., 20, 169
Kenyon Review, 15
Key, Francis Scott, 169
Kilmer, Joyce, 41
Kingbury, Edward, 144
Kipling, Rudyard, 14, 38
Knish, Anne, 49–52
Knoblauch, May Bookstaver, 26, 31
Kreymborg, Alfred, 48–49, 67, 68, 92, 95–96, 112, 113, 114, 119, 130, 132, 138, 140
Kronenberger, Louis, 17, 120
Kuhn, Walt, 36

L

Lagerlöf, Selma, 88–89
Lane, John, 65, 140
Lardner, Ring, 103–04
Larsen, Nella, 26
Lascaux, Elie, 198
Laughlin, James, 161
Laurencin, Marie, 188
Laurie, Annie, 182–83
Lawrence, D. H., 79, 88, 118, 129
Lee, Lynn, 53
Lee, Ulysses G., Jr., 159–60
Léger, Fernand, 108
Levi, Julian, 137
Lewisohn, Ludwig, 97
Lewis, C. S., 14
Lewis, Sinclair, 14, 118
Lewis, Wyndham, 128–29, 132
Life (1883–1936), 7, 8, 13, 24, 39, 58–61, 69, 70–71, 190
Life (1936–2000), 14, 21
Lindsay, Vachel, 169
Lipchitz, Jacques, 85
Literary Guild, 2, 6, 19, 68, 114, 147, 152–53, 186
Little Review, The, 7, 13, 49, 51, 59, 67, 68, 69, 73, 85, 90–92, 98, 108, 109, 117, 181

Loeb, Harold, 68, 92, 119, 121
Loos, Anita, 22, 132
Lorentz, Pare, 195
Loveman, Amy, 11, 153, 178
Lovett, Robert Morse, 11
Lowell, Amy, 14, 24, 40, 50, 57, 78, 88, 91, 92, 161, 169
Loy, Mina, 100, 109
Luce, Clare Boothe, 8, 157, 191
Luce, Henry, 8, 14–15, 59, 85, 191
Luhan, Mabel Dodge, 19, 30–35, 42, 62, 72, 138–39, 142, 150, 181
Lundell, William, 20, 167, 170–71

M

McAlmon, Robert, 68, 99–101, 109, 110, 117, 137
McBride, Henry, 53, 157, 187
McClure's, 116, 184
McDonald, Florin, 10, 147–8
McMillan, Dougald, 69, 98
Macdonald, Dwight, 15
MacDougal, Curtis, 52
MacLeish, Archibald, 170
Macpherson, Kenneth, 99
Malcolm, Janet, 102
Mallarmé, Stéphane, 133
Malone, Ted, 169
Man Who Came to Dinner, The, 20
Mann, Thomas, 14, 84
Mansfield, Katherine, 131
Marek, Jayne, 40–41
Marquis, Don, 8, 19, 53–58, 71, 77, 78, 83
Masters, Edgar Lee, 40, 87, 92
Matisse, Henri, 12, 24, 32, 34, 35, 41, 59, 71, 85, 124, 128, 140, 187–88
Matthews, Edward, 159
Matthews, T. S., 176
Maugham, W. Somerset, 18
Mearson, Lyon, 132
Mellow, James, 32, 42, 69
Mencken, H. L., 18, 19, 46, 81, 87–88, 130, 131, 137
Meredith, George, 89
Millay, Edna St. Vincent, 12, 85–86, 170
Miller, Henry, 141
Miró, Joan, 108
Monroe, Harriet, 38–41, 51, 91, 157
Moore, Marianne, 96, 99, 108, 128, 132, 157, 190
Morgan, Emanuel, 49–52, 114

Morley, Christopher, 11
Morrisson, Mark, 64, 93
Morrow's Almanack (1928), 115
Mumford, Louis, 67, 113, 186
Murphy, Michael, 61
Murray, George, 179

N

Nash, Ogden, 185
Nast, Condé, 71
Nathan, George Jean, 18, 137
Nation, The, 27, 120, 151, 164–66
Niebuhr, Reinhold, 15
New Republic, The, 11, 12, 56–57, 76, 91, 108, 114, 120, 126, 150, 176, 186
New York Herald Tribune, 2, 6, 164–65, 183, 190; *Books*, 6, 8, 11–12, 106, 115, 123, 148–49, 195
New York Times, 2, 10, 11, 31, 83, 94, 98, 103, 107, 108, 113, 127, 130, 134, 167–68, 171, 172, 178, 184, 185, 186; *Book Review*, 7, 11–12, 68, 91, 110–11, 114, 124, 128, 131, 132, 144, 158
New Yorker, The, 3, 12, 13, 14, 17, 20, 97, 107, 108, 121, 127, 129, 135–36, 138, 142, 162, 166, 167, 169, 170, 172, 177, 187
Nichols, John G., 109
Nordstrom, Ludvig, 104
Norman, Dorothy, 186
North, Michael, 64, 111
Norton, Allen, 65
Nott, Stanley, 100

O

O'Brien, Edward, 116, 119
Ochs, Adolph, 10
O'Neill, Eugene, 14, 18, 69, 114
Orgeron, Marsha, 194
Orwell, George, 15
Others, 40, 49, 51, 96

P

Parker, Dorothy, 12, 59, 158
Partisan Review, 15, 189
Pater, Walter, 88
Paterson, Isabel (I. M. P), 8, 11–12, 95, 129, 144, 154–55, 178
Paul, Elliot, 97–98, 106, 130
Payson & Clarke, Ltd., 125

Pearson, Edmund, 58
Pearson, Norman Holmes, 190
Perkins, Maxwell, 120
Pétain, Maréchal, 189
Phillpotts, Eden, 88
Picabia, Francis, 32, 34, 91, 108
Picasso, Pablo, 12, 24, 32, 34, 35, 41, 59, 64, 65, 71, 84, 85, 89, 125, 140, 154, 173, 194
Pickford, Mary, 178
Pirandello, Luigi, 129
Plain Edition, 134–37
Poe, Edgar Allan, 63, 64, 190
Poetry, 5, 13, 32, 38–41, 49, 51, 66, 91, 190
Politics, 15
Porter, Alan, 130
Porter, Katherine Anne, 6, 105–06, 126
Pound, Ezra, 17–18, 24, 39, 57, 68, 73, 92, 100, 102, 112, 117, 119, 140, 169, 190
Proust, Marcel, 73, 102, 105, 129, 133, 169
Provines, June, 179, 197
Publishers' Weekly, 9, 12, 17, 112, 144–45, 168
Putnam, Samuel, 152

R

Radway, Janice, 5–6
Rainey, Lawrence, 8
Rascoe, Burton, 11, 115–16
Reid, Ogden, 11
Reid, Helen, 11
Reid, Marjorie, 68
Renaud, Ralph, 176
Rennels, Mary, 155
Reviewer, The, 93–94, 115
Richardson, Dorothy, 24, 78, 99, 109, 110, 127–28
Riding, Laura, 132–33
Rimbaud, Arthur, 133
Roberts, Kenneth L., 59, 67
Robinson-Wayne, Beatrice, 159
Rogers, Ginger, 20, 191
Rogers, William G., 157, 161, 164–66, 170, 173, 183
Rogue, 24, 53, 65
Roosevelt, Eleanor, 1, 174
Roosevelt, Theodore, 32, 59, 118
Rose, Francis, 195
Rosenfeld, Isaac, 22
Rosenfeld, Paul, 104, 113, 120, 132–33, 178, 186

Ross, David, 169
Ross, Harold, 13, 22, 163–64
Rousseau, Henri, 140
Rubin, Joan Shelley, 5–6
Rugg, Harold, 186
Rukeyser, Muriel, 157
Ruth, Babe, 71
Rutra, Theo, 98

S

Sage, Robert, 110
Salmon, André, 187
Salpeter, Harry, 98
Sandburg, Carl, 14, 17, 92, 111, 130, 169
Saroyan, William, 172
Satie, Erik, 102
Saturday Evening Post, 3, 7, 13, 21, 36, 39, 61, 67, 116, 117, 189–90
Saturday Review of Literature, 2, 6, 11–12, 15, 20, 53, 96, 98, 104–05, 108, 114, 120, 125, 146, 148–49, 164, 177–78
Sauvage, Marcel M., 93–94
Schmalhausen, S. D., 133
Schneider, Isador, 188
Schoenberg, Arnold, 128
Schultz, Susan M., 3
Schuster, Merle, 68
Scudder, Janet, 138
Sedgwick, Ellery, 13–14, 63, 141, 162
Seeley, Evelyn, 166
Selby, John, 150
Seldes, Gilbert, 183
Sewanee Review, 15
Shakespeare, William, 88, 115, 121
Shaw, G. B., 14
Sherman, Stuart, 11, 79–80, 130, 153, 178
Sherwood, Robert, 12
Sinclair, May, 79, 109, 129
Sinclair, Upton, 14
Sitwell, Edith, 100, 107, 108, 109, 128, 130
Skinner, B. F., 162
Smart Set, 18, 81, 184
Smith, Bessie, 73
Smith, Clara, 73
Soil, The, 24, 64–65, 99, 112
Solomons, Leon, 162
Stauffer, Donald, 9
Steell, Willis, 105
Steffens, Lincoln, 139, 152

Stein, Gertrude, writings of: "Absolutely Bob Brown, or, Bobbed Brown," 111; "American Crimes and How They Matter," 183; "American Newspapers," 183; "American Education and Colleges," 183; "American Newspapers," 183; "American States and Cities and How They Differ from each Other," 183; *Autobiography of Alice B. Toklas,* 1,2, 4, 6, 8, 14, 18–19, 27, 41, 53, 59, 63, 107, 108, 122, 124, 136, 138–56, 162, 173, 187, 192–93, 196; "Aux Galeries Lafayette," 53; "B. B. or The Birthplace of Bonnes," 92; *Before the Flowers of Friendship Faded Friendship Faded,* 134; "Benjamin Franklin," 194; "Bundles for Them: A History of Giving Bundles," 92, 181; "Capital Capitals," 117; "The Capital and Capitals of the United States of America," 183; "Composition as Explanation," 107, 160; "Daniel Webster," 195; "An Elucidation," 96–97; *Everybody's Autobiography,* 21, 162, 170, 183, 190, 192, 198; "The Fifteenth of November," 108, 113, 163; *Four Saints in Three Acts,* 1–2, 20, 156–60, 162, 177, 178–79, 195; *Geography and Plays,* 6, 8, 18, 67, 72, 74–85 , 102, 118, 125, 158, 162; "The Great American Army," 62; "Have They Attacked Mary. He Giggled," 13, 61–62; "He and They, Hemingway," 118; *How to Write,* 134; "How Writing is Written," 190; "If I Told Him," 13, 89; "If You Had Three Husbands," 102–03; "An Indian Boy," 93–94, 163; "Ladies Voices," 194; "A League," 60; *Lectures in America,* 167; "A Life of Juan Gris," 190; "A Long Gay Book," 108, 190; *Lucy Church Amiably,* 125, 134–36; "M. Vollard et Cézanne," 53; *The Making of Americans,* 6, 7, 99–107, 115–16, 135, 143; *Matisse Picasso and Gertrude Stein,* 134; "Mildred's Thoughts," 52, 68; "Miss Furr and Miss Skeene," 13; *Mrs. Reynolds,* 22; "One (Van Vechten)," 72; *Operas and Plays,* 134; *Paris France,* 6; "Picasso," 31; "Poartrait of Cézanne," 141; "Portrait of Jo Davidson," 13, 85; "Portrait of Mabel Dodge," 30–35, 44, 72; *Portraits and Prayers,* 167, 185; "Relief Work in France," 60; "Scenery and George Washington: a Novel or a Play," 134; "Still More About Money," 189; *Tender Buttons,* 8, 18, 19, 25, 38, 41–48, 54, 66, 68, 76–78, 80, 99, 102, 110, 111, 115, 143, 162, 190, 191; *They Must. Be Wedded. To Their Wife,* 195; *Three Lives,* 25–30, 73–74, 76, 100, 118, 119, 140, 167, 190; *Useful Knowledge,* 124–26; "Vacation in Brittany," 92; "A Valentine to Sherwood Anderson: Idem the Same," 92 ; "Van or Twenty Years After: A Second Portrait of Carl Van Vechten," 115; "We Came: A History," 112; "What Happened," 194; *World is Round, The,* 6, 195–96

Stein, Leo, 1, 26, 31–32
Sternheim, Carl, 97
Stettheimer, Florine, 157, 159
Stevens, Wallace, 64, 96, 132, 157–58, 190
Stevenson, Robert Louis, 65, 88
Steward, Samuel, 196–97
Stewart, Donald Ogden, 121
Stieglitz, Alfred, 8, 31–32, 64, 96, 128, 186
Story, 186
Strachey, Lytton, 87, 139
Stravinsky, Igor, 159
Strunsky, Robert, 172
Stuart, Henry Longan, 114
Suárez, Juan A., 64
Sullivan, Frank, 115, 142
Sutherland, Donald, 25

T

Tate, Allen, 114, 120
"Testimony Against Gertrude Stein," 187
This Quarter, 117
Thomson, Virgil, 157, 159, 163, 195
Thurber, James, 20, 97, 137, 167

Index

Tischler, Alyson, 21, 54, 69
Time, 6, 8, 12, 14, 15, 51, 58, 116, 147–8, 150–51, 165, 177, 191
Toscanini, Arturo, 158
Toklas, Alice B., 30, 92, 118, 124, 134–35, 140, 143–47, 164, 166, 171, 178, 181, 187
Tolstoy, Leo, 193
Tom Masson's Annual (1925), 67, 115
Top Hat, 20, 191
Tourtellot, Arthur, 185
Towne, Charles Hanson, 184–85
transatlantic review, the, 7, 68, 69, 99–103, 109, 117, 119
transition, 6, 7, 69, 90, 96–98, 109, 110, 112, 117, 124, 130, 132, 187
Trend, The, 47–48
Trilling, Lionel, 15
Trollope, Anthony, 137
Troy, William, 151
Turner, Catherine, 2, 199n3, 50
Twain, Mark, 95, 122, 166
Tzara, Tristan, 187

U
Undset, Singrid, 84
Untermeyer, Louis, 92, 114

V
Vail, Lawrence, 137
Valéry, Paul, 104, 133
Van Doren, Irita, 11
Van Doren, Mark, 114
Van Duym, A. A., 184
Van Gogh, Vincent, 64
Van Vechten, Carl, 8, 26, 30–31, 47–8, 62, 71–74, 81–82, 84, 87, 94, 99, 107, 136, 137, 139, 144, 147, 156, 160, 164, 183, 187, 191, 195, 196; writings of: *The Blind Bow-Boy*, 72–73; *Interpreters and Interpretations*, 72; *Nigger Heaven*, 73–74; *Parties*, 74; *Peter Whiffle*, 72, 139
Van Vuren, Floyd 146
Vanity Fair, 2, 7, 12–13, 21, 58, 60–63, 67, 69, 73, 82, 84–90, 109, 128, 156–57, 162, 183, 190, 191–92
Vogue, 13, 21, 36, 190

W
Wagner-Martin, Linda, 181

Warren, Robert Penn, 41, 114
Waters, Ethel, 73
Watson, Steven, 159
Weeks, Mabel, 26
Wells, H. G., 14, 118
Wescott, Glenway, 108
West, Rebecca, 14, 84
Wharton, Edith, 34, 69, 88
White, E. B., 54, 56, 163
White, Katharine, 13
Whitehead, Alfred North, 154
Whitman, Walt, 63, 64, 88–89, 169, 174
Wicke, Jennifer, 4
Wilde, Oscar, 65
Wilder, Thornton, 169, 184, 193–94, 196
Will, Barbara, 3–4
Willard, Donald, 78–79
Williams, William Carlos, 52, 68, 75, 96, 100, 109, 110, 112, 114, 132, 133, 159, 190
Wilson, Bess, 146
Wilson, Edmund, 6, 12, 15, 18, 26, 71, 82, 85–87, 106, 116, 119, 126–27, 133–34, 150, 178, 186, 191
Wilson, Harry Leon, 182, 184
Wilson, Romer, 129
Wilson, Woodrow, 60
Witaker, Alma, 182
Wodehouse, P. G., 194
Woollcott, Alexander, 8, 12, 17–19, 22, 168
Woolf, Leonard, 8, 100, 107, 112, 131
Woolf, Virginia, 1–2, 6, 8, 14, 79, 84, 100, 102, 107, 112, 123, 129, 131, 139, 153; writings of: *Flush*, 2, 6, 14, 139, 153; *Jacob's Room*, 79; *Orlando* 153
Wordsworth, William, 38
Wright, Frank Lloyd, 128, 180
Wright, Harold Bell, 184
Wright, Richard, 26
Wylie, Elinor, 78, 87–88

Y
Yeats, W. B., 133
Young, F. H., 77

Z
Zayas, Marius de, 31–32

For Product Safety Concerns and Information please contact our EU
representative GPSR@taylorandfrancis.com
Taylor & Francis Verlag GmbH, Kaufingerstraße 24, 80331 München, Germany

www.ingramcontent.com/pod-product-compliance
Lightning Source LLC
Chambersburg PA
CBHW070559300426
44113CB00010B/1322